WITHDRAWN

3 7944 1008 6939 1

D1075929

The Suppression of the African Slave Trade to the United States of America, 1638-1870

W.E.B. Du Bois

Dover Publications, Inc.
Mineola, New York

Published in Canada by General Publishing Company, Ltd., 30 Lesmill Road, Don Mills, Toronto, Ontario.
Published in the United Kingdom by Constable and Company, Ltd., 3 The Lanchesters, 162–164 Fulham Palace Road, London W6 9ER.

Bibliographical Note

The Dover edition, first published in 1970 and reissued in 1999, is an unabridged republication of the work originally published in 1896 by Harvard University Press as Volume I of the Harvard Historical Studies, sponsored by the Henry Warren Torrey Fund. This edition also contains a new Introduction by Philip S. Foner. The publisher gratefully acknowledges the cooperation of Lincoln University Library, which supplied a copy of the work for the purpose of reproduction.

Library of Congress Cataloging-in-Publication Data

Du Bois, W. E. B. (William Edward Burghardt), 1868–1963.
The suppression of the African slave trade to the United States of America, 1638–1870 / W.E.B. Du Bois ; with an introduction by Philip S. Foner.
p. cm.
Originally published: Boston : Harvard University Press, 1896; introd. originally published: 1970.
ISBN 0-486-40910-4 (pbk.)
1. Slave trade—United States—History. I. Title.
E441.D8 1999
382'.44'0973—dc21 99-31505
CIP

Manufactured in the United States of America
Dover Publications, Inc., 31 East 2nd Street, Mineola, N.Y. 11501

INTRODUCTION TO THE DOVER EDITION

IN its report dealing with the annual meeting of the American Historical Association held in Washington, December, 1892, the New York *Independent* noted that among the "three best papers presented" was one on the "enforcement of the Slave Trade Laws." It continued: "The article . . . was written and read by a black man. It was thrilling when one could, for a moment, turn his thoughts from listening to think that scarcely thirty years have elapsed since the war that freed his race, and here was an audience of white men listening to a black man—listening, moreover, to a careful, cool, philosophical history of the laws which had not prevented the enslavement of his race. The voice, the diction, the manner of the speaker was faultless. As one looked at him, one could not help saying, 'Let us not worry about the future of our country in the matter of race distinctions.' "

The black man was W. E. Burghardt Du Bois, a twenty-four-year-old fellow at Harvard University pursuing graduate courses in history and political science. The article was based on his master's thesis, "The Suppression of the Slave Trade," and was published under the title "The Enforcement of the Slave Trade Laws" in the Annual Report of the American Historical Association for 1891.

Du Bois' study of the slave-trade laws was continued and fully developed in his doctoral thesis at Harvard, "The Suppression of the African Slave Trade to the United States." He worked on the subject in 1892 and looked forward to receiving his doctor's degree in about two years. But he was determined to supplement the training in scholarship he had received from Harvard with the best that could be offered in Europe. Logically he chose Germany where the historical seminar in the universities had gained worldwide renown. From 1892 to 1894, through a grant from the Slater Fund, Du Bois studied at the University of Berlin where he worked in economics, history and sociology; for historian

Gustave Schmoller's seminar he wrote a paper entitled "The Plantation and Peasant Proprietorship Systems of Agriculture in the United States." He also tested the conclusions he had reached in his study of the suppression of the African slave trade "by the general principles laid down in German universities."

Upon his return to the United States in 1894, Du Bois submitted his study of the slave trade as his doctoral dissertation to Harvard in partial fulfillment of the degree of Doctor of Philosophy. He then set out to earn a living, and accepted the chair of Classics at Wilberforce University at the annual salary of $800, and was designated a professor of Latin and Greek. In 1895 Harvard awarded him the doctoral degree, and the following year his dissertation was published by Harvard University Press under the title *The Suppression of the African Slave-Trade to the United States of America, 1638-1870*. The volume was the first of the Harvard Historical Studies, published under the direction of the Department of History and Government.

Du Bois' study was based upon historical sources, national and state, colonial statutes, Congressional documents, reports of anti-slavery societies, personal narratives and the existing monographs in the field. In his preface he states that there was difficulty in separating the suppression of the slave trade from the system of American slavery and colonial policy and at the same time "avoid superficiality" and "unscientific narrowness of view." But he added: "While I could not hope entirely to overcome such a difficulty, I nevertheless trust that I have succeeded in rendering this monograph a small contribution to the scientific study of slavery and the American Negro."

In his review of the book in the January 1897 issue of the *African Methodist Church Review,* editor H. T. Kealing declared that the work was "epochal," and that "certainly for faithful and full verification of every statement, for impartiality, for grasp, correct summarizing of the essential meaning of widely divergent actions and seemingly antagonistic motives in the same section, Professor Du Bois' work is monumental among all the writings that the race has produced." While none of the scholarly journals went so far in praising the book, it did receive good reviews in the *American Historical Review,* the *Annals of the American Academy of Political and Social Science,* and the *English Historical Review.* Some of the reviewers, however, were annoyed by Du Bois' eloquent concluding chapter in which he referred bluntly to the fact that Negro enslavement and the African slave trade "arose principally from the cupidity and carelessness of our ancestors," and that the framers of the Constitution engaged in "a bargain largely of dollars and cents" in the slavery and slave-trade compromises. Such judgments, in the eyes of one reviewer, made Du Bois "the advocate rather than the historian."

The Nation's reviewer predicted that the volume would "long remain the authoritative work on the subject." Events have justified this prediction. Du Bois' study of 1896 remains a model of historical research and writing, and has been repeatedly cited in the bibliographies and footnotes in all subsequent works of value concerning the slave trade in the United States. Few historical interpretations withstand the inroads of time so successfully.

Du Bois himself noted later in his life that the study of the suppression of the African slave trade to America had not to be done again "at least in my day." However, when the volume was reprinted in a cloth edition in 1954 by the Social Science Press of New York, Du Bois added a three-page "Apologia" in which he made two major criticisms of his work. First he noted that as an author looking back sixty years to the time when he began the research, he was gratified to realize "how hard and honestly" he had worked on the subject as a young man of twenty-four. "As a piece of documented historical research, it is well done and has in the last half century received very little criticism as to accuracy and completeness." As to self-criticism: the first related to the nature of the monographic method which led to the separation of his subject from "the total flow of history" by an author "when he knows nothing or little of the mass of facts of which his minute study is a part." However, he had been fortunate in the fact that the particular subject he had chosen "was unusually susceptible to segregation without too much danger of misinterpretation from lack of broader understanding."

A more serious criticism was his ignorance at the time he was completing the work "of the significance of the work of Freud and Marx." He had received at Harvard excellent preparation for understanding Freud through William James, Josiah Royce and George Santayana, but knew nothing of the work of Freud and his colleagues when he set out to write the book. As a result, he did not "realize the psychological reasons behind the trends of human action which the African slave-trade involved." This understanding would have made his concluding chapter in which he stressed what men "ought" to have done "less pat and simple."

At Harvard he had heard little of Marx and while in Germany he heard more of Marxism, this was more in rebuttal, and there was "no complete realization of the application of the philosophy of Karl Marx to my subject." Consequently, he had indicated the economic factors involved in slavery and the slave trade, but he had mainly emphasized the influence of "moral lassitude." What he had needed to do was to add to his "terribly conscientious search into the facts of the slave-trade the clear concept of Marx on the class struggle for income and power, beneath which all considerations of right or morals were twisted or utterly crushed." Yet it was too much to expect that he would have had this understanding in 1896, and he concluded: "I am proud to see that at the beginning of my career I made no more mistakes than apparently I did." With this all scholars can agree.

Du Bois' study does not deal with Africa as such, but it was undoubtedly an important influence in directing his attention to his ancestral homeland. Later, in such works as *The Negro, Black Folk: Then and Now, The World and Africa* and other books and articles as well as in the pages of *The Crisis,* which he edited for many years, Du Bois made important contributions to the understanding of Africa's bygone past, and did much to correct the picture of Africa "south of the Sahara" as gigantic jungles which were then and always had been hardly more than haunts of "savage beast and still more savage men." In his research he again paid attention to the African slave trade but this time concentrated on its effects upon Africa itself. He concluded that the trade was one of the primary causes of the decline, decay and final collapse of the cultures, kingdoms and empires which had flourished in Black Africa in earlier times. He pointed out that as a consequence of "organized slave trading in every corner of Africa . . . whole regions were depopulated, and whole tribes disappeared . . . Family ties and government were weakened . . . native industries were disorganized . . . and future advances in civilization became impossible. . . . It was the rape of a continent to an extent never paralleled in ancient or modern times."

PHILIP S. FONER

Lincoln University, Penna.

April 1970

PREFACE.

THIS monograph was begun during my residence as Rogers Memorial Fellow at Harvard University, and is based mainly upon a study of the sources, i. e., national, State, and colonial statutes, Congressional documents, reports of societies, personal narratives, etc. The collection of laws available for this research was, I think, nearly complete; on the other hand, facts and statistics bearing on the economic side of the study have been difficult to find, and my conclusions are consequently liable to modification from this source.

The question of the suppression of the slave-trade is so intimately connected with the questions as to its rise, the system of American slavery, and the whole colonial policy of the eighteenth century, that it is difficult to isolate it, and at the same time to avoid superficiality on the one hand, and unscientific narrowness of view on the other. While I could not hope entirely to overcome such a difficulty, I nevertheless trust that I have succeeded in rendering this monograph a small contribution to the scientific study of slavery and the American Negro.

I desire to express my obligation to Dr. Albert Bushnell Hart, of Harvard University, at whose suggestion I began this work and by whose kind aid and encouragement I have brought it to a close; also I have to thank the trustees of the John F. Slater Fund, whose appointment made it possible to test the conclusions of this study by the general principles laid down in German universities.

W. E. BURGHARDT DU BOIS.

WILBERFORCE UNIVERSITY,
March, 1896.

CONTENTS.

CHAPTER I.

Introductory.

CHAPTER II.

The Planting Colonies.

CHAPTER III.

The Farming Colonies.

CHAPTER IV.

The Trading Colonies.

CHAPTER V.

The Period of the Revolution, 1774–1787.

CHAPTER VI.

The Federal Convention, 1787.

CHAPTER VII.

Toussaint L'Ouverture and Anti-Slavery Effort, 1787–1807.

CHAPTER VIII.

The Period of Attempted Suppression, 1807–1825.

CHAPTER IX.

The International Status of the Slave-Trade, 1783–1862.

CHAPTER X.

The Rise of the Cotton Kingdom, 1820–1850.

CHAPTER XI.

The Final Crisis, 1850–1870.

CHAPTER XII.

THE ESSENTIALS IN THE STRUGGLE.

APPENDICES.

CHAPTER I.

INTRODUCTORY.

1. Plan of the Monograph.
2. The Rise of the English Slave-Trade.

1. **Plan of the Monograph.** This monograph proposes to set forth the efforts made in the United States of America, from early colonial times until the present, to limit and suppress the trade in slaves between Africa and these shores.

The study begins with the colonial period, setting forth in brief the attitude of England and, more in detail, the attitude of the planting, farming, and trading groups of colonies toward the slave-trade. It deals next with the first concerted effort against the trade and with the further action of the individual States. The important work of the Constitutional Convention follows, together with the history of the trade in that critical period which preceded the Act of 1807. The attempt to suppress the trade from 1807 to 1830 is next recounted. A chapter then deals with the slave-trade as an international problem. Finally the development of the crises up to the Civil War is studied, together with the steps leading to the final suppression; and a concluding chapter seeks to sum up the results of the investigation. Throughout the monograph the institution of slavery and the interstate slave-trade are considered only incidentally.

2. **The Rise of the English Slave-Trade.** Any attempt to consider the attitude of the English colonies toward the African slave-trade must be prefaced by a word as to the attitude of England herself and the development of the trade in her hands.[1]

[1] This account is based largely on the *Report of the Lords of the Committee of Council*, etc. (London, 1789).

Sir John Hawkins's celebrated voyage took place in 1562, but probably not until 1631[1] did a regular chartered company undertake to carry on the trade.[2] This company was unsuccessful,[3] and was eventually succeeded by the "Company of Royal Adventurers trading to Africa," chartered by Charles II. in 1662, and including the Queen Dowager and the Duke of York.[4] The company contracted to supply the West Indies with three thousand slaves annually; but contraband trade, misconduct, and war so reduced it that in 1672 it surrendered its charter to another company for £34,000.[5] This new corporation, chartered by Charles II. as the "Royal African Company," proved more successful than its predecessors, and carried on a growing trade for a quarter of a century.

In 1698 Parliamentary interference with the trade began. By the Statute 9 and 10 William and Mary, chapter 26, private traders, on payment of a duty of 10% on English goods exported to Africa, were allowed to participate in the trade. This was brought about by the clamor of the merchants, especially the "American Merchants," who "in their Petition suggest, that it would be a great Benefit to the Kingdom to secure the Trade by maintaining Forts and Castles there, with an equal Duty upon all Goods exported."[6] This plan, being a compromise between maintaining the monopoly intact and entirely abolishing it, was

[1] African trading-companies had previously been erected (e. g. by Elizabeth in 1585 and 1588, and by James I. in 1618); but slaves are not specifically mentioned in their charters, and they probably did not trade in slaves. Cf. Bandinel, *Account of the Slave Trade* (1842), pp. 38-44.

[2] Chartered by Charles I. Cf. Sainsbury, *Cal. State Papers, Col. Ser., America and W. Indies*, 1574-1660, p. 135.

[3] In 1651, during the Protectorate, the privileges of the African trade were granted anew to this same company for fourteen years. Cf. Sainsbury, *Cal. State Papers, Col. Ser., America and W. Indies*, 1574-1660, pp. 342, 355.

[4] Sainsbury, *Cal. State Papers, Col. Ser., America and W. Indies*, 1661-1668, § 408.

[5] Sainsbury, *Cal. State Papers, Col. Ser., America and W. Indies*, 1669-1674, §§ 934, 1095.

[6] Quoted in the above *Report*, under "Most Material Proceedings in the House of Commons," Vol. I. Part I. An import duty of 10% on all goods, except Negroes, imported from Africa to England and the colonies was also laid. The proceeds of these duties went to the Royal African Company.

adopted, and the statute declared the trade "highly Beneficial and Advantageous to this Kingdom, and to the Plantations and Colonies thereunto belonging."

Having thus gained practically free admittance to the field, English merchants sought to exclude other nations by securing a monopoly of the lucrative Spanish colonial slave-trade. Their object was finally accomplished by the signing of the Assiento in 1713.[1]

The Assiento was a treaty between England and Spain by which the latter granted the former a monopoly of the Spanish colonial slave-trade for thirty years, and England engaged to supply the colonies within that time with at least 144,000 slaves, at the rate of 4,800 per year. England was also to advance Spain 200,000 crowns, and to pay a duty of 33½ crowns for each slave imported. The kings of Spain and England were each to receive one-fourth of the profits of the trade, and the Royal African Company were authorized to import as many slaves as they wished above the specified number in the first twenty-five years, and to sell them, except in three ports, at any price they could get.

It is stated that, in the twenty years from 1713 to 1733, fifteen thousand slaves were annually imported into America by the English, of whom from one-third to one-half went to the Spanish colonies.[2] To the company itself the venture proved a financial failure; for during the years 1729–1750 Parliament assisted the Royal Company by annual grants which amounted to £90,000,[3] and by 1739 Spain was a creditor to the extent of £68,000, and threatened to suspend the treaty. The war interrupted the carrying out of the contract, but the Peace of Aix-la-Chapelle extended the limit by four years. Finally, October 5, 1750, this privilege was waived for a money consideration paid to England; the Assiento was ended, and the Royal Company was bankrupt.

[1] Cf. Appendix A.

[2] Bandinel, *Account of the Slave Trade*, p. 59. Cf. Bryan Edwards, *History of the British Colonies in the W. Indies* (London, 1798), Book VI.

[3] From 1729 to 1788, including compensation to the old company, Parliament expended £705,255 on African companies. Cf. *Report*, etc., as above.

By the Statute 23 George II., chapter 31, the old company was dissolved and a new "Company of Merchants trading to Africa" erected in its stead.[1] Any merchant so desiring was allowed to engage in the trade on payment of certain small duties, and such merchants formed a company headed by nine directors. This marked the total abolition of monopoly in the slave-trade, and was the form under which the trade was carried on until after the American Revolution.

That the slave-trade was the very life of the colonies had, by 1700, become an almost unquestioned axiom in British practical economics. The colonists themselves declared slaves "the strength and sinews of this western world,"[2] and the lack of them "the grand obstruction"[3] here, as the settlements "cannot subsist without supplies of them."[4] Thus, with merchants clamoring at home and planters abroad, it easily became the settled policy of England to encourage the slave-trade. Then, too, she readily argued that what was an economic necessity in Jamaica and the Barbadoes could scarcely be disadvantageous to Carolina, Virginia, or even New York. Consequently, the colonial governors were generally instructed to "give all due encouragement and invitation to merchants and others, . . . and in particular to the royal African company of England."[5] Duties laid on the importer, and all acts in any way restricting the trade, were frowned upon and very often disallowed. "Whereas," ran Governor Dobbs's instructions, "Acts have been passed in some of our Plantations in America for laying duties on the importation and exportation of Negroes to the great discouragement of the Merchants trading thither from the

[1] Various amendatory statutes were passed: e. g., 24 George II. ch. 49, 25 George II. ch. 40, 4 George III. ch. 20, 5 George III. ch. 44, 23 George III. ch. 65.

[2] Renatus Enys from Surinam, in 1663: Sainsbury, *Cal. State Papers, Col. Ser., America and W. Indies*, 1661–68, § 577.

[3] Thomas Lynch from Jamaica, in 1665: Sainsbury, *Cal. State Papers, Col. Ser., America and W. Indies*, 1661–68, § 934.

[4] Lieutenant-Governor Willoughby of Barbadoes, in 1666: Sainsbury, *Cal. State Papers, Col. Ser., America and W. Indies*, 1661–68, § 1281.

[5] Smith, *History of New Jersey* (1765), p. 254; Sainsbury, *Cal. State Papers, Col. Ser., America and W. Indies*, 1669–74, §§ 367, 398, 812.

coast of Africa . . . It is our Will and Pleasure that you do not give your assent to or pass any Law imposing duties upon Negroes imported into our Province of North Carolina."[1]

The exact proportions of the slave-trade to America can be but approximately determined. From 1680 to 1688 the African Company sent 249 ships to Africa, shipped there 60,783 Negro slaves, and after losing 14,387 on the middle passage, delivered 46,396 in America. The trade increased early in the eighteenth century, 104 ships clearing for Africa in 1701; it then dwindled until the signing of the Assiento, standing at 74 clearances in 1724. The final dissolution of the monopoly in 1750 led — excepting in the years 1754–57, when the closing of Spanish marts sensibly affected the trade — to an extraordinary development, 192 clearances being made in 1771. The Revolutionary War nearly stopped the traffic; but by 1786 the clearances had risen again to 146.

To these figures must be added the unregistered trade of Americans and foreigners. It is probable that about 25,000 slaves were brought to America each year between 1698 and 1707. The importation then dwindled, but rose after the Assiento to perhaps 30,000. The proportion, too, of these slaves carried to the continent now began to increase. Of about 20,000 whom the English annually imported from 1733 to 1766, South Carolina alone received some 3,000. Before the Revolution, the total exportation to America is variously estimated as between 40,000 and 100,000 each year. Bancroft places the total slave population of the continental colonies at 59,000 in 1714, 78,000 in 1727, and 293,000 in 1754. The census of 1790 showed 697,897 slaves in the United States.[2]

In colonies like those in the West Indies and in South Carolina and Georgia, the rapid importation into America of a mul-

[1] *N. C. Col. Rec.*, V. 1118. For similar instructions, cf. *Penn. Archives*, I. 306; *Doc. rel. Col. Hist. New York*, VI. 34; Gordon, *History of the American Revolution*, I. letter 2; *Mass. Hist. Soc. Coll.*, 4th Ser. X. 642.

[2] These figures are from the above-mentioned *Report*, Vol. II. Part IV. Nos. 1, 5. See also Bancroft, *History of the United States* (1883), II. 274 ff; Bandinel, *Account of the Slave Trade*, p. 63; Benezet, *Caution to Great Britain*, etc., pp. 39–40, and *Historical Account of Guinea*, ch. xiii.

titude of savages gave rise to a system of slavery far different from that which the late Civil War abolished. The strikingly harsh and even inhuman slave codes in these colonies show this. Crucifixion, burning, and starvation were legal modes of punishment.[1] The rough and brutal character of the time and place was partly responsible for this, but a more decisive reason lay in the fierce and turbulent character of the imported Negroes. The docility to which long years of bondage and strict discipline gave rise was absent, and insurrections and acts of violence were of frequent occurrence.[2] Again and again the danger of planters being "cut off by their own negroes"[3] is mentioned, both in the islands and on the continent. This condition of vague dread and unrest not only increased the severity of laws and strengthened the police system, but was the prime motive back of all the earlier efforts to check the further importation of slaves.

On the other hand, in New England and New York the Negroes were merely house servants or farm hands, and were treated neither better nor worse than servants in general in those days. Between these two extremes, the system of slavery varied from a mild serfdom in Pennsylvania and New Jersey to an aristocratic caste system in Maryland and Virginia.

[1] Compare earlier slave codes in South Carolina, Georgia, Jamaica, etc.; also cf. Benezet, *Historical Account of Guinea*, p. 75; *Report*, etc., as above.

[2] Sainsbury, *Cal. State Papers, Col. Ser., America and W. Indies*, 1574–1660, pp. 229, 271, 295; 1661–68, §§ 61, 412, 826, 1270, 1274, 1788; 1669–74, §§ 508, 1244; Bolzius and Von Reck, *Journals* (in Force, *Tracts*, Vol. IV. No. 5, pp. 9, 18); *Proceedings of Governor and Assembly of Jamaica in regard to the Maroon Negroes* (London, 1796).

[3] Sainsbury, *Cal. State Papers, Col. Ser., America and W. Indies*, 1661–68, § 1679.

CHAPTER II.

THE PLANTING COLONIES.

3. Character of these Colonies.
4. Restrictions in Georgia.
5. Restrictions in South Carolina.
6. Restrictions in North Carolina.
7. Restrictions in Virginia.
8. Restrictions in Maryland.
9. General Character of these Restrictions.

3. **Character of these Colonies.** The planting colonies are those Southern settlements whose climate and character destined them to be the chief theatre of North American slavery. The early attitude of these communities toward the slave-trade is therefore of peculiar interest; for their action was of necessity largely decisive for the future of the trade and for the institution in North America. Theirs was the only soil, climate, and society suited to slavery; in the other colonies, with few exceptions, the institution was by these same factors doomed from the beginning. Hence, only strong moral and political motives could in the planting colonies overthrow or check a traffic so favored by the mother country.

4. **Restrictions in Georgia.** In Georgia we have an example of a community whose philanthropic founders sought to impose upon it a code of morals higher than the colonists wished. The settlers of Georgia were of even worse moral fibre than their slave-trading and whiskey-using neighbors in Carolina and Virginia; yet Oglethorpe and the London proprietors prohibited from the beginning both the rum and the slave traffic, refusing to "suffer slavery (which is against the Gospel as well as the fundamental law of England) to be authorised under our

authority."[1] The trustees sought to win the colonists over to their belief by telling them that money could be better expended in transporting white men than Negroes; that slaves would be a source of weakness to the colony; and that the "Produces designed to be raised in the Colony would not require such Labour as to make Negroes necessary for carrying them on."[2]

This policy greatly displeased the colonists, who from 1735, the date of the first law, to 1749, did not cease to clamor for the repeal of the restrictions.[3] As their English agent said, they insisted that "In Spight of all Endeavours to disguise this Point, it is as clear as Light itself, that Negroes are as essentially necessary to the Cultivation of *Georgia*, as Axes, Hoes, or any other Utensil of Agriculture."[4] Meantime, evasions and infractions of the laws became frequent and notorious. Negroes were brought across from Carolina and "hired" for life.[5] "Finally, purchases were openly made in Savannah from African traders: some seizures were made by those who opposed the principle, but as a majority of the magistrates were favorable to the introduction of slaves into the province, legal decisions were suspended from time to time, and a strong disposition evidenced by the courts to evade the operation of the law."[6] At last, in 1749, the colonists prevailed on the trustees and the government, and the trade was thrown open under careful restrictions, which limited importation, required a registry and quarantine on all slaves brought in, and laid a duty.[7] It is probable, however, that these restrictions were never enforced, and that the trade thus established continued unchecked until the Revolution.

[1] Hoare, *Memoirs of Granville Sharp* (1820), p. 157. For the act of prohibition, see W. B. Stevens, *History of Georgia* (1847), I. 311.

[2] [B. Martyn], *Account of the Progress of Georgia* (1741), pp. 9–10.

[3] Cf. Stevens, *History of Georgia*, I. 290 ff.

[4] Stephens, *Account of the Causes*, etc., p. 8. Cf. also *Journal of Trustees*, II. 210; cited by Stevens, *History of Georgia*, I. 306.

[5] McCall, *History of Georgia* (1811), I. 206–7.

[6] *Ibid.*

[7] *Pub. Rec. Office, Board of Trade*, Vol. X.; cited by C. C. Jones, *History of Georgia* (1883), I. 422–5.

5. **Restrictions in South Carolina.**[1] South Carolina had the largest and most widely developed slave-trade of any of the continental colonies. This was owing to the character of her settlers, her nearness to the West Indian slave marts, and the early development of certain staple crops, such as rice, which were adapted to slave labor.[2] Moreover, this colony suffered much less interference from the home government than many other colonies; thus it is possible here to trace the untrammeled development of slave-trade restrictions in a typical planting community.

As early as 1698 the slave-trade to South Carolina had reached such proportions that it was thought that "the great number of negroes which of late have been imported into this Collony may endanger the safety thereof." The immigration of white servants was therefore encouraged by a special law.[3] Increase of immigration reduced this disproportion, but Negroes continued to be imported in such numbers as to afford considerable revenue from a moderate duty on them. About

[1] The following is a summary of the legislation of the colony of South Carolina; details will be found in Appendix A: —

1698,	Act to encourage the immigration of white servants.
1703,	Duty Act: 10*s.* on Africans, 20*s.* on other Negroes.
1714,	" " additional duty.
1714,	" " £2.
1714–15,	" " additional duty.
1716,	" " £3 on Africans, £30 on colonial Negroes.
1717,	" " £40 in addition to existing duties.
1719,	" " £10 on Africans, £30 on colonial Negroes. The Act of 1717, etc., was repealed.
1721,	" " £10 on Africans, £50 on colonial Negroes.
1722,	" " " " " " "
1740,	" " £100 on Africans, £150 on colonial Negroes.
1751,	" " £10 " " £50 " "
1760,	Act prohibiting importation (Disallowed).
1764,	Duty Act: additional duty of £100.
1783,	" " £3 on Africans, £20 on colonial Negroes.
1784,	" " " " £5 " "
1787,	Act and Ordinance prohibiting importation.

[2] Cf. Hewatt, *Historical Account of S. Carolina and Georgia* (1779), I 120 ff.; reprinted in *S. C. Hist. Coll.* (1836), I. 108 ff.

[3] Cooper, *Statutes at Large of S. Carolina*, II. 153.

the time when the Assiento was signed, the slave-trade so increased that, scarcely a year after the consummation of that momentous agreement, two heavy duty acts were passed, because "the number of Negroes do extremely increase in this Province, and through the afflicting providence of God, the white persons do not proportionately multiply, by reason whereof, the safety of the said Province is greatly endangered."[1] The trade, however, by reason of the encouragement abroad and of increased business activity in exporting naval stores at home, suffered scarcely any check, although repeated acts, reciting the danger incident to a "great importation of Negroes," were passed, laying high duties.[2] Finally, in 1717, an additional duty of £40,[3] although due in depreciated currency, succeeded so nearly in stopping the trade that, two years later, all existing duties were repealed and one of £10 substituted.[4] This continued during the time of resistance to the proprietary government, but by 1734 the importation had again reached large proportions. "We must therefore beg leave," the colonists write in that year, "to inform your Majesty, that, amidst our other perilous circumstances, we are subject to many intestine dangers from the great number of negroes that are now among us, who amount at least to twenty-two thousand persons, and are three to one of all your Majesty's white subjects in this province. Insurrections against us have been often attempted."[5] In 1740 an insurrection under a slave, Cato, at Stono, caused such widespread alarm that a prohibitory duty of £100 was immediately laid.[6] Importation was again

[1] The text of the first act is not extant: cf. Cooper, *Statutes*, III. 56. For the second, see Cooper, VII. 365, 367.

[2] Cf. Grimké, *Public Laws of S. Carolina*, p. xvi, No. 362; Cooper, *Statutes*, II. 649. Cf. also *Governor Johnson to the Board of Trade*, Jan. 12, 1719–20; reprinted in Rivers, *Early History of S. Carolina* (1874), App., xii.

[3] Cooper, *Statutes*, VII. 368.

[4] *Ibid.*, III. 56.

[5] From a memorial signed by the governor, President of the Council, and Speaker of the House, dated April 9, 1734, printed in Hewatt, *Historical Account of S. Carolina and Georgia* (1779), II. 39; reprinted in *S. C. Hist. Coll.* (1836), I. 305–6. Cf. *N. C. Col. Rec.*, II. 421.

[6] Cooper, *Statutes*, III. 556; Grimké, *Public Laws*, p. xxxi, No. 694. Cf. Ramsay, *History of S. Carolina*, I. 110.

checked; but in 1751 the colony sought to devise a plan whereby the slightly restricted immigration of Negroes should provide a fund to encourage the importation of white servants, "to prevent the mischiefs that may be attended by the great importation of negroes into this Province."[1] Many white servants were thus encouraged to settle in the colony; but so much larger was the influx of black slaves that the colony, in 1760, totally prohibited the slave-trade. This act was promptly disallowed by the Privy Council and the governor reprimanded;[2] but the colony declared that "an importation of negroes, equal in number to what have been imported of late years, may prove of the most dangerous consequence in many respects to this Province, and the best way to obviate such danger will be by imposing such an additional duty upon them as may totally prevent the evils."[3] A prohibitive duty of £100 was accordingly imposed in 1764.[4] This duty probably continued until the Revolution.

The war made a great change in the situation. It has been computed by good judges that, between the years 1775 and 1783, the State of South Carolina lost twenty-five thousand Negroes, by actual hostilities, plunder of the British, runaways, etc. After the war the trade quickly revived, and considerable revenue was raised from duty acts until 1787, when by act and ordinance the slave-trade was totally prohibited.[5] This prohibition, by renewals from time to time, lasted until 1803.

6. **Restrictions in North Carolina.** In early times there were few slaves in North Carolina;[6] this fact, together with the

[1] Cooper, *Statutes*, III. 739.

[2] The text of this law has not been found. Cf. Burge, *Commentaries on Colonial and Foreign Laws*, I. 737, note; Stevens, *History of Georgia*, I. 286. See instructions of the governor of New Hampshire, June 30, 1761, in Gordon, *History of the American Revolution*, I. letter 2.

[3] Cooper, *Statutes*, IV. 187.

[4] This duty avoided the letter of the English instructions by making the duty payable by the first purchasers, and not by the importers. Cf. Cooper, *Statutes*, IV. 187.

[5] Grimké, *Public Laws*, p. lxviii, Nos. 1485, 1486; Cooper, *Statutes*, VII. 430.

[6] Cf. *N. C. Col. Rec.*, IV. 172.

troubled and turbulent state of affairs during the early colonial period, did not necessitate the adoption of any settled policy toward slavery or the slave-trade. Later the slave-trade to the colony increased; but there is no evidence of any effort to restrict or in any way regulate it before 1786, when it was declared that "the importation of slaves into this State is productive of evil consequences and highly impolitic,"[1] and a prohibitive duty was laid on them.

7. **Restrictions in Virginia.**[2] Next to South Carolina, Virginia had probably the largest slave-trade. Her situation, however, differed considerably from that of her Southern neighbor. The climate, the staple tobacco crop, and the society of Virginia were favorable to a system of domestic slavery, but one which tended to develop into a patriarchal serfdom rather than into a slave-consuming industrial hierarchy. The labor required by the tobacco crop was less unhealthy than that connected with the rice crop, and the Virginians were, perhaps, on a somewhat higher moral plane than the Carolinians. There was consequently no such insatiable demand for slaves in the larger colony. On the other hand, the power of the Virginia executive was peculiarly strong, and it was not possible here

[1] Martin, *Iredell's Acts of Assembly*, I. 413, 492.

[2] The following is a summary of the legislation of the colony of Virginia; details will be found in Appendix A:—

1710,	Duty Act:	proposed duty of £5.		
1723,	" "	prohibitive (?).		
1727,	" "	"		
1732,	" "	5%.		
1736,	" "	"		
1740,	" "	additional duty of 5%.		
1754,	" "	" "	5%.	
1755,	" "	" "	10%	(Repealed, 1760).
1757,	" "	" "	10%	(Repealed, 1761).
1759,	" "	20% on colonial slaves.		
1766,	" "	additional duty of 10% (Disallowed?).		
1769,	" "	" " " "		
1772,	" "	£5 on colonial slaves.		
	Petition of Burgesses *vs.* Slave-trade.			
1776,	Arraignment of the king in the adopted Frame of Government.			
1778,	Importation prohibited.			

to thwart the slave-trade policy of the home government as easily as elsewhere.

Considering all these circumstances, it is somewhat difficult to determine just what was the attitude of the early Virginians toward the slave-trade. There is evidence, however, to show that although they desired the slave-trade, the rate at which the Negroes were brought in soon alarmed them. In 1710 a duty of £5 was laid on Negroes, but Governor Spotswood "soon perceived that the laying so high a Duty on Negros was intended to discourage the importation," and vetoed the measure.[1] No further restrictive legislation was attempted for some years, but whether on account of the attitude of the governor or the desire of the inhabitants, is not clear. With 1723 begins a series of acts extending down to the Revolution, which, so far as their contents can be ascertained, seem to have been designed effectually to check the slave-trade. Some of these acts, like those of 1723 and 1727, were almost immediately disallowed.[2] The Act of 1732 laid a duty of 5%, which was continued until 1769,[3] and all other duties were in addition to this; so that by such cumulative duties the rate on slaves reached 25% in 1755,[4] and 35% at the time of Braddock's expedition.[5] These acts were found "very burthensome," "introductive of many frauds," and "very inconvenient,"[6] and were so far repealed that by 1761 the duty was only 15%. As now the Burgesses became more powerful, two or more bills proposing restrictive duties were passed, but disallowed.[7] By 1772 the anti-slave-trade feeling had become considerably developed, and the Burgesses petitioned the king, declaring that "The importation of slaves into the colonies from the coast of Africa hath long been considered as a trade of great inhumanity, and under its present encouragement, we have too

[1] *Letters of Governor Spotswood*, in *Va. Hist. Soc. Coll.*, New Ser., I. 52.

[2] Hening, *Statutes at Large of Virginia*, IV. 118, 182.

[3] *Ibid.*, IV. 317, 394; V. 28, 160, 318; VI. 217, 353; VII. 281; VIII. 190, 336, 532.

[4] *Ibid.*, V. 92; VI. 417, 419, 461, 466.

[5] *Ibid.*, VII. 69, 81.

[6] *Ibid.*, VII. 363, 383.

[7] *Ibid.*, VIII. 237, 337.

much reason to fear *will endanger the very existence* of your Majesty's American dominions. . . . Deeply impressed with these sentiments, we most humbly beseech your Majesty to remove *all those restraints* on your Majesty's governors of this colony, *which inhibit their assenting to such laws as might check so very pernicious a commerce.*" [1]

Nothing further appears to have been done before the war. When, in 1776, the delegates adopted a Frame of Government, it was charged in this document that the king had perverted his high office into a "detestable and insupportable tyranny, by . . . prompting our negroes to rise in arms among us, those very negroes whom, by an inhuman use of his negative, he hath refused us permission to exclude by law." [2] Two years later, in 1778, an "Act to prevent the further importation of Slaves" stopped definitively the legal slave-trade to Virginia.[3]

8. **Restrictions in Maryland.**[4] Not until the impulse of the Assiento had been felt in America, did Maryland make any attempt to restrain a trade from which she had long enjoyed a comfortable revenue. The Act of 1717, laying a duty of 40*s.*,[5] may have been a mild restrictive measure. The duties were

[1] *Miscellaneous Papers*, 1672–1865, in *Va. Hist. Soc. Coll.*, New Ser., VI. 14; Tucker, *Blackstone's Commentaries*, I. Part II. App., 51.

[2] Hening, *Statutes*, IX. 112.

[3] Importation by sea or by land was prohibited, with a penalty of £1000 for illegal importation and £500 for buying or selling. The Negro was freed, if illegally brought in. This law was revised somewhat in 1785. Cf. Hening, *Statutes*, IX. 471; XII. 182.

[4] The following is a summary of the legislation of the colony of Maryland; details will be found in Appendix A: —

1695,	Duty Act:		10*s.*					
1704,	"	"	20*s.*					
1715,	"	"	"					
1717,	"	"	additional duty of 40*s.* (?).					
1754,	"	"	"	"	10*s.*, total 50*s.*			
1756,	"	"	"	"	20*s.*	"	40*s.* (?).	
1763,	"	"	"	"	£2	"	£4.	
1771,	"	"	"	"	£5	"	£9.	
1783,	Importation prohibited.							

[5] *Compleat Coll. Laws of Maryland* (ed. 1727), p. 191; Bacon, *Laws of Maryland at Large*, 1728, ch. 8.

slowly increased to 50*s.* in 1754,[1] and £4 in 1763.[2] In 1771 a prohibitive duty of £9 was laid;[3] and in 1783, after the war, all importation by sea was stopped and illegally imported Negroes were freed.[4]

Compared with the trade to Virginia and the Carolinas, the slave-trade to Maryland was small, and seems at no time to have reached proportions which alarmed the inhabitants. It was regulated to the economic demand by a slowly increasing tariff, and finally, after 1769, had nearly ceased of its own accord before the restrictive legislation of Revolutionary times.[5] Probably the proximity of Maryland to Virginia made an independent slave-trade less necessary to her.

9. **General Character of these Restrictions.** We find in the planting colonies all degrees of advocacy of the trade, from the passiveness of Maryland to the clamor of Georgia. Opposition to the trade did not appear in Georgia, was based almost solely on political fear of insurrection in Carolina, and sprang largely from the same motive in Virginia, mingled with some moral repugnance. As a whole, it may be said that whatever opposition to the slave-trade there was in the planting colonies was based principally on the political fear of insurrection.

[1] Bacon, *Laws*, 1754, ch. 9, 14.

[2] *Ibid.*, 1763, ch. 28.

[3] *Laws of Maryland since* 1763: 1771, ch. 7. Cf. *Ibid.*: 1777, sess. Feb.–Apr., ch. 18.

[4] *Ibid.*: 1783, sess. Apr.–June, ch. 23.

[5] "The last importation of slaves into Maryland was, as I am credibly informed, in the year 1769": William Eddis, *Letters from America* (London, 1792), p. 65, note.

The number of slaves in Maryland has been estimated as follows: —

In 1704,	4,475.	*Doc. rel. Col. Hist. New York*, V. 605.
" 1710,	7,935.	*Ibid.*
" 1712,	8,330.	Scharf, *History of Maryland*, I. 377.
" 1719,	25,000.	*Doc. rel. Col. Hist. New York*, V. 605.
" 1748,	36,000.	McMahon, *History of Maryland*, I. 313.
" 1755,	46,356.	*Gentleman's Magazine*, XXXIV. 261.
" 1756,	46,225.	McMahon, *History of Maryland*, I. 313.
" 1761,	49,675.	Dexter, *Colonial Population*, p. 21, note.
" 1782,	83,362.	*Encyclopædia Britannica* (9th ed.), XV. 603.
" 1787,	80,000.	Dexter, *Colonial Population*, p. 21, note.

CHAPTER III.

THE FARMING COLONIES.

10. **Character of these Colonies.** The colonies of this group, occupying the central portion of the English possessions, comprise those communities where, on account of climate, physical characteristics, and circumstances of settlement, slavery as an institution found but a narrow field for development. The climate was generally rather cool for the newly imported slaves, the soil was best suited to crops to which slave labor was poorly adapted, and the training and habits of the great body of settlers offered little chance for the growth of a slave system. These conditions varied, of course, in different colonies; but the general statement applies to all. These communities of small farmers and traders derived whatever opposition they had to the slave-trade from three sorts of motives, — economic, political, and moral. First, the importation of slaves did not pay, except to supply a moderate demand for household servants. Secondly, these colonies, as well as those in the South, had a wholesome political fear of a large servile population. Thirdly, the settlers of many of these colonies were of sterner moral fibre than the Southern cavaliers and adventurers, and, in the absence of great counteracting motives, were more easily led to oppose the institution and the trade. Finally, it must be noted that these colonies did not so generally regard themselves as temporary commercial investments as did Virginia and

Carolina. Intending to found permanent States, these settlers from the first more carefully studied the ultimate interests of those States.

11. **The Dutch Slave-Trade.** The Dutch seem to have commenced the slave-trade to the American continent, the Middle colonies and some of the Southern receiving supplies from them. John Rolfe relates that the last of August, 1619, there came to Virginia "a dutch man of warre that sold us twenty Negars."[1] This was probably one of the ships of the numerous private Dutch trading-companies which early entered into and developed the lucrative African slave-trade. Ships sailed from Holland to Africa, got slaves in exchange for their goods, carried the slaves to the West Indies or Brazil, and returned home laden with sugar.[2] Through the enterprise of one of these trading-companies the settlement of New Amsterdam was begun, in 1614. In 1621 the private companies trading in the West were all merged into the Dutch West India Company, and given a monopoly of American trade. This company was very active, sending in four years 15,430 Negroes to Brazil,[3] carrying on war with Spain, supplying even the English plantations,[4] and gradually becoming the great slave carrier of the day.

The commercial supremacy of the Dutch early excited the envy and emulation of the English. The Navigation Ordinance of 1651 was aimed at them, and two wars were necessary to wrest the slave-trade from them and place it in the hands of the English. The final terms of peace among other things surrendered New Netherland to England, and opened the way for England to become henceforth the world's greatest slave-trader. Although the Dutch had thus commenced the continental slave-trade, they had not actually furnished a very large number of slaves to the English colonies outside the West Indies. A small trade had, by 1698, brought a few thousand to New York, and

[1] Smith, *Generall Historie of Virginia* (1626 and 1632), p. 126.

[2] Cf. Southey, *History of Brazil.*

[3] De Laet, in O'Callaghan, *Voyages of the Slavers*, etc., p. viii.

[4] See, e. g., Sainsbury, *Cal. State Papers; Col. Ser., America and W. Indies*, 1574–1660, p. 279.

still fewer to New Jersey.[1] It was left to the English, with their strong policy in its favor, to develop this trade.

12. **Restrictions in New York.**[2] The early ordinances of the Dutch, laying duties, generally of ten per cent, on slaves, probably proved burdensome to the trade, although this was not intentional.[3] The Biblical prohibition of slavery and the slave-trade, copied from New England codes into the Duke of York's Laws, had no practical application,[4] and the trade continued to be encouraged in the governors' instructions. In 1709 a duty of £3 was laid on Negroes from elsewhere than Africa.[5] This was aimed at West India slaves, and was prohibitive. By 1716

[1] Cf. below, pp. 19, 27, notes; also *Freedoms*, XXX., in O'Callaghan, *Laws of New Netherland*, 1638–74 (ed. 1868), p. 10; Brodhead, *History of New York*, I. 312.

[2] The following is a summary of the legislation of the colony of New York; details will be found in Appendix A: —

1709,	Duty Act:	£3 on Negroes not direct from Africa (Continued by the Acts of 1710, 1711).
1711,	Bill to lay further duty, lost in Council.	
1716,	Duty Act:	5 oz. plate on Africans in colony ships.
		10 " " " " other ships.
1728,	" "	40*s*. on Africans, £4 on colonial Negroes.
1732,	" "	" " " " "
1734,	" "	(?)
1753,	" "	40*s*. " " " " (This act was annually continued.)
[1777,	Vermont Constitution does not recognize slavery.]	
1785,	Sale of slaves in State prohibited.	
[1786,	" " Vermont prohibited.]	
1788,	" " State "	

[3] O'Callaghan, *Laws of New Netherland*, 1638–74, pp. 31, 348, etc. The colonists themselves were encouraged to trade, but the terms were not favorable enough: *Doc. rel. Col. Hist. New York*, I. 246; *Laws of New Netherland*, pp. 81–2, note, 127. The colonists declared "that they are inclined to a foreign Trade, and especially to the Coast of *Africa*, . . . in order to fetch thence Slaves": O'Callaghan, *Voyages of the Slavers*, etc., p. 172.

[4] *Charter to William Penn*, etc. (1879), p. 12. First published on Long Island in 1664. Possibly Negro slaves were explicitly excepted. Cf. *Magazine of American History*, XI. 411, and *N. Y. Hist. Soc. Coll.*, I. 322.

[5] *Acts of Assembly*, 1691–1718, pp. 97, 125, 134; *Doc. rel. Col. Hist. New York*, V. 178, 185, 293.

the duty on all slaves was £1 12½*s.*, which was probably a mere revenue figure.[1] In 1728 a duty of 40*s.* was laid, to be continued until 1737.[2] It proved restrictive, however, and on the "humble petition of the Merchants and Traders of the City of Bristol" was disallowed in 1735, as "greatly prejudicial to the Trade and Navigation of this Kingdom."[3] Governor Cosby was also reminded that no duties on slaves payable by the importer were to be laid. Later, in 1753, the 40*s.* duty was restored, but under the increased trade of those days was not felt.[4] No further restrictions seem to have been attempted until 1785, when the sale of slaves in the State was forbidden.[5]

The chief element of restriction in this colony appears to have been the shrewd business sense of the traders, who never flooded the slave market, but kept a supply sufficient for the slowly growing demand. Between 1701 and 1726 only about 2,375 slaves were imported, and in 1774 the total slave population amounted to 21,149.[6] No restriction was ever put by

[1] The Assembly attempted to raise the slave duty in 1711, but the Council objected (*Doc. rel. Col. Hist. New York*, V. 292 ff.), although, as it seems, not on account of the slave duty in particular. Another act was passed between 1711 and 1716, but its contents are not known (cf. title of the Act of 1716). For the Act of 1716, see *Acts of Assembly*, 1691–1718, p. 224.

[2] *Doc. rel. Col. Hist. New York*, VI. 37, 38.

[3] *Ibid.*, VI. 32–4.

[4] *Ibid.*, VII. 907. This act was annually renewed. The slave duty remained a chief source of revenue down to 1774. Cf. *Report of Governor Tryon*, in *Doc. rel. Col. Hist. New York*, VIII. 452.

[5] *Laws of New York*, 1785–88 (ed. 1886), ch. 68, p. 121. Substantially the same act reappears in the revision of the laws of 1788: *Ibid.*, ch. 40, p. 676.

[6] The slave population of New York has been estimated as follows: —

In 1698, 2,170. *Doc. rel. Col. Hist. New York*, IV. 420.
" 1703, 2,258. *N. Y. Col. MSS.*, XLVIII.; cited in Hough, *N. Y. Census*, 1855, Introd.
" 1712, 2,425. *Ibid.*, LVII., LIX. (a partial census).
" 1723, 6,171. *Doc. rel. Col. Hist. New York*, V. 702.
" 1731, 7,743. *Ibid.*, V. 929.
" 1737, 8,941. *Ibid.*, VI. 133.
" 1746, 9,107. *Ibid.*, VI. 392.
" 1749, 10,692. *Ibid.*, VI. 550.
" 1756, 13,548. *London Doc.*, XLIV. 123; cited in Hough, as above.

New York on participation in the trade outside the colony, and in spite of national laws New York merchants continued to be engaged in this traffic even down to the Civil War.[1]

Vermont, who withdrew from New York in 1777, in her first Constitution[2] declared slavery illegal, and in 1786 stopped by law the sale and transportation of slaves within her boundaries.[3]

13. **Restrictions in Pennsylvania and Delaware.**[4] One of the first American protests against the slave-trade came from

In 1771, 19,863. *Ibid.*, XLIV. 144; cited in Hough, as above.
" 1774 21,149. *Ibid.*, " " " " "
" 1786, 18,889. *Deeds in office Sec. of State*, XXII. 35.

Total number of Africans imported from 1701 to 1726, 2,375, of whom 802 were from Africa: O'Callaghan, *Documentary History of New York*, I. 482.

[1] Cf. below, Chapter XI.

[2] *Vermont State Papers*, 1779–86, p. 244. The return of sixteen slaves in Vermont, by the first census, was an error: *New England Record*, XXIX. 249.

[3] *Vermont State Papers*, p. 505.

[4] The following is a summary of the legislation of the colony of Pennsylvania and Delaware; details will be found in Appendix A:—

1705, Duty Act: (?).
1710, " " 40*s*. (Disallowed).
1712, " " £20 "
1712, " " supplementary to the Act of 1710.
1715, " " £5 (Disallowed).
1718, " "
1720, " " (?).
1722, " " (?).
1725–6, " " £10.
1726, " "
1729, " " £2.
1761, " " £10.
1761, " " (?).
1768, " " re-enactment of the Act of 1761.
1773, " " perpetual additional duty of £10; total, £20.
1775, Bill to prohibit importation vetoed by the governor (Delaware).
1775, Bill to prohibit importation vetoed by the governor.
1778, Back duties on slaves ordered collected.
1780, Act for the gradual abolition of slavery.
1787, Act to prevent the exportation of slaves (Delaware).
1788, Act to prevent the slave-trade.

certain German Friends, in 1688, at a Weekly Meeting held in Germantown, Pennsylvania. "These are the reasons," wrote "Garret henderich, derick up de graeff, Francis daniell Pastorius, and Abraham up Den graef," "why we are against the traffick of men-body, as followeth: Is there any that would be done or handled at this manner? . . . Now, tho they are black, we cannot conceive there is more liberty to have them slaves, as it is to have other white ones. There is a saying, that we shall doe to all men like as we will be done ourselves; making no difference of what generation, descent or colour they are. And those who steal or robb men, and those who buy or purchase them, are they not all alike?"[1] This little leaven helped slowly to work a revolution in the attitude of this great sect toward slavery and the slave-trade. The Yearly Meeting at first postponed the matter, "It having so General a Relation to many other Parts."[2] Eventually, however, in 1696, the Yearly Meeting advised "That Friends be careful not to encourage the bringing in of any more Negroes."[3] This advice was repeated in stronger terms for a quarter-century,[4] and by that time Sandiford, Benezet, Lay, and Woolman had begun their crusade. In 1754 the Friends took a step farther and made the purchase of slaves a matter of discipline.[5] Four years later the Yearly Meeting expressed itself clearly as "against every branch of this practice," and declared that if "any professing with us should persist to vindicate it, and be concerned in importing, selling or purchasing slaves, the respective Monthly Meetings to which they belong should manifest their disunion with such persons."[6] Further, manumission was recommended, and in 1776 made compulsory.[7]

[1] From fac-simile copy, published at Germantown in 1880. Cf. Whittier's poem, "Pennsylvania Hall" (*Poetical Works*, Riverside ed., III. 62); and Proud, *History of Pennsylvania* (1797), I. 219.

[2] From fac-simile copy, published at Germantown in 1880.

[3] Bettle, *Notices of Negro Slavery*, in *Penn. Hist. Soc. Mem.* (1864), I. 383.

[4] Cf. Bettle, *Notices of Negro Slavery*, *passim.*

[5] Janney, *History of the Friends*, III. 315–7.

[6] *Ibid.*, III. 317.

[7] Bettle, in *Penn. Hist. Soc. Mem.*, I. 395.

The effect of this attitude of the Friends was early manifested in the legislation of all the colonies where the sect was influential, and particularly in Pennsylvania.

One of the first duty acts (1710) laid a restrictive duty of 40*s.* on slaves, and was eventually disallowed.[1] In 1712 William Southeby petitioned the Assembly totally to abolish slavery. This the Assembly naturally refused to attempt; but the same year, in response to another petition "signed by many hands," they passed an "Act to prevent the Importation of Negroes and Indians,"[2] — the first enactment of its kind in America. This act was inspired largely by the general fear of insurrection which succeeded the "Negro-plot" of 1712 in New York. It declared: "Whereas, divers Plots and Insurrections have frequently happened, not only in the Islands but on the Main Land of *America*, by Negroes, which have been carried on so far that several of the inhabitants have been barbarously Murthered, an Instance whereof we have lately had in our Neighboring Colony of *New York*,"[3] etc. It then proceeded to lay a prohibitive duty of £20 on all slaves imported. These acts were quickly disposed of in England. Three duty acts affecting Negroes, including the prohibitory act, were in 1713 disallowed, and it was directed that "the Dep^ty^ Govr Council and Assembly of Pensilvania, be & they are hereby Strictly Enjoyned & required not to permit the said Laws . . . to be from henceforward put in Execution."[4] The Assembly repealed these laws, but in 1715 passed another laying a duty of £5, which was also eventually disallowed.[5] Other acts, the provisions of which are

[1] *Penn. Col. Rec.* (1852), II. 530; Bettle, in *Penn. Hist. Soc. Mem.*, I. 415.

[2] *Laws of Pennsylvania, collected*, etc., 1714, p. 165; Bettle, in *Penn. Hist. Soc. Mem.*, I. 387.

[3] See preamble of the act.

[4] The Pennsylvanians did not allow their laws to reach England until long after they were passed: *Penn. Archives*, I. 161–2; *Col. Rec.*, II. 572–3. These acts were disallowed Feb. 20, 1713. Another duty act was passed in 1712, supplementary to the Act of 1710 (*Col. Rec.*, II. 553). The contents are unknown.

[5] *Acts and Laws of Pennsylvania*, 1715, p. 270; Chalmers, *Opinions*, II. 118. Before the disallowance was known, the act had been continued by the Act of 1718: Carey and Bioren, *Laws of Pennsylvania*, 1700–1802, I. 118; *Penn. Col. Rec.*, III. 38.

not clear, were passed in 1720 and 1722,[1] and in 1725–1726 the duty on Negroes was raised to the restrictive figure of £10.[2] This duty, for some reason not apparent, was lowered to £2 in 1729,[3] but restored again in 1761.[4] A struggle occurred over this last measure, the Friends petitioning for it, and the Philadelphia merchants against it, declaring that "We, the subscribers, ever desirous to extend the Trade of this Province, have seen, for some time past, the many inconveniencys the Inhabitants have suffer'd for want of Labourers and artificers, . . . have for some time encouraged the importation of Negros;" they prayed therefore at least for a delay in passing the measure.[5] The law, nevertheless, after much debate and altercation with the governor, finally passed.

These repeated acts nearly stopped the trade, and the manumission or sale of Negroes by the Friends decreased the number of slaves in the province. The rising spirit of independence enabled the colony, in 1773, to restore the prohibitive duty of £20 and make it perpetual.[6] After the Revolution unpaid duties on slaves were collected and the slaves registered,[7] and in 1780 an "Act for the gradual Abolition of Slavery" was passed.[8] As there were probably at no time before the war more than 11,000 slaves in Pennsylvania,[9] the task thus accomplished

[1] Carey and Bioren, *Laws*, I. 165; *Penn. Col. Rec.*, III. 171; Bettle, in *Penn. Hist. Soc. Mem.*, I. 389, note.

[2] Carey and Bioren, *Laws*, I. 214; Bettle, in *Penn. Hist. Soc. Mem.*, I. 388. Possibly there were two acts this year.

[3] *Laws of Pennsylvania* (ed. 1742), p. 354, ch. 287. Possibly some change in the currency made this change appear greater than it was.

[4] Carey and Bioren, *Laws*, I. 371; *Acts of Assembly* (ed. 1782), p. 149; Dallas, *Laws*, I. 406, ch. 379. This act was renewed in 1768: Carey and Bioren, *Laws*, I. 451; *Penn. Col. Rec.*, IX. 472, 637, 641.

[5] *Penn. Col. Rec.*, VIII. 576.

[6] A large petition called for this bill. Much altercation ensued with the governor: Dallas, *Laws*, I. 671, ch. 692; *Penn. Col. Rec.*, X. 77; Bettle, in *Penn. Hist. Soc. Mem.*, I. 388–9.

[7] Dallas, *Laws*, I. 782, ch. 810.

[8] *Ibid.*, I. 838, ch. 881.

[9] There exist but few estimates of the number of slaves in this colony: —

In 1721, 2,500–5,000. *Doc. rel. Col. Hist. New York*, V. 604.
" 1754, 11,000. Bancroft, *Hist. of United States* (1883), II. 391.
" 1760, "very few." Burnaby, *Travels through N. Amer.* (2d ed.), p. 81.
" 1775, 2,000. *Penn. Archives*, IV. 597.

was not so formidable as in many other States. As it was, participation in the slave-trade outside the colony was not prohibited until 1788.[1]

It seems probable that in the original Swedish settlements along the Delaware slavery was prohibited.[2] This measure had, however, little practical effect; for as soon as the Dutch got control the slave-trade was opened, although, as it appears, to no large extent. After the fall of the Dutch Delaware came into English hands. Not until 1775 do we find any legislation on the slave-trade. In that year the colony attempted to prohibit the importation of slaves, but the governor vetoed the bill.[3] Finally, in 1776 by the Constitution, and in 1787 by law, importation and exportation were both prohibited.[4]

14. **Restrictions in New Jersey.**[5] Although the freeholders of West New Jersey declared, in 1676, that "all and every Person and Persons Inhabiting the said Province, shall, as far as in us lies, be free from Oppression and Slavery,"[6] yet Negro slaves are early found in the colony.[7] The first restrictive measure was passed, after considerable friction between the Council and the House, in 1713; it laid a duty of £10, currency.[8] Governor Hunter explained to the Board of Trade that the bill was "calculated to Encourage the Importation of

[1] Dallas, *Laws*, II. 586.

[2] Cf. *Argonautica Gustaviana*, pp. 21-3; *Del. Hist. Soc. Papers*, III. 10; *Hazard's Register*, IV. 221, §§ 23, 24; *Hazard's Annals*, p. 372; Armstrong, *Record of Upland Court*, pp. 29-30, and notes.

[3] Force, *American Archives*, 4th Ser., II. 128-9.

[4] *Ibid.*, 5th Ser., I. 1178; *Laws of Delaware*, 1797 (Newcastle ed.), p. 884, ch. 145 b.

[5] The following is a summary of the legislation of the colony of New Jersey; details will be found in Appendix A:—

1713, Duty Act: £10.
1763 (?), Duty Act.
1769, " " £15.
1774, " " £5 on Africans, £10 on colonial Negroes.
1786, Importation prohibited.

[6] Leaming and Spicer, *Grants*, *Concessions*, etc., p. 398. Probably this did not refer to Negroes at all.

[7] Cf. Vincent, *History of Delaware*, I. 159, 381.

[8] *Laws and Acts of New Jersey*, 1703-17 (ed. 1717), p. 43.

white Servants for the better Peopeling that Country."[1] How long this act continued does not appear; probably, not long. No further legislation was enacted until 1762 or 1763, when a prohibitive duty was laid on account of "the inconvenience the Province is exposed to in lying open to the free importation of Negros, when the Provinces on each side have laid duties on them."[2] The Board of Trade declared that while they did not object to "the Policy of imposing a reasonable duty," they could not assent to this, and the act was disallowed.[3] The Act of 1769 evaded the technical objection of the Board of Trade, and laid a duty of £15 on the first purchasers of Negroes, because, as the act declared, "Duties on the Importation of Negroes in several of the neighbouring Colonies hath, on Experience, been found beneficial in the Introduction of sober, industrious Foreigners."[4] In 1774 a bill which, according to the report of the Council to Governor Morris, "plainly intended an entire Prohibition of all Slaves being imported from foreign Parts," was thrown out by the Council.[5] Importation was finally prohibited in 1786.[6]

15. **General Character of these Restrictions.** The main difference in motive between the restrictions which the planting and the farming colonies put on the African slave-trade, lay in the fact that the former limited it mainly from fear of insurrection, the latter mainly because it did not pay. Naturally, the latter motive worked itself out with much less legislation than the former; for this reason, and because they held a smaller number of slaves, most of these colonies have fewer actual statutes than the Southern colonies. In Pennsylvania alone did this

[1] *N. J. Archives*, IV. 196. There was much difficulty in passing the bill: *Ibid.*, XIII. 516–41.

[2] *Ibid.*, IX. 345–6. The exact provisions of the act I have not found.

[3] *Ibid.*, IX. 383, 447, 458. Chiefly because the duty was laid on the importer.

[4] Allinson, *Acts of Assembly*, pp. 315–6.

[5] *N. J. Archives*, VI. 222.

[6] *Acts of the 10th General Assembly*, May 2, 1786. There are two estimates of the number of slaves in this colony:—

In 1738, 3,981. *American Annals*, II. 127.
" 1754, 4,606. " " II. 143.

general economic revolt against the trade acquire a distinct moral tinge. Although even here the institution was naturally doomed, yet the clear moral insight of the Quakers checked the trade much earlier than would otherwise have happened. We may say, then, that the farming colonies checked the slave-trade primarily from economic motives.

CHAPTER IV.

THE TRADING COLONIES.

16. Character of these Colonies.
17. New England and the Slave-Trade.
18. Restrictions in New Hampshire.
19. Restrictions in Massachusetts.
20. Restrictions in Rhode Island.
21. Restrictions in Connecticut.
22. General Character of these Restrictions.

16. **Character of these Colonies.** The rigorous climate of New England, the character of her settlers, and their pronounced political views gave slavery an even slighter basis here than in the Middle colonies. The significance of New England in the African slave-trade does not therefore lie in the fact that she early discountenanced the system of slavery and stopped importation; but rather in the fact that her citizens, being the traders of the New World, early took part in the carrying slave-trade and furnished slaves to the other colonies. An inquiry, therefore, into the efforts of the New England colonies to suppress the slave-trade would fall naturally into two parts: first, and chiefly, an investigation of the efforts to stop the participation of citizens in the carrying slave-trade; secondly, an examination of the efforts made to banish the slave-trade from New England soil.

17. **New England and the Slave-Trade.** Vessels from Massachusetts,[1] Rhode Island,[2] Connecticut,[3] and, to a less extent, from

[1] Cf. Weeden, *Economic and Social History of New England*, II. 449–72; G. H. Moore, *Slavery in Massachusetts;* Charles Deane, *Connection of Massachusetts with Slavery*.

[2] Cf. *American Historical Record*, I. 311, 338.

[3] Cf. W. C. Fowler, *Local Law in Massachusetts and Connecticut*, etc., pp. 122–6.

New Hampshire,[1] were early and largely engaged in the carrying slave-trade. "We know," said Thomas Pemberton in 1795, "that a large trade to Guinea was carried on for many years by the citizens of Massachusetts Colony, who were the proprietors of the vessels and their cargoes, out and home. Some of the slaves purchased in Guinea, and I suppose the greatest part of them, were sold in the West Indies."[2] Dr. John Eliot asserted that "it made a considerable branch of our commerce. . . . It declined very little till the Revolution."[3] Yet the trade of this colony was said not to equal that of Rhode Island. Newport was the mart for slaves offered for sale in the North, and a point of reshipment for all slaves. It was principally this trade that raised Newport to her commercial importance in the eighteenth century.[4] Connecticut, too, was an important slave-trader, sending large numbers of horses and other commodities to the West Indies in exchange for slaves, and selling the slaves in other colonies.

This trade formed a perfect circle. Owners of slavers carried slaves to South Carolina, and brought home naval stores for their ship-building; or to the West Indies, and brought home molasses; or to other colonies, and brought home hogsheads. The molasses was made into the highly prized New England rum, and shipped in these hogsheads to Africa for more slaves.[5]

[1] Cf. W. C. Fowler, *Local Law in Massachusetts and Connecticut*, etc., p. 124.

[2] Deane, *Letters and Documents relating to Slavery in Massachusetts*, in *Mass. Hist. Soc. Coll.*, 5th Ser., III. 392.

[3] *Ibid.*, III. 382.

[4] Weeden, *Economic and Social History of New England*, II. 454.

[5] A typical voyage is that of the brigantine "Sanderson" of Newport. She was fitted out in March, 1752, and carried, beside the captain, two mates and six men, and a cargo of 8,220 gallons of rum, together with "African" iron, flour, pots, tar, sugar, and provisions, shackles, shirts, and water. Proceeding to Africa, the captain after some difficulty sold his cargo for slaves, and in April, 1753, he is expected in Barbadoes, as the consignees write. They also state that slaves are selling at £33 to £56 per head in lots. After a stormy and dangerous voyage, Captain Lindsay arrived, June 17, 1753, with fifty-six slaves, "all in helth & fatt." He also had 40 oz. of gold dust, and 8 or 9 cwt. of pepper. The net proceeds of the sale of all this was £1,324 3*d.* The captain then took on board 55 hhd. of molasses

Thus, the rum-distilling industry indicates to some extent the activity of New England in the slave-trade. In May, 1752, one Captain Freeman found so many slavers fitting out that, in spite of the large importations of molasses, he could get no rum for his vessel.[1] In Newport alone twenty-two stills were at one time running continuously;[2] and Massachusetts annually distilled 15,000 hogsheads of molasses into this "chief manufacture."[3]

Turning now to restrictive measures, we must first note the measures of the slave-consuming colonies which tended to limit the trade. These measures, however, came comparatively late, were enforced with varying degrees of efficiency, and did not seriously affect the slave-trade before the Revolution. The moral sentiment of New England put some check upon the trade. Although in earlier times the most respectable people took ventures in slave-trading voyages, yet there gradually arose a moral sentiment which tended to make the business somewhat disreputable.[4] In the line, however, of definite legal enactments to stop New England citizens from carrying slaves from Africa to any place in the world, there were, before the Revolution, none. Indeed, not until the years 1787–1788 was slave-trading in itself an indictable offence in any New England State.

The particular situation in each colony, and the efforts to restrict the small importing slave-trade of New England, can best be studied in a separate view of each community.

18. Restrictions in New Hampshire. The statistics of slavery in New Hampshire show how weak an institution it always was

and 3 hhd. 27 bbl. of sugar, amounting to £911 17*s*. 2½*d*., received bills on Liverpool for the balance, and returned in safety to Rhode Island. He had done so well that he was immediately given a new ship and sent to Africa again. *American Historical Record*, I. 315–9, 338–42.

[1] *Ibid.*, I. 316.

[2] *Ibid.*, I. 317.

[3] *Ibid.*, I. 344; cf. Weeden, *Economic and Social History of New England*, II. 459.

[4] Cf. *New England Register*, XXXI. 75–6, letter of John Saffin *et al.* to Welstead. Cf. also Sewall, *Protest*, etc.

in that colony.[1] Consequently, when the usual instructions were sent to Governor Wentworth as to the encouragement he must give to the slave-trade, the House replied: "We have considered his Maj[ties] Instruction relating to an Impost on Negroes & Felons, to which this House answers, that there never was any duties laid on either, by this Goverm[t], and so few bro't in that it would not be worth the Publick notice, so as to make an act concerning them."[2] This remained true for the whole history of the colony. Importation was never stopped by actual enactment, but was eventually declared contrary to the Constitution of 1784.[3] The participation of citizens in the trade appears never to have been forbidden.

19. **Restrictions in Massachusetts.** The early Biblical codes of Massachusetts confined slavery to "lawfull Captives taken in iust warres, & such strangers as willingly selle themselves or are sold to us."[4] The stern Puritanism of early days endeavored to carry this out literally, and consequently when a certain Captain Smith, about 1640, attacked an African village and brought some of the unoffending natives home, he was promptly arrested. Eventually, the General Court ordered the Negroes sent home at the colony's expense, "conceiving themselues bound by y[e] first oportunity to bear witnes against y[e] haynos & crying sinn of manstealing, as also to P'scribe such timely redresse for what is past, & such a law for y[e] future as may sufficiently deterr all oth[r]s belonging to us to have to do in such vile & most odious courses, iustly abhored of all good & iust men."[5]

1 The number of slaves in New Hampshire has been estimated as follows:

In 1730,	200.	*N. H. Hist. Soc. Coll.*, I. 229.
" 1767,	633.	*Granite Monthly*, IV. 108.
" 1773,	681.	*Ibid.*
" 1773,	674.	*N. H. Province Papers*, X. 636.
" 1775,	479.	*Granite Monthly*, IV. 108.
" 1790,	158.	*Ibid.*

2 *N. H. Province Papers*, IV. 617.

3 *Granite Monthly*, VI. 377; Poore, *Federal and State Constitutions*, pp. 1280–1.

4 Cf. *The Body of Liberties*, § 91, in Whitmore, *Bibliographical Sketch of the Laws of the Massachusetts Colony*, published at Boston in 1890.

5 *Mass. Col. Rec.*, II. 168, 176; III. 46, 49, 84.

The temptation of trade slowly forced the colony from this high moral ground. New England ships were early found in the West Indian slave-trade, and the more the carrying trade developed, the more did the profits of this branch of it attract Puritan captains. By the beginning of the eighteenth century the slave-trade was openly recognized as legitimate commerce; cargoes came regularly to Boston, and "The merchants of Boston quoted negroes, like any other merchandise demanded by their correspondents."[1] At the same time, the Puritan conscience began to rebel against the growth of actual slavery on New England soil. It was a much less violent wrenching of moral ideas of right and wrong to allow Massachusetts men to carry slaves to South Carolina than to allow cargoes to come into Boston, and become slaves in Massachusetts. Early in the eighteenth century, therefore, opposition arose to the further importation of Negroes, and in 1705 an act "for the Better Preventing of a Spurious and Mixt Issue," laid a restrictive duty of £4 on all slaves imported.[2] One provision of this act plainly illustrates the attitude of Massachusetts: like the acts of many of the New England colonies, it allowed a rebate of the whole duty on re-exportation. The harbors of New England were thus offered as a free exchange-mart for slavers. All the duty acts of the Southern and Middle colonies allowed a rebate of one-half or three-fourths of the duty on the re-exportation of the slave, thus laying a small tax on even temporary importation.

The Act of 1705 was evaded, but it was not amended until 1728, when the penalty for evasion was raised to £100.[3] The act remained in force, except possibly for one period of four years, until 1749. Meantime the movement against importation grew. A bill "for preventing the Importation of Slaves into this Province" was introduced in the Legislature in 1767, but after strong opposition and disagreement between House and Council it was dropped.[4] In 1771 the struggle was renewed.

[1] Weeden, *Economic and Social History of New England*, II. 456.

[2] *Mass. Province Laws*, 1705–6, ch. 10.

[3] *Ibid.*, 1728–9, ch. 16; 1738–9, ch. 27.

[4] For petitions of towns, cf. Felt, *Annals of Salem* (1849), II. 416;

A similar bill passed, but was vetoed by Governor Hutchinson.[1] The imminent war and the discussions incident to it had now more and more aroused public opinion, and there were repeated attempts to gain executive consent to a prohibitory law. In 1774 such a bill was twice passed, but never received assent.[2]

The new Revolutionary government first met the subject in the case of two Negroes captured on the high seas, who were advertised for sale at Salem. A resolution was introduced into the Legislature, directing the release of the Negroes, and declaring "That the selling and enslaving the human species is a direct violation of the natural rights alike vested in all men by their Creator, and utterly inconsistent with the avowed principles on which this, and the other United States, have carried their struggle for liberty even to the last appeal." To this the Council would not consent; and the resolution, as finally passed, merely forbade the sale or ill-treatment of the Negroes.[3] Committees on the slavery question were appointed in 1776 and 1777,[4] and although a letter to Congress on the matter, and a bill for the abolition of slavery were reported, no decisive action was taken.

Boston Town Records, 1758–69, p. 183. Cf. also Otis's anti-slavery speech in 1761: John Adams, *Works*, X. 315. For proceedings, see *House Journal*, 1767, pp. 353, 358, 387, 390, 393, 408, 409–10, 411, 420. Cf. Samuel Dexter's answer to Dr. Belknap's inquiry, Feb. 23, 1795, in Deane (*Mass. Hist. Soc. Coll.*, 5th Ser., III. 385). A committee on slave importation was appointed in 1764. Cf. *House Journal*, 1763–64, p. 170.

[1] *House Journal*, 1771, pp. 211, 215, 219, 228, 234, 236, 240, 242–3; Moore, *Slavery in Massachusetts*, pp. 131–2.

[2] Felt, *Annals of Salem* (1849), II. 416–7; Swan, *Dissuasion to Great Britain*, etc. (1773), p. x; Washburn, *Historical Sketches of Leicester, Mass.*, pp. 442–3; Freeman, *History of Cape Cod*, II. 114; Deane, in *Mass. Hist. Soc. Coll.*, 5th Ser., III. 432; Moore, *Slavery in Massachusetts*, pp. 135–40; Williams, *History of the Negro Race in America*, I. 234–6; *House Journal*, March, 1774, pp. 224, 226, 237, etc.; June, 1774, pp. 27, 41, etc. For a copy of the bill, see Moore.

[3] *Mass. Hist. Soc. Proceedings*, 1855–58, p. 196; Force, *American Archives*, 5th Ser., II. 769; *House Journal*, 1776, pp. 105–9; *General Court Records*, March 13, 1776, etc., pp. 581–9; Moore, *Slavery in Massachusetts*, pp. 149–54. Cf. Moore, pp. 163–76.

[4] Moore, *Slavery in Massachusetts*, pp. 148–9, 181–5.

All such efforts were finally discontinued, as the system was already practically extinct in Massachusetts and the custom of importation had nearly ceased. Slavery was eventually declared by judicial decision to have been abolished.[1] The first step toward stopping the participation of Massachusetts citizens in the slave-trade outside the State was taken in 1785, when a committee of inquiry was appointed by the Legislature.[2] No act was, however, passed until 1788, when participation in the trade was prohibited, on pain of £50 forfeit for every slave and £200 for every ship engaged.[3]

20. **Restrictions in Rhode Island.** In 1652 Rhode Island passed a law designed to prohibit life slavery in the colony. It declared that "Whereas, there is a common course practised amongst English men to buy negers, to that end they may have them for service or slaves forever; for the preventinge of such practices among us, let it be ordered, that no blacke mankind or white being forced by covenant bond, or otherwise, to serve any man or his assighnes longer than ten yeares, or untill they come to bee twentie four yeares of age, if they bee taken in under fourteen, from the time of their cominge within the liber-

[1] Washburn, *Extinction of Slavery in Massachusetts;* Haynes, *Struggle for the Constitution in Massachusetts;* La Rochefoucauld, *Travels through the United States*, II. 166.

[2] Moore, *Slavery in Massachusetts*, p. 225.

[3] *Perpetual Laws of Massachusetts*, 1780–89, p. 235. The number of slaves in Massachusetts has been estimated as follows: —

In 1676,	200.	Randolph's *Report*, in *Hutchinson's Coll. of Papers*, p. 485.
" 1680,	120.	Deane, *Connection of Mass. with Slavery*, p. 28 ff.
" 1708,	550.	*Ibid.*; Moore, *Slavery in Mass.*, p. 50.
" 1720,	2,000.	*Ibid.*
" 1735,	2,600.	Deane, *Connection of Mass. with Slavery*, p. 28 ff.
" 1749,	3,000.	*Ibid.*
" 1754,	4,489.	*Ibid.*
" 1763,	5,000.	*Ibid.*
" 1764–5,	5,779.	*Ibid.*
" 1776,	5,249.	*Ibid.*
" 1784,	4,377.	Moore, *Slavery in Mass.*, p. 51.
" 1786,	4,371.	*Ibid.*
" 1790,	6,001.	*Ibid.*

ties of this Collonie. And at the end or terme of ten yeares to sett them free, as the manner is with the English servants. And that man that will not let them goe free, or shall sell them away elsewhere, to that end that they may bee enslaved to others for a long time, hee or they shall forfeit to the Collonie forty pounds."[1]

This law was for a time enforced,[2] but by the beginning of the eighteenth century it had either been repealed or become a dead letter; for the Act of 1708 recognized perpetual slavery, and laid an impost of £3 on Negroes imported.[3] This duty was really a tax on the transport trade, and produced a steady income for twenty years.[4] From the year 1700 on, the citizens of this State engaged more and more in the carrying trade, until Rhode Island became the greatest slave-trader in America. Although she did not import many slaves for her own use, she became the clearing-house for the trade of other colonies. Governor Cranston, as early as 1708, reported that between 1698 and 1708 one hundred and three vessels were built in the State, all of which were trading to the West Indies and the Southern colonies.[5] They took out lumber and brought back molasses, in most cases making a slave voyage in between. From this, the trade grew. Samuel Hopkins, about 1770, was shocked at the state of the trade: more than thirty distilleries were running in the colony, and one hundred and fifty vessels were in the slave-trade.[6] "Rhode Island," said he, "has been more deeply interested in the slave-trade, and has enslaved more Africans than any other colony in New England." Later, in 1787, he wrote: "The inhabitants of Rhode

[1] *R. I. Col. Rec.*, I. 243.

[2] Cf. letter written in 1681: *New England Register*, XXXI. 75–6. Cf. also Arnold, *History of Rhode Island*, I. 240.

[3] The text of this act is lost (*Col. Rec.*, IV. 34; Arnold, *History of Rhode Island*, II. 31). The Acts of Rhode Island were not well preserved, the first being published in Boston in 1719. Perhaps other whole acts are lost.

[4] E. g., it was expended to pave the streets of Newport, to build bridges, etc.: *R. I. Col. Rec.*, IV. 191–3, 225.

[5] *Ibid.*, IV. 55–60.

[6] Patten, *Reminiscences of Samuel Hopkins* (1843), p. 80.

Island, especially those of Newport, have had by far the greater share in this traffic, of all these United States. This trade in human species has been the first wheel of commerce in Newport, on which every other movement in business has chiefly depended. That town has been built up, and flourished in times past, at the expense of the blood, the liberty, and happiness of the poor Africans; and the inhabitants have lived on this, and by it have gotten most of their wealth and riches."[1]

The Act of 1708 was poorly enforced. The "good intentions" of its framers "were wholly frustrated" by the clandestine "hiding and conveying said negroes out of the town [Newport] into the country, where they lie concealed."[2] The act was accordingly strengthened by the Acts of 1712 and 1715, and made to apply to importations by land as well as by sea.[3] The Act of 1715, however, favored the trade by admitting African Negroes free of duty. The chaotic state of Rhode Island did not allow England often to review her legislation; but as soon as the Act of 1712 came to notice it was disallowed, and accordingly repealed in 1732.[4] Whether the Act of 1715 remained, or whether any other duty act was passed, is not clear.

While the foreign trade was flourishing, the influence of the Friends and of other causes eventually led to a movement against slavery as a local institution. Abolition societies multiplied, and in 1770 an abolition bill was ordered by the Assembly, but it was never passed.[5] Four years later the city of Providence resolved that "as personal liberty is an essential part of the natural rights of mankind," the importation of slaves and the system of slavery should cease in the colony.[6] This movement finally resulted, in 1774, in an act "prohibiting the importation of Negroes into this Colony," — a law which curiously illustrated the attitude of Rhode Island toward the slave-

[1] Hopkins, *Works* (1854), II. 615.

[2] Preamble of the Act of 1712.

[3] *R. I. Col. Rec.*, IV. 131–5, 138, 143, 191–3.

[4] *Ibid.*, IV. 471.

[5] Arnold, *History of Rhode Island*, II. 304, 321, 337. For a probable copy of the bill, see *Narragansett Historical Register*, II. 299.

[6] A man dying intestate left slaves, who became thus the property of the city; they were freed, and the town made the above resolve, May 17, 1774, in town meeting: Staples, *Annals of Providence* (1843), p. 236.

trade. The preamble of the act declared: "Whereas, the inhabitants of America are generally engaged in the preservation of their own rights and liberties, among which, that of personal freedom must be considered as the greatest; as those who are desirous of enjoying all the advantages of liberty themselves, should be willing to extend personal liberty to others;— Therefore," etc. The statute then proceeded to enact "that for the future, no negro or mulatto slave shall be brought into this colony; and in case any slave shall hereafter be brought in, he or she shall be, and are hereby, rendered immediately free. . . ." The logical ending of such an act would have been a clause prohibiting the participation of Rhode Island citizens in the slave-trade. Not only was such a clause omitted, but the following was inserted instead: "Provided, also, that nothing in this act shall extend, or be deemed to extend, to any negro or mulatto slave brought from the coast of Africa, into the West Indies, on board any vessel belonging to this colony, and which negro or mulatto slave could not be disposed of in the West Indies, but shall be brought into this colony. Provided, that the owner of such negro or mulatto slave give bond . . . that such negro or mulatto slave shall be exported out of the colony, within one year from the date of such bond; if such negro or mulatto be alive, and in a condition to be removed."[1]

In 1779 an act to prevent the sale of slaves out of the State was passed,[2] and in 1784, an act gradually to abolish slavery.[3] Not until 1787 did an act pass to forbid participation in the slave-trade. This law laid a penalty of £100 for every slave transported and £1000 for every vessel so engaged.[4]

[1] *R. I. Col. Rec.*, VII. 251–2.

[2] *Bartlett's Index*, p. 329; Arnold, *History of Rhode Island*, II. 444; *R. I. Col. Rec.*, VIII. 618.

[3] *R. I. Col. Rec.*, X. 7–8; Arnold, *History of Rhode Island*, II. 506.

[4] *Bartlett's Index*, p. 333; *Narragansett Historical Register*, II. 298–9. The number of slaves in Rhode Island has been estimated as follows:—

In 1708, 426. *R. I. Col. Rec.*, IV. 59.
" 1730, 1,648. *R. I. Hist. Tracts*, No. 19, pt. 2, p. 99.
" 1749, 3,077. Williams, *History of the Negro Race in America*, I. 281.
" 1756, 4,697. *Ibid.*
" 1774, 3,761. *R. I. Col. Rec.*, VII. 253.

21. **Restrictions in Connecticut.** Connecticut, in common with the other colonies of this section, had a trade for many years with the West Indian slave markets; and though this trade was much smaller than that of the neighboring colonies, yet many of her citizens were engaged in it. A map of Middleton at the time of the Revolution gives, among one hundred families, three slave captains and "three notables" designated as "slave-dealers."[1]

The actual importation was small,[2] and almost entirely unrestricted before the Revolution, save by a few light, general duty acts. In 1774 the further importation of slaves was prohibited, because "the increase of slaves in this Colony is injurious to the poor and inconvenient." The law prohibited importation under any pretext by a penalty of £100 per slave.[3] This was re-enacted in 1784, and provisions were made for the abolition of slavery.[4] In 1788 participation in the trade was forbidden, and the penalty placed at £50 for each slave and £500 for each ship engaged.[5]

22. **General Character of these Restrictions.** Enough has already been said to show, in the main, the character of the opposition to the slave-trade in New England. The system of slavery had, on this soil and amid these surroundings, no economic justification, and the small number of Negroes here furnished no polit-

[1] Fowler, *Local Law*, etc., p. 124.

[2] The number of slaves in Connecticut has been estimated as follows: —

In 1680, 30. *Conn. Col. Rec.*, III. 298.
" 1730, 700. Williams, *History of the Negro Race in America*, I. 259.
" 1756, 3,636. Fowler, *Local Law*, etc., p. 140.
" 1762, 4,590. Williams, *History of the Negro Race in America*, I. 260.
" 1774, 6,562. Fowler, *Local Law*, etc., p. 140.
" 1782, 6,281. *Ibid.*
" 1800, 5,281. *Ibid.*, p. 141.

[3] *Conn. Col. Rec.*, XIV. 329. Fowler (pp. 125-6) says that the law was passed in 1769, as does Sanford (p. 252). I find no proof of this. There was in Connecticut the same Biblical legislation on the trade as in Massachusetts. Cf. *Laws of Connecticut* (repr. 1865), p. 9; also *Col. Rec.*, I. 77. For general duty acts, see *Col. Rec.*, V. 405; VIII. 22; IX. 283; XIII. 72, 125.

[4] *Acts and Laws of Connecticut* (ed. 1784), pp. 233-4.

[5] *Ibid.*, pp. 368, 369, 388.

ical arguments against them. The opposition to the importation was therefore from the first based solely on moral grounds, with some social arguments. As to the carrying trade, however, the case was different. Here, too, a feeble moral opposition was early aroused, but it was swept away by the immense economic advantages of the slave traffic to a thrifty seafaring community of traders. This trade no moral suasion, not even the strong "Liberty" cry of the Revolution, was able wholly to suppress, until the closing of the West Indian and Southern markets cut off the demand for slaves.

CHAPTER V.

THE PERIOD OF THE REVOLUTION. 1774-1787.

23. **The Situation in 1774.** In the individual efforts of the various colonies to suppress the African slave-trade there may be traced certain general movements. First, from 1638 to 1664, there was a tendency to take a high moral stand against the traffic. This is illustrated in the laws of New England, in the plans for the settlement of Delaware and, later, that of Georgia, and in the protest of the German Friends. The second period, from about 1664 to 1760, has no general unity, but is marked by statutes laying duties varying in design from encouragement to absolute prohibition, by some cases of moral opposition, and by the slow but steady growth of a spirit unfavorable to the long continuance of the trade. The last colonial period, from about 1760 to 1787, is one of pronounced effort to regulate, limit, or totally prohibit the traffic. Beside these general movements, there are many waves of legislation, easily distinguishable, which rolled over several or all of the colonies at various times, such as the series of high duties following the Assiento, and the acts inspired by various Negro "plots."

Notwithstanding this, the laws of the colonies before 1774 had no national unity, the peculiar circumstances of each colony determining its legislation. With the outbreak of the Revolution came unison in action with regard to the slave-trade, as with regard to other matters, which may justly be called national. It was, of course, a critical period, — a period when, in the rapid upheaval of a few years, the complicated and diverse forces of decades meet, combine, act, and react, until the resultant seems almost the work of chance. In the settlement of the fate of slavery and the slave-trade, however, the real crisis came in the calm that succeeded the storm, in that day when, in the opinion of most men, the question seemed already settled. And indeed it needed an exceptionally clear and discerning mind, in 1787, to deny that slavery and the slave-trade in the United States of America were doomed to early annihilation. It seemed certainly a legitimate deduction from the history of the preceding century to conclude that, as the system had risen, flourished, and fallen in Massachusetts, New York, and Pennsylvania, and as South Carolina, Virginia, and Maryland were apparently following in the same legislative path, the next generation would in all probability witness the last throes of the system on our soil.

To be sure, the problem had its uncertain quantities. The motives of the law-makers in South Carolina and Pennsylvania were dangerously different; the century of industrial expansion was slowly dawning and awakening that vast economic revolution in which American slavery was to play so prominent and fatal a rôle; and, finally, there were already in the South faint signs of a changing moral attitude toward slavery, which would no longer regard the system as a temporary makeshift, but rather as a permanent though perhaps unfortunate necessity. With regard to the slave-trade, however, there appeared to be substantial unity of opinion; and there were, in 1787, few things to indicate that a cargo of five hundred African slaves would openly be landed in Georgia in 1860.

24. **The Condition of the Slave-Trade.** In 1760 England, the chief slave-trading nation, was sending on an average to Africa 163 ships annually, with a tonnage of 18,000 tons, carrying exports to the value of £163,818. Only about twenty of these ships regularly returned to England. Most of them carried

slaves to the West Indies, and returned laden with sugar and other products. Thus may be formed some idea of the size and importance of the slave-trade at that time, although for a complete view we must add to this the trade under the French, Portuguese, Dutch, and Americans. The trade fell off somewhat toward 1770, but was flourishing again when the Revolution brought a sharp and serious check upon it, bringing down the number of English slavers, clearing, from 167 in 1774 to 28 in 1779, and the tonnage from 17,218 to 3,475 tons. After the war the trade gradually recovered, and by 1786 had reached nearly its former extent. In 1783 the British West Indies received 16,208 Negroes from Africa, and by 1787 the importation had increased to 21,023. In this latter year it was estimated that the British were taking annually from Africa 38,000 slaves; the French, 20,000; the Portuguese, 10,000; the Dutch and Danes, 6,000; a total of 74,000. Manchester alone sent £180,000 annually in goods to Africa in exchange for Negroes.[1]

25. **The Slave-Trade and the "Association."** At the outbreak of the Revolution six main reasons, some of which were old and of slow growth, others peculiar to the abnormal situation of that time, led to concerted action against the slave-trade. The first reason was the economic failure of slavery in the Middle and Eastern colonies; this gave rise to the presumption that like failure awaited the institution in the South. Secondly, the new philosophy of "Freedom" and the "Rights of man," which formed the corner-stone of the Revolution, made the dullest realize that, at the very least, the slave-trade and a struggle for "liberty" were not consistent. Thirdly, the old fear of slave insurrections, which had long played so prominent a part in legislation, now gained new power from the imminence of war and from the well-founded fear that the British might incite servile uprisings. Fourthly, nearly all the American slave markets were, in 1774–1775, overstocked with slaves, and consequently many of the strongest partisans of the system were "bulls" on the market, and desired to raise the value of their

[1] These figures are from the *Report of the Lords of the Committee of Council*, etc. (London, 1789).

slaves by at least a temporary stoppage of the trade. Fifthly, since the vested interests of the slave-trading merchants were liable to be swept away by the opening of hostilities, and since the price of slaves was low,[1] there was from this quarter little active opposition to a cessation of the trade for a season. Finally, it was long a favorite belief of the supporters of the Revolution that, as English exploitation of colonial resources had caused the quarrel, the best weapon to bring England to terms was the economic expedient of stopping all commercial intercourse with her. Since, then, the slave-trade had ever formed an important part of her colonial traffic, it was one of the first branches of commerce which occurred to the colonists as especially suited to their ends.[2]

Such were the complicated moral, political, and economic motives which underlay the first national action against the slave-trade. This action was taken by the "Association," a union of the colonies entered into to enforce the policy of stopping commercial intercourse with England. The movement was not a great moral protest against an iniquitous traffic; although it had undoubtedly a strong moral backing, it was primarily a temporary war measure.

26. **The Action of the Colonies.** The earlier and largely abortive attempts to form non-intercourse associations generally did not mention slaves specifically, although the Virginia House of Burgesses, May 11, 1769, recommended to merchants and traders, among other things, to agree, "That they will not import any slaves, or purchase any imported after the first day of November next, until the said acts are repealed."[3] Later, in 1774, when a Faneuil Hall meeting started the first successful national attempt at non-intercourse, the slave-trade, being at the time especially flourishing, received more attention. Even then

[1] Sheffield, *Observations on American Commerce*, p. 28; P. L. Ford, *The Association of the First Congress*, in *Political Science Quarterly*, VI. 615–7.

[2] Cf., e. g., Arthur Lee's letter to R. H. Lee, March 18, 1774, in which non-intercourse is declared "the only advisable and sure mode of defence": Force, *American Archives*, 4th Ser., I. 229. Cf. also *Ibid.*, p. 240; Ford, in *Political Science Quarterly*, VI. 614–5.

[3] Goodloe, *Birth of the Republic*, p. 260.

slaves were specifically mentioned in the resolutions of but three States. Rhode Island recommended a stoppage of "all trade with Great Britain, Ireland, Africa and the West Indies."[1] North Carolina, in August, 1774, resolved in convention "That we will not import any slave or slaves, or purchase any slave or slaves, imported or brought into this Province by others, from any part of the world, after the first day of *November* next."[2] Virginia gave the slave-trade especial prominence, and was in reality the leading spirit to force her views on the Continental Congress. The county conventions of that colony first took up the subject. Fairfax County thought "that during our present difficulties and distress, no slaves ought to be imported," and said: "We take this opportunity of declaring our most earnest wishes to see an entire stop forever put to such a wicked, cruel, and unnatural trade."[3] Prince George and Nansemond Counties resolved "That the *African* trade is injurious to this Colony, obstructs the population of it by freemen, prevents manufacturers and other useful emigrants from *Europe* from settling amongst us, and occasions an annual increase of the balance of trade against this Colony."[4] The Virginia colonial convention, August, 1774, also declared: "We will neither ourselves import, nor purchase any slave or slaves imported by any other person, after the first day of *November* next, either from *Africa*, the *West Indies*, or any other place."[5]

In South Carolina, at the convention July 6, 1774, decided opposition to the non-importation scheme was manifested, though how much this was due to the slave-trade interest is not certain. Many of the delegates wished at least to limit the powers of their representatives, and the Charleston Chamber of Commerce flatly opposed the plan of an "Association." Finally, however, delegates with full powers were sent to Congress. The arguments leading to this step were not in all cases on the score

[1] Staples, *Annals of Providence* (1843), p. 235.

[2] Force, *American Archives*, 4th Ser., I. 735. This was probably copied from the Virginia resolve.

[3] *Ibid.*, I. 600.

[4] *Ibid.*, I. 494, 530. Cf. pp. 523, 616, 641, etc.

[5] *Ibid.*, I. 687.

of patriotism; a Charleston manifesto argued: "The planters are greatly in arrears to the merchants; a stoppage of importation would give them all an opportunity to extricate themselves from debt. The merchants would have time to settle their accounts, and be ready with the return of liberty to renew trade." [1]

27. **The Action of the Continental Congress.** The first Continental Congress met September 5, 1774, and on September 22 recommended merchants to send no more orders for foreign goods.[2] On September 27 "Mr. Lee made a motion for a non-importation," and it was unanimously resolved to import no goods from Great Britain after December 1, 1774.[3] Afterward, Ireland and the West Indies were also included, and a committee consisting of Low of New York, Mifflin of Pennsylvania, Lee of Virginia, and Johnson of Connecticut were appointed "to bring in a Plan for carrying into Effect the Non-importation, Non-consumption, and Non-exportation resolved on."[4] The next move was to instruct this committee to include in the proscribed articles, among other things, "Molasses, Coffee or Piemento from the *British* Plantations or from *Dominica*," — a motion which cut deep into the slave-trade circle of commerce, and aroused some opposition. "Will, can, the people bear a total interruption of the West India trade?" asked Low of New York; "Can they live without rum, sugar, and molasses? Will not this impatience and vexation defeat the measure?" [5]

The committee finally reported, October 12, 1774, and after three days' discussion and amendment the proposal passed. This document, after a recital of grievances, declared that, in the opinion of the colonists, a non-importation agreement would best secure redress; goods from Great Britain, Ireland, the East

[1] Force, *American Archives*, 4th Ser., I. 511, 526. Cf. also p. 316.

[2] *Journals of Cong.*, I. 20. Cf. Ford, in *Political Science Quarterly*, VI. 615–7.

[3] John Adams, *Works*, II. 382.

[4] *Journals of Cong.*, I. 21.

[5] *Ibid.*, I. 24; Drayton, *Memoirs of the American Revolution*, I. 147; John Adams, *Works*, II. 394.

and West Indies, and Dominica were excluded; and it was resolved that "We will neither import, nor purchase any Slave imported after the First Day of *December* next; after which Time, we will wholly discontinue the Slave Trade, and will neither be concerned in it ourselves, nor will we hire our Vessels, nor sell our Commodities or Manufactures to those who are concerned in it."[1]

Strong and straightforward as this resolution was, time unfortunately proved that it meant very little. Two years later, in this same Congress, a decided opposition was manifested to branding the slave-trade as inhuman, and it was thirteen years before South Carolina stopped the slave-trade or Massachusetts prohibited her citizens from engaging in it. The passing of so strong a resolution must be explained by the motives before given, by the character of the drafting committee, by the desire of America in this crisis to appear well before the world, and by the natural moral enthusiasm aroused by the imminence of a great national struggle.

28. **Reception of the Slave-Trade Resolution.** The unanimity with which the colonists received this "Association" is not perhaps as remarkable as the almost entire absence of comment on the radical slave-trade clause. A Connecticut town-meeting in December, 1774, noticed "with singular pleasure . . . the second Article of the Association, in which it is agreed to import no more Negro Slaves."[2] This comment appears to have been almost the only one. There were in various places some evidences of disapproval; but only in the State of Georgia was this widespread and determined, and based mainly on the slave-trade clause.[3] This opposition delayed the ratification meeting until January 18, 1775, and then delegates from but five of the twelve parishes appeared, and many of these had strong instructions against the approval of the plan. Be-

[1] *Journals of Cong.*, I. 27, 32–8.

[2] Danbury, Dec. 12, 1774: Force, *American Archives*, 4th Ser., I. 1038. This case and that of Georgia are the only ones I have found in which the slave-trade clause was specifically mentioned.

[3] Force, *American Archives*, 4th Ser., I. 1033, 1136, 1160, 1163; II. 279–281, 1544; *Journals of Cong.*, May 13, 15, 17, 1775.

fore this meeting could act, the governor adjourned it, on the ground that it did not represent the province. Some of the delegates signed an agreement, one article of which promised to stop the importation of slaves March 15, 1775, i. e., four months later than the national "Association" had directed. This was not, of course, binding on the province; and although a town like Darien might declare "our disapprobation and abhorrence of the unnatural practice of Slavery in *America*,"[1] yet the powerful influence of Savannah was "not likely soon to give matters a favourable turn. The importers were mostly against any interruption, and the consumers very much divided."[2] Thus the efforts of this Assembly failed, their resolutions being almost unknown, and, as a gentleman writes, "I hope for the honour of the Province ever will remain so."[3] The delegates to the Continental Congress selected by this rump assembly refused to take their seats. Meantime South Carolina stopped trade with Georgia, because it "hath not acceded to the Continental Association,"[4] and the single Georgia parish of St. Johns appealed to the second Continental Congress to except it from the general boycott of the colony. This county had already resolved not to "purchase any Slave imported at *Savannah* (large Numbers of which we understand are there expected) till the Sense of Congress shall be made known to us."[5]

May 17, 1775, Congress resolved unanimously "That all exportations to *Quebec*, *Nova-Scotia*, the Island of *St. John's*, *Newfoundland*, *Georgia*, except the Parish of *St. John's*, and to *East* and *West Florida*, immediately cease."[6] These measures brought the refractory colony to terms, and the Provincial Congress, July 4, 1775, finally adopted the "Association," and resolved, among other things, "That we will neither import or purchase any Slave imported from Africa, or elsewhere, after this day."[7]

The non-importation agreement was in the beginning, at least,

[1] Force, *American Archives*, 4th Ser., I. 1136.

[2] *Ibid.*, II. 279–81. [3] *Ibid.*, I. 1160. [4] *Ibid.*, I. 1163.

[5] *Journals of Cong.*, May 13, 15, 1775.

[6] *Ibid.*, May 17, 1775.

[7] Force, *American Archives*, 4th Ser., II. 1545.

well enforced by the voluntary action of the loosely federated nation. The slave-trade clause seems in most States to have been observed with the others. In South Carolina "a cargo of near three hundred slaves was sent out of the Colony by the consignee, as being interdicted by the second article of the Association."[1] In Virginia the vigilance committee of Norfolk "hold up for your just indignation Mr. *John Brown*, Merchant, of this place," who has several times imported slaves from Jamaica; and he is thus publicly censured "to the end that all such foes to the rights of *British America* may be publickly known . . . as the enemies of *American* Liberty, and that every person may henceforth break off all dealings with him."[2]

29. **Results of the Resolution.** The strain of war at last proved too much for this voluntary blockade, and after some hesitancy Congress, April 3, 1776, resolved to allow the importation of articles not the growth or manufacture of Great Britain, except tea. They also voted "That no slaves be imported into any of the thirteen United Colonies."[3] This marks a noticeable change of attitude from the strong words of two years previous: the former was a definitive promise; this is a temporary resolve, which probably represented public opinion much better than the former. On the whole, the conclusion is inevitably forced on the student of this first national movement against the slave-trade, that its influence on the trade was but temporary and insignificant, and that at the end of the experiment the outlook for the final suppression of the trade was little brighter than before. The whole movement served as a sort of social test of the power and importance of the slave-trade, which proved to be far more powerful than the platitudes of many of the Revolutionists had assumed.

The effect of the movement on the slave-trade in general was to begin, possibly a little earlier than otherwise would have been the case, that temporary breaking up of the trade which

[1] Drayton, *Memoirs of the American Revolution*, I. 182. Cf. pp. 181–7; Ramsay, *History of S. Carolina*, I. 231.

[2] Force, *American Archives*, 4th Ser., II. 33–4.

[3] *Journals of Cong.*, II. 122.

the war naturally caused. "There was a time, during the late war," says Clarkson, "when the slave trade may be considered as having been nearly abolished."[1] The prices of slaves rose correspondingly high, so that smugglers made fortunes.[2] It is stated that in the years 1772–1778 slave merchants of Liverpool failed for the sum of £710,000.[3] All this, of course, might have resulted from the war, without the "Association;" but in the long run the "Association" aided in frustrating the very designs which the framers of the first resolve had in mind; for the temporary stoppage in the end created an extraordinary demand for slaves, and led to a slave-trade after the war nearly as large as that before.

30. **The Slave-Trade and Public Opinion after the War.** The Declaration of Independence showed a significant drift of public opinion from the firm stand taken in the "Association" resolutions. The clique of political philosophers to which Jefferson belonged never imagined the continued existence of the country with slavery. It is well known that the first draft of the Declaration contained a severe arraignment of Great Britain as the real promoter of slavery and the slave-trade in America. In it the king was charged with waging "cruel war against human nature itself, violating its most sacred rights of life and liberty in the persons of a distant people who never offended him, captivating and carrying them into slavery in another hemisphere, or to incur miserable death in their transportation thither. This piratical warfare, the opprobrium of *infidel* powers, is the warfare of the *Christian* king of Great Britain. Determined to keep open a market where *men* should be bought and sold, he has prostituted his negative for suppressing every legislative attempt to prohibit or to restrain this execrable commerce. And that this assemblage of horrors might want no fact of distinguished die, he is now exciting those very people to rise in arms among us, and to purchase that liberty of which he has deprived them, by murdering the people on whom he also obtruded them: thus paying off former crimes committed against

[1] Clarkson, *Impolicy of the Slave-Trade*, pp. 125–8.

[2] *Ibid.*, pp. 25–6.

[3] *Ibid.*

the *liberties* of one people with crimes which he urges them to commit against the *lives* of another." [1]

To this radical and not strictly truthful statement, even the large influence of the Virginia leaders could not gain the assent of the delegates in Congress. The afflatus of 1774 was rapidly subsiding, and changing economic conditions had already led many to look forward to a day when the slave-trade could successfully be reopened. More important than this, the nation as a whole was even less inclined now than in 1774 to denounce the slave-trade uncompromisingly. Jefferson himself says that this clause "was struck out in complaisance to South Carolina and Georgia, who had never attempted to restrain the importation of slaves, and who, on the contrary, still wished to continue it. Our northern brethren also, I believe," said he, "felt a little tender under those censures; for though their people had very few slaves themselves, yet they had been pretty considerable carriers of them to others." [2]

As the war slowly dragged itself to a close, it became increasingly evident that a firm moral stand against slavery and the slave-trade was not a probability. The reaction which naturally follows a period of prolonged and exhausting strife for high political principles now set in. The economic forces of the country, which had suffered most, sought to recover and rearrange themselves; and all the selfish motives that impelled a bankrupt nation to seek to gain its daily bread did not long hesitate to demand a reopening of the profitable African slave-trade. This demand was especially urgent from the fact that the slaves, by pillage, flight, and actual fighting, had become so reduced in numbers during the war that an urgent demand for more laborers was felt in the South.

Nevertheless, the revival of the trade was naturally a matter of some difficulty, as the West India circuit had been cut off, leaving no resort except to contraband traffic and the direct African trade. The English slave-trade after the peace "returned to its former state," and was by 1784 sending 20,000

[1] Jefferson, *Works* (Washington, 1853–4), I. 23–4. On the Declaration as an anti-slavery document, cf. Elliot, *Debates* (1861), I. 89.

[2] Jefferson, *Works* (Washington, 1853–4), I. 19.

slaves annually to the West Indies.[1] Just how large the trade to the continent was at this time there are few means of ascertaining; it is certain that there was a general reopening of the trade in the Carolinas and Georgia, and that the New England traders participated in it. This traffic undoubtedly reached considerable proportions; and through the direct African trade and the illicit West India trade many thousands of Negroes came into the United States during the years 1783–1787.[2]

Meantime there was slowly arising a significant divergence of opinion on the subject. Probably the whole country still regarded both slavery and the slave-trade as temporary; but the Middle States expected to see the abolition of both within a generation, while the South scarcely thought it probable to prohibit even the slave-trade in that short time. Such a difference might, in all probability, have been satisfactorily adjusted, if both parties had recognized the real gravity of the matter. As it was, both regarded it as a problem of secondary importance, to be solved after many other more pressing ones had been disposed of. The anti-slavery men had seen slavery die in their own communities, and expected it to die the same way in others, with as little active effort on their own part. The Southern planters, born and reared in a slave system, thought that some day the system might change, and possibly disappear; but active effort to this end on their part was ever farthest from their thoughts. Here, then, began that fatal policy toward slavery and the slave-trade that characterized the nation for three-quarters of a century, the policy of *laissez-faire, laissez-passer*.

31. **The Action of the Confederation.** The slave-trade was hardly touched upon in the Congress of the Confederation, except in the ordinance respecting the capture of slaves, and on the occasion of the Quaker petition against the trade, although, during the debate on the Articles of Confederation, the counting

[1] Clarkson, *Impolicy of the Slave-Trade*, pp. 25–6; *Report*, etc., as above.

[2] Witness the many high duty acts on slaves, and the revenue derived therefrom. Massachusetts had sixty distilleries running in 1783. Cf. Sheffield, *Observations on American Commerce*, p. 267.

of slaves as well as of freemen in the apportionment of taxes was urged as a measure that would check further importation of Negroes. "It is our duty," said Wilson of Pennsylvania, "to lay every discouragement on the importation of slaves; but this amendment [i. e., to count two slaves as one freeman] would give the *jus trium liberorum* to him who would import slaves."[1] The matter was finally compromised by apportioning requisitions according to the value of land and buildings.

After the Articles went into operation, an ordinance in regard to the recapture of fugitive slaves provided that, if the capture was made on the sea below high-water mark, and the Negro was not claimed, he should be freed. Matthews of South Carolina demanded the yeas and nays on this proposition, with the result that only the vote of his State was recorded against it.[2]

On Tuesday, October 3, 1783, a deputation from the Yearly Meeting of the Pennsylvania, New Jersey, and Delaware Friends asked leave to present a petition. Leave was granted the following day,[3] but no further minute appears. According to the report of the Friends, the petition was against the slave-trade; and "though the Christian rectitude of the concern was by the Delegates generally acknowledged, yet not being vested with the powers of legislation, they declined promoting any public remedy against the gross national iniquity of trafficking in the persons of fellow-men."[4]

The only legislative activity in regard to the trade during the Confederation was taken by the individual States.[5] Before 1778 Connecticut, Vermont, Pennsylvania, Delaware, and Virginia had by law stopped the further importation of slaves, and importation had practically ceased in all the New England and Middle States, including Maryland. In consequence of the revival of the slave-trade after the War, there was then a lull in State activity until 1786, when North Carolina laid a prohibitive

[1] Elliot, *Debates*, I. 72–3. Cf. Art. 8 of the Articles of Confederation.

[2] *Journals of Cong.*, 1781, June 25; July 18; Sept. 21, 27; Nov. 8, 13, 30; Dec. 4.

[3] *Ibid.*, 1782–3, pp. 418–9, 425.

[4] *Annals of Cong.*, 1 Cong. 2 sess. p. 1183.

[5] Cf. above, chapters ii., iii., iv.

duty, and South Carolina, a year later, began her series of temporary prohibitions. In 1787–1788 the New England States forbade the participation of their citizens in the traffic. It was this wave of legislation against the traffic which did so much to blind the nation as to the strong hold which slavery still had on the country.

CHAPTER VI.

THE FEDERAL CONVENTION. 1787.

32. **The First Proposition.** Slavery occupied no prominent place in the Convention called to remedy the glaring defects of the Confederation, for the obvious reason that few of the delegates thought it expedient to touch a delicate subject which, if let alone, bade fair to settle itself in a manner satisfactory to all. Consequently, neither slavery nor the slave-trade is specifically mentioned in the delegates' credentials of any of the States, nor in Randolph's, Pinckney's, or Hamilton's plans, nor in Paterson's propositions. Indeed, the debate from May 14 to June 19, when the Committee of the Whole reported, touched the subject only in the matter of the ratio of representation of slaves. With this same exception, the report of the Committee of the Whole contained no reference to slavery or the slave-trade, and the twenty-three resolutions of the Convention referred to the Committee of Detail, July 23 and 26, maintain the same silence.

The latter committee, consisting of Rutledge, Randolph, Gorham, Ellsworth, and Wilson, reported a draft of the Constitution August 6, 1787. The committee had, in its deliberations, probably made use of a draft of a national Constitution made by Edmund Randolph.[1] One clause of this provided that

[1] Conway, *Life and Papers of Edmund Randolph*, ch. ix.

"no State shall lay a duty on imports;" and, also, "1. No duty on exports. 2. No prohibition on such inhabitants as the United States think proper to admit. 3. No duties by way of such prohibition." It does not appear that any reference to Negroes was here intended. In the extant copy, however, notes in Edward Rutledge's handwriting change the second clause to "No prohibition on such inhabitants or people as the several States think proper to admit."[1] In the report, August 6, these clauses take the following form: —

> "Article VII. Section 4. No tax or duty shall be laid by the legislature on articles exported from any state; nor on the migration or importation of such persons as the several states shall think proper to admit; nor shall such migration or importation be prohibited."[2]

33. **The General Debate.** This, of course, referred both to immigrants ("migration") and to slaves ("importation").[3] Debate on this section began Tuesday, August 22, and lasted two days. Luther Martin of Maryland precipitated the discussion by a proposition to alter the section so as to allow a prohibition or tax on the importation of slaves. The debate immediately became general, being carried on principally by Rutledge, the Pinckneys, and Williamson from the Carolinas; Baldwin of Georgia; Mason, Madison, and Randolph of Virginia; Wilson and Gouverneur Morris of Pennsylvania; Dickinson of Delaware; and Ellsworth, Sherman, Gerry, King, and Langdon of New England.[4]

In this debate the moral arguments were prominent. Colonel George Mason of Virginia denounced the traffic in slaves as "infernal;" Luther Martin of Maryland regarded it as "inconsistent with the principles of the revolution, and dishonorable to the American character." "Every principle of honor and safety," declared John Dickinson of Delaware, "demands the exclusion of slaves." Indeed, Mason solemnly averred that the

[1] Conway, *Life and Papers of Edmund Randolph*, p. 78.

[2] Elliot, *Debates*, I. 227.

[3] Cf. Conway, *Life and Papers of Edmund Randolph*, pp. 78–9.

[4] For the following debate, Madison's notes (Elliot, *Debates*, V. 457 ff.) are mainly followed.

crime of slavery might yet bring the judgment of God on the nation. On the other side, Rutledge of South Carolina bluntly declared that religion and humanity had nothing to do with the question, that it was a matter of "interest" alone. Gerry of Massachusetts wished merely to refrain from giving direct sanction to the trade, while others contented themselves with pointing out the inconsistency of condemning the slave-trade and defending slavery.

The difficulty of the whole argument, from the moral standpoint, lay in the fact that it was completely checkmated by the obstinate attitude of South Carolina and Georgia. Their delegates — Baldwin, the Pinckneys, Rutledge, and others — asserted flatly, not less than a half-dozen times during the debate, that these States "can never receive the plan if it prohibits the slave-trade;" that "if the Convention thought" that these States would consent to a stoppage of the slave-trade, "the expectation is vain."[1] By this stand all argument from the moral standpoint was virtually silenced, for the Convention evidently agreed with Roger Sherman of Connecticut that "it was better to let the Southern States import slaves than to part with those States."

In such a dilemma the Convention listened not unwillingly to the *non possumus* arguments of the States' Rights advocates. The "morality and wisdom" of slavery, declared Ellsworth of Connecticut, "are considerations belonging to the States themselves;" let every State "import what it pleases;" the Confederation has not "meddled" with the question, why should the Union? It is a dangerous symptom of centralization, cried Baldwin of Georgia; the "central States" wish to be the "vortex for everything," even matters of "a local nature." The national government, said Gerry of Massachusetts, had nothing to do with slavery in the States; it had only to refrain from giving direct sanction to the system. Others opposed this whole argument, declaring, with Langdon of New Hampshire, that Congress ought to have this power, since, as Dickinson tartly remarked, "The true question was, whether the national happiness would be promoted or impeded by the importation;

[1] Cf. Elliot, *Debates*, V., *passim*.

and this question ought to be left to the national government, not to the states particularly interested."

Beside these arguments as to the right of the trade and the proper seat of authority over it, many arguments of general expediency were introduced. From an economic standpoint, for instance, General C. C. Pinckney of South Carolina "contended, that the importation of slaves would be for the interest of the whole Union. The more slaves, the more produce." Rutledge of the same State declared: "If the Northern States consult their interest, they will not oppose the increase of slaves, which will increase the commodities of which they will become the carriers." This sentiment found a more or less conscious echo in the words of Ellsworth of Connecticut, "What enriches a part enriches the whole." It was, moreover, broadly hinted that the zeal of Maryland and Virginia against the trade had an economic rather than a humanitarian motive, since they had slaves enough and to spare, and wished to sell them at a high price to South Carolina and Georgia, who needed more. In such case restrictions would unjustly discriminate against the latter States. The argument from history was barely touched upon. Only once was there an allusion to "the example of all the world" "in all ages" to justify slavery,[1] and once came the counter declaration that "Greece and Rome were made unhappy by their slaves."[2] On the other hand, the military weakness of slavery in the late war led to many arguments on that score. Luther Martin and George Mason dwelt on the danger of a servile class in war and insurrection; while Rutledge hotly replied that he "would readily exempt the other states from the obligation to protect the Southern against them;" and Ellsworth thought that the very danger would "become a motive to kind treatment." The desirability of keeping slavery out of the West was once mentioned as an argument against the trade: to this all seemed tacitly to agree.[3]

Throughout the debate it is manifest that the Convention had no desire really to enter upon a general slavery argument.

[1] By Charles Pinckney.

[2] By John Dickinson.

[3] Mentioned in the speech of George Mason.

The broader and more theoretic aspects of the question were but lightly touched upon here and there. Undoubtedly, most of the members would have much preferred not to raise the question at all; but, as it was raised, the differences of opinion were too manifest to be ignored, and the Convention, after its first perplexity, gradually and perhaps too willingly set itself to work to find some "middle ground" on which all parties could stand. The way to this compromise was pointed out by the South. The most radical pro-slavery arguments always ended with the opinion that "if the Southern States were let alone, they will probably of themselves stop importations."[1] To be sure, General Pinckney admitted that, "candidly, he did not think South Carolina would stop her importations of slaves in any short time;" nevertheless, the Convention "observed," with Roger Sherman, "that the abolition of slavery seemed to be going on in the United States, and that the good sense of the several states would probably by degrees complete it." Economic forces were evoked to eke out moral motives: when the South had its full quota of slaves, like Virginia it too would abolish the trade; free labor was bound finally to drive out slave labor. Thus the chorus of "*laissez-faire*" increased; and compromise seemed at least in sight, when Connecticut cried, "Let the trade alone!" and Georgia denounced it as an "evil." Some few discordant notes were heard, as, for instance, when Wilson of Pennsylvania made the uncomforting remark, "If South Carolina and Georgia were themselves disposed to get rid of the importation of slaves in a short time, as had been suggested, they would never refuse to unite because the importation might be prohibited."

With the spirit of compromise in the air, it was not long before the general terms were clear. The slavery side was strongly intrenched, and had a clear and definite demand. The forces of freedom were, on the contrary, divided by important conflicts of interest, and animated by no very strong and decided anti-slavery spirit with settled aims. Under such circumstances,

[1] Charles Pinckney. Baldwin of Georgia said that if the State were left to herself, "she may probably put a stop to the evil": Elliot, *Debates*, V. 459.

it was easy for the Convention to miss the opportunity for a really great compromise, and to descend to a scheme that savored unpleasantly of "log-rolling." The student of the situation will always have good cause to believe that a more sturdy and definite anti-slavery stand at this point might have changed history for the better.

34. **The Special Committee and the "Bargain."** Since the debate had, in the first place, arisen from a proposition to tax the importation of slaves, the yielding of this point by the South was the first move toward compromise. To all but the doctrinaires, who shrank from taxing men as property, the argument that the failure to tax slaves was equivalent to a bounty, was conclusive. With this point settled, Randolph voiced the general sentiment, when he declared that he "was for committing, in order that some middle ground might, if possible, be found." Finally, Gouverneur Morris discovered the "middle ground," in his suggestion that the whole subject be committed, "including the clauses relating to taxes on exports and to a navigation act. These things," said he, "may form a bargain among the Northern and Southern States." This was quickly assented to; and sections four and five, on slave-trade and capitation tax, were committed by a vote of 7 to 3,[1] and section six, on navigation acts, by a vote of 9 to 2.[2] All three clauses were referred to the following committee: Langdon of New Hampshire, King of Massachusetts, Johnson of Connecticut, Livingston of New Jersey, Clymer of Pennsylvania, Dickinson of Delaware, Martin of Maryland, Madison of Virginia, Williamson of North Carolina, General Pinckney of South Carolina, and Baldwin of Georgia.

The fullest account of the proceedings of this committee is given in Luther Martin's letter to his constituents, and is confirmed in its main particulars by similar reports of other delegates. Martin writes: "A committee of *one* member from each state was chosen by ballot, to take this part of the system

[1] *Affirmative:* Connecticut, New Jersey, Maryland, Virginia, North Carolina, South Carolina, Georgia, — 7. *Negative:* New Hampshire, Pennsylvania, Delaware, — 3. *Absent:* Massachusetts, — 1.

[2] *Negative:* Connecticut and New Jersey.

under their consideration, and to endeavor to agree upon some report which should reconcile those states [i. e., South Carolina and Georgia]. To this committee also was referred the following proposition, which had been reported by the committee of detail, viz.: 'No navigation act shall be passed without the assent of two thirds of the members present in each house'—a proposition which the staple and commercial states were solicitous to retain, lest their commerce should be placed too much under the power of the Eastern States, but which these last States were as anxious to reject. This committee—of which also I had the honor to be a member—met, and took under their consideration the subjects committed to them. I found the *Eastern* States, notwithstanding their *aversion to slavery*, were very willing to indulge the Southern States at least with a temporary liberty to prosecute the slave trade, provided the Southern States would, in their turn, gratify *them*, by laying no restriction on navigation acts; and after a very little time, the committee, by a great majority, agreed on a report, by which the general government was to be prohibited from preventing the importation of slaves for a limited time, and the restrictive clause relative to navigation acts was to be omitted."[1]

That the "bargain" was soon made is proven by the fact that the committee reported the very next day, Friday, August 24, and that on Saturday the report was taken up. It was as follows: "Strike out so much of the fourth section as was referred to the committee, and insert 'The migration or importation of such persons as the several states, now existing, shall think proper to admit, shall not be prohibited by the legislature prior to the year 1800; but a tax or duty may be imposed on such migration or importation, at a rate not exceeding the average of the duties laid on imports.' The fifth section to remain as in the report. The sixth section to be stricken out."[2]

35. **The Appeal to the Convention.** The ensuing debate,[3] which lasted only a part of the day, was evidently a sort of

[1] Luther Martin's letter, in Elliot, *Debates*, I. 373. Cf. explanations of delegates in the South Carolina, North Carolina, and other conventions.

[2] Elliot, *Debates*, V. 471.

[3] Saturday, Aug. 25, 1787.

appeal to the House on the decisions of the committee. It throws light on the points of disagreement. General Pinckney first proposed to extend the slave-trading limit to 1808, and Gorham of Massachusetts seconded the motion. This brought a spirited protest from Madison: "Twenty years will produce all the mischief that can be apprehended from the liberty to import slaves. So long a term will be more dishonorable to the American character than to say nothing about it in the Constitution."[1] There was, however, evidently another "bargain" here; for, without farther debate, the South and the East voted the extension, 7 to 4, only New Jersey, Pennsylvania, Delaware, and Virginia objecting. The ambiguous phraseology of the whole slave-trade section as reported did not pass without comment; Gouverneur Morris would have it read: "The importation of slaves into North Carolina, South Carolina, and Georgia, shall not be prohibited," etc.[2] This emendation was, however, too painfully truthful for the doctrinaires, and was, amid a score of objections, withdrawn. The taxation clause also was manifestly too vague for practical use, and Baldwin of Georgia wished to amend it by inserting "common impost on articles not enumerated," in lieu of the "average" duty.[3] This minor point gave rise to considerable argument: Sherman and Madison deprecated any such recognition of property in man as taxing would imply; Mason and Gorham argued that the tax restrained the trade; while King, Langdon, and General Pinckney contented themselves with the remark that this clause was "the price of the first part." Finally, it was unanimously agreed to make the duty "not exceeding ten dollars for each person."[4]

Southern interests now being safe, some Southern members attempted, a few days later, to annul the "bargain" by restoring the requirement of a two-thirds vote in navigation acts. Charles Pinckney made the motion, in an elaborate speech designed to show the conflicting commercial interests of the States; he declared that "The power of regulating commerce was a pure

[1] Elliot, *Debates*, V. 477.

[2] *Ibid.* Dickinson made a similar motion, which was disagreed to: *Ibid.*

[3] *Ibid.*, V. 478.

[4] *Ibid.*

concession on the part of the Southern States." [1] Martin and Williamson of North Carolina, Butler of South Carolina, and Mason of Virginia defended the proposition, insisting that it would be a dangerous concession on the part of the South to leave navigation acts to a mere majority vote. Sherman of Connecticut, Morris of Pennsylvania, and Spaight of North Carolina declared that the very diversity of interest was a security. Finally, by a vote of 7 to 4, Maryland, Virginia, North Carolina, and Georgia being in the minority, the Convention refused to consider the motion, and the recommendation of the committee passed.[2]

When, on September 10, the Convention was discussing the amendment clause of the Constitution, the ever-alert Rutledge, perceiving that the results of the laboriously settled "bargain" might be endangered, declared that he "never could agree to give a power by which the articles relating to slaves might be altered by the states not interested in that property." [3] As a result, the clause finally adopted, September 15, had the proviso: "Provided, that no amendment which may be made prior to the year 1808 shall in any manner affect the 1st and 4th clauses in the 9th section of the 1st article." [4]

36. **Settlement by the Convention.** Thus, the slave-trade article of the Constitution stood finally as follows: —

> "Article I. Section 9. The Migration or Importation of such Persons as any of the States now existing shall think proper to admit, shall not be prohibited by the Congress prior to the Year one thousand eight hundred and eight, but a Tax or duty may be imposed on such Importation, not exceeding ten dollars for each Person."

This settlement of the slavery question brought out distinct differences of moral attitude toward the institution, and yet differences far from hopeless. To be sure, the South apologized for slavery, the Middle States denounced it, and the East could only tolerate it from afar; and yet all three sections united in considering it a temporary institution, the corner-stone of which was the slave-trade. No one of them had ever seen a system

[1] Aug. 29: Elliot, *Debates*, V. 489.
[2] *Ibid.*, V. 492.
[3] *Ibid.*, V. 532.
[4] *Ibid.*, I. 317.

of slavery without an active slave-trade; and there were probably few members of the Convention who did not believe that the foundations of slavery had been sapped merely by putting the abolition of the slave-trade in the hands of Congress twenty years hence. Here lay the danger; for when the North called slavery "temporary," she thought of twenty or thirty years, while the "temporary" period of the South was scarcely less than a century. Meantime, for at least a score of years, a policy of strict *laissez-faire*, so far as the general government was concerned, was to intervene. Instead of calling the whole moral energy of the people into action, so as gradually to crush this portentous evil, the Federal Convention lulled the nation to sleep by a "bargain," and left to the vacillating and unripe judgment of the States one of the most threatening of the social and political ills which they were so courageously seeking to remedy.

37. **Reception of the Clause by the Nation.** When the proposed Constitution was before the country, the slave-trade article came in for no small amount of condemnation and apology. In the pamphlets of the day it was much discussed. One of the points in Mason's "Letter of Objections" was that "the general legislature is restrained from prohibiting the further importation of slaves for twenty odd years, though such importations render the United States weaker, more vulnerable, and less capable of defence."[1] To this Iredell replied, through the columns of the *State Gazette* of North Carolina: "If all the States had been willing to adopt this regulation [i. e., to prohibit the slave-trade], I should as an individual most heartily have approved of it, because even if the importation of slaves in fact rendered us stronger, less vulnerable and more capable of defence, I should rejoice in the prohibition of it, as putting an end to a trade which has already continued too long for the honor and humanity of those concerned in it. But as it was well known that South Carolina and Georgia thought a further continuance of such importations useful to them, and would not perhaps otherwise have agreed to the new constitu-

[1] P. L. Ford, *Pamphlets on the Constitution*, p. 331.

tion, those States which had been importing till they were satisfied, could not with decency have insisted upon their relinquishing advantages themselves had already enjoyed. Our situation makes it necessary to bear the evil as it is. It will be left to the future legislatures to allow such importations or not. If any, in violation of their clear conviction of the injustice of this trade, persist in pursuing it, this is a matter between God and their own consciences. The interests of humanity will, however, have gained something by the prohibition of this inhuman trade, though at a distance of twenty odd years." [1]

"Centinel," representing the Quaker sentiment of Pennsylvania, attacked the clause in his third letter, published in the *Independent Gazetteer, or The Chronicle of Freedom*, November 8, 1787: "We are told that the objects of this article are slaves, and that it is inserted to secure to the southern states the right of introducing negroes for twenty-one years to come, against the declared sense of the other states to put an end to an odious traffic in the human species, which is especially scandalous and inconsistent in a people, who have asserted their own liberty by the sword, and which dangerously enfeebles the districts wherein the laborers are bondsmen. The words, dark and ambiguous, such as no plain man of common sense would have used, are evidently chosen to conceal from Europe, that in this enlightened country, the practice of slavery has its advocates among men in the highest stations. When it is recollected that no poll tax can be imposed on *five* negroes, above what *three* whites shall be charged; when it is considered, that the imposts on the consumption of Carolina field negroes must be trifling, and the excise nothing, it is plain that the proportion of contributions, which can be expected from the southern states under the new constitution, will be unequal, and yet they are to be allowed to enfeeble themselves by the further importation of negroes till the year 1808. Has not the concurrence of the five southern states (in the convention) to the new system, been purchased too dearly by the rest?" [2]

1 P. L. Ford, *Pamphlets on the Constitution*, p. 367.

2 McMaster and Stone, *Pennsylvania and the Federal Convention*, pp. 599–600. Cf. also p. 773.

Noah Webster's "Examination" (1787) addressed itself to such Quaker scruples: "But, say the enemies of slavery, negroes may be imported for twenty-one years. This exception is addressed to the quakers, and a very pitiful exception it is. The truth is, Congress cannot prohibit the importation of slaves during that period; but the laws against the importation into particular states, stand unrepealed. An immediate abolition of slavery would bring ruin upon the whites, and misery upon the blacks, in the southern states. The constitution has therefore wisely left each state to pursue its own measures, with respect to this article of legislation, during the period of twenty-one years."[1]

The following year the "Examination" of Tench Coxe said: "The temporary reservation of any particular matter must ever be deemed an admission that it should be done away. This appears to have been well understood. In addition to the arguments drawn from liberty, justice and religion, opinions against this practice [i. e., of slave-trading], founded in sound policy, have no doubt been urged. Regard was necessarily paid to the peculiar situation of our southern fellow-citizens; but they, on the other hand, have not been insensible of the delicate situation of our national character on this subject."[2]

From quite different motives Southern men defended this section. For instance, Dr. David Ramsay, a South Carolina member of the Convention, wrote in his "Address": "It is farther objected, that they have stipulated for a right to prohibit the importation of negroes after 21 years. On this subject observe, as they are bound to protect us from domestic violence, they think we ought not to increase our exposure to that evil, by an unlimited importation of slaves. Though Congress may forbid the importation of negroes after 21 years, it does not follow that they will. On the other hand, it is probable that they will not. The more rice we make, the more business will be for their shipping; their interest will therefore coincide with ours. Besides, we have other sources of supply —the importation of the ensuing 20 years, added to the natural

[1] See Ford, *Pamphlets*, etc., p. 54. [2] *Ibid.*, p. 146.

increase of those we already have, and the influx from our northern neighbours who are desirous of getting rid of their slaves, will afford a sufficient number for cultivating all the lands in this state."[1]

Finally, *The Federalist*, No. 41, written by James Madison, commented as follows: "It were doubtless to be wished, that the power of prohibiting the importation of slaves had not been postponed until the year 1808, or rather, that it had been suffered to have immediate operation. But it is not difficult to account, either for this restriction on the General Government, or for the manner in which the whole clause is expressed. It ought to be considered as a great point gained in favor of humanity, that a period of twenty years may terminate forever, within these States, a traffic which has so long and so loudly upbraided the barbarism of modern policy; that within that period, it will receive a considerable discouragement from the Federal Government, and may be totally abolished, by a concurrence of the few States which continue the unnatural traffic, in the prohibitory example which has been given by so great a majority of the Union. Happy would it be for the unfortunate Africans, if an equal prospect lay before them of being redeemed from the oppressions of their European brethren!

"Attempts have been made to pervert this clause into an objection against the Constitution, by representing it on one side as a criminal toleration of an illicit practice, and on another, as calculated to prevent voluntary and beneficial emigrations from Europe to America. I mention these misconstructions, not with a view to give them an answer, for they deserve none; but as specimens of the manner and spirit, in which some have thought fit to conduct their opposition to the proposed Government."[2]

38. **Attitude of the State Conventions.** The records of the proceedings in the various State conventions are exceedingly meagre. In nearly all of the few States where records exist

[1] "Address to the Freemen of South Carolina on the Subject of the Federal Constitution": *Ibid.*, p. 378.

[2] Published in the *New York Packet*, Jan. 22, 1788; reprinted in Dawson's *Fœderalist*, I. 290–1.

there is found some opposition to the slave-trade clause. The opposition was seldom very pronounced or bitter; it rather took the form of regret, on the one hand that the Convention went so far, and on the other hand that it did not go farther. Probably, however, the Constitution was never in danger of rejection on account of this clause.

Extracts from a few of the speeches, *pro* and *con*, in various States will best illustrate the character of the arguments. In reply to some objections expressed in the Pennsylvania convention, Wilson said, December 3, 1787: "I consider this as laying the foundation for banishing slavery out of this country; and though the period is more distant than I could wish, yet it will produce the same kind, gradual change, which was pursued in Pennsylvania."[1] Robert Barnwell declared in the South Carolina convention, January 17, 1788, that this clause "particularly pleased" him. "Congress," he said, "has guarantied this right for that space of time, and at its expiration may continue it as long as they please. This question then arises — What will their interest lead them to do? The Eastern States, as the honorable gentleman says, will become the carriers of America. It will, therefore, certainly be their interest to encourage exportation to as great an extent as possible; and if the quantum of our products will be diminished by the prohibition of negroes, I appeal to the belief of every man, whether he thinks those very carriers will themselves dam up the sources from whence their profit is derived. To think so is so contradictory to the general conduct of mankind, that I am of opinion, that, without we ourselves put a stop to them, the traffic for negroes will continue forever."[2]

In Massachusetts, January 30, 1788, General Heath said: "The gentlemen who have spoken have carried the matter rather too far on both sides. I apprehend that it is not in our power to do anything for or against those who are in slavery in the southern States. . . . Two questions naturally arise, if we ratify the Constitution: Shall we do anything by our act to hold the blacks in slavery? or shall we become partakers of other

[1] Elliot, *Debates*, II. 452.

[2] *Ibid.*, IV. 296–7.

men's sins? I think neither of them. Each State is sovereign and independent to a certain degree, and they have a right, and will regulate their own internal affairs, as to themselves appears proper."[1] Iredell said, in the North Carolina convention, July 26, 1788: "When the entire abolition of slavery takes place, it will be an event which must be pleasing to every generous mind, and every friend of human nature. . . . But as it is, this government is nobly distinguished above others by that very provision."[2]

Of the arguments against the clause, two made in the Massachusetts convention are typical. The Rev. Mr. Neal said, January 25, 1788, that "unless his objection [to this clause] was removed, he could not put his hand to the Constitution."[3] General Thompson exclaimed, "Shall it be said, that after we have established our own independence and freedom, we make slaves of others?"[4] Mason, in the Virginia convention, June 15, 1788, said: "As much as I value a union of all the states, I would not admit the Southern States into the Union unless they agree to the discontinuance of this disgraceful trade. . . . Yet they have not secured us the property of the slaves we have already. So that 'they have done what they ought not to have done, and have left undone what they ought to have done.'"[5] Joshua Atherton, who led the opposition in the New Hampshire convention, said: "The idea that strikes those who are opposed to this clause so disagreeably and so forcibly is, — hereby it is conceived (if we ratify the Constitution) that we become *consenters to* and *partakers in* the sin and guilt of this abominable traffic, at least for a certain period, without any positive stipulation that it shall even then be brought to an end."[6]

In the South Carolina convention Lowndes, January 16, 1788, attacked the slave-trade clause. "Negroes," said he, "were

[1] Published in *Debates of the Massachusetts Convention*, 1788, p. 217 ff.

[2] Elliot, *Debates*, IV. 100–1.

[3] Published in *Debates of the Massachusetts Convention*, 1788, p. 208.

[4] *Ibid.*

[5] Elliot, *Debates*, III. 452–3.

[6] Walker, *Federal Convention of New Hampshire*, App. 113; Elliot, *Debates*, II. 203.

our wealth, our only natural resource; yet behold how our kind friends in the north were determined soon to tie up our hands, and drain us of what we had! The Eastern States drew their means of subsistence, in a great measure, from their shipping; and, on that head, they had been particularly careful not to allow of any burdens. . . . Why, then, call this a reciprocal bargain, which took all from one party, to bestow it on the other!"[1]

In spite of this discussion in the different States, only one State, Rhode Island, went so far as to propose an amendment directing Congress to "promote and establish such laws and regulations as may effectually prevent the importation of slaves of every description, into the United States."[2]

39. **Acceptance of the Policy.** As in the Federal Convention, so in the State conventions, it is noticeable that the compromise was accepted by the various States from widely different motives.[3] Nevertheless, these motives were not fixed and unchangeable, and there was still discernible a certain underlying agreement in the dislike of slavery. One cannot help thinking that if the devastation of the late war had not left an extraordinary demand for slaves in the South, — if, for instance,

[1] Elliot, *Debates*, IV. 273.

[2] Updike's *Minutes*, in Staples, *Rhode Island in the Continental Congress*, pp. 657–8, 674–9. Adopted by a majority of one in a convention of seventy.

[3] In five States I have found no mention of the subject (Delaware, New Jersey, Georgia, Connecticut, and Maryland). In the Pennsylvania convention there was considerable debate, partially preserved in Elliot's and Lloyd's *Debates*. In the Massachusetts convention the debate on this clause occupied a part of two or three days, reported in published debates. In South Carolina there were several long speeches, reported in Elliot's *Debates*. Only three speeches made in the New Hampshire convention seem to be extant, and two of these are on the slave-trade: cf. Walker and Elliot. The Virginia convention discussed the clause to considerable extent: see Elliot. The clause does not seem to have been a cause of North Carolina's delay in ratification, although it occasioned some discussion: see Elliot. In Rhode Island "much debate ensued," and in this State alone was an amendment proposed: see Staples, *Rhode Island in the Continental Congress*. In New York the Committee of the Whole "proceeded through sections 8, 9 . . . with little or no debate": Elliot, *Debates*, II. 406.

there had been in 1787 the same plethora in the slave-market as in 1774, — the future history of the country would have been far different. As it was, the twenty-one years of *laissez-faire* were confirmed by the States, and the nation entered upon the constitutional period with the slave-trade legal in three States,[1] and with a feeling of quiescence toward it in the rest of the Union.

[1] South Carolina, Georgia, and North Carolina. North Carolina had, however, a prohibitive duty.

CHAPTER VII.

TOUSSAINT L'OUVERTURE AND ANTI-SLAVERY EFFORT, 1787–1806.

40. **Influence of the Haytian Revolution.** The rôle which the great Negro Toussaint, called L'Ouverture, played in the history of the United States has seldom been fully appreciated. Representing the age of revolution in America, he rose to leadership through a bloody terror, which contrived a Negro "problem" for the Western Hemisphere, intensified and defined the anti-slavery movement, became one of the causes, and probably the prime one, which led Napoleon to sell Louisiana for a song, and finally, through the interworking of all these effects, rendered more certain the final prohibition of the slave-trade by the United States in 1807.

From the time of the reorganization of the Pennsylvania Abolition Society, in 1787, anti-slavery sentiment became active. New York, New Jersey, Rhode Island, Delaware, Maryland, and

Virginia had strong organizations, and a national convention was held in 1794. The terrible upheaval in the West Indies, beginning in 1791, furnished this rising movement with an irresistible argument. A wave of horror and fear swept over the South, which even the powerful slave-traders of Georgia did not dare withstand; the Middle States saw their worst dreams realized, and the mercenary trade interests of the East lost control of the New England conscience.

41. **Legislation of the Southern States.** In a few years the growing sentiment had crystallized into legislation. The Southern States took immediate measures to close their ports, first against West India Negroes, finally against all slaves. Georgia, who had had legal slavery only from 1755, and had since passed no restrictive legislation, felt compelled in 1793 [1] to stop the entry of free Negroes, and in 1798 [2] to prohibit, under heavy penalties, the importation of all slaves. This provision was placed in the Constitution of the State, and, although miserably enforced, was never repealed.

South Carolina was the first Southern State in which the exigencies of a great staple crop rendered the rapid consumption of slaves more profitable than their proper maintenance. Alternating, therefore, between a plethora and a dearth of Negroes, she prohibited the slave-trade only for short periods. In 1788 [3] she had forbidden the trade for five years, and in 1792,[4] being peculiarly exposed to the West Indian insurrection, she quickly found it "inexpedient" to allow Negroes "from Africa, the West India Islands, or other place beyond sea" to enter for two years. This act continued to be extended, although

[1] Prince, *Digest of the Laws of Georgia*, p. 786; Marbury and Crawford, *Digest of the Laws of Georgia*, pp. 440, 442. The exact text of this act appears not to be extant. Section I. is stated to have been "re-enacted by the constitution." Possibly this act prohibited slaves also, although this is not certain. Georgia passed several regulative acts between 1755 and 1793. Cf. Renne, *Colonial Acts of Georgia*, pp. 73–4, 164, note.

[2] Marbury and Crawford, *Digest*, p. 30, § 11. The clause was penned by Peter J. Carnes of Jefferson. Cf. W. B. Stevens, *History of Georgia* (1847), II. 501.

[3] Grimké, *Public Laws*, p. 466.

[4] Cooper and McCord, *Statutes*, VII. 431.

with lessening penalties, until 1803.[1] The home demand in view of the probable stoppage of the trade in 1808, the speculative chances of the new Louisiana Territory trade, and the large already existing illicit traffic combined in that year to cause the passage of an act, December 17, reopening the African slave-trade, although still carefully excluding "West India" Negroes.[2] This action profoundly stirred the Union, aroused anti-slavery sentiment, led to a concerted movement for a constitutional amendment, and, failing in this, to an irresistible demand for a national prohibitory act at the earliest constitutional moment.

North Carolina had repealed her prohibitory duty act in 1790,[3] but in 1794 she passed an "Act to prevent further importation and bringing of slaves," etc.[4] Even the body-servants of West India immigrants and, naturally, all free Negroes, were eventually prohibited.[5]

42. **Legislation of the Border States.** The Border States, Virginia and Maryland, strengthened their non-importation laws, Virginia freeing illegally imported Negroes,[6] and Maryland prohibiting even the interstate trade.[7] The Middle States took action chiefly in the final abolition of slavery within their borders, and the prevention of the fitting out of slaving vessels in their ports. Delaware declared, in her Act of 1789, that "it is inconsistent with that spirit of general liberty which pervades the constitution of this state, that vessels should be fitted out, or equipped, in any of the ports thereof, for the purpose of receiving and transporting the natives of Africa to places where they are held in slavery,"[8] and forbade such a practice under penalty of £500 for each person so engaged. The Pennsylvania

[1] Cooper and McCord, *Statutes*, VII. 433–6, 444, 447.

[2] *Ibid.*, VII. 449.

[3] Martin, *Iredell's Acts of Assembly*, I. 492.

[4] *Ibid.*, II. 53.

[5] Cf. *Ibid.*, II. 94; *Laws of North Carolina* (revision of 1819), I. 786.

[6] Virginia codified her whole slave legislation in 1792 (*Va. Statutes at Large*, New Ser., I. 122), and amended her laws in 1798 and 1806 (*Ibid.*, III. 251).

[7] Dorsey, *Laws of Maryland*, 1796, I. 334.

[8] *Laws of Delaware*, 1797 (Newcastle ed.), p. 942, ch. 194 b.

Act of 1788[1] had similar provisions, with a penalty of £1000; and New Jersey followed with an act in 1798.[2]

43. **Legislation of the Eastern States.** In the Eastern States, where slavery as an institution was already nearly defunct, action was aimed toward stopping the notorious participation of citizens in the slave-trade outside the State. The prime movers were the Rhode Island Quakers. Having early secured a law against the traffic in their own State, they turned their attention to others. Through their remonstrances Connecticut, in 1788,[3] prohibited participation in the trade by a fine of £500 on the vessel, £50 on each slave, and loss of insurance; this act was strengthened in 1792,[4] the year after the Haytian revolt. Massachusetts, after many fruitless attempts, finally took advantage of an unusually bold case of kidnapping, and passed a similar act in 1788.[5] "This," says Belknap, "was the utmost which could be done by our legislatures; we still have to regret the impossibility of making a law *here*, which shall restrain our citizens from carrying on this trade *in foreign bottoms*, and from committing the crimes which this act prohibits, *in foreign countries*, as it is said some of them have done since the enacting of these laws." [6]

Thus it is seen how, spurred by the tragedy in the West Indies, the United States succeeded by State action in prohibiting the slave-trade from 1798 to 1803, in furthering the cause of abolition, and in preventing the fitting out of slave-trade expeditions in United States ports. The country had good cause to congratulate itself. The national government hastened to supplement State action as far as possible, and the

[1] Dallas, *Laws*, II. 586.

[2] Paterson, *Digest of the Laws of New Jersey* (1800), pp. 307–13. In 1804 New Jersey passed an act gradually to abolish slavery. The legislation of New York at this period was confined to regulating the exportation of slave criminals (1790), and to passing an act gradually abolishing slavery (1799). In 1801 she codified all her acts.

[3] *Acts and Laws of Connecticut* (ed. 1784), pp. 368, 369, 388.

[4] *Ibid.*, p. 412.

[5] *Perpetual Laws of Massachusetts*, 1780–89, pp. 235–6.

[6] *Queries Respecting Slavery*, etc., in *Mass. Hist. Soc. Coll.*, 1st Ser., IV. 205.

prophecies of the more sanguine Revolutionary fathers seemed about to be realized, when the ill-considered act of South Carolina showed the weakness of the constitutional compromise.

44. **First Debate in Congress, 1789.** The attention of the national government was early directed to slavery and the trade by the rise, in the first Congress, of the question of taxing slaves imported. During the debate on the duty bill introduced by Clymer's committee, Parker of Virginia moved, May 13, 1789, to lay a tax of ten dollars *per capita* on slaves imported. He plainly stated that the tax was designed to check the trade, and that he was "sorry that the Constitution prevented Congress from prohibiting the importation altogether." The proposal was evidently unwelcome, and caused an extended debate.[1] Smith of South Carolina wanted to postpone a matter so "big with the most serious consequences to the State he represented." Roger Sherman of Connecticut "could not reconcile himself to the insertion of human beings as an article of duty, among goods, wares, and merchandise." Jackson of Georgia argued against any restriction, and thought such States as Virginia "ought to let their neighbors get supplied, before they imposed such a burden upon the importation." Tucker of South Carolina declared it "unfair to bring in such an important subject at a time when debate was almost precluded," and denied the right of Congress to "consider whether the importation of slaves is proper or not."

Mr. Parker was evidently somewhat abashed by this onslaught of friend and foe, but he "had ventured to introduce the subject after full deliberation, and did not like to withdraw it." He desired Congress, "if possible," to "wipe off the stigma under which America labored." This brought Jackson of Georgia again to his feet. He believed, in spite of the "fashion of the day," that the Negroes were better off as slaves than as freedmen, and that, as the tax was partial, "it would be the most odious tax Congress could impose." Such sentiments were a distinct advance in pro-slavery doctrine, and called for a protest from Madison of Virginia. He thought the discussion proper,

[1] *Annals of Cong.*, 1 Cong. 1 sess. pp. 336–41.

denied the partiality of the tax, and declared that, according to the spirit of the Constitution and his own desire, it was to be hoped "that, by expressing a national disapprobation of this trade, we may destroy it, and save ourselves from reproaches, and our posterity the imbecility ever attendant on a country filled with slaves." Finally, to Burke of South Carolina, who thought "the gentlemen were contending for nothing," Madison sharply rejoined, "If we contend for nothing, the gentlemen who are opposed to us do not contend for a great deal."

It now became clear that Congress had been whirled into a discussion of too delicate and lengthy a nature to allow its further prolongation. Compromising councils prevailed; and it was agreed that the present proposition should be withdrawn and a separate bill brought in. This bill was, however, at the next session dexterously postponed "until the next session of Congress."[1]

45. **Second Debate in Congress, 1790.** It is doubtful if Congress of its own initiative would soon have resurrected the matter, had not a new anti-slavery weapon appeared in the shape of urgent petitions from abolition societies. The first petition, presented February 11, 1790,[2] was from the same interstate Yearly Meeting of Friends which had formerly petitioned the Confederation Congress.[3] They urged Congress to inquire "whether, notwithstanding such seeming impediments, it be not in reality within your power to exercise justice and mercy, which, if adhered to, we cannot doubt, must produce the abolition of the slave trade," etc. Another Quaker petition from New York was also presented,[4] and both were about to be referred, when Smith of South Carolina objected, and precipitated a sharp debate.[5] This debate had a distinctly different tone from that of the preceding one, and represents another step in pro-slavery doctrine. The key-note of these utterances was struck by Stone of Maryland, who "feared that if Con-

[1] *Annals of Cong.*, 1 Cong. 1 sess. p. 903.
[2] *Ibid.*, 1 Cong. 2 sess. pp. 1182–3.
[3] *Journals of Cong.*, 1782–3, pp. 418–9. Cf. above, p. 51.
[4] *Annals of Cong.*, 1 Cong. 2 sess. p. 1184.
[5] *Ibid.*, pp. 1182–91.

gress took any measures indicative of an intention to interfere with the kind of property alluded to, it would sink it in value very considerably, and might be injurious to a great number of the citizens, particularly in the Southern States. He thought the subject was of general concern, and that the petitioners had no more right to interfere with it than any other members of the community. It was an unfortunate circumstance, that it was the disposition of religious sects to imagine they understood the rights of human nature better than all the world besides."

In vain did men like Madison disclaim all thought of unconstitutional "interference," and express only a desire to see "If anything is within the Federal authority to restrain such violation of the rights of nations and of mankind, as is supposed to be practised in some parts of the United States." A storm of disapproval from Southern members met such sentiments. "The rights of the Southern States ought not to be threatened," said Burke of South Carolina. "Any extraordinary attention of Congress to this petition," averred Jackson of Georgia, would put slave property "in jeopardy," and "evince to the people a disposition towards a total emancipation." Smith and Tucker of South Carolina declared that the request asked for "unconstitutional" measures. Gerry of Massachusetts, Hartley of Pennsylvania, and Lawrence of New York rather mildly defended the petitioners; but after considerable further debate the matter was laid on the table.

The very next day, however, the laid ghost walked again in the shape of another petition from the "Pennsylvania Society for promoting the Abolition of Slavery," signed by its venerable president, Benjamin Franklin. This petition asked Congress to "step to the very verge of the power vested in you for discouraging every species of traffic in the persons of our fellow-men."[1] Hartley of Pennsylvania called up the memorial of the preceding day, and it was read a second time and a motion for commitment made. Plain words now came from Tucker of South Carolina. "The petition," he said, "contained

[1] *Annals of Cong.*, 1 Cong. 2 sess. pp. 1197–1205.

an unconstitutional request." The commitment would alarm the South. These petitions were "mischievous" attempts to imbue the slaves with false hopes. The South would not submit to a general emancipation without "civil war." The commitment would "blow the trumpet of sedition in the Southern States," echoed his colleague, Burke. The Pennsylvania men spoke just as boldly. Scott declared the petition constitutional, and was sorry that the Constitution did not interdict this "most abominable" traffic. "Perhaps, in our Legislative capacity," he said, "we can go no further than to impose a duty of ten dollars, but I do not know how far I might go if I was one of the Judges of the United States, and those people were to come before me and claim their emancipation; but I am sure I would go as far as I could." Jackson of Georgia rejoined in true Southern spirit, boldly defending slavery in the light of religion and history, and asking if it was "good policy to bring forward a business at this moment likely to light up the flame of civil discord; for the people of the Southern States will resist one tyranny as soon as another. The other parts of the Continent may bear them down by force of arms, but they will never suffer themselves to be divested of their property without a struggle. The gentleman says, if he was a Federal Judge, he does not know to what length he would go in emancipating these people; but I believe his judgment would be of short duration in Georgia, perhaps even the existence of such a Judge might be in danger." Baldwin, his New-England-born colleague, urged moderation by reciting the difficulty with which the constitutional compromise was reached, and declaring, "the moment we go to jostle on that ground, I fear we shall feel it tremble under our feet." Lawrence of New York wanted to commit the memorials, in order to see how far Congress might constitutionally interfere. Smith of South Carolina, in a long speech, said that his constituents entered the Union "from political, not from moral motives," and that "we look upon this measure as an attack upon the palladium of the property of our country." Page of Virginia, although a slave owner, urged commitment, and Madison again maintained the appropriateness of the request, and suggested that "regulations might be made in relation to the introduction of them [i. e., slaves] into the new States to be formed out of the Western Territory." Even conservative Gerry of Massachusetts declared, with regard to the whole trade, that the fact that "we have a right to regulate this business, is as clear as that we have any rights whatever."

Finally, by a vote of 43 to 11, the memorials were committed, the South Carolina and Georgia delegations, Bland and Coles of Virginia, Stone of Maryland, and Sylvester of New York voting in the negative.[1] A committee, consisting of Foster of New Hampshire, Huntington of Connecticut, Gerry of Massachusetts, Lawrence of New York, Sinnickson of New Jersey, Hartley of Pennsylvania, and Parker of Virginia, was charged with the matter, and reported Friday, March 5. The absence of Southern members on this committee compelled it to make this report a sort of official manifesto on the aims of Northern anti-slavery politics. As such, it was sure to meet with vehement opposition in the House, even though conservatively worded. Such proved to be the fact when the committee reported. The onslaught to "negative the whole report" was prolonged and bitter, the debate *pro* and *con* lasting several days.[2]

46. **The Declaration of Powers, 1790.** The result is best seen by comparing the original report with the report of the Committee of the Whole, adopted by a vote of 29 to 25 Monday, March 23, 1790:[3]—

REPORT OF THE SELECT COMMITTEE.	REPORT OF THE COMMITTEE OF THE WHOLE.
That, from the nature of the matters contained in these memorials, they were induced to examine the powers vested in Congress, under the present Constitution, relating to the Abolition of Slavery, and are clearly of opinion,	
First. That the General Government is expressly restrained from prohibiting	*First.* That the migration or importation of such persons as any of the States

[1] *House Journal* (repr. 1826), 1 Cong. 2 sess. I. 157–8.

[2] *Annals of Cong.*, 1 Cong. 2 sess. pp. 1413–7.

[3] For the reports and debates, cf. *Annals of Cong.*, 1 Cong. 2 sess. pp. 1413–7, 1450–74; *House Journal* (repr. 1826), 1 Cong. 2 sess. I. 168–81.

the importation of such persons 'as any of the States now existing shall think proper to admit, until the year one thousand eight hundred and eight.'

Secondly. That Congress, by a fair construction of the Constitution, are equally restrained from interfering in the emancipation of slaves, who already are, or who may, within the period mentioned, be imported into, or born within, any of the said States.

Thirdly. That Congress have no authority to interfere in the internal regulations of particular States, relative to the instructions of slaves in the principles of morality and religion; to their comfortable clothing, accommodations, and subsistence; to the regulation of their marriages, and the prevention of the violation of the rights thereof, or to the separation of children from their parents; to a comfortable provision in cases of sickness, age, or infirmity; or to the seizure, transportation, or sale of free negroes; but have the fullest confidence in the wisdom and humanity of the Legislatures of the several States, that they will revise their laws from time to time, when necessary, and promote the objects mentioned in the memorials, and every other measure that may tend to the happiness of slaves.

Fourthly. That, nevertheless, Congress have authority, if they shall think it necessary, to lay at any time a tax or duty, not exceeding ten dollars for each person of any description, the importation of whom shall be by any of the States admitted as aforesaid.

Fifthly. That Congress have authority to interdict,[1] or (so far as it is or may be carried on by citizens of the United States, for supplying foreigners) to regulate[1] the African trade, and to make provision for the humane treatment of slaves, in all cases while on their pas-

now existing shall think proper to admit, cannot be prohibited by Congress, prior to the year one thousand eight hundred and eight.

Secondly. That Congress have no authority to interfere in the emancipation of slaves, or in the treatment of them within any of the States; it remaining with the several States alone to provide any regulation therein, which humanity and true policy may require.

Thirdly. That Congress have authority to restrain the citizens of the United States from carrying on the African trade, for the purpose of supplying foreigners with slaves, and of providing, by proper regulations, for the humane treatment, during their passage, of slaves im-

[1] A clerical error in the original: "interdict" and "regulate" should be interchanged.

sage to the United States, or to foreign ports, so far as respects the citizens of the United States.

Sixthly. That Congress have also authority to prohibit foreigners from fitting out vessels in any port of the United States, for transporting persons from Africa to any foreign port.

Seventhly. That the memorialists be informed, that in all cases to which the authority of Congress extends, they will exercise it for the humane objects of the memorialists, so far as they can be promoted on the principles of justice, humanity, and good policy.

ported by the said citizens into the States admitting such importation.

Fourthly. That Congress have authority to prohibit foreigners from fitting out vessels in any port of the United States for transporting persons from Africa to any foreign port.

47. **The Act of 1794.** This declaration of the powers of the central government over the slave-trade bore early fruit in the second Congress, in the shape of a shower of petitions from abolition societies in Massachusetts, Rhode Island, Connecticut, New York, Pennsylvania, Maryland, and Virginia.[1] In some of these slavery was denounced as "an outrageous violation of one of the most essential rights of human nature,"[2] and the slave-trade as a traffic "degrading to the rights of man" and "repugnant to reason."[3] Others declared the trade "injurious to the true commercial interest of a nation,"[4] and asked Congress that, having taken up the matter, they do all in their power to limit the trade. Congress was, however, determined to avoid as long as possible so unpleasant a matter, and, save an angry attempt to censure a Quaker petitioner,[5] nothing was heard of the slave-trade until the third Congress.

Meantime, news came from the seas southeast of Carolina and Georgia which influenced Congress more powerfully than humanitarian arguments had done. The wild revolt of despised slaves, the rise of a noble black leader, and the birth of a new

[1] See *Memorials presented to Congress*, etc. (1792), published by the Pennsylvania Abolition Society.

[2] From the Virginia petition.

[3] From the petition of Baltimore and other Maryland societies.

[4] From the Providence Abolition Society's petition.

[5] *House Journal* (repr. 1826), 2 Cong. 2 sess. I. 627–9; *Annals of Cong.*, 2 Cong. 2 sess. pp. 728–31.

nation of Negro freemen frightened the pro-slavery advocates and armed the anti-slavery agitation. As a result, a Quaker petition for a law against the transport traffic in slaves was received without a murmur in 1794,[1] and on March 22 the first national act against the slave-trade became a law.[2] It was designed "to prohibit the carrying on the Slave Trade from the United States to any foreign place or country," or the fitting out of slavers in the United States for that country. The penalties for violation were forfeiture of the ship, a fine of $1000 for each person engaged, and of $200 for each slave transported. If the Quakers thought this a triumph of anti-slavery sentiment, they were quickly undeceived. Congress might willingly restrain the country from feeding West Indian turbulence, and yet be furious at a petition like that of 1797,[3] calling attention to "the oppressed state of our brethren of the African race" in this country, and to the interstate slave-trade. "Considering the present extraordinary state of the West India Islands and of Europe," young John Rutledge insisted "that 'sufficient for the day is the evil thereof,' and that they ought to shut their door against any thing which had a tendency to produce the like confusion in this country." After excited debate and some investigation by a special committee, the petition was ordered, in both Senate and House, to be withdrawn.

48. **The Act of 1800.** In the next Congress, the sixth, another petition threw the House into paroxysms of slavery debate. Waln of Pennsylvania presented the petition of certain free colored men of Pennsylvania praying for a revision of the slave-trade laws and of the fugitive-slave law, and for prospective emancipation.[4] Waln moved the reference of this memorial to a committee already appointed on the revision of the loosely drawn and poorly enforced Act of 1794.[5] Rutledge of South

[1] *Annals of Cong.*, 3 Cong. 1 sess. pp. 64, 70, 72; *House Journal* (repr. 1826), 3 Cong. 1 sess. II. 76, 84–5, 96–100; *Senate Journal* (repr. 1820), 3 Cong. 1 sess. II. 51.

[2] *Statutes at Large*, I. 347–9.

[3] *Annals of Cong.*, 5 Cong. 2 sess. pp. 656–70, 945–1033.

[4] *Annals of Cong.*, 6 Cong. 1 sess. p. 229.

[5] Dec. 12, 1799: *House Journal* (repr. 1826), 6 Cong. 1 sess. III. 535. For the debate, see *Annals of Cong.*, 6 Cong. 1 sess. pp. 230–45.

Carolina immediately arose. He opposed the motion, saying, that these petitions were continually coming in and stirring up discord; that it was a good thing the Negroes were in slavery; and that already "too much of this new-fangled French philosophy of liberty and equality" had found its way among them. Others defended the right of petition, and declared that none wished Congress to exceed its powers. Brown of Rhode Island, a new figure in Congress, a man of distinguished services and from a well-known family, boldly set forth the commercial philosophy of his State. "We want money," said he, "we want a navy; we ought therefore to use the means to obtain it. We ought to go farther than has yet been proposed, and repeal the bills in question altogether, for why should we see Great Britain getting all the slave trade to themselves; why may not our country be enriched by that lucrative traffic? There would not be a slave the more sold, but we should derive the benefits by importing from Africa as well as that nation." Waln, in reply, contended that they should look into "the slave trade, much of which was still carrying on from Rhode Island, Boston and Pennsylvania." Hill of North Carolina called the House back from this general discussion to the petition in question, and, while willing to remedy any existing defect in the Act of 1794, hoped the petition would not be received. Dana of Connecticut declared that the paper "contained nothing but a farrago of the French metaphysics of liberty and equality;" and that "it was likely to produce some of the dreadful scenes of St. Domingo." The next day Rutledge again warned the House against even discussing the matter, as "very serious, nay, dreadful effects, must be the inevitable consequence." He held up the most lurid pictures of the fatuity of the French Convention in listening to the overtures of the "three emissaries from St. Domingo," and thus yielding "one of the finest islands in the world" to "scenes which had never been practised since the destruction of Carthage." "But, sir," he continued, "we have lived to see these dreadful scenes. These horrid effects have succeeded what was conceived once to be trifling. Most important consequences may be the result, although gentlemen little apprehend it. But we know the situation of things there, although they do not, and knowing we deprecate it. There have been emissaries amongst us in the Southern States; they have begun their war upon us; an actual organization has commenced; we have had them meeting in their club rooms, and debating on that subject. . . . Sir, I do believe that persons have been sent from France to feel the pulse of this country, to know whether these [i. e., the Negroes] are the proper engines to make use of: these people have been talked to; they have been tampered with, and this is going on."

Finally, after censuring certain parts of this Negro petition, Congress committed the part on the slave-trade to the committee already appointed. Meantime, the Senate sent down a bill to amend the Act of 1794, and the House took this bill under consideration.[1] Prolonged debate ensued. Brown of Rhode Island again made a most elaborate plea for throwing open the foreign slave-trade. Negroes, he said, bettered their condition by being enslaved, and thus it was morally wrong and commercially indefensible to impose "a heavy fine and imprisonment . . . for carrying on a trade so advantageous;" or, if the trade must be stopped, then equalize the matter and abolish slavery too. Nichols of Virginia thought that surely the gentlemen would not advise the importation of more Negroes; for while it "was a fact, to be sure," that they would thus improve their condition, "would it be policy so to do?" Bayard of Delaware said that "a more dishonorable item of revenue" than that derived from the slave-trade "could not be established." Rutledge opposed the new bill as defective and impracticable: the former act, he said, was enough; the States had stopped the trade, and in addition the United States had sought to placate philanthropists by stopping the use of our ships in the trade. "This was going very far indeed." New England first began the trade, and why not let them enjoy its profits now as well as the English? The trade could not be stopped.

The bill was eventually recommitted and reported again.[2]

[1] *Senate Journal* (repr. 1821), 6 Cong. 1 sess. III. 72, 77, 88, 92; see *Ibid.*, Index, Bill No. 62; *House Journal* (repr. 1826), 6 Cong. 1 sess. III., Index, House Bill No. 247. For the debate, see *Annals of Cong.*, 6 Cong. 1 sess. pp. 686–700.

[2] *Annals of Cong.*, 6 Cong. 1 sess. p. 697.

"On the question for its passing, a long and warm debate ensued," and several attempts to postpone it were made; it finally passed, however, only Brown of Rhode Island, Dent of Maryland, Rutledge and Huger of South Carolina, and Dickson of North Carolina voting against it, and 67 voting for it.[1] This Act of May 10, 1800,[2] greatly strengthened the Act of 1794. The earlier act had prohibited citizens from equipping slavers for the foreign trade; but this went so far as to forbid them having any interest, direct or indirect, in such voyages, or serving on board slave-ships in any capacity. Imprisonment for two years was added to the former fine of $2000, and United States commissioned ships were directed to capture such slavers as prizes. The slaves though forfeited by the owner, were not to go to the captor; and the act omitted to say what disposition should be made of them.

49. **The Act of 1803.** The Haytian revolt, having been among the main causes of two laws, soon was the direct instigation to a third. The frightened feeling in the South, when freedmen from the West Indies began to arrive in various ports, may well be imagined. On January 17, 1803, the town of Wilmington, North Carolina, hastily memorialized Congress, stating the arrival of certain freed Negroes from Guadeloupe, and apprehending "much danger to the peace and safety of the people of the Southern States of the Union" from the "admission of persons of that description into the United States."[3] The House committee which considered this petition hastened to agree "That the system of policy stated in the said memorial to exist, and to be now pursued in the French colonial government, of the West Indies, is fraught with danger to the peace and safety of the United States. That the fact stated to have occurred in the prosecution of that system of policy, demands the prompt interference of the Government of the United States, as well Legislative as Executive."[4] The result was a bill providing for the forfeiture of any ship which should bring into

[1] *Annals of Cong.*, 6 Cong. 1 sess. pp. 699–700.

[2] *Statutes at Large*, II. 70.

[3] *Annals of Cong.*, 7 Cong. 2 sess. pp. 385–6.

[4] *Ibid.*, p. 424.

States prohibiting the same "any negro, mulatto, or other person of color;" the captain of the ship was also to be punished. After some opposition[1] the bill became a law, February 28, 1803.[2]

50. **State of the Slave-Trade from 1789 to 1803.** Meantime, in spite of the prohibitory State laws, the African slave-trade to the United States continued to flourish. It was notorious that New England traders carried on a large traffic.[3] Members stated on the floor of the House that "it was much to be regretted that the severe and pointed statute against the slave trade had been so little regarded. In defiance of its forbiddance and its penalties, it was well known that citizens and vessels of the United States were still engaged in that traffic. . . . In various parts of the nation, outfits were made for slave-voyages, without secrecy, shame, or apprehension. . . . Countenanced by their fellow-citizens at home, who were as ready to buy as they themselves were to collect and to bring to market, they approached our Southern harbors and inlets, and clandestinely disembarked the sooty offspring of the Eastern, upon the ill fated soil of the Western hemisphere. In this way, it had been computed that, during the last twelve months, twenty thousand enslaved negroes had been transported from Guinea, and, by smuggling, added to the plantation stock of Georgia and South Carolina. So little respect seems to have been paid to the existing prohibitory statute, that it may almost be considered as disregarded by common consent."[4]

These voyages were generally made under the flag of a foreign nation, and often the vessel was sold in a foreign port to escape confiscation. South Carolina's own Congressman confessed that although the State had prohibited the trade since 1788, she "was unable to enforce" her laws. "With navigable rivers running into the heart of it," said he, "it was impossible,

[1] See House Bills Nos. 89 and 101; *Annals of Cong.*, 7 Cong. 2 sess. pp. 424, 459–67. For the debate, see *Ibid.*, pp. 459–72.

[2] *Statutes at Large*, II. 205.

[3] Cf. Fowler, *Local Law in Massachusetts and Connecticut*, etc., p. 126.

[4] Speech of S. L. Mitchell of New York, Feb. 14, 1804: *Annals of Cong.*, 8 Cong. 1 sess. p. 1000. Cf. also speech of Bedinger: *Ibid.*, pp. 997–8.

with our means, to prevent our Eastern brethren, who, in some parts of the Union, in defiance of the authority of the General Government, have been engaged in this trade, from introducing them into the country. The law was completely evaded, and, for the last year or two [1802–3], Africans were introduced into the country in numbers little short, I believe, of what they would have been had the trade been a legal one."[1] The same tale undoubtedly might have been told of Georgia.

51. **The South Carolina Repeal of 1803.** This vast and apparently irrepressible illicit traffic was one of three causes which led South Carolina, December 17, 1803, to throw aside all pretence and legalize her growing slave-trade; the other two causes were the growing certainty of total prohibition of the traffic in 1808, and the recent purchase of Louisiana by the United States, with its vast prospective demand for slave labor. Such a combination of advantages, which meant fortunes to planters and Charleston slave-merchants, could not longer be withheld from them; the prohibition was repealed, and the United States became again, for the first time in at least five years, a legal slave mart. This action shocked the nation, frightening Southern States with visions of an influx of untrained barbarians and servile insurrections, and arousing and intensifying the anti-slavery feeling of the North, which had long since come to think of the trade, so far as legal enactment went, as a thing of the past.

Scarcely a month after this repeal, Bard of Pennsylvania solemnly addressed Congress on the matter. "For many reasons," said he, "this House must have been justly surprised by a recent measure of one of the Southern States. The impressions, however, which that measure gave my mind, were deep and painful. Had I been informed that some formidable foreign Power had invaded our country, I would not, I ought not, be more alarmed than on hearing that South Carolina had repealed her law prohibiting the importation of slaves. . . . Our hands are tied, and we are obliged to stand confounded, while we see the flood-gate opened, and pouring incalculable miseries

[1] Speech of Lowndes in the House, Feb. 14, 1804: *Annals of Cong.*, 8 Cong., 1 sess. p. 992. Cf. Stanton's speech later: *Ibid.*, 9 Cong. 2 sess. p. 240.

into our country."[1] He then moved, as the utmost legal measure, a tax of ten dollars per head on slaves imported.

Debate on this proposition did not occur until February 14, when Lowndes explained the circumstances of the repeal, and a long controversy took place.[2] Those in favor of the tax argued that the trade was wrong, and that the tax would serve as some slight check; the tax was not inequitable, for if a State did not wish to bear it she had only to prohibit the trade; the tax would add to the revenue, and be at the same time a moral protest against an unjust and dangerous traffic. Against this it was argued that if the tax furnished a revenue it would defeat its own object, and make prohibition more difficult in 1808; it was inequitable, because it was aimed against one State, and would fall exclusively on agriculture; it would give national sanction to the trade; it would look "like an attempt in the General Government to correct a State for the undisputed exercise of its constitutional powers;" the revenue would be inconsiderable, and the United States had nothing to do with the moral principle; while a prohibitory tax would be defensible, a small tax like this would be useless as a protection and criminal as a revenue measure.

The whole debate hinged on the expediency of the measure, few defending South Carolina's action.[3] Finally, a bill was ordered to be brought in, which was done on the 17th.[4] Another long debate took place, covering substantially the same ground. It was several times hinted that if the matter were dropped South Carolina might again prohibit the trade. This, and the vehement opposition, at last resulted in the postponement of the bill, and it was not heard from again during the session.

52. **The Louisiana Slave-Trade, 1803–1805.** About this time

[1] *Annals of Cong.*, 8 Cong. 1 sess. pp. 820, 876.

[2] *Ibid.*, pp. 992–1036.

[3] Huger of South Carolina declared that the whole South Carolina Congressional delegation opposed the repeal of the law, although they maintained the State's right to do so if she chose: *Ibid.*, p. 1005.

[4] *Ibid.*, pp. 1020–36; *House Journal* (repr. 1826), 8 Cong. 1 sess. IV. 523, 578, 580, 581–5.

the cession of Louisiana brought before Congress the question of the status of slavery and the slave-trade in the Territories. Twice or thrice before had the subject called for attention. The first time was in the Congress of the Confederation, when, by the Ordinance of 1787,[1] both slavery and the slave-trade were excluded from the Northwest Territory. In 1790 Congress had accepted the cession of North Carolina back lands on the express condition that slavery there be undisturbed.[2] Nothing had been said as to slavery in the South Carolina cession (1787),[3] but it was tacitly understood that the provision of the Northwest Ordinance would not be applied. In 1798 the bill introduced for the cession of Mississippi contained a specific declaration that the anti-slavery clause of 1787 should not be included.[4] The bill passed the Senate, but caused long and excited debate in the House.[5] It was argued, on the one hand, that the case in Mississippi was different from that in the Northwest Territory, because slavery was a legal institution in all the surrounding country, and to prohibit the institution was virtually to prohibit the settling of the country. On the other hand, Gallatin declared that if this amendment should not obtain, "he knew not how slaves could be prevented from being introduced by way of New Orleans, by persons who are not citizens of the United States." It was moved to strike out the excepting clause; but the motion received only twelve votes, — an apparent indication that Congress either did not appreciate the great precedent it was establishing, or was reprehensibly careless. Harper of South Carolina then succeeded in building up the Charleston slave-trade interest by a section forbidding the slave traffic from "without the limits of the United States." Thatcher moved to strike out the last clause of this amendment, and thus to prohibit the interstate trade, but he failed to get a second.[6] Thus the act passed, punishing the introduction of

[1] On slavery in the Territories, cf. Welling, in *Report Amer. Hist. Assoc.*, 1891, pp. 133–60.

[2] *Statutes at Large*, I. 108.

[3] *Journals of Cong.*, XII. 137–8.

[4] *Annals of Cong.*, 5 Cong. 1 sess. pp. 511, 515, 532–3.

[5] *Ibid.*, 5 Cong. 2 sess. pp. 1235, 1249, 1277–84, 1296–1313.

[6] *Ibid.*, p. 1313.

slaves from without the country by a fine of $300 for each slave, and freeing the slave.[1]

In 1804 President Jefferson communicated papers to Congress on the status of slavery and the slave-trade in Louisiana.[2] The Spanish had allowed the traffic by edict in 1793, France had not stopped it, and Governor Claiborne had refrained from interference. A bill erecting a territorial government was already pending.[3] The Northern "District of Louisiana" was placed under the jurisdiction of Indiana Territory, and was made subject to the provisions of the Ordinance of 1787. Various attempts were made to amend the part of the bill referring to the Southern Territory: first, so as completely to prohibit the slave-trade;[4] then to compel the emancipation at a certain age of all those imported;[5] next, to confine all importation to that from the States;[6] and, finally, to limit it further to slaves imported before South Carolina opened her ports.[7] The last two amendments prevailed, and the final act also extended to the Territory the Acts of 1794 and 1803. Only slaves imported before May 1, 1798, could be introduced, and those must be slaves of actual settlers.[8] All slaves illegally imported were freed.

This stringent act was limited to one year. The next year, in accordance with the urgent petition of the inhabitants, a bill was introduced against these restrictions.[9] By dexterous wording, this bill, which became a law March 2, 1805,[10] swept away

[1] *Statutes at Large*, I. 549.

[2] *Amer. State Papers, Miscellaneous*, I. No. 177.

[3] *Annals of Cong.*, 8 Cong. 1 sess. pp. 106, 211, 223, 231, 233–4, 238.

[4] *Ibid.*, pp. 240, 1186.

[5] *Ibid.*, p. 241.

[6] *Ibid.*, p. 240.

[7] *Ibid.*, p. 242.

[8] For further proceedings, see *Ibid.*, pp. 240–55, 1038–79, 1128–9, 1185–9. For the law, see *Statutes at Large*, II. 283–9.

[9] First, a bill was introduced applying the Northwest Ordinance to the Territory (*Annals of Cong.*, 8 Cong. 2 sess. pp. 45–6); but this was replaced by a Senate bill (*Ibid.*, p. 68; *Senate Journal*, repr. 1821, 8 Cong. 2 sess. III. 464). For the petition of the inhabitants, see *Annals of Cong.*, 8 Cong. 2 sess. p. 727–8.

[10] The bill was hurried through, and there are no records of debate. Cf. *Annals of Cong.*, 8 Cong. 2 sess. pp. 28–69, 727, 871, 957, 1016–20, 1213–5. In *Senate Journal* (repr. 1821), III., see Index, Bill No. 8. Importation

all restrictions upon the slave-trade except that relating to foreign ports, and left even this provision so ambiguous that, later, by judicial interpretation of the law,[1] the foreign slave-trade was allowed, at least for a time.

Such a stream of slaves now poured into the new Territory that the following year a committee on the matter was appointed by the House.[2] The committee reported that they "are in possession of the fact, that African slaves, lately imported into Charleston, have been thence conveyed into the territory of Orleans, and, in their opinion, this practice will be continued to a very great extent, while there is no law to prevent it."[3] The House ordered a bill checking this to be prepared; and such a bill was reported, but was soon dropped.[4] Importations into South Carolina during this time reached enormous proportions. Senator Smith of that State declared from official returns that, between 1803 and 1807, 39,075 Negroes were imported into Charleston, most of whom went to the Territories.[5]

of slaves was allowed by a clause erecting a Frame of Government "similar" to that of the Mississippi Territory.

[1] *Annals of Cong.*, 9 Cong. 1 sess. p. 443. The whole trade was practically foreign, for the slavers merely entered the Negroes at Charleston and immediately reshipped them to New Orleans. Cf. *Annals of Cong.*, 16 Cong. 1 sess. p. 264.

[2] *House Journal* (repr. 1826), 9 Cong. 1 sess. V. 264; *Annals of Cong.*, 9 Cong. 1 sess. pp. 445, 878.

[3] *House Reports*, 9 Cong. 1 sess. Feb. 17, 1806.

[4] House Bill No. 123.

[5] *Annals of Cong.*, 16 Cong. 2 sess. pp. 73–7. This report covers the time from Jan. 1, 1804, to Dec. 31, 1807. During that time the following was the number of ships engaged in the traffic: —

From Charleston,	61	From Connecticut,	1
" Rhode Island,	59	" Sweden,	1
" Baltimore,	4	" Great Britain,	70
" Boston,	1	" France,	3
" Norfolk,	2		202

The consignees of these slave ships were natives of

Charleston	13
Rhode Island	88
Great Britain	91
France	10
	202

53. **Last Attempts at Taxation, 1805–1806.** So alarming did the trade become that North Carolina passed a resolution in December, 1804,[1] proposing that the States give Congress power to prohibit the trade. Massachusetts,[2] Vermont,[3] New Hampshire,[4] and Maryland[5] responded; and a joint resolution was introduced in the House, proposing as an amendment to the Constitution "That the Congress of the United States shall have power to prevent the further importation of slaves into the United States and the Territories thereof."[6] Nothing came of this effort; but meantime the project of taxation was revived. A motion to this effect, made in February, 1805, was referred to a Committee of the Whole, but was not discussed. Early in the first session of the ninth Congress the motion of 1805 was renewed; and although again postponed on the assurance that South Carolina was about to stop the trade,[7] it finally came up for debate January 20, 1806.[8] Then occurred a most stubborn legislative battle, which lasted during the whole session.[9] Several amendments to the motion were first introduced,

The following slaves were imported: —

By British vessels	19,949	
" French "	1,078	
		21,027
By American vessels: —		
" Charleston merchants	2,006	
" Rhode Island "	7,958	
" Foreign "	5,717	
" other Northern "	930	
" " Southern "	1,437	18,048
Total number of slaves imported, 1804–7		39,075

It is, of course, highly probable that the Custom House returns were much below the actual figures.

[1] McMaster, *History of the People of the United States*, III. p. 517.

[2] *House Journal* (repr. 1826), 8 Cong. 2 sess. V. 171; *Mass. Resolves*, May, 1802, to March, 1806, Vol. II. A. (State House ed., p. 239).

[3] *House Journal* (repr. 1826), 9 Cong. 1 sess. V. 238.

[4] *Ibid.*, V. 266.

[5] *Senate Journal* (repr. 1821), 9 Cong. 1 sess. IV. 76, 77, 79.

[6] *House Journal* (repr. 1826), 8 Cong. 2 sess. V. 171.

[7] *Annals of Cong.*, 9 Cong. 1 sess. p. 274.

[8] *Ibid.*, pp. 272–4, 323.

[9] *Ibid.*, pp. 346–52, 358–75, etc., to 520.

so as to make it apply to all immigrants, and again to all "persons of color." As in the former debate, it was proposed to substitute a resolution of censure on South Carolina. All these amendments were lost. A long debate on the expediency of the measure followed, on the old grounds. Early of Georgia dwelt especially on the double taxation it would impose on Georgia; others estimated that a revenue of one hundred thousand dollars might be derived from the tax, a sum sufficient to replace the tax on pepper and medicines. Angry charges and counter-charges were made, — e. g., that Georgia, though ashamed openly to avow the trade, participated in it as well as South Carolina. "Some recriminations ensued between several members, on the participation of the traders of some of the New England States in carrying on the slave trade." Finally, January 22, by a vote of 90 to 25, a tax bill was ordered to be brought in.[1] One was reported on the 27th.[2] Every sort of opposition was resorted to. On the one hand, attempts were made to amend it so as to prohibit importation after 1807, and to prevent importation into the Territories; on the other hand, attempts were made to recommit and postpone the measure. It finally got a third reading, but was recommitted to a select committee, and disappeared until February 14.[3] Being then amended so as to provide for the forfeiture of smuggled cargoes, but saying nothing as to the disposition of the slaves, it was again relegated to a committee, after a vote of 69 to 42 against postponement.[4] On March 4 it appeared again, and a motion to reject it was lost. Finally, in the midst of the war scare and the question of non-importation of British goods, the bill was apparently forgotten, and the last attempt to tax imported slaves ended, like the others, in failure.

54. **Key-Note of the Period.** One of the last acts of this period strikes again the key-note which sounded throughout the whole of it. On February 20, 1806, after considerable opposition, a bill to prohibit trade with San Domingo passed the Senate.[5] In

[1] *Annals of Cong.*, 9 Cong. 1 sess. pp. 374–5.

[2] See House Bill No. 94.

[3] *Annals of Cong.*, 9 Cong. 1 sess. p. 466.

[4] *Ibid.*, pp. 519–20.

[5] *Ibid.*, pp. 21, 52, 75, etc., to 138, 485–515, 1228. See House Bill No. 168. Cf. *Statutes at Large*, II. 421–2.

the House it was charged by one side that the measure was dictated by France, and by the other, that it originated in the fear of countenancing Negro insurrection. The bill, however, became a law, and by continuations remained on the statute-books until 1809. Even at that distance the nightmare of the Haytian insurrection continued to haunt the South, and a proposal to reopen trade with the island caused wild John Randolph to point out the "dreadful evil" of a "direct trade betwixt the town of Charleston and the ports of the island of St. Domingo."[1]

Of the twenty years from 1787 to 1807 it can only be said that they were, on the whole, a period of disappointment so far as the suppression of the slave-trade was concerned. Fear, interest, and philanthropy united for a time in an effort which bade fair to suppress the trade; then the real weakness of the constitutional compromise appeared, and the interests of the few overcame the fears and the humanity of the many.

[1] A few months later, at the expiration of the period, trade was quietly reopened. *Annals of Cong.*, 11 Cong. 1 sess. pp. 443–6.

CHAPTER VIII.

THE PERIOD OF ATTEMPTED SUPPRESSION. 1807–1825.

55. **The Act of 1807.** The first great goal of anti-slavery effort in the United States had been, since the Revolution, the suppression of the slave-trade by national law. It would hardly be too much to say that the Haytian revolution, in addition to its influence in the years from 1791 to 1806, was one of the main causes that rendered the accomplishment of this aim possible at the earliest constitutional moment. To the great influence of the fears of the South was added the failure of the French designs on Louisiana, of which Toussaint L'Ouverture was the most probable cause. The cession of Louisiana in 1803 challenged and aroused the North on the slavery question again; put the Carolina and Georgia slave-traders in the saddle, to the dismay of the Border States; and brought the whole slave-trade question vividly before the public conscience. Another scarcely less potent influence was, naturally, the great

anti-slavery movement in England, which after a mighty struggle of eighteen years was about to gain its first victory in the British Act of 1807.

President Jefferson, in his pacificatory message of December 2, 1806, said: "I congratulate you, fellow-citizens, on the approach of the period at which you may interpose your authority constitutionally, to withdraw the citizens of the United States from all further participation in those violations of human rights which have been so long continued on the unoffending inhabitants of Africa, and which the morality, the reputation, and the best interests of our country, have long been eager to proscribe. Although no law you may pass can take prohibitory effect till the first day of the year one thousand eight hundred and eight, yet the intervening period is not too long to prevent, by timely notice, expeditions which cannot be completed before that day."[1]

In pursuance of this recommendation, the very next day Senator Bradley of Vermont introduced into the Senate a bill which, after a complicated legislative history, became the Act of March 2, 1807, prohibiting the African slave-trade.[2]

Three main questions were to be settled by this bill: first, and most prominent, that of the disposal of illegally imported Africans; second, that of the punishment of those concerned in the importation; third, that of the proper limitation of the interstate traffic by water.

The character of the debate on these three questions, as well as the state of public opinion, is illustrated by the fact that forty of the sixty pages of officially reported debates are devoted to the first question, less than twenty to the second, and only two to the third. A sad commentary on the previous enforcement of State and national laws is the readiness with which it was admitted that wholesale violations of the law would take place; indeed, Southern men declared that no strict law against the slave-trade could be executed in the South, and that it was only by playing on the motives of personal interest that the trade

1 *House Journal* (repr. 1826), 9 Cong. 2 sess. V. 468.

2 Cf. below, § 59.

could be checked. The question of punishment indicated the slowly changing moral attitude of the South toward the slave system. Early boldly said, "A large majority of people in the Southern States do not consider slavery as even an evil."[1] The South, in fact, insisted on regarding man-stealing as a minor offence, a "misdemeanor" rather than a "crime." Finally, in the short and sharp debate on the interstate coastwise trade, the growing economic side of the slavery question came to the front, the vested interests' argument was squarely put, and the future interstate trade almost consciously provided for.

From these considerations, it is doubtful as to how far it was expected that the Act of 1807 would check the slave traffic; at any rate, so far as the South was concerned, there seemed to be an evident desire to limit the trade, but little thought that this statute would definitively suppress it.

56. **The First Question: How shall illegally imported Africans be disposed of?** The dozen or more propositions on the question of the disposal of illegally imported Africans may be divided into two chief heads, representing two radically opposed parties: 1. That illegally imported Africans be free, although they might be indentured for a term of years or removed from the country. 2. That such Africans be sold as slaves.[2] The arguments on

[1] *Annals of Cong.*, 9 Cong. 2 sess. p. 238.

[2] There were at least twelve distinct propositions as to the disposal of the Africans imported: —

1. That they be forfeited and sold by the United States at auction (Early's bill, reported Dec. 15: *Ibid.*, pp. 167–8).

2. That they be forfeited and left to the disposal of the States (proposed by Bidwell and Early: *Ibid.*, pp. 181, 221, 477. This was the final settlement.)

3. That they be forfeited and sold, and that the proceeds go to charities, education, or internal improvements (Early, Holland, and Masters: *Ibid.*, p. 273).

4. That they be forfeited and indentured for life (Alston and Bidwell: *Ibid.*, pp. 170–1).

5. That they be forfeited and indentured for 7, 8, or 10 years (Pitkin: *Ibid.*, p. 186).

6. That they be forfeited and given into the custody of the President, and by him indentured in free States for a term of years (bill reported from the

these two propositions, which were many and far-reaching, may be roughly divided into three classes, political, constitutional, and moral.

The political argument, reduced to its lowest terms, ran thus: those wishing to free the Negroes illegally imported declared that to enslave them would be to perpetrate the very evil which the law was designed to stop. "By the same law," they said, "we condemn the man-stealer and become the receivers of his stolen goods. We punish the criminal, and then step into his place, and complete the crime." [1] They said that the objection to free Negroes was no valid excuse; for if the Southern people really feared this class, they would consent to the imposing of such penalties on illicit traffic as would stop the importation of a single slave.[2] Moreover, "forfeiture" and sale of the Negroes implied a property right in them which did not exist.[3] Waiving this technical point, and allowing them to be "forfeited" to the government, then the government should either immediately set them free, or, at the most, indenture them for a term of years; otherwise, the law would be an encouragement to violators. "It certainly will be," said they, "if the importer can find means to evade the penalty of the act; for there he has all the advantage of a market enhanced by our ineffectual attempt to prohibit." [4] They claimed that even the indenturing of the ignorant barbarian for life was better than slavery; and Sloan declared that

Senate Jan. 28: *House Journal* (repr. 1826), 9 Cong. 2 sess. V. 575; *Annals of Cong.*, 9 Cong. 2 sess. p. 477. Cf. also *Ibid.*, p. 272.)

7. That the Secretary of the Treasury dispose of them, at his discretion, in service (Quincy: *Annals of Cong.*, 9 Cong. 2 sess. p. 183).

8. That those imported into slave States be returned to Africa or bound out in free States (Sloan: *Ibid.*, p. 254).

9. That all be sent back to Africa (Smilie: *Ibid.*, p. 176).

10. That those imported into free States be free, those imported into slave States be returned to Africa or indentured (Sloan: *Ibid.*, p. 226).

11. That they be forfeited but not sold (Sloan and others: *Ibid.*, p. 270).

12. That they be free (Sloan: *Ibid.*, p. 168; Bidwell: *House Journal* (repr. 1826), 9 Cong. 2 sess. V. 515).

[1] Bidwell, Cook, and others: *Annals of Cong.*, 9 Cong. 2 sess. p. 201.

[2] Bidwell: *Ibid.*, p. 172.

[3] Fisk: *Ibid.*, pp. 224–5; Bidwell: *Ibid.*, p. 221.

[4] Quincy: *Ibid.*, p. 184.

the Northern States would receive the freed Negroes willingly rather than have them enslaved.[1]

The argument of those who insisted that the Negroes should be sold was tersely put by Macon: "In adopting our measures on this subject, we must pass such a law as can be executed." [2] Early expanded this: "It is a principle in legislation, as correct as any which has ever prevailed, that to give effect to laws you must not make them repugant to the passions and wishes of the people among whom they are to operate. How then, in this instance, stands the fact? Do not gentlemen from every quarter of the Union prove, on the discussion of every question that has ever arisen in the House, having the most remote bearing on the giving freedom to the Africans in the bosom of our country, that it has excited the deepest sensibility in the breasts of those where slavery exists? And why is this so? It is, because those who, from experience, know the extent of the evil, believe that the most formidable aspect in which it can present itself, is by making these people free among them. Yes, sir, though slavery is an evil, regretted by every man in the country, to have among us in any considerable quantity persons of this description, is an evil far greater than slavery itself. Does any gentleman want proof of this? I answer that all proof is useless; no fact can be more notorious. With this belief on the minds of the people where slavery exists, and where the importation will take place, if at all, we are about to turn loose in a state of freedom all persons brought in after the passage of this law. I ask gentlemen to reflect and say whether such a law, opposed to the ideas, the passions, the views, and the affections of the people of the Southern States, can be executed? I tell them, no; it is impossible — why? Because no man will inform — why? Because to inform will be to lead to an evil which will be deemed greater than the offence of which information is given, because it will be opposed to the principle of self-preservation, and to the love of family. No, no man will be disposed to jeopard his life, and the lives of his countrymen. And if no one dare

[1] *Annals of Cong.*, 9 Cong. 2 sess. p. 478; Bidwell: *Ibid.*, p. 171.
[2] *Ibid.*, p. 172.

inform, the whole authority of the Government cannot carry the law into effect. The whole people will rise up against it. Why? Because to enforce it would be to turn loose, in the bosom of the country, firebrands that would consume them."[1]

This was the more tragic form of the argument; it also had a mercenary side, which was presented with equal emphasis. It was repeatedly said that the only way to enforce the law was to play off individual interests against each other. The profit from the sale of illegally imported Negroes was declared to be the only sufficient "inducement to give information of their importation."[2] "Give up the idea of forfeiture, and I challenge the gentleman to invent fines, penalties, or punishments of any sort, sufficient to restrain the slave trade."[3] If such Negroes be freed, "I tell you that slaves will continue to be imported as heretofore. . . . You cannot get hold of the ships employed in this traffic. Besides, slaves will be brought into Georgia from East Florida. They will be brought into the Mississippi Territory from the bay of Mobile. You cannot inflict any other penalty, or devise any other adequate means of prevention, than a forfeiture of the Africans in whose possession they may be found after importation."[4] Then, too, when foreigners smuggled in Negroes, "who then . . . could be operated on, but the purchasers? There was the rub — it was their interest alone which, by being operated on, would produce a check. Snap their purse-strings, break open their strong box, deprive them of their slaves, and by destroying the temptation to buy, you put an end to the trade, . . . nothing short of a forfeiture of the slave would afford an effectual remedy."[5] Again, it was argued that it was impossible to prevent imported Negroes from becoming slaves, or, what was just as bad, from being sold as vagabonds or indentured for life.[6] Even our own laws, it was said, recognize the title of the African slave factor in the transported Negroes;

[1] *Annals of Cong.*, 9 Cong. 2 sess. pp. 173–4.
[2] Alston: *Ibid.*, p. 170.
[3] D. R. Williams: *Ibid.*, p. 183.
[4] Early: *Ibid.*, pp. 184–5.
[5] Lloyd, Early, and others: *Ibid.*, p. 203.
[6] Alston: *Ibid.*, p. 170.

and if the importer have no title, why do we legislate? Why not let the African immigrant alone to get on as he may, just as we do the Irish immigrant?[1] If he should be returned to Africa, his home could not be found, and he would in all probability be sold into slavery again.[2]

The constitutional argument was not urged as seriously as the foregoing; but it had a considerable place. On the one hand, it was urged that if the Negroes were forfeited, they were forfeited to the United States government, which could dispose of them as it saw fit;[3] on the other hand, it was said that the United States, as owner, was subject to State laws, and could not free the Negroes contrary to such laws.[4] Some alleged that the freeing of such Negroes struck at the title to all slave property;[5] others thought that, as property in slaves was not recognized in the Constitution, it could not be in a statute.[6] The question also arose as to the source of the power of Congress over the slave-trade. Southern men derived it from the clause on commerce, and declared that it exceeded the power of Congress to declare Negroes imported into a slave State, free, against the laws of that State; that Congress could not determine what should or should not be property in a State.[7] Northern men replied that, according to this principle, forfeiture and sale in Massachusetts would be illegal; that the power of Congress over the trade was derived from the restraining clause, as a non-existent power could not be restrained; and that the United States could act under her general powers as executor of the Law of Nations.[8]

The moral argument as to the disposal of illegally imported Negroes was interlarded with all the others. On the one side, it began with the "Rights of Man," and descended to a stickling

[1] Quincy: *Annals of Cong.*, 9 Cong. 2 sess. p. 222; Macon: *Ibid.*, p. 225.

[2] Macon: *Ibid.*, p. 177.

[3] Barker: *Ibid.*, p. 171; Bidwell: *Ibid.*, p. 172.

[4] Clay, Alston, and Early: *Ibid.*, p. 266.

[5] *Ibid.*

[6] Bidwell: *Ibid.*, p. 221.

[7] Sloan and others: *Ibid.*, p. 271; Early and Alston: *Ibid.*, pp. 168, 171.

[8] Ely, Bidwell, and others: *Ibid.*, pp. 179, 181, 271: Smilie and Findley: *Ibid.*, pp. 225, 226.

for the decent appearance of the statute-book; on the other side, it began with the uplifting of the heathen, and descended to a denial of the applicability of moral principles to the question. Said Holland of North Carolina: "It is admitted that the condition of the slaves in the Southern States is much superior to that of those in Africa. Who, then, will say that the trade is immoral?"[1] But, in fact, "morality has nothing to do with this traffic,"[2] for, as Joseph Clay declared, "it must appear to every man of common sense, that the question could be considered in a commercial point of view only."[3] The other side declared that, "by the laws of God and man," these captured Negroes are "entitled to their freedom as clearly and absolutely as we are;"[4] nevertheless, some were willing to leave them to the tender mercies of the slave States, so long as the statute-book was disgraced by no explicit recognition of slavery.[5] Such arguments brought some sharp sarcasm on those who seemed anxious "to legislate for the honor and glory of the statute book;"[6] some desired "to know what honor you will derive from a law that will be broken every day of your lives."[7] They would rather boldly sell the Negroes and turn the proceeds over to charity.

The final settlement of the question was as follows: —

"SECTION 4. . . . And neither the importer, nor any person or persons claiming from or under him, shall hold any right or title whatsoever to any negro, mulatto, or person of color, nor to the service or labor thereof, who may be imported or brought within the United States, or territories thereof, in violation of this law, but the same shall remain subject to any regulations not contravening the provisions of this act, which the Legislatures of the several States or Territories at any time hereafter may make, for disposing of any such negro, mulatto, or person of color."[8]

[1] *Annals of Cong.*, 9 Cong. 2 sess. p. 240. Cf. Lloyd: *Ibid.*, p. 236.
[2] Holland: *Ibid.*, p. 241.
[3] *Ibid.*, p. 227; Macon: *Ibid.*, p. 225.
[4] Bidwell, Cook, and others: *Ibid.*, p. 201.
[5] Bidwell: *Ibid.*, p. 221. Cf. *Ibid.*, p. 202.
[6] Early: *Ibid.*, p. 239.
[7] *Ibid.*
[8] *Ibid.*, p. 1267.

57. **The Second Question: How shall Violations be punished?** The next point in importance was that of the punishment of offenders. The half-dozen specific propositions reduce themselves to two: 1. A violation should be considered a crime or felony, and be punished by death; 2. A violation should be considered a misdemeanor, and be punished by fine and imprisonment.[1]

Advocates of the severer punishment dwelt on the enormity of the offence. It was "one of the highest crimes man could commit," and "a captain of a ship engaged in this traffic was guilty of murder."[2] The law of God punished the crime with death, and any one would rather be hanged than be enslaved.[3] It was a peculiarly deliberate crime, in which the offender did not act in sudden passion, but had ample time for reflection.[4] Then, too, crimes of much less magnitude are punished with death. Shall we punish the stealer of $50 with death, and the man-stealer with imprisonment only?[5] Piracy, forgery, and fraudulent sinking of vessels are punishable with death, "yet these are crimes only against property; whereas the importation of slaves, a crime committed against the liberty of man, and inferior only to murder or treason, is accounted nothing but a misdemeanor."[6] Here, indeed, lies the remedy for the evil of freeing illegally imported Negroes, — in making the penalty so severe that none will be brought in; if the South is sincere,

[1] There were about six distinct punishments suggested: —

1. Forfeiture, and fine of $5000 to $10,000 (Early's bill: *Annals of Cong.*, 9 Cong. 2 sess. p. 167).

2. Forfeiture and imprisonment (amendment to Senate bill: *Ibid.*, pp. 231, 477, 483).

3. Forfeiture, imprisonment from 5 to 10 years, and fine of $1000 to $10,000 (amendment to amendment of Senate bill: *Ibid.*, pp. 228, 483).

4. Forfeiture, imprisonment from 5 to 40 years, and fine of $1000 to $10,000 (Chandler's amendment: *Ibid.*, p. 228).

5. Forfeiture of all property, and imprisonment (Pitkin: *Ibid.*, p. 188).

6. Death (Smilie: *Ibid.*, pp. 189–90; bill reported to House, Dec. 19: *Ibid.*, p. 190; Senate bill as reported to House, Jan. 28).

[2] Smilie: *Ibid.*, pp. 189–90.

[3] Tallmadge: *Ibid.*, p. 233; Olin: *Ibid.*, p. 237.

[4] Ely: *Ibid.*, p. 237.

[5] Smilie: *Ibid.*, p. 236. Cf. Sloan: *Ibid.*, p. 232.

[6] Hastings: *Ibid.*, p. 228.

"they will unite to a man to execute the law."[1] To free such Negroes is dangerous; to enslave them, wrong; to return them, impracticable; to indenture them, difficult, — therefore, by a death penalty, keep them from being imported.[2] Here the East had a chance to throw back the taunts of the South, by urging the South to unite with them in hanging the New England slave-traders, assuring the South that "so far from charging their Southern brethren with cruelty or severity in hanging them, they would acknowledge the favor with gratitude."[3] Finally, if the Southerners would refuse to execute so severe a law because they did not consider the offence great, they would probably refuse to execute any law at all for the same reason.[4]

The opposition answered that the death penalty was more than proportionate to the crime, and therefore "immoral."[5] "I cannot believe," said Stanton of Rhode Island, "that a man ought to be hung for only stealing a negro."[6] It was argued that the trade was after all but a "transfer from one master to another;"[7] that slavery was worse than the slave-trade, and the South did not consider slavery a crime: how could it then punish the trade so severely and not reflect on the institution?[8] Severity, it was said, was also inexpedient: severity often increases crime; if the punishment is too great, people will sympathize with offenders and will not inform against them. Said Mr. Mosely: "When the penalty is excessive or disproportioned to the offence, it will naturally create a repugnance to the law, and render its execution odious."[9] John Randolph argued against even fine and imprisonment, "on the ground that such an excessive penalty could not, in such case, be constitutionally

[1] Dwight: *Annals of Cong.*, 9 Cong. 2 sess. p. 241; Ely: *Ibid.*, p. 232.

[2] Mosely: *Ibid.*, pp. 234–5.

[3] Tallmadge: *Ibid.*, pp. 232, 234. Cf. Dwight: *Ibid.*, p. 241.

[4] Varnum: *Ibid.*, p. 243.

[5] Elmer: *Ibid.*, p. 235.

[6] *Ibid.*, p. 240.

[7] Holland: *Ibid.*, p. 240.

[8] Early: *Ibid.*, pp. 238–9; Holland: *Ibid.*, p. 239.

[9] *Ibid.*, p. 233. Cf. Lloyd: *Ibid.*, p. 237; Ely: *Ibid.*, p. 232; **Early**: *Ibid.*, pp. 238–9.

imposed by a Government possessed of the limited powers of the Government of the United States." [1]

The bill as passed punished infractions as follows: —

For equipping a slaver, a fine of $20,000 and forfeiture of the ship.

For transporting Negroes, a fine of $5000 and forfeiture of the ship and Negroes.

For transporting and selling Negroes, a fine of $1000 to $10,000, imprisonment from 5 to 10 years, and forfeiture of the ship and Negroes.

For knowingly buying illegally imported Negroes, a fine of $800 for each Negro, and forfeiture.

58. **The Third Question: How shall the Interstate Coastwise Slave-Trade be protected?** The first proposition was to prohibit the coastwise slave-trade altogether,[2] but an amendment reported to the House allowed it "in any vessel or species of craft whatever." It is probable that the first proposition would have prevailed, had it not been for the vehement opposition of Randolph and Early.[3] They probably foresaw the value which Virginia would derive from this trade in the future, and consequently Randolph violently declared that if the amendment did not prevail, "the Southern people would set the law at defiance. He would begin the example." He maintained that by the first proposition "the proprietor of sacred and chartered rights is prevented the Constitutional use of his property." [4] The Conference Committee finally arranged a compromise, forbidding the coastwise trade for purposes of sale in vessels under forty tons.[5] This did not suit Early, who declared that the law with this provision "would not prevent the introduction of a single slave." [6] Randolph, too, would "rather lose the bill, he had rather lose all the bills of the session, he had rather lose every bill passed since the establishment of the Government, than agree to the provision contained in this slave bill." [7] He predicted the severance of the slave and the free States, if disunion

[1] *Annals of Cong.*, 9 Cong. 2 sess. p. 484.

[2] This was the provision of the Senate bill as reported to the House. It was over the House amendment to this that the Houses disagreed. Cf. *Ibid.*, p. 484.

[3] Cf. *Ibid.*, pp. 527–8.

[4] *Ibid.*, p. 528.

[5] *Ibid.*, p. 626.

[6] *Ibid.*

[7] *Ibid.*

should ever come. Congress was, however, weary with the dragging of the bill, and it passed both Houses with the compromise provision. Randolph was so dissatisfied that he had a committee appointed the next day, and introduced an amendatory bill. Both this bill and another similar one, introduced at the next session, failed of consideration.[1]

59. **Legislative History of the Bill.**[2] On December 12, 1805, Senator Stephen R. Bradley of Vermont gave notice of a bill to prohibit the introduction of slaves after 1808. By a vote of 18 to 9 leave was given, and the bill read a first time on the 17th. On the 18th, however, it was postponed until "the first Monday in December, 1806." The presidential message mentioning the matter, Senator Bradley, December 3, 1806, gave notice of a similar bill, which was brought in on the 8th, and on the 9th referred to a committee consisting of Bradley, Stone, Giles, Gaillard, and Baldwin. This bill passed, after some consideration, January 27. It provided, among other things, that violations of the act should be felony, punishable with death, and forbade the interstate coast-trade.[3]

Meantime, in the House, Mr. Bidwell of Massachusetts had proposed, February 4, 1806, as an amendment to a bill taxing slaves imported, that importation after December 31, 1807, be prohibited, on pain of fine and imprisonment and forfeiture of ship.[4] This was rejected by a vote of 86 to 17. On December 3, 1806, the House, in appointing committees on the message, "*Ordered*, That Mr. Early, Mr. Thomas M. Randolph, Mr. John Campbell, Mr. Kenan, Mr. Cook, Mr. Kelly, and Mr. Van Rensselaer be appointed a committee" on the slave-trade. This committee reported a bill on the 15th, which was considered, but finally, December 18, recommitted. It was re-

[1] *Annals of Cong.*, 9 Cong. 2 sess. pp. 636–8; *House Journal* (repr. 1826), 9 Cong. 2 sess. V. 616, and House Bill No. 219; *Ibid.*, 10 Cong. 1 sess. VI. 27, 50; *Annals of Cong.*, 10 Cong. 1 sess. pp. 854–5, 961.

[2] On account of the meagre records it is difficult to follow the course of this bill. I have pieced together information from various sources, and trust that this account is approximately correct.

[3] Cf. *Senate Journal* (repr. 1821), 9 Cong. 2 sess. IV., Senate Bill No. 41.

[4] *Annals of Cong.*, 9 Cong. 1 sess. p. 438. Cf. above, § 53.

ported in an amended form on the 19th, and amended in Committee of the Whole so as to make violation a misdemeanor punishable by fine and imprisonment, instead of a felony punishable by death.[1] A struggle over the disposal of the cargo then ensued. A motion by Bidwell to except the cargo from forfeiture was lost, 77 to 39. Another motion by Bidwell may be considered the crucial vote on the whole bill: it was an amendment to the forfeiture clause, and read, "*Provided, that no person shall be sold as a slave by virtue of this act.*"[2] This resulted in a tie vote, 60 to 60; but the casting vote of the Speaker, Macon of North Carolina, defeated it. New England voted solidly in favor of it, the Middle States stood 4 for and 2 against it, and the six Southern States stood solid against it. On January 8 the bill went again to a select committee of seventeen, by a vote of 76 to 46. The bill was reported back amended January 20, and on the 28th the Senate bill was also presented to the House. On the 9th, 10th, and 11th of February both bills were considered in Committee of the Whole, and the Senate bill finally replaced the House bill, after several amendments had been made.[3] The bill was then passed, by a vote of 113 to 5.[4] The Senate agreed to the amendments, including that substituting fine and imprisonment for the death penalty, but asked for a conference on the provision which left the interstate coast-trade free. The six conferees succeeded in bringing the Houses to agree, by limiting the trade to vessels over forty tons and requiring registry of the slaves.[5]

[1] This amendment of the Committee of the Whole was adopted by a vote of 63 to 53. The New England States stood 3 to 2 for the death penalty; the Middle States were evenly divided, 3 and 3; and the South stood 5 to 0 against it, with Kentucky evenly divided. Cf. *House Journal* (repr. 1826), 9 Cong. 2 sess. V. 504.

[2] *Ibid.*, V. 514–5.

[3] The substitution of the Senate bill was a victory for the anti-slavery party, as all battles had to be fought again. The Southern party, however, succeeded in carrying all its amendments.

[4] Messrs. Betton of New Hampshire, Chittenden of Vermont, Garnett and Trigg of Virginia, and D. R. Williams of South Carolina voted against the bill: *House Journal* (repr. 1826), 9 Cong. 2 sess. V. 585–6.

[5] *Annals of Cong.*, 9 Cong. 2 sess. pp. 626–7.

The following diagram shows in graphic form the legislative history of the act: —

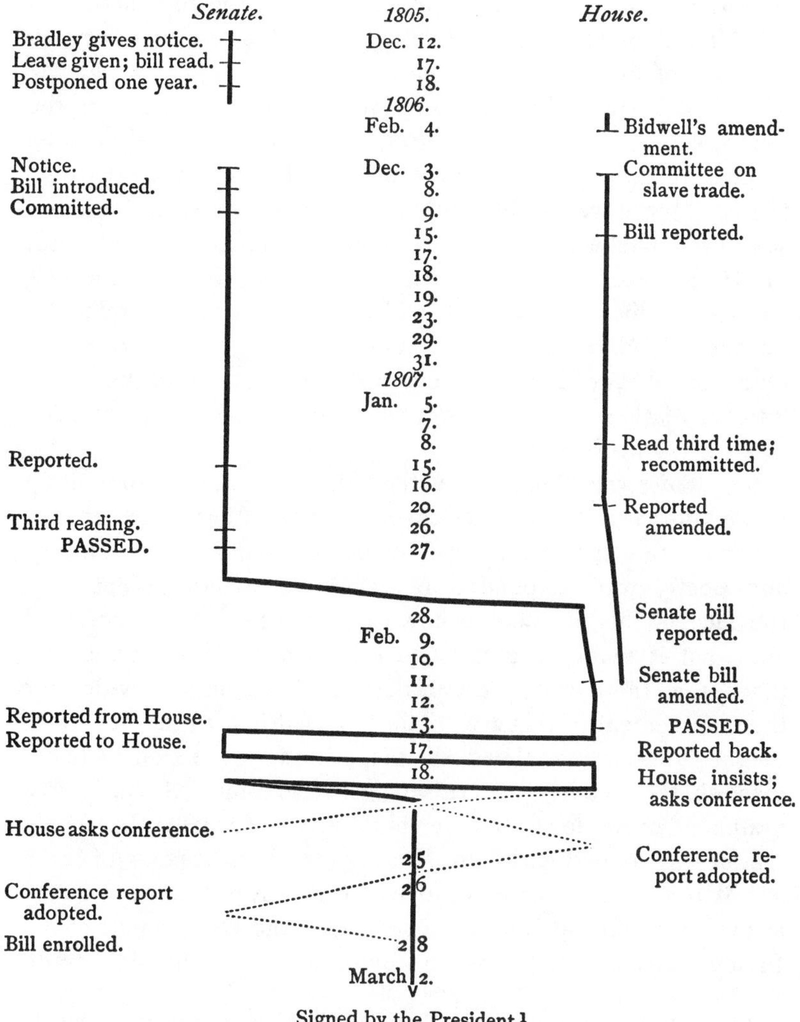

[1] The unassigned dates refer to debates, etc. The history of the amendments and debates on the measure may be traced in the following references: —

Senate (Bill No. 41).

Annals of Cong., 9 Cong. 1 sess. pp. 20–1; 9 Cong. 2 sess. pp. 16, 19, 23, 33, 36, 45, 47, 68, 69, 70, 71, 79, 87, 93, etc.

Senate Journal (repr. 1826), 9 Cong. 1–2 sess. IV. 11, 112, 123, 124, 132, 133, 150, 158, 164, 165, 167, 168, etc.

House (Bill No. 148).

Annals of Cong., 9 Cong. 1 sess. p. 438; 9 Cong. 2 sess. pp. 114, 151, 167–8, 173–4, 180, 183, 189, 200, 202–4, 220, 228, 231, 240, 254, 264, 266–7, 270, 273, 373, 427, 477, 481, 484–6, 527, 528, etc.

House Journal (repr. 1826), 9 Cong. 1–2 sess. V. 470, 482, 488, 490, 491, 496, 500, 504, 510, 513–6, 517, 540, 557, 575, 579, 581, 583–4, 585, 592, 594, 610, 613–5, 623, 638, 640, etc.

This bill received the approval of President Jefferson, March 2, 1807, and became thus the "Act to prohibit the importation of Slaves into any port or place within the jurisdiction of the United States, from and after the first day of January, in the year of our Lord one thousand eight hundred and eight."[1] The debates in the Senate were not reported. Those in the House were prolonged and bitter, and hinged especially on the disposal of the slaves, the punishment of offenders, and the coast-trade. Men were continually changing their votes, and the bill see-sawed backward and forward, in committee and out, until the House was thoroughly worn out. On the whole, the strong anti-slavery men, like Bidwell and Sloan, were outgeneraled by Southerners, like Early and Williams; and, considering the immense moral backing of the anti-slavery party from the Revolutionary fathers down, the bill of 1807 can hardly be regarded as a great anti-slavery victory.

60. **Enforcement of the Act.** The period so confidently looked forward to by the constitutional fathers had at last arrived; the slave-trade was prohibited, and much oratory and poetry were expended in celebration of the event. In the face of this, let us see how the Act of 1807 was enforced and what it really accomplished. It is noticeable, in the first place, that there was no especial set of machinery provided for the enforcement of this act. The work fell first to the Secretary of the Treasury, as head of the customs collection. Then, through the activity of cruisers, the Secretary of the Navy gradually came to have oversight, and eventually the whole matter was lodged with him, although the Departments of State and War were more or less active on different occasions. Later, at the advent of the Lincoln government, the Department of the Interior was charged with the enforcement of the slave-trade

[1] *Statutes at Large*, II. 426. There were some few attempts to obtain laws of relief from this bill: see, e. g., *Annals of Cong.*, 10 Cong. 1 sess. p. 1243; 11 Cong. 1 sess. pp. 34, 36–9, 41, 43, 48, 49, 380, 465, 688, 706, 2209; *House Journal* (repr. 1826), 11 Cong. 1–2 sess. VII. 100, 102, 124, etc., and Index, Senate Bill No. 8. Cf. *Amer. State Papers, Miscellaneous*, II. No. 269. There was also one proposed amendment to make the prohibition perpetual: *Amer. State Papers, Miscellaneous*, I. No. 244.

laws. It would indeed be surprising if, amid so much uncertainty and shifting of responsibility, the law were not poorly enforced. Poor enforcement, moreover, in the years 1808 to 1820 meant far more than at almost any other period; for these years were, all over the European world, a time of stirring economic change, and the set which forces might then take would in a later period be unchangeable without a cataclysm. Perhaps from 1808 to 1814, in the midst of agitation and war, there was some excuse for carelessness. From 1814 on, however, no such palliation existed, and the law was probably enforced as the people who made it wished it enforced.

Most of the Southern States rather tardily passed the necessary supplementary acts disposing of illegally imported Africans. A few appear not to have passed any. Some of these laws, like the Alabama-Mississippi Territory Act of 1815,[1] directed such Negroes to be "sold by the proper officer of the court, to the highest bidder, at public auction, for ready money." One-half the proceeds went to the informer or to the collector of customs, the other half to the public treasury. Other acts, like that of North Carolina in 1816,[2] directed the Negroes to "be sold and disposed of for the use of the state." One-fifth of the proceeds went to the informer. The Georgia Act of 1817[3] directed that the slaves be either sold or given to the Colonization Society for transportation, providing the society reimburse the State for all expense incurred, and pay for the transportation. In this manner, machinery of somewhat clumsy build and varying pattern was provided for the carrying out of the national act.

61. **Evidence of the Continuance of the Trade.** Undoubtedly, the Act of 1807 came very near being a dead letter. The testimony supporting this view is voluminous. It consists of presidential messages, reports of cabinet officers, letters of collectors of revenue, letters of district attorneys, reports of committees of Congress, reports of naval commanders, statements made on

[1] Toulmin, *Digest of the Laws of Alabama*, p. 637.

[2] *Laws of North Carolina* (revision of 1819), II. 1350.

[3] Prince, *Digest*, p. 793.

the floor of Congress, the testimony of eye-witnesses, and the complaints of home and foreign anti-slavery societies.

"When I was young," writes Mr. Fowler of Connecticut, "the slave-trade was still carried on, by Connecticut ship-masters and Merchant adventurers, for the supply of southern ports. This trade was carried on by the consent of the Southern States, under the provisions of the Federal Constitution, until 1808, and, after that time, clandestinely. There was a good deal of conversation on the subject, in private circles." Other States were said to be even more involved than Connecticut.[1] The African Society of London estimated that, down to 1816, fifteen of the sixty thousand slaves annually taken from Africa were shipped by Americans. "Notwithstanding the prohibitory act of America, which was passed in 1807, ships bearing the American flag continued to trade for slaves until 1809, when, in consequence of a decision in the English prize appeal courts, which rendered American slave ships liable to capture and condemnation, that flag suddenly disappeared from the coast. Its place was almost instantaneously supplied by the Spanish flag, which, with one or two exceptions, was now seen for the first time on the African coast, engaged in covering the slave trade. This sudden substitution of the Spanish for the American flag seemed to confirm what was established in a variety of instances by more direct testimony, that the slave trade, which now, for the first time, assumed a Spanish dress, was in reality only the trade of other nations in disguise."[2]

So notorious did the participation of Americans in the traffic become, that President Madison informed Congress in his message, December 5, 1810, that "it appears that American citizens are instrumental in carrying on a traffic in enslaved Africans, equally in violation of the laws of humanity, and in defiance of those of their own country. The same just and benevolent motives which produced the interdiction in force against this criminal conduct, will doubtless be felt by Congress, in devising

[1] Fowler, *Historical Status of the Negro in Connecticut*, in *Local Law*, etc., pp. 122, 126.

[2] *House Reports*, 17 Cong. 1 sess. II. No. 92, p. 32.

further means of suppressing the evil."[1] The Secretary of the Navy wrote the same year to Charleston, South Carolina: "I hear, not without great concern, that the law prohibiting the importation of slaves has been violated in frequent instances, near St. Mary's."[2] Testimony as to violations of the law and suggestions for improving it also came in from district attorneys.[3]

The method of introducing Negroes was simple. A slave smuggler says: "After resting a few days at St. Augustine, . . . I agreed to accompany Diego on a land trip through the United States, where a *kaffle* of negroes was to precede us, for whose disposal the shrewd Portuguese had already made arrangements with my uncle's consignees. I soon learned how readily, and at what profits, the Florida negroes were sold into the neighboring American States. The *kaffle*, under charge of negro drivers, was to strike up the Escambia River, and thence cross the boundary into Georgia, where some of our wild Africans were mixed with various squads of native blacks, and driven inland, till sold off, singly or by couples, on the road. At this period [1812], the United States had declared the African slave trade illegal, and passed stringent laws to prevent the importation of negroes; yet the Spanish possessions were thriving on this inland exchange of negroes and mulattoes; Florida was a sort of nursery for slave-breeders, and many American citizens grew rich by trafficking in Guinea negroes, and smuggling them continually, in small parties, through the southern United States. At the time I mention, the business was a lively one, owing to the war then going on between the States and England, and the unsettled condition of affairs on the border."[4]

The Spanish flag continued to cover American slave-traders. The rapid rise of privateering during the war was not caused

[1] *House Journal* (repr. 1826), 11 Cong. 3 sess. VII. p. 435.

[2] *House Doc.*, 15 Cong. 2 sess. IV. No. 84, p. 5.

[3] See, e. g., *House Journal* (repr. 1826), 11 Cong. 3 sess. VII. p. 575.

[4] Drake, *Revelations of a Slave Smuggler*, p. 51. Parts of this narrative are highly colored and untrustworthy; this passage, however, has every earmark of truth, and is confirmed by many incidental allusions.

solely by patriotic motives; for many armed ships fitted out in the United States obtained a thin Spanish disguise at Havana, and transported thousands of slaves to Brazil and the West Indies. Sometimes all disguise was thrown aside, and the American flag appeared on the slave coast, as in the cases of the "Paz,"[1] the "Rebecca," the "Rosa"[2] (formerly the privateer "Commodore Perry"), the "Dorset" of Baltimore,[3] and the "Saucy Jack."[4] Governor McCarthy of Sierra Leone wrote, in 1817: "The slave trade is carried on most vigorously by the Spaniards, Portuguese, Americans and French. I have had it affirmed from several quarters, and do believe it to be a fact, that there is a greater number of vessels employed in that traffic than at any former period."[5]

62. **Apathy of the Federal Government.** The United States cruisers succeeded now and then in capturing a slaver, like the "Eugene," which was taken when within four miles of the New Orleans bar.[6] President Madison again, in 1816, urged Congress to act on account of the "violations and evasions which, it is suggested, are chargeable on unworthy citizens, who mingle in the slave trade under foreign flags, and with foreign ports; and by collusive importations of slaves into the United States, through adjoining ports and territories."[7] The executive was continually in receipt of ample evidence of this illicit trade and of the helplessness of officers of the law. In 1817 it was reported to the Secretary of the Navy that most of the goods

[1] For accounts of these slavers, see *House Reports*, 17 Cong. 1 sess. II. No. 92, pp. 30–50. The "Paz" was an armed slaver flying the American flag.

[2] Said to be owned by an Englishman, but fitted in America and manned by Americans. It was eventually captured by H. M. S. "Bann," after a hard fight.

[3] Also called Spanish schooner "Triumvirate," with American supercargo, Spanish captain, and American, French, Spanish, and English crew. It was finally captured by a British vessel.

[4] An American slaver of 1814, which was boarded by a British vessel. All the above cases, and many others, were proven before British courts.

[5] *House Reports*, 17 Cong. 1 sess. II. No. 92, p. 51.

[6] *House Doc.*, 15 Cong. 1 sess. II. No. 12, pp. 22, 38. This slaver was after capture sent to New Orleans, — an illustration of the irony of the Act of 1807.

[7] *House Journal*, 14 Cong. 2 sess. p. 15.

carried to Galveston were brought into the United States; "the more valuable, and the slaves are smuggled in through the numerous inlets to the westward, where the people are but too much disposed to render them every possible assistance. Several hundred slaves are now at Galveston, and persons have gone from New-Orleans to purchase them. Every exertion will be made to intercept them, but I have little hopes of success."[1] Similar letters from naval officers and collectors showed that a system of slave piracy had arisen since the war, and that at Galveston there was an establishment of organized brigands, who did not go to the trouble of sailing to Africa for their slaves, but simply captured slavers and sold their cargoes into the United States. This Galveston nest had, in 1817, eleven armed vessels to prosecute the work, and "the most shameful violations of the slave act, as well as our revenue laws, continue to be practised."[2] Cargoes of as many as three hundred slaves were arriving in Texas. All this took place under Aury, the buccaneer governor; and when he removed to Amelia Island in 1817 with the McGregor raid, the illicit traffic in slaves, which had been going on there for years,[3] took an impulse that brought it even to the somewhat deaf ears of Collector Bullock. He reported, May 22, 1817: "I have just received information from a source on which I can implicitly rely, that it has already become the practice to introduce into the state of Georgia, across the St. Mary's River, from Amelia Island, East Florida, Africans, who have been carried into the Port of Fernandina, subsequent to the capture of it by the Patriot army now in possession of it . . .; were the legislature to pass an act giving compensation in some manner to informers, it would have a tendency in a great degree to prevent the practice; as the

[1] *House Doc.*, 16 Cong. 1 sess. III. No. 36, p. 5.

[2] *Ibid.*, 15 Cong. 1 sess. II. No. 12, pp. 8–14. See Chew's letter of Oct. 17, 1817: *Ibid.*, pp. 14–16.

[3] By the secret Joint Resolution and Act of 1811 (*Statutes at Large*, III. 471), Congress gave the President power to suppress the Amelia Island establishment, which was then notorious. The capture was not accomplished until 1817.

thing now is, no citizen will take the trouble of searching for and detecting the slaves. I further understand, that the evil will not be confined altogether to Africans, but will be extended to the worst class of West India slaves."[1]

Undoubtedly, the injury done by these pirates to the regular slave-trading interests was largely instrumental in exterminating them. Late in 1817 United States troops seized Amelia Island, and President Monroe felicitated Congress and the country upon escaping the "annoyance and injury" of this illicit trade.[2] The trade, however, seems to have continued, as is shown by such letters as the following, written three and a half months later: —

PORT OF DARIEN, March 14, 1818.

. . . It is a painful duty, sir, to express to you, that I am in possession of undoubted information, that African and West India negroes are almost daily illicitly introduced into Georgia, for sale or settlement, or passing through it to the territories of the United States for similar purposes; these facts are notorious; and it is not unusual to see such negroes in the streets of St. Mary's, and such too, recently captured by our vessels of war, and ordered to Savannah, were illegally bartered by hundreds in that city, *for* this bartering or bonding (as *it is called*, but in reality *selling*,) actually took place before any decision had [been] passed by the court respecting them. I cannot but again express to you, sir, that these irregularities and mocking of the laws, by men who understand them, and who, it was presumed, would have respected them, are such, that it requires the immediate interposition of Congress to effect a suppression of this traffic; for, as things are, should a faithful officer of the government apprehend such negroes, to avoid the penalties imposed by the laws, the proprietors disclaim them, and some agent of the executive demands a delivery of the same to him, who may employ them as he pleases, or effect a sale by way of a bond, for the restoration of the negroes when legally called on so to do; which bond, it is *understood*, is to be *forfeited*, as the amount of the bond is so much less than the value of the property. . . . There are many negroes . . . recently

[1] *House Doc.*, 16 Cong. 1 sess. III. No. 42, pp. 10–11. Cf. Report of the House Committee, Jan. 10, 1818: "It is but too notorious that numerous infractions of the law prohibiting the importation of slaves into the United States have been perpetrated with impunity upon our southern frontier." *Amer. State Papers, Miscellaneous*, II. No. 441.

[2] Special message of Jan. 13, 1818: *House Journal*, 15 Cong. 1 sess. pp. 137–9.

introduced into this state and the Alabama territory, and which can be apprehended. The undertaking would be great; but to be sensible that we shall possess your approbation, and that we are carrying the views and wishes of the government into execution, is all we wish, and it shall be done, independent of every personal consideration.

I have, etc.[1]

This "approbation" failed to come to the zealous collector, and on the 5th of July he wrote that, "not being favored with a reply," he has been obliged to deliver over to the governor's agents ninety-one illegally imported Negroes.[2] Reports from other districts corroborate this testimony. The collector at Mobile writes of strange proceedings on the part of the courts.[3] General D. B. Mitchell, ex-governor of Georgia and United States Indian agent, after an investigation in 1821 by Attorney-General Wirt, was found "guilty of having prostituted his power, as agent for Indian affairs at the Creek agency, to the purpose of aiding and assisting in a conscious breach of the act of Congress of 1807, in prohibition of the slave trade—and this from mercenary motives."[4] The indefatigable Collector Chew of New Orleans wrote to Washington that, "to put a stop to that traffic, a naval force suitable to those waters is indispensable," and that "vast numbers of slaves will be introduced to an alarming extent, unless prompt and effectual measures are adopted by the general government."[5] Other collectors continually reported infractions, complaining that they could get no assistance from the citizens,[6] or plaintively asking the services of "one small cutter."[7]

Meantime, what was the response of the government to such representations, and what efforts were made to enforce the act? A few unsystematic and spasmodic attempts are recorded. In 1811 some special instructions were sent out,[8] and the President

[1] Collector McIntosh, of the District of Brunswick, Ga., to the Secretary of the Treasury. *House Doc.*, 16 Cong. 1 sess. III. No. 42, pp. 8–9.

[2] *Ibid.*, pp. 6–7.

[3] *Ibid.*, pp. 11–12.

[4] *Amer. State Papers, Miscellaneous*, II. No. 529.

[5] *House Doc.*, 16 Cong. 1 sess. III. No. 42, p. 7.

[6] *Ibid.*, p. 6.

[7] *House Reports*, 21 Cong. 1 sess. III. No. 348, p. 82.

[8] They were not general instructions, but were directed to Commander Campbell. Cf. *House Doc.*, 15 Cong. 2 sess. IV. No. 84, pp. 5–6.

was authorized to seize Amelia Island.[1] Then came the war; and as late as November 15, 1818, in spite of the complaints of collectors, we find no revenue cutter on the Gulf coast.[2] During the years 1817 and 1818[3] some cruisers went there irregularly, but they were too large to be effective; and the partial suppression of the Amelia Island pirates was all that was accomplished. On the whole, the efforts of the government lacked plan, energy, and often sincerity. Some captures of slavers were made;[4] but, as the collector at Mobile wrote, anent certain cases, "this was owing rather to accident, than any well-timed arrangement." He adds: "from the Chandalier Islands to the Perdido river, including the coast, and numerous other islands, we have only a small boat, with four men and an inspector, to oppose to the whole confederacy of smugglers and pirates."[5]

To cap the climax, the government officials were so negligent that Secretary Crawford, in 1820, confessed to Congress that "it appears, from an examination of the records of this office, that no particular instructions have ever been given, by the Secretary of the Treasury, under the original or supplementary acts prohibiting the introduction of slaves into the United States."[6] Beside this inactivity, the government was criminally negligent in not prosecuting and punishing offenders when captured. Urgent appeals for instruction from prosecuting attorneys were too often received in official silence; complaints as to the violation of law by State officers went unheeded;[7] informers were unprotected and sometimes driven

[1] *Statutes at Large*, III. 471 ff.

[2] *House Doc.*, 15 Cong. 2 sess. VI. No. 107, pp. 8–9.

[3] *Ibid.*, IV. No. 84. Cf. Chew's letters in *House Reports*, 21 Cong. 1 sess. III. No. 348.

[4] *House Doc.*, 15 Cong. 1 sess. II. No. 12, pp. 22, 38; 15 Cong. 2 sess. VI. No. 100, p. 13; 16 Cong. 1 sess. III. No. 42, p. 9, etc.; *House Reports*, 21 Cong. 1 sess. III. No. 348, p. 85.

[5] *House Doc.*, 15 Cong. 2 sess. VI. No. 107, pp. 8–9.

[6] *House Reports*, 21 Cong. 1 sess. III. No. 348, p. 77.

[7] Cf. *House Doc.*, 16 Cong. 1 sess. III. No. 42, p. 11: "The Grand Jury found true bills against the owners of the vessels, masters, and a supercargo — all of whom are discharged; why or wherefore I cannot say, except that it could not be for want of proof against them."

from home.[1] Indeed, the most severe comment on the whole period is the report, January 7, 1819, of the Register of the Treasury, who, after the wholesale and open violation of the Act of 1807, reported, in response to a request from the House, "that it doth not appear, from an examination of the records of this office, and particularly of the accounts (to the date of their last settlement) of the collectors of the customs, and of the several marshals of the United States, that any forfeitures had been incurred under the said act."[2]

63. **Typical Cases.** At this date (January 7, 1819), however, certain cases were stated to be pending, a history of which will fitly conclude this discussion. In 1818 three American schooners sailed from the United States to Havana; on June 2 they started back with cargoes aggregating one hundred and seven slaves. The schooner "Constitution" was captured by one of Andrew Jackson's officers under the guns of Fort Barancas. The "Louisa" and "Marino" were captured by Lieutenant McKeever of the United States Navy. The three vessels were duly proceeded against at Mobile, and the case began slowly to drag along. The slaves, instead of being put under the care of the zealous marshal of the district, were placed in the hands of three bondsmen, friends of the judge. The marshal notified the government of this irregularity, but apparently received no answer. In 1822 the three vessels were condemned as forfeited, but the court "reserved" for future order the distribution of the slaves. Nothing whatever either then or later was done to the slave-traders themselves. The owners of the ships promptly appealed to the Supreme Court of the United States, and that tribunal, in 1824, condemned the three vessels and the slaves on two of them.[3] These slaves, considerably reduced in number "from various causes," were sold at auction for the

[1] E. g, in July, 1818, one informer "will have to leave that part of the country to save his life": *Ibid.*, 15 Cong. 2 sess. VI. No. 100, p. 9.

[2] Joseph Nourse, Register of the Treasury, to Hon. W. H. Crawford, Secretary of the Treasury: *Ibid.*, 15 Cong. 2 sess. VI. No. 107, p. 5.

[3] The slaves on the "Constitution" were not condemned, for the technical reason that she was not captured by a commissioned officer of the United States navy.

benefit of the State, in spite of the Act of 1819. Meantime, before the decision of the Supreme Court, the judge of the Supreme Court of West Florida had awarded to certain alleged Spanish claimants of the slaves indemnity for nearly the whole number seized, at the price of $650 per head, and the Secretary of the Treasury had actually paid the claim.[1] In 1826 Lieutenant McKeever urgently petitions Congress for his prize-money of $4,415.15, which he has not yet received.[2] The "Constitution" was for some inexplicable reason released from bond, and the whole case fades in a very thick cloud of official mist. In 1831 Congress sought to inquire into the final disposition of the slaves. The information given was never printed; but as late as 1836 a certain Calvin Mickle petitions Congress for reimbursement for the slaves sold, for their hire, for their natural increase, for expenses incurred, and for damages.[3]

64. **The Supplementary Acts, 1818–1820.** To remedy the obvious defects of the Act of 1807 two courses were possible: one, to minimize the crime of transportation, and, by encouraging informers, to concentrate efforts against the buying of smuggled slaves; the other, to make the crime of transportation so great that no slaves would be imported. The Act of 1818 tried the first method; that of 1819, the second.[4] The latter was obviously the more upright and logical, and the only method deserving thought even in 1807; but the Act of 1818 was the natural descendant of that series of compromises which began

[1] These proceedings are very obscure, and little was said about them. The Spanish claimants were, it was alleged with much probability, but representatives of Americans. The claim was paid under the provisions of the Treaty of Florida, and included slaves whom the court afterward declared forfeited.

[2] An act to relieve him was finally passed, Feb. 8, 1827, nine years after the capture. See *Statutes at Large*, VI. 357.

[3] It is difficult to get at the exact facts in this complicated case. The above statement is, I think, much milder than the real facts would warrant, if thoroughly known. Cf. *House Reports*, 19 Cong. 1 sess. II. No. 231; 21 Cong. 1 sess. III. No. 348, pp. 62–3, etc.; 24 Cong. 1 sess. I. No. 209; *Amer. State Papers*, *Naval*, II. No. 308.

[4] The first method, represented by the Act of 1818, was favored by the South, the Senate, and the Democrats; the second method, represented by the Act of 1819, by the North, the House, and by the as yet undeveloped but growing Whig party.

in the Constitutional Convention, and which, instead of postponing the settlement of critical questions to more favorable times, rather aggravated and complicated them.

The immediate cause of the Act of 1818 was the Amelia Island scandal.[1] Committees in both Houses reported bills, but that of the Senate finally passed. There does not appear to have been very much debate.[2] The sale of Africans for the benefit of the informer and of the United States was strongly urged "as the only means of executing the laws against the slave trade as experience had fully demonstrated since the origin of the prohibition."[3] This proposition was naturally opposed as "inconsistent with the principles of our Government, and calculated to throw as wide open the door to the importation of slaves as it was before the existing prohibition."[4] The act, which became a law April 20, 1818,[5] was a poorly constructed compromise, which virtually acknowledged the failure of efforts to control the trade, and sought to remedy defects by pitting cupidity against cupidity, informer against thief. One-

[1] Committees on the slave-trade were appointed by the House in 1810 and 1813; the committee of 1813 recommended a revision of the laws, but nothing was done: *Annals of Cong.*, 11 Cong. 3 sess. p. 387; 12 Cong. 2 sess. pp. 1074, 1090. The presidential message of 1816 led to committees on the trade in both Houses. The committee of the House of Representatives reported a joint resolution on abolishing the traffic and colonizing the Negroes, also looking toward international action. This never came to a vote: *Senate Journal*, 14 Cong. 2 sess. pp. 46, 179, 180; *House Journal*, 14 Cong. 2 sess. pp. 25, 27, 380; *House Doc.*, 14 Cong. 2 sess. II. No. 77. Finally, the presidential message of 1817 (*House Journal*, 15 Cong. 1 sess. p. 11), announcing the issuance of orders to suppress the Amelia Island establishment, led to two other committees in both Houses. The House committee under Middleton made a report with a bill (*Amer. State Papers, Miscellaneous*, II. No. 441), and the Senate committee also reported a bill.

[2] The Senate debates were entirely unreported, and the report of the House debates is very meagre. For the proceedings, see *Senate Journal*, 15 Cong. 1 sess. pp. 243, 304, 315, 333, 338, 340, 348, 377, 386, 388, 391, 403, 406; *House Journal*, 15 Cong. 1 sess. pp. 19, 20, 29, 51, 92, 131, 362, 410, 450, 452, 456, 468, 479, 484, 492, 505.

[3] Simkins of South Carolina, Edwards of North Carolina, and Pindall: *Annals of Cong.*, 15 Cong. 1 sess. p. 1740.

[4] Hugh Nelson of Virginia: *Annals of Cong.*, 15 Cong. 1 sess. p. 1740.

[5] *Statutes at Large*, III. 450. By this act the first six sections of the Act of 1807 were repealed.

half of all forfeitures and fines were to go to the informer, and penalties for violation were changed as follows: —

For equipping a slaver, instead of a fine of $20,000, a fine of $1000 to $5000 and imprisonment from 3 to 7 years.

For transporting Negroes, instead of a fine of $5000 and forfeiture of ship and Negroes, a fine of $1000 to $5000 and imprisonment from 3 to 7 years.

For actual importation, instead of a fine of $1000 to $10,000 and imprisonment from 5 to 10 years, a fine of $1000 to $10,000, and imprisonment from 3 to 7 years.

For knowingly buying illegally imported Negroes, instead of a fine of $800 for each Negro and forfeiture, a fine of $1000 for each Negro.

The burden of proof was laid on the defendant, to the extent that he must prove that the slave in question had been imported at least five years before the prosecution. The slaves were still left to the disposal of the States.

This statute was, of course, a failure from the start,[1] and at the very next session Congress took steps to revise it. A bill was reported in the House, January 13, 1819, but it was not discussed till March.[2] It finally passed, after "much debate."[3] The Senate dropped its own bill, and, after striking out the provision for the death penalty, passed the bill as it came from the House.[4] The House acquiesced, and the bill became a law, March 3, 1819,[5] in the midst of the Missouri trouble. This act directed the President to use armed cruisers on the coasts of the

[1] Or, more accurately speaking, every one realized, in view of the increased activity of the trade, that it would be a failure.

[2] Nov. 18, 1818, the part of the presidential message referring to the slave-trade was given to a committee of the House, and this committee also took in hand the House bill of the previous session which the Senate bill had replaced: *House Journal*, 15 Cong. 2 sess. pp. 9–19, 42, 150, 179, 330, 334, 341, 343, 352.

[3] Of which little was reported: *Annals of Cong.*, 15 Cong. 2 sess. pp. 1430–31. Strother opposed, "for various reasons of expediency," the bounties for captors. Nelson of Virginia advocated the death penalty, and, aided by Pindall, had it inserted. The vote on the bill was 57 to 45.

[4] The Senate had also had a committee at work on a bill which was reported Feb. 8, and finally postponed: *Senate Journal*, 15 Cong. 2 sess. pp. 234, 244, 311–2, 347. The House bill was taken up March 2: *Annals of Cong.*, 15 Cong. 2 sess. p. 280.

[5] *Statutes at Large*, III. 532.

United States and Africa to suppress the slave-trade; one-half the proceeds of the condemned ship were to go to the captors as bounty, provided the Africans were safely lodged with a United States marshal and the crew with the civil authorities. These provisions were seriously marred by a proviso which Butler of Louisiana, had inserted, with a "due regard for the interests of the State which he represented," viz., that a captured slaver must always be returned to the port whence she sailed.[1] This, of course, secured decided advantages to Southern slave-traders. The most radical provision of the act was that which directed the President to "make such regulations and arrangements as he may deem expedient for the safe keeping, support, and removal beyond the limits of the United States, of all such negroes, mulattoes, or persons of colour, as may be so delivered and brought within their jurisdiction;" and to appoint an agent in Africa to receive such Negroes.[2] Finally, an appropriation of $100,000 was made to enforce the act.[3] This act was in some measure due to the new colonization movement; and the return of Africans recaptured was a distinct recognition of its efforts, and the real foundation of Liberia.

To render this straightforward act effective, it was necessary to add but one measure, and that was a penalty commensurate with the crime of slave stealing. This was accomplished by the Act of May 15, 1820,[4] a law which may be regarded as the

[1] *Annals of Cong.*, 15 Cong. 2 sess. p. 1430. This insured the trial of slave-traders in a sympathetic slave State, and resulted in the "disappearance" of many captured Negroes.

[2] *Statutes at Large*, III. 533.

[3] The first of a long series of appropriations extending to 1869, of which a list is given on the next page. The totals are only approximately correct. Some statutes may have escaped me, and in the reports of moneys the surpluses of previous years are not always clearly distinguishable.

[4] In the first session of the sixteenth Congress, two bills on piracy were introduced into the Senate, one of which passed, April 26. In the House there was a bill on piracy, and a slave-trade committee reported recommending that the slave-trade be piracy. The Senate bill and this bill were considered in Committee of the Whole, May 11, and a bill was finally passed declaring, among other things, the traffic piracy. In the Senate there was "some discussion, rather on the form than the substance of these amendments," and "they were agreed to without a division": *Senate Journal*, 16 Cong. 1 sess. pp. 238, 241, 268, 287, 314, 331, 346, 350, 409, 412, 417, 420,

last of the Missouri Compromise measures. The act originated from the various bills on piracy which were introduced early in

STATUTES AT LARGE.		DATE.	AMOUNT APPROPRIATED.
VOL.	PAGE		
III.	533–4	March 3, 1819	$100,000
"	764	" 3, 1823	50,000
IV.	141	" 14, 1826	32,000
"	208	March 2, 1827	36,710 20,000
"	302	May 24, 1828	30,000
"	354	March 2, 1829	16,000
"	462	" 2, 1831	16,000
"	615	Feb. 20, 1833	5,000
"	671	Jan. 24, 1834	5,000
V.	157–8	March 3, 1837	11,413.57
"	501	Aug. 4, 1842	10,543.42
"	615	March 3, 1843	5,000
IX.	96	Aug. 10, 1846	25,000
XI.	90	" 18, 1856	8,000
"	227	March 3, 1857	8,000
"	404	" 3, 1859	75,000
XII.	21	May 26, 1860	40,000
"	132	Feb. 19, 1861	900,000
"	219	March 2, 1861	900,000
"	639	Feb. 4, 1863	17,000
XIII.	424	Jan. 24, 1865	17,000
XIV.	226	July 25, 1866	17,000
"	415	Feb. 28, 1867	17,000
XV.	58	March 30, 1868	12,500
"	321	March 3, 1869	12,500

Total, 50 years	$2.386,666.99
Minus surpluses re-appropriated (approximate) .	48,666.99?
	$2,338,000
Cost of squadron, 1843–58, @ $384,500 per year (*House Exec. Doc.*, 31 Cong. 1 sess. IX. No. 73)	5,767,500
Returning slaves on "Wildfire" (*Statutes at Large*, XII. 41)	250,000
Approximate cost of squadron, 1858–66, probably not less than $500,000 per year	4,000,000?
Approximate money cost of suppressing the slave-trade	$12,355,500?

Cf. Kendall's Report: *Senate Doc.*, 21 Cong. 2 sess. I. No. 1, pp. 211–8; *Amer. State Papers, Naval*, III. No. 429 E.; also Reports of the Secretaries of the Navy from 1819 to 1860.

422, 424, 425; *House Journal*, 16 Cong. 1 sess. pp. 113, 280, 453, 454, 494, 518, 520, 522, 537; *Annals of Cong.*, 16 Cong. 1 sess. pp. 693–4, 2231, 2236–7, etc. The debates were not reported.

the sixteenth Congress. The House bill, in spite of opposition, was amended so as to include slave-trading under piracy, and passed. The Senate agreed without a division. This law provided that direct participation in the slave-trade should be piracy, punishable with death.[1]

65. **Enforcement of the Supplementary Acts, 1818–1825.** A somewhat more sincere and determined effort to enforce the slave-trade laws now followed; and yet it is a significant fact that not until Lincoln's administration did a slave-trader suffer death for violating the laws of the United States. The participation of Americans in the trade continued, declining somewhat between 1825 and 1830, and then reviving, until it reached its highest activity between 1840 and 1860. The development of a vast internal slave-trade, and the consequent rise in the South of vested interests strongly opposed to slave smuggling, led to a falling off in the illicit introduction of Negroes after 1825, until the fifties; nevertheless, smuggling never entirely ceased, and large numbers were thus added to the plantations of the Gulf States.

Monroe had various constitutional scruples as to the execution of the Act of 1819;[2] but, as Congress took no action, he at last put a fair interpretation on his powers, and appointed Samuel Bacon as an agent in Africa to form a settlement for recaptured Africans. Gradually the agency thus formed became merged with that of the Colonization Society on Cape Mesurado; and from this union Liberia was finally evolved.[3]

Meantime, during the years 1818 to 1820, the activity of the

[1] *Statutes at Large*, III. 600–1. This act was in reality a continuation of the piracy Act of 1819, and was only temporary. The provision was, however, continued by several acts, and finally made perpetual by the Act of Jan. 30, 1823: *Statutes at Large*, III. 510–4, 721. On March 3, 1823, it was slightly amended so as to give district courts jurisdiction.

[2] Attorney-General Wirt advised him, October, 1819, that no part of the appropriation could be used to purchase land in Africa or tools for the Negroes, or as salary for the agent: *Opinions of Attorneys-General*, I. 314–7. Monroe laid the case before Congress in a special message Dec. 20, 1819 (*House Journal*, 16 Cong. 1 sess. p. 57); but no action was taken there.

[3] Cf. Kendall's Report, August, 1830: *Senate Doc.*, 21 Cong. 2 sess. I. No. 1, pp. 211–8; also see below, Chapter X.

slave-traders was prodigious. General James Tallmadge declared in the House, February 15, 1819: "Our laws are already highly penal against their introduction, and yet, it is a well known fact, that about fourteen thousand slaves have been brought into our country this last year."[1] In the same year Middleton of South Carolina and Wright of Virginia estimated illicit introduction at 13,000 and 15,000 respectively.[2] Judge Story, in charging a jury, took occasion to say: "We have but too many proofs from unquestionable sources, that it [the slave-trade] is still carried on with all the implacable rapacity of former times. Avarice has grown more subtle in its evasions, and watches and seizes its prey with an appetite quickened rather than suppressed by its guilty vigils. American citizens are steeped to their very mouths (I can hardly use too bold a figure) in this stream of iniquity."[3] The following year, 1820, brought some significant statements from various members of Congress. Said Smith of South Carolina: "Pharaoh was, for his temerity, drowned in the Red Sea, in pursuing them [the Israelites] contrary to God's express will; but our Northern friends have not been afraid even of that, in their zeal to furnish the Southern States with Africans. They are better seamen than Pharaoh, and calculate by that means to elude the vigilance of Heaven; which they seem to disregard, if they can but elude the violated laws of their country."[4] As late as May he saw little hope of suppressing the traffic.[5] Sergeant of Pennsylvania declared: "It is notorious that, in spite of the utmost vigilance that can be employed, African negroes are clandestinely brought in and sold as slaves."[6] Plumer of New Hampshire stated that "of the unhappy beings, thus in violation of all laws transported to our shores, and thrown by force into the mass of our black population, scarcely one in a

[1] Speech in the House of Representatives, Feb. 15, 1819, p. 18; published in Boston, 1849.

[2] Jay, *Inquiry into American Colonization* (1838), p. 59, note.

[3] Quoted in Friends' *Facts and Observations on the Slave Trade* (ed. 1841), pp. 7–8.

[4] *Annals of Cong.*, 16 Cong. 1 sess. pp. 270–1.

[5] *Ibid.*, p. 698.

[6] *Ibid.*, p. 1207.

hundred is ever detected by the officers of the General Government, in a part of the country, where, if we are to believe the statement of Governor Rabun, 'an officer who would perform his duty, by attempting to enforce the law [against the slave trade] is, by many, considered as an officious meddler, and treated with derision and contempt; ' . . . I have been told by a gentleman, who has attended particularly to this subject, that ten thousand slaves were in one year smuggled into the United States; and that, even for the last year, we must count the number not by hundreds, but by thousands."[1] In 1821 a committee of Congress characterized prevailing methods as those "of the grossest fraud that could be practised to deceive the officers of government."[2] Another committee, in 1822, after a careful examination of the subject, declare that they "find it impossible to measure with precision the effect produced upon the American branch of the slave trade by the laws above mentioned, and the seizures under them. They are unable to state, whether those American merchants, the American capital and seamen which heretofore aided in this traffic, have abandoned it altogether, or have sought shelter under the flags of other nations." They then state the suspicious circumstance that, with the disappearance of the American flag from the traffic, "the trade, notwithstanding, increases annually, under the flags of other nations." They complain of the spasmodic efforts of the executive. They say that the first United States cruiser arrived on the African coast in March, 1820, and remained a "few weeks;" that since then four others had in two years made five visits in all; but "since the middle of last November, the commencement of the healthy season on that coast, no vessel has been, nor, as your committee is informed, is, under orders for that service."[3] The United States African agent, Ayres, reported in 1823: "I was informed by an American officer who had been on the coast in 1820, that he had boarded 20 American vessels in one morning, lying in the port of Gallinas, and

[1] *Annals of Cong.*, 16 Cong. 1 sess. p. 1433.

[2] Referring particularly to the case of the slaver "Plattsburg." Cf. *House Reports*, 17 Cong. 1 sess. II. No. 92, p. 10.

[3] *House Reports*, 17 Cong. 1 sess. II. No. 92, p. 2. The President had in

fitted for the reception of slaves. It is a lamentable fact, that most of the harbours, between the Senegal and the line, were visited by an equal number of American vessels, and for the sole purpose of carrying away slaves. Although for some years the coast had been occasionally visited by our cruizers, their short stay and seldom appearance had made but slight impression on those traders, rendered hardy by repetition of crime, and avaricious by excessive gain. They were enabled by a regular system to gain intelligence of any cruizer being on the coast."[1]

Even such spasmodic efforts bore abundant fruit, and indicated what vigorous measures might have accomplished. Between May, 1818, and November, 1821, nearly six hundred Africans were recaptured and eleven American slavers taken.[2] Such measures gradually changed the character of the trade, and opened the international phase of the question. American slavers cleared for foreign ports, there took a foreign flag and papers, and then sailed boldly past American cruisers, although their real character was often well known. More stringent clearance laws and consular instructions might have greatly reduced this practice; but nothing was ever done, and gradually the laws became in large measure powerless to deal with the bulk of the illicit trade. In 1820, September 16, a British officer, in his official report, declares that, in spite of United States laws, "American vessels, American subjects, and American capital, are unquestionably engaged in the trade, though under other

his message spoken in exhilarating tones of the success of the government in suppressing the trade. The House Committee appointed in pursuance of this passage made the above report. Their conclusions are confirmed by British reports: *Parliamentary Papers*, 1822, Vol. XXII., *Slave Trade*, Further Papers, III. p. 44. So, too, in 1823, Ashmun, the African agent, reports that thousands of slaves are being abducted.

[1] Ayres to the Secretary of the Navy, Feb. 24, 1823; reprinted in *Friends' View of the African Slave-Trade* (1824), p. 31.

[2] *House Reports*, 17 Cong. 1 sess. II. No. 92, pp. 5–6. The slavers were the "Ramirez," "Endymion," "Esperanza," "Plattsburg," "Science," "Alexander," "Eugene," "Mathilde," "Daphne," "Eliza," and "La Pensée." In these 573 Africans were taken. The naval officers were greatly handicapped by the size of the ships, etc. (cf. *Friends' View*, etc., pp. 33–41). They nevertheless acted with great zeal.

colours and in disguise."[1] The United States ship "Cyane" at one time reported ten captures within a few days, adding: "Although they are evidently owned by Americans, they are so completely covered by Spanish papers that it is impossible to condemn them."[2] The governor of Sierra Leone reported the rivers Nunez and Pongas full of renegade European and American slave-traders;[3] the trade was said to be carried on "to an extent that almost staggers belief."[4] Down to 1824 or 1825, reports from all quarters prove this activity in slave-trading.

The execution of the laws within the country exhibits grave defects and even criminal negligence. Attorney-General Wirt finds it necessary to assure collectors, in 1819, that "it is against public policy to dispense with prosecutions for violation of the law to prohibit the Slave trade."[5] One district attorney writes: "It appears to be almost impossible to enforce the laws of the United States against offenders after the negroes have been landed in the state."[6] Again, it is asserted that "when vessels engaged in the slave trade have been detained by the American cruizers, and sent into the slave-holding states, there appears at once a difficulty in securing the freedom to these captives which the laws of the United States have decreed for them."[7] In some cases, one man would smuggle in the Africans and hide them in the woods; then his partner would "rob" him, and so all trace be lost.[8] Perhaps 350 Africans were officially reported as brought in contrary to law from 1818 to 1820: the absurdity of this figure is apparent.[9] A circular

[1] *Parliamentary Papers*, 1821, Vol. XXIII., *Slave Trade*, Further Papers, A, p. 76. The names and description of a dozen or more American slavers are given: *Ibid.*, pp. 18–21.

[2] *House Reports*, 17 Cong. 1 sess. II. No. 92, pp. 15–20.

[3] *House Doc.*, 18 Cong. 1 sess. VI. No. 119, p. 13.

[4] *Parliamentary Papers*, 1823, Vol. XVIII., *Slave Trade*, Further Papers, A, pp. 10–11.

[5] *Opinions of Attorneys-General*, V. 717.

[6] R. W. Habersham to the Secretary of the Navy, August, 1821; reprinted in *Friends' View*, etc., p. 47.

[7] *Ibid.*, p. 42.

[8] *Ibid.*, p. 43.

[9] Cf. above, p. 124.

letter to the marshals, in 1821, brought reports of only a few well-known cases, like that of the "General Ramirez;" the marshal of Louisiana had "no information."[1]

There appears to be little positive evidence of a large illicit importation into the country for a decade after 1825. It is hardly possible, however, considering the activity in the trade, that slaves were not largely imported. Indeed, when we note how the laws were continually broken in other respects, absence of evidence of petty smuggling becomes presumptive evidence that collusive or tacit understanding of officers and citizens allowed the trade to some extent.[2] Finally, it must be noted that during all this time scarcely a man suffered for participating in the trade, beyond the loss of the Africans and, more rarely, of his ship. Red-handed slavers, caught in the act and convicted, were too often, like La Coste of South Carolina, the subjects of executive clemency.[3] In certain cases there were those who even

[1] *Friends' View*, etc., p. 42.

[2] A few accounts of captures here and there would make the matter less suspicious; these, however, do not occur. How large this suspected illicit traffic was, it is of course impossible to say; there is no reason why it may not have reached many hundreds per year.

[3] Cf. editorial in *Niles's Register*, XXII. 114. Cf. also the following instances of pardons:—

PRESIDENT JEFFERSON: March 1, 1808, Phillip M. Topham, convicted for "carrying on an illegal slave-trade" (pardoned twice). *Pardons and Remissions*, I. 146, 148–9.

PRESIDENT MADISON: July 29, 1809, fifteen vessels arrived at New Orleans from Cuba, with 666 white persons and 683 negroes. Every penalty incurred under the Act of 1807 was remitted. (Note: "Several other pardons of this nature were granted.") *Ibid.*, I. 179.

Nov. 8, 1809, John Hopkins and Lewis Le Roy, convicted for importing a slave. *Ibid.*, I. 184–5.

Feb. 12, 1810, William Sewall, convicted for importing slaves. *Ibid.*, I. 194, 235, 240.

May 5, 1812, William Babbit, convicted for importing slaves. *Ibid.*, I. 248.

PRESIDENT MONROE: June 11, 1822, Thomas Shields, convicted for bringing slaves into New Orleans. *Ibid.*, IV. 15.

Aug. 24, 1822, J. F. Smith, sentenced to five years' imprisonment and $3000 fine; served twenty-five months and was then pardoned. *Ibid.*, IV. 22.

July 23, 1823, certain parties liable to penalties for introducing slaves into Alabama. *Ibid.*, IV. 63.

had the effrontery to ask Congress to cancel their own laws. For instance, in 1819 a Venezuelan privateer, secretly fitted out and manned by Americans in Baltimore, succeeded in capturing several American, Portuguese, and Spanish slavers, and appropriating the slaves; being finally wrecked herself, she transferred her crew and slaves to one of her prizes, the "Antelope," which was eventually captured by a United States cruiser and the 280 Africans sent to Georgia. After much litigation, the United States Supreme Court ordered those captured from Spaniards to be surrendered, and the others to be returned to Africa. By some mysterious process, only 139 Africans now remained, 100 of whom were sent to Africa. The Spanish claimants of the remaining thirty-nine sold them to a certain Mr. Wilde, who gave bond to transport them out of the country. Finally, in December, 1827, there came an innocent petition to Congress to *cancel this bond*.[1] A bill to that effect passed and was approved, May 2, 1828,[2] and in consequence these Africans remained as slaves in Georgia.

On the whole, it is plain that, although in the period from 1807 to 1820 Congress laid down broad lines of legislation sufficient, save in some details, to suppress the African slave trade to America, yet the execution of these laws was criminally lax.

Aug. 15, 1823, owners of schooner "Mary," convicted of importing slaves. *Pardons and Remissions.*, IV. 66.

PRESIDENT J. Q. ADAMS: March 4, 1826, Robert Perry; his ship was forfeited for slave-trading. *Ibid.*, IV. 140.

Jan. 17, 1827, Jesse Perry; forfeited ship, and was convicted for introducing slaves. *Ibid.*, IV. 158.

Feb. 13, 1827, Zenas Winston; incurred penalties for slave-trading. *Ibid.*, IV. 161. The four following cases are similar to that of Winston: —

Feb. 24, 1827, John Tucker and William Morbon. *Ibid.*, IV. 162.

March 25, 1828, Joseph Badger. *Ibid.*, IV. 192.

Feb. 19, 1829, L. R. Wallace. *Ibid.*, IV. 215.

PRESIDENT JACKSON: Five cases. *Ibid.*, IV. 225, 270, 301, 393, 440.

The above cases were taken from manuscript copies of the Washington records, made by Mr. W. C. Endicott, Jr., and kindly loaned me.

[1] See *Senate Journal*, 20 Cong. 1 sess. pp. 60, 66, 340, 341, 343, 348, 352, 355; *House Journal*, 20 Cong. 1 sess. pp. 59, 76, 123, 134, 156, 169, 173, 279, 634, 641, 646, 647, 688, 692.

[2] *Statutes at Large*, VI. 376.

Moreover, by the facility with which slavers could disguise their identity, it was possible for them to escape even a vigorous enforcement of our laws. This situation could properly be met only by energetic and sincere international co-operation. The next chapter will review efforts directed toward this end.[1]

[1] Among interesting minor proceedings in this period were two Senate bills to register slaves so as to prevent illegal importation. They were both dropped in the House; a House proposition to the same effect also came to nothing: *Senate Journal*, 15 Cong. 1 sess. pp. 147, 152, 157, 165, 170, 188, 201, 203, 232, 237; 15 Cong. 2 sess. pp. 63, 74, 77, 202, 207, 285, 291, 297; *House Journal*, 15 Cong. 1 sess. p. 332; 15 Cong. 2 sess. pp. 303, 305, 316; 16 Cong. 1 sess. p. 150. Another proposition was contained in the Meigs resolution presented to the House, Feb. 5, 1820, which proposed to devote the public lands to the suppression of the slave-trade. This was ruled out of order. It was presented again and laid on the table in 1821: *House Journal*, 16 Cong. 1 sess. pp. 196, 200, 227; 16 Cong. 2 sess. p. 238.

CHAPTER IX.

THE INTERNATIONAL STATUS OF THE SLAVE-TRADE.
1783–1862.

66. **The Rise of the Movement against the Slave-Trade, 1788–1807.** At the beginning of the nineteenth century England held 800,000 slaves in her colonies; France, 250,000; Denmark, 27,000; Spain and Portugal, 600,000; Holland, 50,000; Sweden, 600; there were also about 2,000,000 slaves in Brazil, and about 900,000 in the United States.[1] This was the powerful basis of the demand for the slave-trade; and against the economic forces which these four and a half millions of enforced laborers represented, the battle for freedom had to be fought.

Denmark first responded to the denunciatory cries of the eighteenth century against slavery and the slave-trade. In 1792, by royal order, this traffic was prohibited in the Danish possessions after 1802. The principles of the French Revolution logically called for the extinction of the slave system by France. This was, however, accomplished more precipitately than the Convention anticipated; and in a whirl of enthusiasm engendered by the appearance of the Dominican deputies, slavery and the slave-trade were abolished in all French colonies February 4,

[1] Cf. Augustin Cochin, in Lalor, *Cyclopædia*, III. 723.

1794.[1] This abolition was short-lived; for at the command of the First Consul slavery and the slave-trade were restored in An X (1799).[2] The trade was finally abolished by Napoleon during the Hundred Days by a decree, March 29, 1815, which briefly declared: "À dater de la publication du présent Décret, la Traite des Noirs est abolie."[3] The Treaty of Paris eventually confirmed this law.[4]

In England, the united efforts of Sharpe, Clarkson, and Wilberforce early began to arouse public opinion by means of agitation and pamphlet literature. May 21, 1788, Sir William Dolben moved a bill regulating the trade, which passed in July and was the last English measure countenancing the traffic.[5] The report of the Privy Council on the subject in 1789[6] precipitated the long struggle. On motion of Pitt, in 1788, the House had resolved to take up at the next session the question of the abolition of the trade.[7] It was, accordingly, called up by Wilberforce, and a remarkable parliamentary battle ensued, which lasted continuously until 1805. The Grenville-Fox min-

[1] By a law of Aug. 11, 1792, the encouragement formerly given to the trade was stopped. Cf. *Choix de rapports, opinions et discours prononcés à la tribune nationale depuis* 1789 (Paris, 1821), XIV. 425; quoted in Cochin, *The Results of Emancipation* (Booth's translation, 1863), pp. 33, 35–8.

[2] Cochin, *The Results of Emancipation* (Booth's translation, 1863), pp. 42–7.

[3] *British and Foreign State Papers*, 1815–6, p. 196.

[4] *Ibid.*, pp. 195–9, 292–3; 1816–7, p. 755. It was eventually confirmed by royal ordinance, and the law of April 15, 1818.

[5] *Statute* 28 *George III.*, ch. 54. Cf. *Statute* 29 *George III.*, ch. 66.

[6] Various petitions had come in praying for an abolition of the slave-trade; and by an order in Council, Feb. 11, 1788, a committee of the Privy Council was ordered to take evidence on the subject. This committee presented an elaborate report in 1789. See published *Report*, London, 1789.

[7] For the history of the Parliamentary struggle, cf. Clarkson's and Copley's histories. The movement was checked in the House of Commons in 1789, 1790, and 1791. In 1792 the House of Commons resolved to abolish the trade in 1796. The Lords postponed the matter to take evidence. A bill to prohibit the foreign slave-trade was lost in 1793, passed the next session, and was lost in the House of Lords. In 1795, 1796, 1798, and 1799 repeated attempts to abolish the trade were defeated. The matter then rested until 1804, when the battle was renewed with more success.

istry now espoused the cause. This ministry first prohibited the trade with such colonies as England had acquired by conquest during the Napoleonic wars; then, in 1806, they prohibited the foreign slave-trade; and finally, March 25, 1807, enacted the total abolition of the traffic.[1]

67. **Concerted Action of the Powers, 1783–1814.** During the peace negotiations between the United States and Great Britain in 1783, it was proposed by Jay, in June, that there be a proviso inserted as follows: "Provided that the subjects of his Britannic Majesty shall not have any right or claim under the convention, to carry or import, into the said States any slaves from any part of the world; it being the intention of the said States entirely to prohibit the importation thereof."[2] Fox promptly replied: "If that be their policy, it never can be competent to us to dispute with them their own regulations."[3] No mention of this was, however, made in the final treaty, probably because it was thought unnecessary.

In the proposed treaty of 1806, signed at London December 31, Article 24 provided that "The high contracting parties engage to communicate to each other, without delay, all such laws as have been or shall be hereafter enacted by their respective Legislatures, as also all measures which shall have been taken for the abolition or limitation of the African slave trade; and they further agree to use their best endeavors to procure the co-operation of other Powers for the final and complete abolition of a trade so repugnant to the principles of justice and humanity."[4]

This marks the beginning of a long series of treaties between England and other powers looking toward the prohibition of the traffic by international agreement. During the years 1810–1814 she signed treaties relating to the subject with Portugal, Denmark, and Sweden.[5] May 30, 1814, an additional article

[1] *Statute* 46 *George III.*, ch. 52, 119; 47 *George III.*, sess. I. ch. 36.

[2] Sparks, *Diplomatic Correspondence*, X. 154.

[3] Fox to Hartley, June 10, 1783; quoted in Bancroft, *History of the Constitution of the United States*, I. 61.

[4] *Amer. State Papers, Foreign*, III. No. 214, p. 151.

[5] *British and Foreign State Papers*, 1815–6, pp. 886, 937 (quotation).

to the Treaty of Paris, between France and Great Britain, engaged these powers to endeavor to induce the approaching Congress at Vienna "to decree the abolition of the Slave Trade, so that the said Trade shall cease universally, as it shall cease definitively, under any circumstances, on the part of the French Government, in the course of 5 years; and that during the said period no Slave Merchant shall import or sell Slaves, except in the Colonies of the State of which he is a Subject."[1] In addition to this, the next day a circular letter was despatched by Castlereagh to Austria, Russia, and Prussia, expressing the hope "that the Powers of Europe, when restoring Peace to Europe, with one common interest, will crown this great work by interposing their benign offices in favour of those Regions of the Globe, which yet continue to be desolated by this unnatural and inhuman traffic."[2] Meantime additional treaties were secured: in 1814 by royal decree Netherlands agreed to abolish the trade;[3] Spain was induced by her necessities to restrain her trade to her own colonies, and to endeavor to prevent the fraudulent use of her flag by foreigners;[4] and in 1815 Portugal agreed to abolish the slave-trade north of the equator.[5]

68. **Action of the Powers from 1814 to 1820.** At the Congress of Vienna, which assembled late in 1814, Castlereagh was indefatigable in his endeavors to secure the abolition of the trade. France and Spain, however, refused to yield farther than they had already done, and the other powers hesitated to go to the lengths he recommended. Nevertheless, he secured the institution of annual conferences on the matter, and a declaration by the Congress strongly condemning the trade and declaring that "the public voice in all civilized countries was raised to demand its suppression as soon as possible," and that, while the definitive

[1] *British and Foreign State Papers*, 1815–6, pp. 890–1.

[2] *Ibid.*, p. 887. Russia, Austria, and Prussia returned favorable replies: *Ibid.*, pp. 887–8.

[3] *Ibid.*, p. 889.

[4] She desired a loan, which England made on this condition: *Ibid.*, pp. 921–2.

[5] *Ibid.*, pp. 937–9. Certain financial arrangements secured this concession.

period of termination would be left to subsequent negotiation, the sovereigns would not consider their work done until the trade was entirely suppressed.[1]

In the Treaty of Ghent, between Great Britain and the United States, ratified February 17, 1815, Article 10, proposed by Great Britain, declared that, "Whereas the traffic in slaves is irreconcilable with the principles of humanity and justice," the two countries agreed to use their best endeavors in abolishing the trade.[2] The final overthrow of Napoleon was marked by a second declaration of the powers, who, "desiring to give effect to the measures on which they deliberated at the Congress of Vienna, relative to the complete and universal abolition of the Slave Trade, and having, each in their respective Dominions, prohibited without restriction their Colonies and Subjects from taking any part whatever in this Traffic, engage to renew conjointly their efforts, with the view of securing final success to those principles which they proclaimed in the Declaration of the 4th February, 1815, and of concerting, without loss of time, through their Ministers at the Courts of London and of Paris, the most effectual measures for the entire and definitive abolition of a Commerce so odious, and so strongly condemned by the laws of religion and of nature."[3]

Treaties further restricting the trade continued to be made by Great Britain: Spain abolished the trade north of the equator in 1817,[4] and promised entire abolition in 1820; Spain, Portugal, and Holland also granted a mutual limited Right of Search to England, and joined in establishing mixed courts.[5] The effort, however, to secure a general declaration of the powers urging, if not compelling, the abolition of the trade in 1820, as well as the attempt to secure a qualified international Right of

[1] *British and Foreign State Papers*, 1815–6, pp. 939–75.

[2] *Amer. State Papers, Foreign*, III. No. 271, pp. 735–48; *U. S. Treaties and Conventions* (ed. 1889), p. 405.

[3] This was inserted in the Treaty of Paris, Nov. 20, 1815: *British and Foreign State Papers*, 1815–6, p. 292.

[4] *Ibid.*, 1816–7, pp. 33–74 (English version, 1823–4, p. 702 ff.).

[5] Cf. *Ibid.*, 1817–8, p. 125 ff.

Visit, failed, although both propositions were strongly urged by England at the Conference of 1818.[1]

69. **The Struggle for an International Right of Search, 1820–1840.** Whatever England's motives were, it is certain that only a limited international Right of Visit on the high seas could suppress or greatly limit the slave-trade. Her diplomacy was therefore henceforth directed to this end. On the other hand, the maritime supremacy of England, so successfully asserted during the Napoleonic wars, would, in case a Right of Search were granted, virtually make England the policeman of the seas; and if nations like the United States had already, under present conditions, had just cause to complain of violations by England of their rights on the seas, might not any extension of rights by international agreement be dangerous? It was such considerations that for many years brought the powers to a dead-lock in their efforts to suppress the slave-trade.

At first it looked as if England might attempt, by judicial decisions in her own courts, to seize even foreign slavers.[2] After the war, however, her courts disavowed such action,[3] and the right was sought for by treaty stipulation. Castlereagh took early opportunity to approach the United States on the matter, suggesting to Minister Rush, June 20, 1818, a mutual but strictly limited Right of Search.[4] Rush was ordered to give him assurances of the solicitude of the United States to suppress the traffic, but to state that the concessions asked for appeared of a

[1] This was the first meeting of the London ministers of the powers according to agreement; they assembled Dec. 4, 1817, and finally called a meeting of plenipotentiaries on the question of suppression at Aix-la-Chapelle, beginning Oct. 24, 1818. Among those present were Metternich, Richelieu, Wellington, Castlereagh, Hardenberg, Bernstorff, Nesselrode, and Capodistrias. Castlereagh made two propositions: 1. That the five powers join in urging Portugal and Brazil to abolish the trade May 20, 1820; 2. That the powers adopt the principle of a mutual qualified Right of Search. Cf. *British and Foreign State Papers*, 1818–9, pp. 21–88; *Amer. State Papers, Foreign*, V. No. 346, pp. 113–122.

[2] For cases, see 1 *Acton*, 240, the "Amedie," and 1 *Dodson*, 81, the "Fortuna;" quoted in U. S. Reports, 10 *Wheaton*, 66.

[3] Cf. the case of the French ship "Le Louis": 2 *Dodson*, 238; and also the case of the "San Juan Nepomuceno": 1 *Haggard*, 267.

[4] *British and Foreign State Papers*, 1819–20, pp. 375–9; also pp. 220–2.

character not adaptable to our institutions. Negotiations were then transferred to Washington; and the new British minister, Mr. Stratford Canning, approached Adams with full instructions in December, 1820.[1]

Meantime, it had become clear to many in the United States that the individual efforts of States could never suppress or even limit the trade without systematic co-operation. In 1817 a committee of the House had urged the opening of negotiations looking toward such international co-operation,[2] and a Senate motion to the same effect had caused long debate.[3] In 1820 and 1821 two House committee reports, one of which recommended the granting of a Right of Search, were adopted by the House, but failed in the Senate.[4] Adams, notwithstanding this, saw constitutional objections to the plan proposed by Canning, and wrote to him, December 30: "A Compact, giving the power to the Naval Officers of one Nation to search the Merchant Vessels of another for Offenders and offences against the Laws of the latter, backed by a further power to seize and carry into a Foreign Port, and there subject to the decision of a Tribunal composed of at least one half Foreigners, irresponsible to the Supreme Corrective tribunal of this Union, and not amenable to the controul of impeachment for official misdemeanors, was an investment of power, over the persons, property and reputation of the Citizens of this Country, not only unwarranted by any delegation of Sovereign Power to the National Government, but so adverse to the elementary principles and indispensable securities of individual rights, . . . that not even the most unqualified approbation of the ends . . . could justify the transgression." He then suggested co-opera-

[1] *British and Foreign State Papers*, 1820–21, pp. 395–6.

[2] *House Doc.*, 14 Cong. 2 sess. II. No. 77.

[3] *Annals of Cong.*, 15 Cong. 1 sess. pp. 71, 73–78, 94–109. The motion was opposed largely by Southern members, and passed by a vote of 17 to 16.

[4] One was reported, May 9, 1820, by Mercer's committee, and passed May 12: *House Journal*, 16 Cong. 1 sess. pp. 497, 518, 520, 526; *Annals of Cong.*, 16 Cong. 1 sess. pp. 697–9. A similar resolution passed the House next session, and a committee reported in favor of the Right of Search: *Ibid.*, 16 Cong. 2 sess. pp. 1064–71. Cf. *Ibid.*, pp. 476, 743, 865, 1469.

tion of the fleets on the coast of Africa, a proposal which was promptly accepted.[1]

The slave-trade was again a subject of international consideration at the Congress of Verona in 1822. Austria, France, Great Britain, Russia, and Prussia were represented. The English delegates declared that, although only Portugal and Brazil allowed the trade, yet the traffic was at that moment carried on to a greater extent than ever before. They said that in seven months of the year 1821 no less than 21,000 slaves were abducted, and three hundred and fifty-two vessels entered African ports north of the equator. "It is obvious," said they, "that this crime is committed in contravention of the Laws of every Country of Europe, and of America, excepting only of one, and that it requires something more than the ordinary operation of Law to prevent it." England therefore recommended: —

1. That each country denounce the trade as piracy, with a view of founding upon the aggregate of such separate declarations a general law to be incorporated in the Law of Nations.

2. A withdrawing of the flags of the Powers from persons not natives of these States, who engage in the traffic under the flags of these States.

3. A refusal to admit to their domains the produce of the colonies of States allowing the trade, a measure which would apply to Portugal and Brazil alone.

These proposals were not accepted. Austria would agree to the first two only; France refused to denounce the trade as piracy; and Prussia was non-committal. The utmost that could be gained was another denunciation of the trade couched in general terms.[2]

70. **Negotiations of 1823–1825.** England did not, however, lose hope of gaining some concession from the United States. Another House committee had, in 1822, reported that the only method of suppressing the trade was by granting a Right of Search.[3] The House agreed, February 28, 1823, to request the President to enter into negotiations with the maritime powers of

[1] *British and Foreign State Papers*, 1820–21, pp. 397–400.

[2] *Ibid.*, 1822–3, pp. 94–110.

[3] *House Reports*, 17 Cong. 1 sess. II. No. 92.

Europe to denounce the slave-trade as piracy; an amendment "that we agree to a qualified right of search" was, however, lost.[1] Meantime, the English minister was continually pressing the matter upon Adams, who proposed in turn to denounce the trade as piracy. Canning agreed to this, but only on condition that it be piracy under the Law of Nations and not merely by statute law. Such an agreement, he said, would involve a Right of Search for its enforcement; he proposed strictly to limit and define this right, to allow captured ships to be tried in their own courts, and not to commit the United States in any way to the question of the belligerent Right of Search. Adams finally sent a draft of a proposed treaty to England, and agreed to recognize the slave-traffic "as piracy under the law of nations, namely: that, although seizable by the officers and authorities of every nation, they should be triable only by the tribunals of the country of the slave trading vessel."[2]

Rush presented this *projet* to the government in January, 1824. England agreed to all the points insisted on by the United States; viz., that she herself should denounce the trade as piracy; that slavers should be tried in their own country; that the captor should be laid under the most effective responsibility for his conduct; and that vessels under convoy of a ship of war of their own country should be exempt from search. In addition, England demanded that citizens of either country captured under the flag of a third power should be sent home for trial, and that citizens of either country chartering vessels of a third country should come under these stipulations.[3]

This convention was laid before the Senate April 30, 1824, but was not acted upon until May 21, when it was so amended as to make it terminable at six months' notice. The same day, President Monroe, "apprehending, from the delay in the decision, that some difficulty exists," sent a special message to the Senate, giving at length the reasons for signing the treaty, and

[1] *House Journal*, 17 Cong. 2 sess. pp. 212, 280; *Annals of Cong.*, 17 Cong. 2 sess. pp. 922, 1147–1155.

[2] *British and Foreign State Papers*, 1823–4, pp. 409–21; 1824–5, pp. 828–47; *Amer. State Papers, Foreign*, V. No. 371, pp. 333–7.

[3] *Ibid.*

saying that "should this Convention be adopted, there is every reason to believe, that it will be the commencement of a system destined to accomplish the entire Abolition of the Slave Trade." It was, however, a time of great political pot-boiling, and consequently an unfortunate occasion to ask senators to settle any great question. A systematic attack, led by Johnson of Louisiana, was made on all the vital provisions of the treaty: the waters of America were excepted from its application, and those of the West Indies barely escaped exception; the provision which, perhaps, aimed the deadliest blow at American slave-trade interests was likewise struck out; namely, the application of the Right of Search to citizens chartering the vessels of a third nation.[1]

The convention thus mutilated was not signed by England, who demanded as the least concession the application of the Right of Search to American waters. Meantime the United States had invited nearly all nations to denounce the trade as piracy; and the President, the Secretary of the Navy, and a House committee had urgently favored the granting of the Right of Search. The bad faith of Congress, however, in the matter of the Colombian treaty broke off for a time further negotiations with England.[2]

[1] *Amer. State Papers, Foreign*, V. No. 374, p. 344 ff., No. 379, pp. 360–2.

[2] *House Reports*, 18 Cong. 2 sess. I. No. 70; *Amer. State Papers, Foreign*, V. No. 379, pp. 364–5, No. 414, p. 783, etc. Among the nations invited by the United States to co-operate in suppressing the trade was the United States of Colombia. Mr. Anderson, our minister, expressed "the certain belief that the Republic of Colombia will not permit herself to be behind any Government in the civilized world in the adoption of energetic measures for the suppression of this disgraceful traffic": *Ibid.*, No. 407, p. 729. The little republic replied courteously; and, as a *projet* for a treaty, Mr. Anderson offered the proposed English treaty of 1824, including the Senate amendments. Nevertheless, the treaty thus agreed to was summarily rejected by the Senate, March 9, 1825: *Ibid.*, p. 735. Another result of this general invitation of the United States was a proposal by Colombia that the slave-trade and the status of Hayti be among the subjects for discussion at the Panama Congress. As a result of this, a Senate committee recommended that the United States take no part in the Congress. This report was finally disagreed to by a vote of 19 to 24: *Ibid.*, No. 423, pp. 837, 860, 876, 882.

71. **The Attitude of the United States and the State of the Slave-Trade.** In 1824 the Right of Search was established between England and Sweden, and in 1826 Brazil promised to abolish the trade in three years.[1] In 1831 the cause was greatly advanced by the signing of a treaty between Great Britain and France, granting mutually a geographically limited Right of Search.[2] This led, in the next few years, to similar treaties with Denmark, Sardinia,[3] the Hanse towns,[4] and Naples.[5] Such measures put the trade more and more in the hands of Americans, and it began greatly to increase. Mercer sought repeatedly in the House to have negotiations reopened with England, but without success.[6] Indeed, the chances of success were now for many years imperilled by the recurrence of deliberate search of American vessels by the British.[7] In the majority of cases the vessels proved to be slavers, and some of them fraudulently flew the American flag; nevertheless, their molestation by British cruisers created much feeling, and hindered all steps toward an understanding: the United States was loath to have her criminal negligence in enforcing her own laws thus exposed by foreigners. Other international questions connected with the trade also strained the relations of the two countries: three different vessels engaged in the domestic slave-trade, driven by stress of weather, or, in the "Creole" case, captured by Negroes on board, landed slaves in British possessions; England freed them, and refused to pay for such as were landed after emancipation had been proclaimed in the West Indies.[8] The case

[1] *British and Foreign State Papers*, 1823–4, and 1826–7. Brazil abolished the trade in 1830.

[2] This treaty was further defined in 1833: *Ibid.*, 1830–1, p. 641 ff.; 1832–3, p. 286 ff.

[3] *Ibid.*, 1833–4, pp. 218 ff., 1059 ff.

[4] *Ibid.*, 1837–8, p. 268 ff.

[5] *Ibid.*, 1838–9, p. 792 ff.

[6] Viz., Feb. 28, 1825; April 7, 1830; Feb. 16, 1831; March 3, 1831. The last resolution passed the House: *House Journal*, 21 Cong. 2 sess. pp. 426–8.

[7] Cf. *House Doc.*, 26 Cong. 2 sess. V. No. 115, pp. 35–6, etc.; *House Reports*, 27 Cong. 3 sess. III. No. 283, pp. 730–55, etc.

[8] These were the celebrated cases of the "Encomium," "Enterprize," and "Comet." Cf. *Senate Doc.*, 24 Cong. 2 sess. II. No. 174; 25 Cong. 3 sess. III. No. 216. Cf. also case of the "Creole": *Ibid.*, 27 Cong. 2 sess. II.–III. Nos. 51, 137.

of the slaver "L'Amistad" also raised difficulties with Spain. This Spanish vessel, after the Negroes on board had mutinied and killed their owners, was seized by a United States vessel and brought into port for adjudication. The court, however, freed the Negroes, on the ground that under Spanish law they were not legally slaves; and although the Senate repeatedly tried to indemnify the owners, the project did not succeed.[1]

Such proceedings well illustrate the new tendency of the pro-slavery party to neglect the enforcement of the slave-trade laws, in a frantic defence of the remotest ramparts of slave property. Consequently, when, after the treaty of 1831, France and England joined in urging the accession of the United States to it, the British minister was at last compelled to inform Palmerston, December, 1833, that "the Executive at Washington appears to shrink from bringing forward, in any shape, a question, upon which depends the completion of their former object — the utter and universal Abolition of the Slave Trade — from an apprehension of alarming the Southern States."[2] Great Britain now offered to sign the proposed treaty of 1824 as amended; but even this Forsyth refused, and stated that the United States had determined not to become "a party of any Convention on the subject of the Slave Trade."[3]

Estimates as to the extent of the slave-trade agree that the traffic to North and South America in 1820 was considerable, certainly not much less than 40,000 slaves annually. From that time to about 1825 it declined somewhat, but afterward

[1] *Senate Doc.*, 26 Cong. 2 sess. IV. No. 179; *Senate Exec. Doc.*, 31 Cong. 2 sess. III. No. 29; 32 Cong. 2 sess. III. No. 19; *Senate Reports*, 31 Cong. 2 sess. No. 301; 32 Cong. 1 sess. I. No. 158; 35 Cong. 1 sess. I. No. 36; *House Doc.*, 26 Cong. 1 sess. IV. No. 185; 27 Cong. 3 sess. V. No. 191; 28 Cong. 1 sess. IV. No. 83; *House Exec. Doc.*, 32 Cong. 2 sess. III. No. 20; *House Reports*, 26 Cong. 2 sess. No. 51; 28 Cong. 1 sess. II. No. 426; 29 Cong. 1 sess. IV. No. 753; also Decisions of the U. S. Supreme Court, 15 *Peters*, 518. Cf. Drake, *Revelations of a Slave Smuggler*, p. 98.

[2] *British and Foreign State Papers*, 1834–5, p. 136.

[3] *Ibid.*, pp. 135–47. Great Britain made treaties meanwhile with Hayti, Uruguay, Venezuela, Bolivia, Argentine Confederation, Mexico, Texas, etc. Portugal prohibited the slave-trade in 1836, except between her African colonies. Cf. *Ibid.*, from 1838 to 1841.

increased enormously, so that by 1837 the American importation was estimated as high as 200,000 Negroes annually. The total abolition of the African trade by American countries then brought the traffic down to perhaps 30,000 in 1842. A large and rapid increase of illicit traffic followed; so that by 1847 the importation amounted to nearly 100,000 annually. One province of Brazil is said to have received 173,000 in the years 1846–1849. In the decade 1850–1860 this activity in slave-trading continued, and reached very large proportions.

The traffic thus carried on floated under the flags of France, Spain, and Portugal, until about 1830; from 1830 to 1840 it began gradually to assume the United States flag; by 1845, a large part of the trade was under the stars and stripes; by 1850 fully one-half the trade, and in the decade, 1850–1860 nearly all the traffic, found this flag its best protection.[1]

72. **The Quintuple Treaty, 1839–1842.** In 1839 Pope Gregory XVI. stigmatized the slave-trade "as utterly unworthy of the Christian name;" and at the same time, although proscribed by the laws of every civilized State, the trade was flourishing with pristine vigor. Great advantage was given the traffic by the fact that the United States, for two decades after the abortive attempt of 1824, refused to co-operate with the rest of the civilized world, and allowed her flag to shelter and protect the slave-trade. If a fully equipped slaver sailed from New York, Havana, Rio Janeiro, or Liverpool, she had only to hoist the

[1] These estimates are from the following sources: *British and Foreign State Papers*, 1822–3, pp. 94–110; *Parliamentary Papers*, 1823, XVIII., *Slave Trade*, Further Papers, A., pp. 10–11; 1838–9, XLIX., *Slave Trade*, Class A, Further Series, pp. 115, 119, 121; *House Doc.*, 19 Cong. 1 sess. I. No. 1, p. 93; 20 Cong. 1 sess. III. No. 99; 26 Cong. 1 sess. VI. No. 211; *House Exec. Doc.*, 31 Cong. 2 sess. I. No. 1, p. 193; *House Reports*, 21 Cong. 1 sess. III. No. 348; *Senate Doc.*, 28 Cong. 1 sess. IV. No. 217; 31 Cong. 1 sess. XIV. No. 66; 31 Cong. 2 sess. II. No. 6; *Amer. State Papers, Naval*, I. No. 249; Buxton, *The African Slave Trade and its Remedy*, pp. 44–59; Friends' *Facts and Observations on the Slave Trade* (ed. 1841); Friends' *Exposition of the Slave Trade*, 1840–50; *Annual Reports of the American and Foreign Anti-Slavery Society*.

The annexed table gives the dates of the abolition of the slave-trade by the various nations: —

stars and stripes in order to proceed unmolested on her piratical voyage; for there was seldom a United States cruiser to be met with, and there were, on the other hand, diplomats at Washington so jealous of the honor of the flag that they would prostitute it to crime rather than allow an English or a French cruiser in any way to interfere. Without doubt, the contention of the United States as to England's pretensions to a Right of Visit was technically correct. Nevertheless, it was clear that if the slave-trade was to be suppressed, each nation must either zealously keep her flag from fraudulent use, or, as a labor-saving device, depute to others this duty for limited places and under special circumstances. A failure of any one nation to do one of these two things meant that the efforts of all other nations were to be fruitless. The United States had invited the world to join her in denouncing the slave-trade as piracy; yet, when such a pirate was waylaid by an English vessel, the United States complained or demanded reparation. The only answer which this country for years returned to the long-continued exposures of American slave-traders and of the fraudulent use of the American flag, was a recital of cases where Great Britain had gone beyond

Date.	Slave-trade Abolished by	Right of Search Treaty with Great Britain, made by	Arrangements for Joint Cruising with Great Britain, made by
1802	Denmark.		
1807	Great Britain; United States.		
1813	Sweden.		
1814	Netherlands.		
1815	Portugal (north of the equator).		
1817	Spain (north of the equator).	Portugal; Spain.	
1818	France.	Netherlands.	
1820	Spain.		
1824		Sweden.	
1829	Brazil (?).		
1830	Portugal.		
1831–33		France.	
1833–39		Denmark, Hanse Towns, etc.	
1841		Quintuple Treaty (Austria, Russia, Prussia).	
1842			United States.
1844		Texas.	
1845		Belgium.	France.
1862		United States.	

her legal powers in her attempt to suppress the slave-trade.[1] In the face of overwhelming evidence to the contrary, Secretary of State Forsyth declared, in 1840, that the duty of the United States in the matter of the slave-trade "has been faithfully performed, and if the traffic still exists as a disgrace to humanity, it is to be imputed to nations with whom Her Majesty's Government has formed and maintained the most intimate connexions, and to whose Governments Great Britain has paid for the right of active intervention in order to its complete extirpation."[2] So zealous was Stevenson, our minister to England, in denying the Right of Search, that he boldly informed Palmerston, in 1841, "that there is no shadow of pretence for excusing, much less justifying, the exercise of any such right. That it is wholly immaterial, whether the vessels be equipped for, or actually engaged in slave traffic or not, and consequently the right to search or detain even slave vessels, must be confined to the ships or vessels of those nations with whom it may have treaties on the subject."[3] Palmerston courteously replied that he could not think that the United States seriously intended to make its flag a refuge for slave-traders;[4] and Aberdeen pertinently declared: "Now, it can scarcely be maintained by Mr. Stevenson that Great Britain should be bound to permit her own subjects, with British vessels and British capital, to carry on, before the eyes of British officers, this detestable traffic in human beings, which the law has declared to be piracy, merely because they had the audacity to commit an additional offence by fraudulently usurping the American flag."[5] Thus the dispute, even after the advent of Webster, went on for a time, involving itself in metaphysical subtleties, and apparently leading no nearer to an understanding.[6]

In 1838 a fourth conference of the powers for the consideration of the slave-trade took place at London. It was attended

[1] Cf. *British and Foreign State Papers*, from 1836 to 1842.

[2] *Ibid.*, 1839–40, p. 940.

[3] *House Doc.*, 27 Cong. 1 sess. No. 34, pp. 5–6.

[4] *Senate Doc.*, 29 Cong. 1 sess. VIII. No. 377, p. 56.

[5] *Ibid.*, p. 72.

[6] *Ibid.*, pp. 133–40, etc.

by representatives of England, France, Russia, Prussia, and Austria. England laid the *projet* of a treaty before them, to which all but France assented. This so-called Quintuple Treaty, signed December 20, 1841, denounced the slave-trade as piracy, and declared that "the High Contracting Parties agree by common consent, that those of their ships of war which shall be provided with special warrants and orders . . . may search every merchant-vessel belonging to any one of the High Contracting Parties which shall, on reasonable grounds, be suspected of being engaged in the traffic in slaves." All captured slavers were to be sent to their own countries for trial.[1]

While the ratification of this treaty was pending, the United States minister to France, Lewis Cass, addressed an official note to Guizot at the French foreign office, protesting against the institution of an international Right of Search, and rather grandiloquently warning the powers against the use of force to accomplish their ends.[2] This extraordinary epistle, issued on the minister's own responsibility, brought a reply denying that the creation of any "new principle of international law, whereby the vessels even of those powers which have not participated in the arrangement should be subjected to the right of search," was ever intended, and affirming that no such extraordinary interpretation could be deduced from the Convention. Moreover, M. Guizot hoped that the United States, by agreeing to this treaty, would "aid, by its most sincere endeavors, in the definitive abolition of the trade."[3] Cass's theatrical protest was, consciously or unconsciously, the manifesto of that growing class in the United States who wanted no further measures taken for the suppression of the slave-trade; toward that, as toward the institution of slavery, this party favored a policy of strict *laissez-faire*.

73. **Final Concerted Measures, 1842–1862.** The Treaty of Washington, in 1842, made the first effective compromise in the matter and broke the unpleasant dead-lock, by substituting joint

[1] *British and Foreign State Papers*, 1841–2, p. 269 ff.

[2] See below, Appendix B.

[3] *Senate Doc.*, 29 Cong. 1 sess. VIII. No. 377, p. 201.

cruising by English and American squadrons for the proposed grant of a Right of Search. In submitting this treaty, Tyler said: "The treaty which I now submit to you proposes no alteration, mitigation, or modification of the rules of the law of nations. It provides simply that each of the two Governments shall maintain on the coast of Africa a sufficient squadron to enforce separately and respectively the laws, rights, and obligations of the two countries for the suppression of the slave trade."[1] This provision was a part of the treaty to settle the boundary disputes with England. In the Senate, Benton moved to strike out this article; but the attempt was defeated by a vote of 37 to 12, and the treaty was ratified.[2]

This stipulation of the treaty of 1842 was never properly carried out by the United States for any length of time.[3] Consequently the same difficulties as to search and visit by English vessels continued to recur. Cases like the following were frequent. The "Illinois," of Gloucester, Massachusetts, while lying at Whydah, Africa, was boarded by a British officer, but having American papers was unmolested. Three days later she hoisted Spanish colors and sailed away with a cargo of slaves. Next morning she fell in with another British vessel and hoisted American colors; the British ship had then no right to molest her; but the captain of the slaver feared that she would, and therefore ran his vessel aground, slaves and all. The senior English officer reported that "had Lieutenant Cumberland brought to and boarded the 'Illinois,' notwithstanding the American colors which she hoisted, . . . the American master of the 'Illinois' . . . would have complained to his Government of the detention of his vessel."[4] Again, a vessel which had been boarded by British officers and found with American flag

[1] *Senate Exec. Journal*, VI. 123.

[2] *U.S. Treaties and Conventions* (ed. 1889), pp. 436–7. For the debates in the Senate, see *Congressional Globe*, 27 Cong. 3 sess. Appendix. Cass resigned on account of the acceptance of this treaty without a distinct denial of the Right of Search, claiming that this compromised his position in France. Cf. *Senate Doc.*, 27 Cong. 3 sess. II., IV. Nos. 52, 223; 29 Cong. 1 sess. VIII. No. 377.

[3] Cf. below, Chapter X.

[4] *Senate Exec. Doc.*, 28 Cong. 2 sess. IX. No. 150, p. 72.

and papers was, a little later, captured under the Spanish flag with four hundred and thirty slaves. She had in the interim complained to the United States government of the boarding.[1]

Meanwhile, England continued to urge the granting of a Right of Search, claiming that the stand of the United States really amounted to the wholesale protection of pirates under her flag.[2] The United States answered by alleging that even the Treaty of 1842 had been misconstrued by England,[3] whereupon there was much warm debate in Congress, and several attempts were made to abrogate the slave-trade article of the treaty.[4] The pro-slavery party had become more and more suspicious of England's motives, since they had seen her abolition of the slave-trade blossom into abolition of the system itself, and they seized every opportunity to prevent co-operation with her. At the same time, European interest in the question showed some signs of weakening, and no decided action was taken. In 1845 France changed her Right of Search stipulations of 1833 to one for joint cruising,[5] while the Germanic Federation,[6] Portugal,[7] and Chili[8] denounced the trade as piracy. In 1844 Texas granted the Right of Search to England,[9] and in 1845 Belgium signed the Quintuple Treaty.[10]

Discussion between England and the United States was revived when Cass held the State portfolio, and, strange to say, the author of "Cass's Protest" went farther than any of his predecessors in acknowledging the justice of England's demands.

[1] *Senate Exec. Doc.*, 28 Cong. 2 sess. IX. No. 150, p. 77.

[2] *House Doc.*, 27 Cong. 3 sess. V. No. 192, p. 4. Cf. *British and Foreign State Papers*, 1842–3, p. 708 ff.

[3] *House Journal*, 27 Cong. 3 sess. pp. 431, 485–8. Cf. *House Doc.*, 27 Cong. 3 sess. V. No. 192.

[4] Cf. below, Chapter X.

[5] With a fleet of 26 vessels, reduced to 12 in 1849: *British and Foreign State Papers*, 1844–5, p. 4 ff.; 1849–50, p. 480.

[6] *Ibid.*, 1850–1, p. 953.

[7] Portugal renewed her Right of Search treaty in 1842: *Ibid.*, 1841–2, p. 527 ff.; 1842–3, p. 450.

[8] *Ibid.*, 1843–4, p. 316.

[9] *Ibid.*, 1844–5, p. 592. There already existed some such privileges between England and Texas.

[10] *Ibid.*, 1847–8, p. 397 ff.

Said he, in 1859: "If The United States maintained that, by carrying their flag at her masthead, any vessel became thereby entitled to the immunity which belongs to American vessels, they might well be reproached with assuming a position which would go far towards shielding crimes upon the ocean from punishment; but they advance no such pretension, while they concede that, if in the honest examination of a vessel sailing under American colours, but accompanied by strongly-marked suspicious circumstances, a mistake is made, and she is found to be entitled to the flag she bears, but no injury is committed, and the conduct of the boarding party is irreproachable, no Government would be likely to make a case thus exceptional in its character a subject of serious reclamation."[1] While admitting this and expressing a desire to co-operate in the suppression of the slave-trade, Cass nevertheless steadily refused all further overtures toward a mutual Right of Search.

The increase of the slave-traffic was so great in the decade 1850–1860 that Lord John Russell proposed to the governments of the United States, France, Spain, Portugal, and Brazil, that they instruct their ministers to meet at London in May or June, 1860, to consider measures for the final abolition of the trade. He stated: "It is ascertained, by repeated instances, that the practice is for vessels to sail under the American flag. If the flag is rightly assumed, and the papers correct, no British cruizer can touch them. If no slaves are on board, even though the equipment, the fittings, the water-casks, and other circumstances prove that the ship is on a Slave Trade venture, no American cruizer can touch them."[2] Continued representations of this kind were made to the paralyzed United States government; indeed, the slave-trade of the world seemed now to float securely under her flag. Nevertheless, Cass refused even to participate in the proposed conference, and later refused to accede to a proposal for joint cruising off the coast of Cuba.[3] Great Britain offered to relieve the United States of any embarrassment by receiving all captured Africans into the West Indies; but Presi-

[1] *British and Foreign State Papers*, 1858–9, pp. 1121, 1129.
[2] *Ibid.*, 1859–60, pp. 902–3.
[3] *House Exec. Doc.*, 36 Cong. 2 sess. IV. No. 7.

dent Buchanan "could not contemplate any such arrangement," and obstinately refused to increase the suppressing squadron.[1]

On the outbreak of the Civil War, the Lincoln administration, through Secretary Seward, immediately expressed a willingness to do all in its power to suppress the slave-trade.[2] Accordingly, June 7, 1862, a treaty was signed with Great Britain granting a mutual limited Right of Search, and establishing mixed courts for the trial of offenders at the Cape of Good Hope, Sierra Leone, and New York.[3] The efforts of a half-century of diplomacy were finally crowned; Seward wrote to Adams, "Had such a treaty been made in 1808, there would now have been no sedition here."[4]

[1] *House Exec. Doc.*, 36 Cong. 2 sess. IV. No. 7.

[2] *Senate Exec. Doc.*, 37 Cong. 2 sess. V. No. 57.

[3] *Senate Exec. Journal*, XII. 230–1, 240, 254, 256, 391, 400, 403; *Diplomatic Correspondence*, 1862, pp. 141, 158; *U. S. Treaties and Conventions* (ed. 1889), pp. 454–9.

[4] *Diplomatic Correspondence*, 1862, pp. 64–5. This treaty was revised in 1863. The mixed court in the West Indies had, by February, 1864, liberated 95,206 Africans: *Senate Exec. Doc.*, 38 Cong. 1 sess. No. 56, p. 24.

CHAPTER X.

THE RISE OF THE COTTON KINGDOM. 1820–1850.

74. **The Economic Revolution.** The history of slavery and the slave-trade after 1820 must be read in the light of the industrial revolution through which the civilized world passed in the first half of the nineteenth century. Between the years 1775 and 1825 occurred economic events and changes of the highest importance and widest influence. Though all branches of industry felt the impulse of this new industrial life, yet, "if we consider single industries, cotton manufacture has, during the nineteenth century, made the most magnificent and gigantic advances."[1] This fact is easily explained by the remarkable series of inventions that revolutionized this industry between 1738 and 1830, including Arkwright's, Watt's, Compton's, and Cartwright's epoch-making contrivances.[2] The effect which

[1] Beer, *Geschichte des Welthandels im 19ten Jahrhundert*, II. 67.

[2] A list of these inventions most graphically illustrates this advance:—

1738, John Jay, fly-shuttle.
John Wyatt, spinning by rollers.
1748, Lewis Paul, carding-machine.
1760, Robert Kay, drop-box.
1769, Richard Arkwright, water-frame and throstle.
James Watt, steam-engine.
1772, James Lees, improvements on carding-machine.
1775, Richard Arkwright, series of combinations.
1779, Samuel Compton, mule.

these inventions had on the manufacture of cotton goods is best illustrated by the fact that in England, the chief cotton market of the world, the consumption of raw cotton rose steadily from 13,000 bales in 1781, to 572,000 in 1820, to 871,000 in 1830, and to 3,366,000 in 1860.[1] Very early, therefore, came the query whence the supply of raw cotton was to come. Tentative experiments on the rich, broad fields of the Southern United States, together with the indispensable invention of Whitney's cotton-gin, soon answered this question: a new economic future was opened up to this land, and immediately the whole South began to extend its cotton culture, and more and more to throw its whole energy into this one staple.

Here it was that the fatal mistake of compromising with slavery in the beginning, and of the policy of *laissez-faire* pursued thereafter, became painfully manifest; for, instead now of a healthy, normal, economic development along proper industrial lines, we have the abnormal and fatal rise of a slave-labor large-farming system, which, before it was realized, had so intertwined itself with and braced itself upon the economic forces of an industrial age, that a vast and terrible civil war was necessary to displace it. The tendencies to a patriarchal serfdom, recognizable in the age of Washington and Jefferson, began slowly but surely to disappear; and in the second quarter of the century Southern slavery was irresistibly changing from a family institution to an industrial system.

The development of Southern slavery has heretofore been viewed so exclusively from the ethical and social standpoint that we are apt to forget its close and indissoluble connection with the world's cotton market. Beginning with 1820, a little after the close of the Napoleonic wars, when the industry of

1785, Edmund Cartwright, power-loom.
1803–4, Radcliffe and Johnson, dressing-machine.
1817, Roberts, fly-frame.
1818, William Eaton, self-acting frame.
1825–30, Roberts, improvements on mule.

Cf. Baines, *History of the Cotton Manufacture*, pp. 116–231; *Encyclopædia Britannica*, 9th ed., article "Cotton."

[1] Baines, *History of the Cotton Manufacture*, p. 215. A bale weighed from 375 lbs. to 400 lbs.

cotton manufacture had begun its modern development and the South had definitely assumed her position as chief producer of raw cotton, we find the average price of cotton per pound, 8½*d.* From this time until 1845 the price steadily fell, until in the latter year it reached 4*d.*; the only exception to this fall was in the years 1832–1839, when, among other things, a strong increase in the English demand, together with an attempt of the young slave power to "corner" the market, sent the price up as high as 11*d.* The demand for cotton goods soon outran a crop which McCullough had pronounced "prodigious," and after 1845 the price started on a steady rise, which, except for the checks suffered during the continental revolutions and the Crimean War, continued until 1860.[1] The steady increase in the production of cotton explains the fall in price down to 1845. In 1822 the crop was a half-million bales; in 1831, a million; in 1838, a million and a half; and in 1840–1843, two million. By this time the world's consumption of cotton goods began to increase so rapidly that, in spite of the increase in Southern crops, the price kept rising. Three million bales were gathered in 1852, three and a half million in 1856, and the remarkable crop of five million bales in 1860.[2]

Here we have data to explain largely the economic development of the South. By 1822 the large-plantation slave system had gained footing; in 1838–1839 it was able to show its power in the cotton "corner;" by the end of the next decade it had not only gained a solid economic foundation, but it had built a closed oligarchy with a political policy. The changes in price during the next few years drove out of competition many survivors of the small-farming free-labor system, and put the slave *régime* in position to dictate the policy of the nation. The zenith of the system and the first inevitable signs of decay came in the years 1850–1860, when the rising price of cotton threw the whole economic energy of the South into its cultivation, leading to a terrible consumption of soil and slaves, to a great increase in the size of plantations, and to increasing power and effrontery on the part of the slave barons. Finally, when a

[1] The prices cited are from Newmarch and Tooke, and refer to the London market. The average price in 1855–60 was about 7*d.*

[2] From United States census reports.

rising moral crusade conjoined with threatened economic disaster, the oligarchy, encouraged by the state of the cotton market, risked all on a political *coup-d'état*, which failed in the war of 1861–1865.[1]

75. **The Attitude of the South.** The attitude of the South toward the slave-trade changed *pari passu* with this development of the cotton trade. From 1808 to 1820 the South half wished to get rid of a troublesome and abnormal institution, and yet saw no way to do so. The fear of insurrection and of the further spread of the disagreeable system led her to consent to the partial prohibition of the trade by severe national enactments. Nevertheless, she had in the matter no settled policy: she refused to support vigorously the execution of the laws she had helped to make, and at the same time she acknowledged the theoretical necessity of these laws. After 1820, however, there came a gradual change. The South found herself supplied with a body of slave laborers, whose number had been augmented by large illicit importations, with an abundance of rich land, and with all other natural facilities for raising a crop which was in large demand and peculiarly adapted to slave labor. The increasing crop caused a new demand for slaves, and an interstate slave-traffic arose between the Border and the Gulf States, which turned the former into slave-breeding districts, and bound them to the slave States by ties of strong economic interest.

As the cotton crop continued to increase, this source of supply became inadequate, especially as the theory of land and slave consumption broke down former ethical and prudential bounds. It was, for example, found cheaper to work a slave to death in a few years, and buy a new one, than to care for him in sickness and old age; so, too, it was easier to despoil rich, new land in a few years of intensive culture, and move on to the Southwest, than to fertilize and conserve the soil.[2] Consequently, there early came a demand for land and slaves greater than the country could supply. The demand for land showed itself in the annexation of Texas, the conquest of Mexico, and

[1] Cf. United States census reports; and Olmsted, *The Cotton Kingdom*.
[2] Cf. *Ibid.*

the movement toward the acquisition of Cuba. The demand for slaves was manifested in the illicit traffic that noticeably increased about 1835, and reached large proportions by 1860. It was also seen in a disposition to attack the government for stigmatizing the trade as criminal,[1] then in a disinclination to take any measures which would have rendered our repressive laws effective; and finally in such articulate declarations by prominent men as this: "Experience having settled the point, that this Trade *cannot be abolished by the use of force*, and that blockading squadrons serve only to make it more profitable and more cruel, I am surprised that the attempt is persisted in, unless as it serves as a cloak to some other purposes. It would be far better than it now is, for the African, if the trade was free from all restrictions, and left to the mitigation and decay which time and competition would surely bring about."[2]

76. **The Attitude of the North and Congress.** With the North as yet unawakened to the great changes taking place in the South, and with the attitude of the South thus in process of development, little or no constructive legislation could be expected on the subject of the slave-trade. As the divergence in sentiment became more and more pronounced, there were various attempts at legislation, all of which proved abortive. The pro-slavery party attempted, as early as 1826, and again in 1828, to abolish the African agency and leave the Africans practically at the mercy of the States;[3] one or two attempts were made to relax

[1] As early as 1836 Calhoun declared that he should ever regret that the term "piracy" had been applied to the slave-trade in our laws: Benton, *Abridgment of Debates*, XII. 718.

[2] Governor J. H. Hammond of South Carolina, in *Letters to Clarkson*, No. 1, p. 2.

[3] In 1826 Forsyth of Georgia attempted to have a bill passed abolishing the African agency, and providing that the Africans imported be disposed of in some way that would entail no expense on the public treasury: *House Journal*, 19 Cong. 1 sess. p. 258. In 1828 a bill was reported to the House to abolish the agency and make the Colonization Society the agents, if they would agree to the terms. The bill was so amended as merely to appropriate money for suppressing the slave-trade: *Ibid.*, 20 Cong. 1 sess., House Bill No. 190.

the few provisions which restrained the coastwise trade;[1] and, after the treaty of 1842, Benton proposed to stop appropriations for the African squadron until England defined her position on the Right of Search question.[2] The anti-slavery men presented several bills to amend and strengthen previous laws;[3] they sought, for instance, in vain to regulate the Texan trade, through which numbers of slaves indirectly reached the United States.[4] Presidents and consuls earnestly recommended legislation to restrict the clearances of vessels bound on slave-trading voyages, and to hinder the facility with which slavers obtained fraudulent papers.[5] Only one such bill succeeded in passing the Senate, and that was dropped in the House.[6]

The only legislation of this period was confined to a few appropriation bills. Only one of these acts, that of 1823, appropriating $50,000,[7] was designed materially to aid in the suppression of the trade, all the others relating to expenses incurred after violations. After 1823 the appropriations dwindled, being made at intervals of one, two, and three years, down to 1834, when the amount was $5,000. No further appropriations were made until 1842, when a few thousands above an unexpended surplus were appropriated. In 1843 $5,000 were given, and finally, in 1846, $25,000 were secured; but this was the last sum obtainable until 1856.[8] Nearly all of these meagre appro-

[1] *House Journal*, 20 Cong. 1 sess. pp. 121, 135; 20 Cong. 2 sess. pp. 58–9, 84, 215.

[2] *Congressional Globe*, 27 Cong. 3 sess. pp. 328, 331–6.

[3] Cf. Mercer's bill, *House Journal*, 21 Cong. 1 sess. p. 512; also Strange's two bills, *Senate Journal*, 25 Cong. 3 sess. pp. 200, 313; 26 Cong. 1 sess., Senate Bill No. 123.

[4] *Senate Journal*, 25 Cong. 2 sess. pp. 297–8, 300.

[5] *Senate Doc.*, 28 Cong. 1 sess. IV. No. 217, p. 19; *Senate Exec. Doc.*, 31 Cong. 2 sess. II. No. 6, pp. 3, 10, etc.; 33 Cong. 1 sess. VIII. No. 47, pp. 5–6; 34 Cong. 1 sess. XV. No. 99, p. 80; *House Journal*, 26 Cong. 1 sess. pp. 117–8; cf. *Ibid.*, 20 Cong. 1 sess. p. 650, etc.; 21 Cong. 2 sess. p. 194, 27 Cong. 1 sess. pp. 31, 184; *House Doc.*, 29 Cong. 1 sess. III. No. 43, p. 11; *House Exec. Doc.*, 31 Cong. 1 sess. III. pt. 1, No. 5, pp. 7–8.

[6] *Senate Journal*, 26 Cong. 1 sess., Senate Bill No. 335; *House Journal*, 26 Cong. 1 sess. pp. 1138, 1228, 1257.

[7] *Statutes at Large*, III. 764.

[8] Cf. above, Chapter VIII. p. 122.

priations went toward reimbursing Southern plantation owners for the care and support of illegally imported Africans, and the rest to the maintenance of the African agency. Suspiciously large sums were paid for the first purpose, considering the fact that such Africans were always worked hard by those to whom they were farmed out, and often "disappeared" while in their hands. In the accounts we nevertheless find many items like that of $20,286.98 for the maintenance of Negroes imported on the "Ramirez;"[1] in 1827, $5,442.22 for the "bounty, subsistence, clothing, medicine," etc., of fifteen Africans;[2] in 1835, $3,613 for the support of thirty-eight slaves for two months (including a bill of $1,038 for medical attendance).[3]

The African agency suffered many vicissitudes. The first agent, Bacon, who set out early in 1820, was authorized by President Monroe "to form an establishment on the island of Sherbro, or elsewhere on the coast of Africa," and to build barracks for three hundred persons. He was, however, warned "not to connect your agency with the views or plans of the Colonization Society, with which, under the law, the Government of the United States has no concern." Bacon soon died, and was followed during the next four years by Winn and Ayres; they succeeded in establishing a government agency on Cape Mesurado, in conjunction with that of the Colonization Society. The agent of that Society, Jehudi Ashmun, became after 1822, the virtual head of the colony; he fortified and enlarged it, and laid the foundations of an independent community. The succeeding government agents came to be merely official representatives of the United States, and the distribution of free rations for liberated Africans ceased in 1827.

Between 1819 and 1830 two hundred and fifty-two recaptured Africans were sent to the agency, and $264,710 were expended. The property of the government at the agency was valued at $18,895. From 1830 to 1840, nearly $20,000 more were expended, chiefly for the agents' salaries. About 1840 the appointment of an agent ceased, and the colony became gradually

[1] Cf. *Report of the Secretary of the Navy*, 1827.

[2] *Ibid.*

[3] *House Reports*, 24 Cong. 1 sess. I. No. 223.

self-supporting and independent. It was proclaimed as the Republic of Liberia in 1847.[1]

77. **Imperfect Application of the Laws.** In reviewing efforts toward the suppression of the slave-trade from 1820 to 1850, it must be remembered that nearly every cabinet had a strong, if not a predominating, Southern element, and that consequently the efforts of the executive were powerfully influenced by the changing attitude of the South. Naturally, under such circumstances, the government displayed little activity and no enthusiasm in the work. In 1824 a single vessel of the Gulf squadron was occasionally sent to the African coast to return by the route usually followed by the slavers; no wonder that "none of these or any other of our public ships have found vessels engaged in the slave trade under the flag of the United States, . . . although it is known that the trade still exists to a most lamentable extent."[2] Indeed, all that an American slaver need do was to run up a Spanish or a Portuguese flag, to be absolutely secure from all attack or inquiry on the part of United States vessels. Even this desultory method of suppression was not regular: in 1826 "no vessel has been despatched to the coast of Africa for several months,"[3] and from that time until 1839 this country probably had no slave-trade police upon the seas, except in the Gulf of Mexico. In 1839 increasing violations led to the sending of two fast-sailing vessels to the African coast, and these were kept there more or less regularly;[4] but even after the signing of the treaty

[1] This account is taken exclusively from government documents: *Amer. State Papers, Naval*, III. Nos. 339, 340, 357, 429 E; IV. Nos. 457 R (1 and 2), 486 H, I, p. 161 and 519 R, 564 P, 585 P; *House Reports*, 19 Cong. 1 sess. I. No. 65; *House Doc.*, 19 Cong. 2 sess. IV. No. 69; 21 Cong. 2 sess. I. No. 2, pp. 42–3, 211–8; 22 Cong. 1 sess. I. No. 2, pp. 45, 272–4; 22 Cong. 2 sess. I. No. 2, pp. 48, 229; 23 Cong. 1 sess. I. No. 1, pp. 238, 269; 23 Cong. 2 sess. I. No. 2, pp. 315, 363; 24 Cong. 1 sess. I. No. 2, pp. 336, 378; 24 Cong. 2 sess. I. No. 2, pp. 450, 506; 25 Cong. 2 sess. I. No. 3, pp. 771, 850; 26 Cong. 1 sess. I. No. 2, pp. 534, 612; 26 Cong. 2 sess. I. No. 2, pp. 405, 450. It is probable that the agent became eventually the United States consul and minister; I cannot however cite evidence for this supposition.

[2] *Report of the Secretary of the Navy*, 1824.

[3] *Ibid.*, 1826.

[4] *Ibid.*, 1839.

of 1842 the Secretary of the Navy reports: "On the coast of Africa we have *no* squadron. The small appropriation of the present year was believed to be scarcely sufficient."[1] Between 1843 and 1850 the coast squadron varied from two to six vessels, with from thirty to ninety-eight guns;[2] "but the force habitually and actively engaged in cruizing on the ground frequented by slavers has probably been less by one-fourth, if we consider the size of the ships employed and their withdrawal for purposes of recreation and health, and the movement of the reliefs, whose arrival does not correspond exactly with the departure of the vessels whose term of service has expired."[3] The reports of the navy show that in only four of the eight years mentioned was the fleet, at the time of report, at the stipulated size of eighty guns; and at times it was much below this, even as late as 1848, when only two vessels are reported on duty along the African coast.[4] As the commanders themselves acknowledged, the squadron was too small and the cruising-ground too large to make joint cruising effective.[5]

The same story comes from the Brazil station: "Nothing effectual can be done towards stopping the slave trade, as our squadron is at present organized," wrote the consul at Rio Janeiro in 1847; "when it is considered that the Brazil station extends from north of the equator to Cape Horn on this continent, and includes a great part of Africa south of the equator, on both sides of the Cape of Good Hope, it must be admitted that one frigate and one brig is a very insufficient force to protect American commerce, and repress the participation in the slave trade by our own vessels."[6] In the Gulf of Mexico cruisers were stationed most of the time, although even here there were

[1] *Report of the Secretary of the Navy*, 1842.

[2] *British and Foreign State Papers*, 1857–8, p. 1250.

[3] Lord Napier to Secretary of State Cass, Dec. 24, 1857: *British and Foreign State Papers*, 1857–8, p. 1249.

[4] *Parliamentary Papers*, 1847–8, Vol. LXIV. No. 133, *Papers Relative to the Suppression of the Slave Trade on the Coast of Africa*, p. 2.

[5] Report of Perry: *Senate Doc.*, 28 Cong. 2 sess. IX. No. 150, p. 118.

[6] Consul Park at Rio Janeiro to Secretary Buchanan, Aug. 20, 1847: *House Exec. Doc.*, 30 Cong. 2 sess. VII. No. 61, p. 7.

at times urgent representations that the scarcity or the absence of such vessels gave the illicit trade great license.[1]

Owing to this general negligence of the government, and also to its anxiety on the subject of the theoretic Right of Search, many officials were kept in a state of chronic deception in regard to the trade. The enthusiasm of commanders was dampened by the lack of latitude allowed and by the repeated insistence in their orders on the non-existence of a Right of Search.[2] When one commander, realizing that he could not cover the trading-track with his fleet, requested English commanders to detain suspicious American vessels until one of his vessels came up, the government annulled the agreement as soon as it reached their ears, rebuked him, and the matter was alluded to in Congress long after with horror.[3] According to the orders of cruisers, only slavers with slaves actually on board could be seized. Consequently, fully equipped slavers would sail past the American fleet, deliberately make all preparations for shipping a cargo, then, when the English were not near, "sell" the ship to a Spaniard, hoist the Spanish flag, and again sail gayly past the American fleet with a cargo of slaves. An English commander reported: "The officers of the United States' navy are extremely active and zealous in the cause, and

[1] Suppose "an American vessel employed to take in negroes at some point on this coast. There is no American man-of-war here to obtain intelligence. What risk does she run of being searched? But suppose that there is a man-of-war in port. What is to secure the master of the merchantman against her [the man-of-war's] commander's knowing all about his [the merchant-man's] intention, or suspecting it in time to be upon him [the merchant-man] before he shall have run a league on his way to Texas?" Consul Trist to Commander Spence: *House Doc.*, 27 Cong. 1 sess. No. 34, p. 41.

[2] A typical set of instructions was on the following plan: 1. You are charged with the protection of legitimate commerce. 2. While the United States wishes to suppress the slave-trade, she will not admit a Right of Search by foreign vessels. 3. You are to arrest slavers. 4. You are to allow in no case an exercise of the Right of Search or any great interruption of legitimate commerce. — To Commodore Perry, March 30, 1843: *House Exec. Doc.*, 35 Cong. 2 sess. IX. No. 104.

[3] *House Reports*, 27 Cong. 3 sess. III. No. 283, pp. 765–8. Cf. Benton's speeches on the treaty of 1842.

no fault can be attributed to them, but it is greatly to be lamented that this blemish should in so great a degree nullify our endeavours." [1]

78. **Responsibility of the Government.** Not only did the government thus negatively favor the slave-trade, but also many conscious, positive acts must be attributed to a spirit hostile to the proper enforcement of the slave-trade laws. In cases of doubt, when the law needed executive interpretation, the decision was usually in favor of the looser construction of the law; the trade from New Orleans to Mobile was, for instance, declared not to be coastwise trade, and consequently, to the joy of the Cuban smugglers, was left utterly free and unrestricted.[2] After the conquest of Mexico, even vessels bound to California, by the way of Cape Horn, were allowed to clear coastwise, thus giving our flag to "the slave-pirates of the whole world." [3] Attorney-General Nelson declared that the selling to a slave-trader of an American vessel, to be delivered on the coast of Africa, was not aiding or abetting the slave-trade.[4] So easy was it for slavers to sail that corruption among officials was hinted at. "There is certainly a want of proper vigilance at Havana," wrote Commander Perry in 1844, "and perhaps at the ports of the United States;" and again, in the same year, "I cannot but think that the custom-house authorities in the United States are not sufficiently rigid in looking after vessels of suspicious character." [5]

In the courts it was still next to impossible to secure the punishment of the most notorious slave-trader. In 1847 a consul writes: "The slave power in this city [i. e., Rio Janeiro] is extremely great, and a consul doing his duty needs to be supported kindly and effectually at home. In the case of the

[1] Report of Hotham to Admiralty, April 7, 1847: *Parliamentary Papers*, 1847–8, Vol. LXIV. No. 133, *Papers Relative to the Suppression of the Slave Trade on the Coast of Africa*, p. 13.

[2] *Opinions of Attorneys-General*, III. 512.

[3] *Tenth Annual Report of the Amer. and Foreign Anti-Slav. Soc.*, May 7, 1850, p. 149.

[4] *Opinions of Attorneys-General*, IV. 245.

[5] *Senate Doc.*, 28 Cong. 2 sess. IX. No. 150, pp. 108, 132.

'Fame,' where the vessel was diverted from the business intended by her owners and employed in the slave trade — both of which offences are punishable with death, if I rightly read the laws — I sent home the two mates charged with these offences, for trial, the first mate to Norfolk, the second mate to Philadelphia. What was done with the first mate I know not. In the case of the man sent to Philadelphia, Mr. Commissioner Kane states that a clear prima facie case is made out, and then holds him to bail in the sum of *one thousand dollars*, which would be paid by any slave trader in Rio, on the *presentation of a draft.* In all this there is little encouragement for exertion."[1] Again, the "Perry" in 1850 captured a slaver which was about to ship 1,800 slaves. The captain admitted his guilt, and was condemned in the United States District Court at New York. Nevertheless, he was admitted to bail of $5,000; this being afterward reduced to $3,000, he forfeited it and escaped. The mate was sentenced to two years in the penitentiary.[2] Also several slavers sent home to the United States by the British, with clear evidence of guilt, escaped condemnation through technicalities.[3]

79. **Activity of the Slave-Trade, 1820–1850.** The enhanced price of slaves throughout the American slave market, brought about by the new industrial development and the laws against the slave-trade, was the irresistible temptation that drew American capital and enterprise into that traffic. In the United States, in spite of the large interstate traffic, the average price of slaves rose from about $325 in 1840, to $360 in 1850, and to $500 in 1860.[4] Brazil and Cuba offered similar inducements to smugglers, and the American flag was ready to protect such pirates. As a result, the American slave-trade finally came to be carried on principally by United States capital, in United States ships, officered by United States citizens, and under the United States flag.

Executive reports repeatedly acknowledged this fact. In

[1] *House Exec. Doc.*, 30 Cong. 2 sess. VII. No. 61, p. 18.

[2] Foote, *Africa and the American Flag*, pp. 286–90.

[3] *British and Foreign State Papers*, 1839–40, pp. 913–4.

[4] Cf. United States census reports; and Olmsted, *Cotton Kingdom.*

1839 "a careful revision of these laws" is recommended by the President, in order that "the integrity and honor of our flag may be carefully preserved."[1] In June, 1841, the President declares: "There is reason to believe that the traffic is on the increase," and advocates "vigorous efforts."[2] His message in December of the same year acknowledges: "That the American flag is grossly abused by the abandoned and profligate of other nations is but too probable."[3] The special message of 1845 explains at length that "it would seem" that a regular policy of evading the laws is carried on: American vessels with the knowledge of the owners are chartered by notorious slave dealers in Brazil, aided by English capitalists, with this intent.[4] The message of 1849 "earnestly" invites the attention of Congress "to an amendment of our existing laws relating to the African slave-trade, with a view to the effectual suppression of that barbarous traffic. It is not to be denied," continues the message, "that this trade is still, in part, carried on by means of vessels built in the United States, and owned or navigated by some of our citizens."[5] Governor Buchanan of Liberia reported in 1839: "The chief obstacle to the success of the very active measures pursued by the British government for the suppression of the slave-trade on the coast, is the *American flag*. Never was the proud banner of freedom so extensively used by those pirates upon liberty and humanity, as at this season."[6] One well-known American slaver was boarded fifteen times and twice taken into port, but always escaped by means of her papers.[7] Even American officers report that the English are doing all they can, but that the American flag protects the trade.[8] The evidence which literally poured in from our consuls and ministers at Brazil adds to the story of the

[1] *House Journal*, 26 Cong. 1 sess. p. 118.
[2] *Ibid.*, 27 Cong. 1 sess. pp. 31, 184.
[3] *Ibid.*, 27 Cong. 2 sess. pp. 14, 15, 86, 113.
[4] *Senate Journal*, 28 Cong. 2 sess. pp. 191, 227.
[5] *House Exec. Doc.*, 31 Cong. 1 sess. III. pt. I. No. 5, p. 7.
[6] Foote, *Africa and the American Flag*, p. 152.
[7] *Ibid.*, pp. 152–3.
[8] *Ibid.*, p. 241.

guilt of the United States.[1] It was proven that the participation of United States citizens in the trade was large and systematic. One of the most notorious slave merchants of Brazil said: "I am worried by the Americans, who insist upon my hiring their vessels for slave-trade."[2] Minister Proffit stated, in 1844, that the "slave-trade is almost entirely carried on under our flag, in American-built vessels."[3] So, too, in Cuba: the British commissioners affirm that American citizens were openly engaged in the traffic; vessels arrived undisguised at Havana from the United States, and cleared for Africa as slavers after an alleged sale.[4] The American consul, Trist, was proven to have consciously or unconsciously aided this trade by the issuance of blank clearance papers.[5]

The presence of American capital in these enterprises, and the connivance of the authorities, were proven in many cases and known in scores. In 1837 the English government informed the United States that from the papers of a captured slaver it appeared that the notorious slave-trading firm, Blanco and Carballo of Havana, who owned the vessel, had correspondents in the United States: "at Baltimore, Messrs. Peter Harmony and Co., in New York, Robert Barry, Esq."[6] The slaver "Martha" of New York, captured by the "Perry," contained among her papers curious revelations of the guilt of persons in America who were little suspected.[7] The slaver "Prova," which was allowed to lie in the harbor of Charleston, South Carolina, and refit, was after-

[1] Cf. e. g. *House Doc.*, 28 Cong. 2 sess. IV. pt. I. No. 148; 29 Cong. 1 sess. III. No. 43; *House Exec. Doc.*, 30 Cong. 2 sess. VII. No. 61; *Senate Exec. Doc.*, 30 Cong. 1 sess. IV. No. 28; 31 Cong. 2 sess. II. No. 6; 33 Cong. 1 sess. VIII. No. 47.

[2] Foote, *Africa and the American Flag*, p. 218.

[3] *Ibid.*, p. 221.

[4] Palmerston to Stevenson: *House Doc.*, 26 Cong. 2 sess. V. No. 115, p. 5. In 1836 five such slavers were known to have cleared; in 1837, eleven; in 1838, nineteen; and in 1839, twenty-three: *Ibid.*, pp. 220–1.

[5] *Parliamentary Papers*, 1839, Vol. XLIX., *Slave Trade*, class A, Further Series, pp. 58–9; class B, Further Series, p. 110; class D, Further Series, p. 25. Trist pleaded ignorance of the law: Trist to Forsyth, *House Doc.*, 26 Cong. 2 sess. V. No. 115.

[6] *House Doc.*, 26 Cong. 2 sess. V. No. 115.

[7] Foote, *Africa and the American Flag*, p. 290.

wards captured with two hundred and twenty-five slaves on board.[1] The real reason that prevented many belligerent Congressmen from pressing certain search claims against England lay in the fact that the unjustifiable detentions had unfortunately revealed so much American guilt that it was deemed wiser to let the matter end in talk. For instance, in 1850 Congress demanded information as to illegal searches, and President Fillmore's report showed the uncomfortable fact that, of the ten American ships wrongly detained by English men-of-war, nine were proven red-handed slavers.[2]

The consul at Havana reported, in 1836, that whole cargoes of slaves fresh from Africa were being daily shipped to Texas in American vessels, that 1,000 had been sent within a few months, that the rate was increasing, and that many of these slaves "can scarcely fail to find their way into the United States." Moreover, the consul acknowledged that ships frequently cleared for the United States in ballast, taking on a cargo at some secret point.[3] When with these facts we consider the law facilitating "recovery" of slaves from Texas,[4] the repeated refusals to regulate the Texan trade, and the shelving of a proposed congressional investigation into these matters,[5] conjecture becomes a practical certainty. It was estimated in 1838 that 15,000 Africans were annually taken to Texas, and "there are even grounds for suspicion that there are other places . . . where slaves are introduced." [6] Between 1847 and 1853 the slave smuggler Drake had a slave depot in the Gulf, where sometimes as many as 1,600 Negroes were on hand, and

[1] *House Doc.*, 26 Cong. 2 sess. V. No. 115, pp. 121, 163–6.

[2] *Senate Exec. Doc.*, 31 Cong. 1 sess. XIV. No. 66.

[3] Trist to Forsyth: *House Doc.*, 26 Cong. 2 sess. V. No. 115. "The business of supplying the United States with Africans from this island is one that must necessarily exist," because "slaves are a hundred *per cent*, or more, higher in the United States than in Cuba," and this profit "is a temptation which it is not in human nature as modified by American institutions to withstand": *Ibid.*

[4] *Statutes at Large*, V. 674.

[5] Cf. above, p. 156, note 4.

[6] Buxton, *The African Slave Trade and its Remedy*, pp. 44–5. Cf. *2d Report of the London African Soc.*, p. 22.

the owners were continually importing and shipping. "The joint-stock company," writes this smuggler, "was a very extensive one, and connected with leading American and Spanish mercantile houses. Our island[1] was visited almost weekly, by agents from Cuba, New York, Baltimore, Philadelphia, Boston, and New Orleans. . . . The seasoned and instructed slaves were taken to Texas, or Florida, overland, and to Cuba, in sailing-boats. As no squad contained more than half a dozen, no difficulty was found in posting them to the United States, without discovery, and generally without suspicion. . . . The Bay Island plantation sent ventures weekly to the Florida Keys. Slaves were taken into the great American swamps, and there kept till wanted for the market. Hundreds were sold as captured runaways from the Florida wilderness. We had agents in every slave State; and our coasters were built in Maine, and came out with lumber. I could tell curious stories . . . of this business of smuggling Bozal negroes into the United States. It is growing more profitable every year, and if you should hang all the Yankee merchants engaged in it, hundreds would fill their places."[2] Inherent probability and concurrent testimony confirm the substantial truth of such confessions. For instance, one traveller discovers on a Southern plantation Negroes who can speak no English.[3] The careful reports of the Quakers "apprehend that many [slaves] are also introduced into the United States."[4] Governor Mathew of the Bahama Islands reports that "in more than one instance, Bahama vessels with coloured crews have been purposely wrecked on the coast of Florida, and the crews forcibly sold." This was brought to the notice of the United States authorities, but the district attorney of Florida could furnish no information.[5]

[1] I. e., Bay Island in the Gulf of Mexico, near the coast of Honduras.

[2] *Revelations of a Slave Smuggler*, p. 98.

[3] Mr. H. Moulton in *Slavery as it is*, p. 140; cited in *Facts and Observations on the Slave Trade* (Friends' ed. 1841), p. 8.

[4] In a memorial to Congress, 1840: *House Doc.*, 26 Cong. 1 sess. VI. No. 211.

[5] *British and Foreign State Papers*, 1845–6, pp. 883, 968, 989–90. The governor wrote in reply: "The United States, if properly served by their law officers in the Floridas, will not experience any difficulty in obtaining

Such was the state of the slave-trade in 1850, on the threshold of the critical decade which by a herculean effort was destined finally to suppress it.

the requisite knowledge of these illegal transactions, which, I have reason to believe, were the subject of common notoriety in the neighbourhood where they occurred, and of boast on the part of those concerned in them": *British and Foreign State Papers*, 1845–6, p. 990.

CHAPTER XI.

THE FINAL CRISIS. 1850–1870.

80. **The Movement against the Slave-Trade Laws.** It was not altogether a mistaken judgment that led the constitutional fathers to consider the slave-trade as the backbone of slavery. An economic system based on slave labor will find, sooner or later, that the demand for the cheapest slave labor cannot long be withstood. Once degrade the laborer so that he cannot assert his own rights, and there is but one limit below which his price cannot be reduced. That limit is not his physical well-being, for it may be, and in the Gulf States it was, cheaper to work him rapidly to death; the limit is simply the cost of procuring him and keeping him alive a profitable length of time. Only the moral sense of a community can keep helpless labor from sinking to this level; and when a community has once been debauched by slavery, its moral sense offers little resistance to economic demand. This was the case in the West Indies and Brazil; and although better moral stamina held the crisis back longer in the United States,

yet even here the ethical standard of the South was not able to maintain itself against the demands of the cotton industry. When, after 1850, the price of slaves had risen to a monopoly height, the leaders of the plantation system, brought to the edge of bankruptcy by the crude and reckless farming necessary under a slave *régime*, and baffled, at least temporarily, in their quest of new rich land to exploit, began instinctively to feel that the only salvation of American slavery lay in the reopening of the African slave-trade.

It took but a spark to put this instinctive feeling into words, and words led to deeds. The movement first took definite form in the ever radical State of South Carolina. In 1854 a grand jury in the Williamsburg district declared, "as our unanimous opinion, that the Federal law abolishing the African Slave Trade is a public grievance. We hold this trade has been and would be, if re-established, a blessing to the American people, and a benefit to the African himself."[1] This attracted only local attention; but when, in 1856, the governor of the State, in his annual message, calmly argued at length for a reopening of the trade, and boldly declared that "if we cannot supply the demand for slave labor, then we must expect to be supplied with a species of labor we do not want,"[2] such words struck even Southern ears like "a thunder clap in a calm day."[3] And yet it needed but a few years to show that South Carolina had merely been the first to put into words the inarticulate thought of a large minority, if not a majority, of the inhabitants of the Gulf States.

81. **Commercial Conventions of 1855–56.** The growth of the movement is best followed in the action of the Southern Commercial Convention, an annual gathering which seems to have been fairly representative of a considerable part of Southern opinion. In the convention that met at New Orleans in 1855, McGimsey of Louisiana introduced a resolution instructing the Southern Congressmen to secure the repeal of the slave-trade laws. This resolution went to the Committee on Resolutions,

[1] *British and Foreign State Papers*, 1854–5, p. 1156.

[2] Cluskey, *Political Text-Book* (14th ed.), p. 585.

[3] *De Bow's Review*, XXII. 223; quoted from Andrew Hunter of Virginia.

and was not reported.[1] In 1856, in the convention at Savannah, W. B. Goulden of Georgia moved that the members of Congress be requested to bestir themselves energetically to have repealed all laws which forbade the slave-trade. By a vote of 67 to 18 the convention refused to debate the motion, but appointed a committee to present at the next convention the facts relating to a reopening of the trade.[2] In regard to this action a pamphlet of the day said: "There were introduced into the convention two leading measures, viz.: the laying of a State tariff on northern goods, and the reopening of the slave-trade; the one to advance our commercial interest, the other our agricultural interest, and which, when taken together, as they were doubtless intended to be, and although they have each been attacked by presses of doubtful service to the South, are characterized in the private judgment of politicians as one of the completest southern remedies ever submitted to popular action. . . . The proposition to revive, or more properly to reopen, the slave trade is as yet but imperfectly understood, in its intentions and probable results, by the people of the South, and but little appreciated by them. It has been received in all parts of the country with an undefined sort of repugnance, a sort of squeamishness, which is incident to all such violations of moral prejudices, and invariably wears off on familiarity with the subject. The South will commence by enduring, and end by embracing the project."[3] The matter being now fully before the public through these motions, Governor Adams's message, and newspaper and pamphlet discussion, the radical party pushed the project with all energy.

82. **Commercial Conventions of 1857–58.** The first piece of regular business that came before the Commercial Convention at Knoxville, Tennessee, August 10, 1857, was a proposal to recommend the abrogation of the 8th Article of the Treaty of Washington, on the slave-trade. An amendment offered by

[1] *De Bow's Review*, XVIII. 628.

[2] *Ibid.*, XXII. 91, 102, 217, 221–2.

[3] From a pamphlet entitled "A New Southern Policy, or the Slave Trade as meaning Union and Conservatism;" quoted in Etheridge's speech, Feb. 21, 1857: *Congressional Globe*, 34 Cong. 3 sess., Appendix, p. 366.

Sneed of Tennessee, declaring it inexpedient and against settled policy to reopen the trade, was voted down, Alabama, Arkansas, Florida, Louisiana, Mississippi, South Carolina, and Virginia refusing to agree to it. The original motion then passed; and the radicals, satisfied with their success in the first skirmish, again secured the appointment of a committee to report at the next meeting on the subject of reopening the slave-trade.[1] This next meeting assembled May 10, 1858, in a Gulf State, Alabama, in the city of Montgomery. Spratt of South Carolina, the slave-trade champion, presented an elaborate majority report from the committee, and recommended the following resolutions: —

1. *Resolved*, That slavery is right, and that being right, there can be no wrong in the natural means to its formation.

2. *Resolved*, That it is expedient and proper that the foreign slave trade should be re-opened, and that this Convention will lend its influence to any legitimate measure to that end.

3. *Resolved*, That a committee, consisting of one from each slave State, be appointed to consider of the means, consistent with the duty and obligations of these States, for re-opening the foreign slave-trade, and that they report their plan to the next meeting of this Convention.

Yancey, from the same committee, presented a minority report, which, though it demanded the repeal of the national prohibitory laws, did not advocate the reopening of the trade by the States.

Much debate ensued. Pryor of Virginia declared the majority report "a proposition to dissolve the Union." Yancey declared that "he was for disunion now. [Applause.]" He defended the principle of the slave-trade, and said: "If it is right to buy slaves in Virginia and carry them to New Orleans, why is it not right to buy them in Cuba, Brazil, or Africa, and carry them there?" The opposing speeches made little attempt to meet

[1] *De Bow's Review*, XXIII. 298–320. A motion to table the motion on the 8th article was supported only by Kentucky, Tennessee, North Carolina, and Maryland. Those voting for Sneed's motion were Georgia, Maryland, North Carolina, and Tennessee. The appointment of a slave-trade committee was at first defeated by a vote of 48 to 44. Finally a similar motion was passed, 52 to 40.

this uncomfortable logic; but, nevertheless, opposition enough was developed to lay the report on the table until the next convention, with orders that it be printed, in the mean time, as a radical campaign document. Finally the convention passed a resolution: —

That it is inexpedient for any State, or its citizens, to attempt to re-open the African slave-trade while that State is one of the United States of America.[1]

83. **Commercial Convention of 1859.** The Convention of 1859 met at Vicksburg, Mississippi, May 9–19, and the slave-trade party came ready for a fray. On the second day Spratt called up his resolutions, and the next day the Committee on Resolutions recommended that, "*in the opinion of this Convention, all laws, State or Federal, prohibiting the African slave trade, ought to be repealed.*" Two minority reports accompanied this resolution: one proposed to postpone action, on account of the futility of the attempt at that time; the other report recommended that, since repeal of the national laws was improbable, nullification by the States impracticable, and action by the Supreme Court unlikely, therefore the States should bring in the Africans as apprentices, a system the legality of which "is incontrovertible." "The only difficult question," it was said, "is the future status of the apprentices after the expiration of their term of servitude."[2] Debate on these propositions began in the afternoon. A brilliant speech on the resumption of the importation of slaves, says Foote of Mississippi, "was listened to with breathless attention and applauded vociferously. Those of us who rose in opposition were looked upon by the excited assemblage present as *traitors* to the best interests of the South, and only worthy of expulsion from the body. The excitement at last grew so high that personal violence was menaced, and some dozen of the more conservative members of the convention withdrew from the hall in which it was holding its sittings."[3]

[1] *De Bow's Review*, XXIV. 473–491, 579–605. The Louisiana delegation alone did not vote for the last resolution, the vote of her delegation being evenly divided.

[2] *Ibid.*, XXVII. 94–235.

[3] H. S. Foote, in *Bench and Bar of the South and Southwest*, p. 69.

"It was clear," adds De Bow, "that the people of Vicksburg looked upon it [i. e., the convention] with some distrust."[1] When at last a ballot was taken, the first resolution passed by a vote of 40 to 19.[2] Finally, the 8th Article of the Treaty of Washington was again condemned; and it was also suggested, in the newspaper which was the official organ of the meeting, that "the Convention raise a fund to be dispensed in premiums for the best sermons in favor of reopening the African Slave Trade."[3]

84. **Public Opinion in the South.** This record of the Commercial Conventions probably gives a true reflection of the development of extreme opinion on the question of reopening the slave-trade. First, it is noticeable that on this point there was a distinct divergence of opinion and interest between the Gulf and the Border States, and it was this more than any moral repugnance that checked the radicals. The whole movement represented the economic revolt of the slave-consuming cotton-belt against their base of labor supply. This revolt was only prevented from gaining its ultimate end by the fact that the Gulf States could not get on without the active political co-operation of the Border States. Thus, although such hot-heads as Spratt were not able, even as late as 1859, to carry a substantial majority of the South with them in an attempt to reopen the trade at all hazards, yet the agitation did succeed in sweeping away nearly all theoretical opposition to the trade, and left

[1] *De Bow's Review*, XXVII. 115.

[2] *Ibid.*, p. 99. The vote was: —

Yea.		*Nay.*	
Alabama,	5 votes.	Tennessee,	12 votes.
Arkansas,	4 "	Florida,	3 "
South Carolina,	4 "	South Carolina,	4 "
Louisiana,	6 "		—
Texas,	4 "	Total	19
Georgia,	10 "		
Mississippi,	7 "		
	—		
Total	40		

Virginia, Maryland, Kentucky, and North Carolina did not vote; they either withdrew or were not represented.

[3] Quoted in *26th Report of the Amer. Anti-slav. Soc.*, p. 38. The official organ was the *True Southron*.

the majority of Southern people in an attitude which regarded the reopening of the African slave-trade as merely a question of expediency.

This growth of Southern opinion is clearly to be followed in the newspapers and pamphlets of the day, in Congress, and in many significant movements. The Charleston *Standard* in a series of articles strongly advocated the reopening of the trade; the Richmond *Examiner*, though opposing the scheme as a Virginia paper should, was brought to "acknowledge that the laws which condemn the Slave-trade imply an aspersion upon the character of the South.[1] In March, 1859, the *National Era* said: "There can be no doubt that the idea of reviving the African Slave Trade is gaining ground in the South. Some two months ago we could quote strong articles from ultra Southern journals against the traffic; but of late we have been sorry to observe in the same journals an ominous silence upon the subject, while the advocates of 'free trade in negroes' are earnest and active."[2] The Savannah *Republican*, which at first declared the movement to be of no serious intent, conceded, in 1859, that it was gaining favor, and that nine-tenths of the Democratic Congressional Convention favored it, and that even those who did not advocate a revival demanded the abolition of the laws.[3] A correspondent from South Carolina writes, December 18, 1859: "The nefarious project of opening it [i. e., the slave trade] has been started here in that prurient temper of the times which manifests itself in disunion schemes. . . . My State is strangely and terribly infected with all this sort of thing. . . . One feeling that gives a countenance to the opening of the slave trade is, that it will be a sort of spite to the North and defiance of their opinions."[4] The New Orleans *Delta* declared that those who voted for the slave-trade in Congress were men "whose names will be honored hereafter for the unflinching manner in which they

[1] Quoted in *24th Report of the Amer. Anti-slav. Soc.*, p. 54.

[2] Quoted in *26th Report*, *Ibid.*, p. 43.

[3] *27th Report*, *Ibid.*, pp. 19–20.

[4] Letter of W. C. Preston, in the *National Intelligencer*, April 3, 1863. Also published in the pamphlet, *The African Slave Trade: The Secret Purpose*, etc., p. 26.

stood up for principle, for truth, and consistency, as well as the vital interests of the South."[1]

85. **The Question in Congress.** Early in December, 1856, the subject reached Congress; and although the agitation was then new, fifty-seven Southern Congressmen refused to declare a re-opening of the slave-trade "shocking to the moral sentiment of the enlightened portion of mankind," and eight refused to call the reopening even "unwise" and "inexpedient."[2] Three years later, January 31, 1859, it was impossible, in a House of one hundred and ninety-nine members, to get a two-thirds vote in order even to consider Kilgore's resolutions, which declared "that no legislation can be too thorough in its measures, nor can any penalty known to the catalogue of modern punishment for crime be too severe against a traffic so inhuman and unchristian."[3]

Congressmen and other prominent men hastened with the rising tide.[4] Dowdell of Alabama declared the repressive acts "highly offensive;" J. B. Clay of Kentucky was "opposed to all these laws;"[5] Seward of Georgia declared them "wrong, and a violation of the Constitution;"[6] Barksdale of Mississippi agreed with this sentiment; Crawford of Georgia threatened a reopening of the trade; Miles of South Carolina was for "sweeping away" all restrictions;[7] Keitt of South Carolina wished to withdraw the African squadron, and to cease to brand slave-trading as piracy;[8] Brown of Mississippi "would repeal the law instantly;"[9] Alexander Stephens, in his farewell address to his constituents, said: "Slave states cannot be made with-

[1] Quoted in Etheridge's speech: *Congressional Globe*, 34 Cong. 3 sess. Appen., p. 366.

[2] *House Journal*, 34 Cong. 3 sess. pp. 105–10; *Congressional Globe*, 34 Cong. 3 sess. pp. 123–6; Cluskey, *Political Text-Book* (14th ed.), p. 589.

[3] *House Journal*, 35 Cong. 2 sess. pp. 298–9. Cf. *26th Report of the Amer. Anti-slav. Soc.*, p. 45.

[4] Cf. *Reports of the Amer. Anti-slav. Soc.*, especially the 26th, pp. 43–4.

[5] *Ibid.*, p. 43. He referred especially to the Treaty of 1842.

[6] *Ibid.; Congressional Globe*, 35 Cong. 2 sess., Appen., pp. 248–50.

[7] *26th Report of the Amer. Anti-slav. Soc.*, p. 44.

[8] *Ibid.; 27th Report*, pp. 13–4.

[9] *26th Report, Ibid.*, p. 44.

out Africans. . . . [My object is] to bring clearly to your mind the great truth that without an increase of African slaves from abroad, you may not expect or look for many more slave States."[1] Jefferson Davis strongly denied "any coincidence of opinion with those who prate of the inhumanity and sinfulness of the trade. The interest of Mississippi," said he, "not of the African, dictates my conclusion." He opposed the immediate reopening of the trade in Mississippi for fear of a paralyzing influx of Negroes, but carefully added: "This conclusion, in relation to Mississippi, is based upon my view of her *present* condition, *not* upon any *general theory*. It is not supposed to be applicable to Texas, to New Mexico, or to any *future acquisitions* to be made south of the Rio Grande."[2] John Forsyth, who for seven years conducted the slave-trade diplomacy of the nation, declared, about 1860: "But one stronghold of its [i. e., slavery's] enemies remains to be carried, to *complete its triumph* and assure its welfare, — that is the existing prohibition of the African Slave-trade."[3] Pollard, in his *Black Diamonds*, urged the importation of Africans as "laborers." "This I grant you," said he, "would be practically the re-opening of the African slave trade; but . . . you will find that it very often becomes necessary to evade the letter of the law, in some of the greatest measures of social happiness and patriotism."[4]

86. **Southern Policy in 1860.** The matter did not rest with mere words. During the session of the Vicksburg Convention, an "African Labor Supply Association" was formed, under the presidency of J. D. B. De Bow, editor of *De Bow's Review*, and ex-superintendent of the seventh census. The object of the association was "to promote the supply of African labor."[5] In 1857 the committee of the South Carolina legislature to

[1] Quoted in Lalor, *Cyclopædia*, III. 733; Cairnes, *The Slave Power* (New York, 1862), p. 123, note; *27th Report of the Amer. Anti-slav. Soc.*, p. 15.

[2] Quoted in Cairnes, *The Slave Power*, p. 123, note; *27th Report of the Amer. Anti-slav. Soc.*, p. 19.

[3] *27th Report*, *Ibid.*, p. 16; quoted from the Mobile *Register*.

[4] Edition of 1859, pp. 63–4.

[5] *De Bow's Review*, XXVII. 121, 231–5.

whom the Governor's slave-trade message was referred made an elaborate report, which declared in italics: "*The South at large does need a re-opening of the African slave trade.*" Pettigrew, the only member who disagreed to this report, failed of re-election. The report contained an extensive argument to prove the kingship of cotton, the perfidy of English philanthropy, and the lack of slaves in the South, which, it was said, would show a deficit of six hundred thousand slaves by 1878.[1] In Georgia, about this time, an attempt to expunge the slave-trade prohibition in the State Constitution lacked but one vote of passing.[2] From these slower and more legal movements came others less justifiable. The long argument on the "apprentice" system finally brought a request to the collector of the port at Charleston, South Carolina, from E. Lafitte & Co., for a clearance to Africa for the purpose of importing African "emigrants." The collector appealed to the Secretary of the Treasury, Howell Cobb of Georgia, who flatly refused to take the bait, and replied that if the "emigrants" were brought in as slaves, it would be contrary to United States law; if as freemen, it would be contrary to their own State law.[3] In Louisiana a still more radical movement was attempted, and a bill passed the House of Representatives authorizing a company to import two thousand five hundred Africans, "indentured" for fifteen years "at least." The bill lacked but two votes of passing the Senate.[4] It was said that the *Georgian*, of Savannah, contained a notice of an agricultural society which "unanimously resolved to offer a premium of $25 for the best specimen of a live African imported into the United States within the last twelve months."[5]

It would not be true to say that there was in the South in 1860 substantial unanimity on the subject of reopening the

1 *Report of the Special Committee*, etc. (1857), pp. 24–5.

2 *26th Report of the Amer. Anti-slav. Soc.*, p. 40. The vote was 47 to 46.

3 *House Exec. Doc.*, 36 Cong. 2 sess. IV. No. 7, pp. 632–6. For the State law, cf. above, Chapter II. This refusal of Cobb's was sharply criticised by many Southern papers. Cf. *26th Report of the Amer. Anti-slav. Soc.*, p. 39.

4 New York *Independent*, March 11 and April 1, 1858.

5 *26th Report of the Amer. Anti-slav. Soc.*, p. 41.

slave-trade; nevertheless, there certainly was a large and influential minority, including perhaps a majority of citizens of the Gulf States, who favored the project, and, in defiance of law and morals, aided and abetted its actual realization. Various movements, it must be remembered, gained much of their strength from the fact that their success meant a partial nullification of the slave-trade laws. The admission of Texas added probably seventy-five thousand recently imported slaves to the Southern stock; the movement against Cuba, which culminated in the "Ostend Manifesto" of Buchanan, Mason, and Soulé, had its chief impetus in the thousands of slaves whom Americans had poured into the island. Finally, the series of filibustering expeditions against Cuba, Mexico, and Central America were but the wilder and more irresponsible attempts to secure both slave territory and slaves.

87. **Increase of the Slave-Trade from 1850 to 1860.** The long and open agitation for the reopening of the slave-trade, together with the fact that the South had been more or less familiar with violations of the laws since 1808, led to such a remarkable increase of illicit traffic and actual importations in the decade 1850–1860, that the movement may almost be termed a reopening of the slave-trade.

In the foreign slave-trade our own officers continue to report "how shamefully our flag has been used;"[1] and British officers write "that at least one half of the successful part of the slave trade is carried on under the American flag," and this because "the number of American cruisers on the station is so small, in proportion to the immense extent of the slave-dealing coast."[2] The fitting out of slavers became a flourishing business in the United States, and centred at New York City. "Few of our readers," writes a periodical of the day, "are aware of the extent to which this infernal traffic is carried on, by vessels clearing from New York, and in close alliance with our legitimate trade; and that down-town merchants of wealth

[1] Gregory to the Secretary of the Navy, June 8, 1850: *Senate Exec. Doc.*, 31 Cong. 1 sess. XIV. No. 66, p. 2. Cf. *Ibid.*, 31 Cong. 2 sess. II. No. 6.

[2] Cumming to Commodore Fanshawe, Feb. 22, 1850: *Senate Exec. Doc.*, 31 Cong. 1 sess. XIV. No. 66, p. 8.

and respectability are extensively engaged in buying and selling African Negroes, and have been, with comparatively little interruption, for an indefinite number of years."[1] Another periodical says: "The number of persons engaged in the slave-trade, and the amount of capital embarked in it, exceed our powers of calculation. The city of New York has been until of late [1862] the principal port of the world for this infamous commerce; although the cities of Portland and Boston are only second to her in that distinction. Slave dealers added largely to the wealth of our commercial metropolis; they contributed liberally to the treasuries of political organizations, and their bank accounts were largely depleted to carry elections in New Jersey, Pennsylvania, and Connecticut."[2] During eighteen months of the years 1859–1860 eighty-five slavers are reported to have been fitted out in New York harbor,[3] and these alone transported from 30,000 to 60,000 slaves annually.[4] The United States deputy marshal of that district declared in 1856 that the business of fitting out slavers "was never prosecuted with greater energy than at present. The occasional interposition of the legal authorities exercises no apparent influence for its suppression. It is seldom that one or more vessels cannot be designated at the wharves, respecting which there is evidence that she is either in or has been concerned in the Traffic."[5] On the coast of Africa "it is a well-known fact that most of the Slave ships which visit the river are sent from New York and New Orleans."[6]

[1] New York *Journal of Commerce*, 1857; quoted in *24th Report of the Amer. Anti-slav. Soc.*, p. 56.

[2] "The Slave-Trade in New York," in the *Continental Monthly*, January, 1862, p. 87.

[3] New York *Evening Post;* quoted in Lalor, *Cyclopædia*, III. 733.

[4] Lalor, *Cyclopædia*, III. 733; quoted from a New York paper.

[5] *Friends' Appeal on behalf of the Coloured Races* (1858), Appendix, p. 41; quoted from the *Journal of Commerce*.

[6] *26th Report of the Amer. Anti-slav. Soc.*, pp. 53–4; quoted from the African correspondent of the Boston *Journal*. From April, 1857, to May, 1858, twenty-one of twenty-two slavers which were seized by British cruisers proved to be American, from New York, Boston, and New Orleans. Cf. *25th Report, Ibid.*, p. 122. De Bow estimated in 1856 that forty slavers

The absence of United States war-ships at the Brazilian station enabled American smugglers to run in cargoes, in spite of the prohibitory law. One cargo of five hundred slaves was landed in 1852, and the *Correio Mercantil* regrets "that it was the flag of the United States which covered this act of piracy, sustained by citizens of that great nation."[1] When the Brazil trade declined, the illicit Cuban trade greatly increased, and the British consul reported: "Almost all the slave expeditions for some time past have been fitted out in the United States, chiefly at New York."[2]

88. **Notorious Infractions of the Laws.** This decade is especially noteworthy for the great increase of illegal importations into the South. These became bold, frequent, and notorious. Systematic introduction on a considerable scale probably commenced in the forties, although with great secrecy. "To have boldly ventured into New Orleans, with negroes freshly imported from Africa, would not only have brought down upon the head of the importer the vengeance of our very philanthropic Uncle Sam, but also the anathemas of the whole sect of philanthropists and negrophilists everywhere. To import them for years, however, into quiet places, evading with impunity the penalty of the law, and the ranting of the thin-skinned sympathizers with Africa, was gradually to popularize the traffic by creating a demand for laborers, and thus to pave the way for the *gradual revival of the slave trade.* To this end, a few men, bold and energetic, determined, ten or twelve years ago [1848 or 1850], to commence the business of importing negroes, slowly at first, but surely; and for this purpose they selected a few secluded places on the coast of Florida, Georgia and Texas, for the purpose of concealing their stock until it could be sold out. Without specifying other places, let me draw your attention to a deep and abrupt pocket or indentation in the coast of Texas, about thirty miles from Brazos Santiago. Into this pocket a slaver could run at any

cleared annually from Eastern harbors, clearing yearly $17,000,000: *De Bow's Review*, XXII. 430–1.

[1] *Senate Exec. Doc.*, 33 Cong. 1 sess. VIII. No. 47, p. 13.

[2] *House Exec. Doc.*, 34 Cong. 1 sess. XII. No. 105, p. 38.

hour of the night, because there was no hindrance at the entrance, and here she could discharge her cargo of movables upon the projecting bluff, and again proceed to sea inside of three hours. The live stock thus landed could be marched a short distance across the main island, over a porous soil which refuses to retain the recent foot-prints, until they were again placed in boats, and were concealed upon some of the innumerable little islands which thicken on the waters of the Laguna in the rear. These islands, being covered with a thick growth of bushes and grass, offer an inscrutable hiding place for the 'black diamonds.'"[1] These methods became, however, toward 1860, too slow for the radicals, and the trade grew more defiant and open. The yacht "Wanderer," arrested on suspicion in New York and released, landed in Georgia six months later four hundred and twenty slaves, who were never recovered.[2] The Augusta *Despatch* says: "Citizens of our city are probably interested in the enterprise. It is hinted that this is the third cargo landed by the same company, during the last six months."[3] Two parties of Africans were brought into Mobile with impunity. One bark, strongly suspected of having landed a cargo of slaves, was seized on the Florida coast; another vessel was reported to be landing slaves near Mobile; a letter from Jacksonville, Florida, stated that a bark had left there for Africa to ship a cargo for Florida and Georgia.[4] Stephen A. Douglas said "that there was not the shadow of doubt that the Slave-trade had been carried on quite extensively for a long time back, and that there had been more Slaves imported into the southern States, during the last year, than had ever been imported before in any one year, even when the Slave-trade was legal. It was his confident belief, that over fifteen thousand Slaves had been brought into this country during the past year [1859.] He had seen, with his

[1] New York *Herald*, Aug. 5, 1860; quoted in Drake, *Revelations of a Slave Smuggler*, Introd., pp. vii.–viii.

[2] *House Exec. Doc.*, 35 Cong. 2 sess. IX. No. 89. Cf. *26th Report of the Amer. Anti-slav. Soc.*, pp. 45–9.

[3] Quoted in *26th Report*, *Ibid.*, p. 46.

[4] For all the above cases, cf. *Ibid.*, p. 49.

own eyes, three hundred of those recently-imported, miserable beings, in a Slave-pen in Vicksburg, Miss., and also large numbers at Memphis, Tenn."[1] It was currently reported that depots for these slaves existed in over twenty large cities and towns in the South, and an interested person boasted to a senator, about 1860, that "twelve vessels would discharge their living freight upon our shores within ninety days from the 1st of June last," and that between sixty and seventy cargoes had been successfully introduced in the last eighteen months.[2] The New York *Tribune* doubted the statement; but 'John C. Underwood, formerly of Virginia, wrote to the paper saying that he was satisfied that the correspondent was correct. "I have," he said, "had ample evidences of the fact, that reopening the African Slave-trade is a thing already accomplished, and the traffic is brisk, and rapidly increasing. In fact, the most vital question of the day is not the opening of this trade, but its suppression. The arrival of cargoes of negroes, fresh from Africa, in our southern ports, is an event of frequent occurrence."[3]

Negroes, newly landed, were openly advertised for sale in the public press, and bids for additional importations made. In reply to one of these, the Mobile *Mercury* facetiously remarks: "Some negroes who never learned to talk English, went up the railroad the other day."[4] Congressmen declared on the floor of the House: "The slave trade may therefore be regarded

[1] Quoted in *27th Report, Ibid.*, p. 20. Cf. *Report of the Secretary of the Navy*, 1859: *Senate Exec. Doc.*, 36 Cong. 1 sess. III. No. 2.

[2] *27th Report of the Amer. Anti-slav. Soc.*, p. 21.

[3] Quoted in *Ibid.*

[4] Issue of July 22, 1860; quoted in Drake, *Revelations of a Slave Smuggler*, Introd., p. vi. The advertisement referred to was addressed to the "Shipowners and Masters of our Mercantile Marine," and appeared in the Enterprise (Miss.) *Weekly News*, April 14, 1859. William S. Price and seventeen others state that they will "pay three hundred dollars per head for one thousand native Africans, between the ages of fourteen and twenty years, (of sexes equal,) likely, sound, and healthy, to be delivered within twelve months from this date, at some point accessible by land, between Pensacola, Fla., and Galveston, Texas; the contractors giving thirty days' notice as to time and place of delivery": Quoted in *26th Report of the Amer. Anti-slav. Soc.*, pp. 41–2.

as practically re-established;"[1] and petitions like that from the American Missionary Society recited the fact that "this piratical and illegal trade — this inhuman invasion of the rights of men, — this outrage on civilization and Christianity — this violation of the laws of God and man — is openly countenanced and encouraged by a portion of the citizens of some of the States of this Union."[2]

From such evidence it seems clear that the slave-trade laws, in spite of the efforts of the government, in spite even of much opposition to these extra-legal methods in the South itself, were grossly violated, if not nearly nullified, in the latter part of the decade 1850–1860.

89. **Apathy of the Federal Government.** During the decade there was some attempt at reactionary legislation, chiefly directed at the Treaty of Washington. June 13, 1854, Slidell, from the Committee on Foreign Relations, made an elaborate report to the Senate, advocating the abrogation of the 8th Article of that treaty, on the ground that it was costly, fatal to the health of the sailors, and useless, as the trade had actually increased under its operation.[3] Both this and a similar attempt in the House failed,[4] as did also an attempt to substitute life imprisonment for the death penalty.[5] Most of the actual legislation naturally took the form of appropriations. In 1853 there was an attempt to appropriate $20,000.[6] This failed, and the appropriation of

[1] *Congressional Globe*, 35 Cong. 1 sess. p. 1362. Cf. the speech of a delegate from Georgia to the Democratic Convention at Charleston, 1860: "If any of you northern democrats will go home with me to my plantation, I will show you some darkies that I bought in Virginia, some in Delaware, some in Florida, and I will also show you the pure African, the noblest Roman of them all. I represent the African slave trade interest of my section:" Lalor, *Cyclopædia*, III. 733.

[2] *Senate Misc. Doc.*, 36 Cong. 1 sess. No. 8.

[3] *Senate Journal*, 34 Cong. 1–2 sess. pp. 396, 695–8; *Senate Reports*, 34 Cong. 1 sess. I. No. 195.

[4] *House Journal*, 31 Cong. 2 sess. p. 64. There was still another attempt by Sandidge. Cf. *26th Report of the Amer. Anti-Slav. Soc.*, p. 44.

[5] *Senate Journal*, 36 Cong. 1 sess. p. 274; *Congressional Globe*, 36 Cong. 1 sess. p. 1245.

[6] *Congressional Globe*, 32 Cong. 2 sess. p. 1072.

$8,000 in 1856 was the first for ten years.[1] The following year brought a similar appropriation,[2] and in 1859 [3] and 1860 [4] $75,000 and $40,000 respectively were appropriated. Of attempted legislation to strengthen the laws there was plenty: e. g., propositions to regulate the issue of sea-letters and the use of our flag; [5] to prevent the "coolie" trade, or the bringing in of "apprentices" or "African laborers;" [6] to stop the coastwise trade; [7] to assent to a Right of Search; [8] and to amend the Constitution by forever prohibiting the slave-trade.[9]

The efforts of the executive during this period were criminally lax and negligent. "The General Government did not exert itself in good faith to carry out either its treaty stipulations or the legislation of Congress in regard to the matter. If a vessel was captured, her owners were permitted to bond her, and thus continue her in the trade; and if any man was convicted of this form of piracy, the executive always interposed between him and the penalty of his crime. The laws providing for the seizure of vessels engaged in the traffic were so constructed as to render the duty unremunerative; and marshals now find their fees for such

[1] I. e., since 1846: *Statutes at Large*, XI. 90.

[2] *Ibid.*, XI. 227.

[3] *Ibid.*, XI. 404.

[4] *Ibid.*, XII. 21.

[5] E. g., Clay's resolutions: *Congressional Globe*, 31 Cong. 2 sess. pp. 304–9. Clayton's resolutions: *Senate Journal*, 33 Cong. 1 sess. p. 404; *House Journal*, 33 Cong. 1 sess. pp. 1093, 1332–3; *Congressional Globe*, 33 Cong. 1 sess. pp. 1591–3, 2139. Seward's bill: *Senate Journal*, 33 Cong. 1 sess. pp. 448, 451.

[6] Mr. Blair of Missouri asked unanimous consent in Congress, Dec. 23, 1858, to a resolution instructing the Judiciary Committee to bring in such a bill; Houston of Alabama objected: *Congressional Globe*, 35 Cong. 2 sess. p. 198; *26th Report of the Amer. Anti-slav. Soc.*, p. 44.

[7] This was the object of attack in 1851 and 1853 by Giddings: *House Journal*, 32 Cong. 1 sess. p. 42; 33 Cong. 1 sess. p. 147. Cf. *House Journal*, 38 Cong. 1 sess. p. 46.

[8] By Mr. Wilson, March 20, 1860: *Senate Journal*, 36 Cong. 1 sess. p. 274.

[9] Four or five such attempts were made: Dec. 12, 1860, *House Journal*, 36 Cong. 2 sess. pp. 61–2; Jan. 7, 1861, *Congressional Globe*, 36 Cong. 2 sess. p. 279; Jan. 23, 1861, *Ibid.*, p. 527; Feb. 1, 1861, *Ibid.*, p. 690; Feb. 27, 1861, *Ibid.*, pp. 1243, 1259.

services to be actually less than their necessary expenses. No one who bears this fact in mind will be surprised at the great indifference of these officers to the continuing of the slave-trade; in fact, he will be ready to learn that the laws of Congress upon the subject had become a dead letter, and that the suspicion was well grounded that certain officers of the Federal Government had actually connived at their violation."[1] From 1845 to 1854, in spite of the well-known activity of the trade, but five cases obtained cognizance in the New York district. Of these, Captains Mansfield and Driscoll forfeited their bonds of $5,000 each, and escaped; in the case of the notorious Canot, nothing had been done as late as 1856, although he was arrested in 1847; Captain Jefferson turned State's evidence, and, in the case of Captain Mathew, a *nolle prosequi* was entered.[2] Between 1854 and 1856 thirty-two persons were indicted in New York, of whom only thirteen had at the latter date been tried, and only one of these convicted.[3] These dismissals were seldom on account of insufficient evidence. In the notorious case of the "Wanderer," she was arrested on suspicion, released, and soon after she landed a cargo of slaves in Georgia; some who attempted to seize the Negroes were arrested for larceny, and in spite of the efforts of Congress the captain was never punished. The yacht was afterwards started on another voyage, and being brought back to Boston was sold to her former owner for about one third her value.[4] The bark "Emily" was seized on suspicion and released, and finally caught red-handed on the coast of Africa; she was sent to New York for trial, but "disappeared" under a certain slave captain, Townsend, who had, previous to this, in the face of the most convincing evidence, been acquitted at Key West.[5]

The squadron commanders of this time were by no means as

1 "The Slave-Trade in New York," in the *Continental Monthly*, January, 1862, p. 87.

2 New York *Herald*, July 14, 1856.

3 *Ibid.* Cf. *Senate Exec. Doc.*, 37 Cong. 2 sess. V. No. 53.

4 *27th Report of the Amer. Anti-slav. Soc.*, pp. 25–6. Cf. *26th Report, Ibid.*, pp. 45–9.

5 *27th Report, Ibid.*, pp. 26–7.

efficient as their predecessors, and spent much of their time, apparently, in discussing the Right of Search. Instead of a number of small light vessels, which by the reports of experts were repeatedly shown to be the only efficient craft, the government, until 1859, persisted in sending out three or four great frigates. Even these did not attend faithfully to their duties. A letter from on board one of them shows that, out of a fifteen months' alleged service, only twenty-two days were spent on the usual cruising-ground for slavers, and thirteen of these at anchor; eleven months were spent at Madeira and Cape Verde Islands, 300 miles from the coast and 3,000 miles from the slave market.[1] British commanders report the apathy of American officers and the extreme caution of their instructions, which allowed many slavers to escape.[2]

The officials at Washington often remained in blissful, and perhaps willing, ignorance of the state of the trade. While Americans were smuggling slaves by the thousands into Brazil, and by the hundreds into the United States, Secretary Graham was recommending the abrogation of the 8th Article of the Treaty of Washington;[3] so, too, when the Cuban slave-trade was reaching unprecedented activity, and while slavers were being fitted out in every port on the Atlantic seaboard, Secretary Kennedy naïvely reports: "The time has come, perhaps, when it may be properly commended to the notice of Congress to inquire into the necessity of further continuing the regular employment of a squadron on this [i. e., the African] coast."[4] Again, in 1855, the government has "advices that the slave trade south of the equator is entirely broken up;"[5] in 1856, the reports are "favorable;"[6] in 1857 a British commander writes: "No vessel has been seen here for one year, certainly; I think for nearly three years there have been no American cruizers on these waters, where a valuable and extensive Ameri-

[1] *26th Report of the Amer. Anti-Slav. Soc.*, p. 54.

[2] *British and Foreign State Papers*, 1859–60, pp. 899, 973.

[3] Nov. 29, 1851: *House Exec. Doc.*, 32 Cong. 1 sess. II. pt. 2, No. 2, p. 4.

[4] Dec. 4, 1852: *Ibid.*, 32 Cong. 2 sess. I. pt. 2, No. 1, p. 293.

[5] *Ibid.*, 34 Cong. 1 sess. I. pt. 3, No. 1, p. 5.

[6] *Ibid.*, 34 Cong. 3 sess. I. pt. 2, No. 1, p. 407.

can commerce is carried on. I cannot, therefore, but think that this continued absence of foreign cruizers looks as if they were intentionally withdrawn, and as if the Government did not care to take measures to prevent the American flag being used to cover Slave Trade transactions;"[1] nevertheless, in this same year, according to Secretary Toucey, "the force on the coast of Africa has fully accomplished its main object."[2] Finally, in the same month in which the "Wanderer" and her mates were openly landing cargoes in the South, President Buchanan, who seems to have been utterly devoid of a sense of humor, was urging the annexation of Cuba to the United States as the only method of suppressing the slave-trade![3]

About 1859 the frequent and notorious violations of our laws aroused even the Buchanan government; a larger appropriation was obtained, swift light steamers were employed, and, though we may well doubt whether after such a carnival illegal importations "entirely" ceased, as the President informed Congress,[4] yet some sincere efforts at suppression were certainly begun. From 1850 to 1859 we have few notices of captured slavers, but in 1860 the increased appropriation of the thirty-fifth Congress resulted in the capture of twelve vessels with 3,119 Africans.[5] The Act of June 16, 1860, enabled the President to contract with the Colonization Society for the return of recaptured Africans; and by a long-needed arrangement cruisers were to proceed direct to Africa with such cargoes, instead of first landing them in this country.[6]

1 Commander Burgess to Commodore Wise, Whydah, Aug. 12, 1857: *Parliamentary Papers*, 1857–8, vol. LXI. *Slave Trade*, Class A, p. 136.

2 *House Exec. Doc.*, 35 Cong. 1 sess. II. pt. 3, No. 2, p. 576.

3 *Ibid.*, 35 Cong. 2 sess. II. pt. 1, No. 2, pp. 14–15, 31–33.

4 *Senate Exec. Doc.*, 36 Cong. 2 sess. I. No. 1, p. 24. The Report of the Secretary of the Navy, 1859, contains this ambiguous passage: "What the effect of breaking up the trade will be upon the United States or Cuba it is not necessary to inquire; certainly, under the laws of Congress and our treaty obligations, it is the duty of the executive government to see that our citizens shall not be engaged in it": *Ibid.*, 36 Cong. 1 sess. III. No. 2, pp. 1138–9.

5 *Ibid.*, 36 Cong. 2 sess. III. pt. 1, No. 1, pp. 8–9.

6 *Statutes at Large*, XII. 40.

90. **Attitude of the Southern Confederacy.** The attempt, initiated by the constitutional fathers, to separate the problem of slavery from that of the slave-trade had, after a trial of half a century, signally failed, and for well-defined economic reasons. The nation had at last come to the parting of the ways, one of which led to a free-labor system, the other to a slave system fed by the slave-trade. Both sections of the country naturally hesitated at the cross-roads: the North clung to the delusion that a territorially limited system of slavery, without a slave-trade, was still possible in the South; the South hesitated to fight for her logical object — slavery and free trade in Negroes — and, in her moral and economic dilemma, sought to make autonomy and the Constitution her object. The real line of contention was, however, fixed by years of development, and was unalterable by the present whims or wishes of the contestants, no matter how important or interesting these might be: the triumph of the North meant free labor; the triumph of the South meant slavery and the slave-trade.

It is doubtful if many of the Southern leaders ever deceived themselves by thinking that Southern slavery, as it then was, could long be maintained without a general or a partial reopening of the slave-trade. Many had openly declared this a few years before, and there was no reason for a change of opinion. Nevertheless, at the outbreak of actual war and secession, there were powerful and decisive reasons for relegating the question temporarily to the rear. In the first place, only by this means could the adherence of important Border States be secured, without the aid of which secession was folly. Secondly, while it did no harm to laud the independence of the South and the kingship of cotton in "stump" speeches and conventions, yet, when it came to actual hostilities, the South sorely needed the aid of Europe; and this a nation fighting for slavery and the slave-trade stood poor chance of getting. Consequently, after attacking the slave-trade laws for a decade, and their execution for a quarter-century, we find the Southern leaders inserting, in both the provisional and the permanent Constitutions of the Confederate States, the following article: —

The importation of negroes of the African race, from any foreign country other than the slaveholding States or Territories of the United States of America, is hereby forbidden; and Congress is required to pass such laws as shall effectually prevent the same.

Congress shall also have power to prohibit the introduction of slaves from any State not a member of, or Territory not belonging to, this Confederacy.[1]

The attitude of the Confederate government toward this article is best illustrated by its circular of instructions to its foreign ministers: —

It has been suggested to this Government, from a source of unquestioned authenticity, that, after the recognition of our independence by the European Powers, an expectation is generally entertained by them that in our treaties of amity and commerce a clause will be introduced making stipulations against the African slave trade. It is even thought that neutral Powers may be inclined to insist upon the insertion of such a clause as a *sine qua non*.

You are well aware how firmly fixed in our Constitution is the policy of this Confederacy against the opening of that trade, but we are informed that false and insidious suggestions have been made by the agents of the United States at European Courts of our intention to change our constitution as soon as peace is restored, and of authorizing the importation of slaves from Africa. If, therefore, you should find, in your intercourse with the Cabinet to which you are accredited, that any such impressions are entertained, you will use every proper effort to remove them, and if an attempt is made to introduce into any treaty which you may be charged with negotiating stipulations on the subject just mentioned, you will assume, in behalf of your Government, the position which, under the direction of the President, I now proceed to develop.

The Constitution of the Confederate States is an agreement made between independent States. By its terms all the powers of Government are separated into classes as follows, viz.: —

1st. Such powers as the States delegate to the General Government.

2d. Such powers as the States agree to refrain from exercising, although they do not delegate them to the General Government.

3d. Such powers as the States, without delegating them to the Gen-

[1] *Confederate States of America Statutes at Large*, 1861, p. 15, Constitution, Art. 1, sect. 9, §§ 1, 2.

eral Government, thought proper to exercise by direct agreement between themselves contained in the Constitution.

4th. All remaining powers of sovereignty, which not being delegated to the Confederate States by the Constitution nor prohibited by it to the States, are reserved to the States respectively, or to the people thereof. . . . Especially in relation to the importation of African negroes was it deemed important by the States that no power to permit it should exist in the Confederate Government. . . . It will thus be seen that no power is delegated to the Confederate Government over this subject, but that it is included in the third class above referred to, of powers exercised directly by the States. . . . This Government unequivocally and absolutely denies its possession of any power whatever over the subject, and cannot entertain any proposition in relation to it. . . . The policy of the Confederacy is as fixed and immutable on this subject as the imperfection of human nature permits human resolve to be. No additional agreements, treaties, or stipulations can commit these States to the prohibition of the African slave trade with more binding efficacy than those they have themselves devised. A just and generous confidence in their good faith on this subject exhibited by friendly Powers will be far more efficacious than persistent efforts to induce this Government to assume the exercise of powers which it does not possess. . . . We trust, therefore, that no unnecessary discussions on this matter will be introduced into your negotiations. If, unfortunately, this reliance should prove ill-founded, you will decline continuing negotiations on your side, and transfer them to us at home. . . .[1]

This attitude of the conservative leaders of the South, if it meant anything, meant that individual State action could, when it pleased, reopen the slave-trade. The radicals were, of course, not satisfied with any veiling of the ulterior purpose of the new slave republic, and attacked the constitutional provision violently. "If," said one, "the clause be carried into the permanent government, our whole movement is defeated. It will

[1] From an intercepted circular despatch from J. P. Benjamin, "Secretary of State," addressed in this particular instance to Hon. L. Q. C. Lamar, "Commissioner, etc., St. Petersburg, Russia," and dated Richmond, Jan. 15, 1863; published in the *National Intelligencer*, March 31, 1863; cf. also the issues of Feb. 19, 1861, April 2, 3, 25, 1863; also published in the pamphlet, *The African Slave-Trade: The Secret Purpose*, etc. The editors vouch for its authenticity, and state it to be in Benjamin's own handwriting.

abolitionize the Border Slave States — it will brand our institution. Slavery cannot share a government with Democracy, — it cannot bear a brand upon it; thence another revolution . . . having achieved one revolution to escape democracy at the North, it must still achieve another to escape it at the South. That it will ultimately triumph none can doubt." [1]

91. **Attitude of the United States.** In the North, with all the hesitation in many matters, there existed unanimity in regard to the slave-trade; and the new Lincoln government ushered in the new policy of uncompromising suppression by hanging the first American slave-trader who ever suffered the extreme penalty of the law.[2] One of the earliest acts of President Lincoln was a step which had been necessary since 1808, but had never been taken, viz., the unification of the whole work of suppression into the hands of one responsible department. By an order, dated May 2, 1861, Caleb B. Smith, Secretary of the Interior, was charged with the execution of the slave-trade laws,[3] and he immediately began energetic work. Early in 1861, as soon as the withdrawal of the Southern members untied the hands of Congress, two appropriations of $900,000 each were made to suppress the slave trade, the first appropriations commensurate with the vastness of the task. These were followed by four appropriations of $17,000 each in the years 1863 to 1867, and two of $12,500 each in 1868 and 1869.[4] The first work of the new secretary was to obtain a corps of efficient assistants. To this end, he assembled all the marshals of the loyal seaboard States at New York, and gave them instruction and opportunity to inspect actual slavers. Congress also, for

[1] L. W. Spratt of South Carolina, in the *Southern Literary Messenger*, June, 1861, XXXII. 414, 420. Cf. also the Charleston *Mercury*, Feb. 13, 1861, and the *National Intelligencer*, Feb. 19, 1861.

[2] Captain Godon of the slaver "Erie;" condemned in the U. S. District Court for Southern New York in 1862. Cf. *Senate Exec. Doc.*, 37 Cong. 2 sess. I. No. 1, p. 13.

[3] *Ibid.*, pp. 453–4.

[4] *Statutes at Large*, XII. 132, 219, 639; XIII. 424; XIV. 226, 415; XV. 58, 321. The sum of $250,000 was also appropriated to return the slaves on the "Wildfire": *Ibid.*, XII. 40–41.

the first time, offered them proper compensation.[1] The next six months showed the effect of this policy in the fact that five vessels were seized and condemned, and four slave-traders were convicted and suffered the penalty of their crimes. "This is probably the largest number [of convictions] ever obtained, and certainly the only ones for many years."[2]

Meantime the government opened negotiations with Great Britain, and the treaty of 1862 was signed June 7, and carried out by Act of Congress, July 11.[3] Specially commissioned war vessels of either government were by this agreement authorized to search merchant vessels on the high seas and specified coasts, and if they were found to be slavers, or, on account of their construction or equipment, were suspected to be such, they were to be sent for condemnation to one of the mixed courts established at New York, Sierra Leone, and the Cape of Good Hope. These courts, consisting of one judge and one arbitrator on the part of each government, were to judge the facts without appeal, and upon condemnation by them, the culprits were to be punished according to the laws of their respective countries. The area in which this Right of Search could be exercised was somewhat enlarged by an additional article to the treaty, signed in 1863. In 1870 the mixed courts were abolished, but the main part of the treaty was left in force. The Act of July 17, 1862, enabled the President to contract with foreign governments for the apprenticing of recaptured Africans in the West Indies,[4] and in 1864 the coastwise slave-trade was forever prohibited.[5] By these measures the trade was soon checked, and before the end of the war entirely suppressed.[6] The vigilance of the government, however, was not checked, and as late as 1866 a squadron of ten ships, with one hundred and thirteen guns, patrolled

[1] *Statutes at Large*, XII. 368–9.

[2] *Senate Exec. Doc.*, 37 Cong. 2 sess. I. No. 1, pp. 453–4.

[3] *Statutes at Large*, XII. 531.

[4] For a time not exceeding five years: *Ibid.*, pp. 592–3.

[5] By section 9 of an appropriation act for civil expenses, July 2, 1864: *Ibid.*, XIII. 353.

[6] British officers attested this: *Diplomatic Correspondence*, 1862, p. 285.

the slave coast.[1] Finally, the Thirteenth Amendment legally confirmed what the war had already accomplished, and slavery and the slave-trade fell at one blow.[2]

[1] *Report of the Secretary of the Navy*, 1866; *House Exec. Doc.*, 39 Cong. 2 sess. IV. p. 12.

[2] There were some later attempts to legislate. Sumner tried to repeal the Act of 1803: *Congressional Globe*, 41 Cong. 2 sess. pp. 2894, 2932, 4953, 5594. Banks introduced a bill to prohibit Americans owning or dealing in slaves abroad: *House Journal*, 42 Cong. 2 sess. p. 48. For the legislation of the Confederate States, cf. Mason, *Veto Power*, 2d ed., Appendix C, No. 1.

CHAPTER XII.

THE ESSENTIALS IN THE STRUGGLE.

92. **How the Question Arose.** We have followed a chapter of history which is of peculiar interest to the sociologist. Here was a rich new land, the wealth of which was to be had in return for ordinary manual labor. Had the country been conceived of as existing primarily for the benefit of its actual inhabitants, it might have waited for natural increase or immigration to supply the needed hands; but both Europe and the earlier colonists themselves regarded this land as existing chiefly for the benefit of Europe, and as designed to be exploited, as rapidly and ruthlessly as possible, of the boundless wealth of its resources. This was the primary excuse for the rise of the African slave-trade to America.

Every experiment of such a kind, however, where the moral standard of a people is lowered for the sake of a material advantage, is dangerous in just such proportion as that advantage is great. In this case it was great. For at least a century, in the West Indies and the southern United States, agriculture flourished, trade increased, and English manufactures were nourished, in just such proportion as Americans stole Negroes and worked them to death. This advantage, to be sure, became much smaller in later times, and at one critical period was, at least in the Southern States, almost *nil;* but energetic efforts were wanting, and, before the nation was aware, slavery had seized a new and well-nigh immovable footing in the Cotton Kingdom.

The colonists averred with perfect truth that they did not commence this fatal traffic, but that it was imposed upon them from without. Nevertheless, all too soon did they lay aside scruples against it and hasten to share its material benefits. Even those who braved the rough Atlantic for the highest moral motives fell early victims to the allurements of this system. Thus, throughout colonial history, in spite of many honest attempts to stop the further pursuit of the slave-trade, we notice back of nearly all such attempts a certain moral apathy, an indisposition to attack the evil with the sharp weapons which its nature demanded. Consequently, there developed steadily, irresistibly, a vast social problem, which required two centuries and a half for a nation of trained European stock and boasted moral fibre to solve.

93. **The Moral Movement.** For the solution of this problem there were, roughly speaking, three classes of efforts made during this time, — moral, political, and economic: that is to say, efforts which sought directly to raise the moral standard of the nation; efforts which sought to stop the trade by legal enactment; efforts which sought to neutralize the economic advantages of the slave-trade. There is always a certain glamour about the idea of a nation rising up to crush an evil simply because it is wrong. Unfortunately, this can seldom be realized in real life; for the very existence of the evil usually argues a moral weakness in the very place where extraordinary moral strength is called for. This was the case in the early history of the colonies; and experience proved that an appeal to moral rectitude was unheard in Carolina when rice had become a great crop, and in Massachusetts when the rum-slave-traffic was paying a profit of 100 %. That the various abolition societies and anti-slavery movements did heroic work in rousing the national conscience is certainly true; unfortunately, however, these movements were weakest at the most critical times. When, in 1774 and 1804, the material advantages of the slave-trade and the institution of slavery were least, it seemed possible that moral suasion might accomplish the abolition of both. A fatal spirit of temporizing, however, seized the nation at these points; and although the

slave-trade was, largely for political reasons, forbidden, slavery was left untouched. Beyond this point, as years rolled by, it was found well-nigh impossible to rouse the moral sense of the nation. Even in the matter of enforcing its own laws and co-operating with the civilized world, a lethargy seized the country, and it did not awake until slavery was about to destroy it. Even then, after a long and earnest crusade, the national sense of right did not rise to the entire abolition of slavery. It was only a peculiar and almost fortuitous commingling of moral, political, and economic motives that eventually crushed African slavery and its handmaid, the slave-trade in America.

94. **The Political Movement.** The political efforts to limit the slave-trade were the outcome partly of moral reprobation of the trade, partly of motives of expediency. This legislation was never such as wise and powerful rulers may make for a nation, with the ulterior purpose of calling in the respect which the nation has for law to aid in raising its standard of right. The colonial and national laws on the slave-trade merely registered, from time to time, the average public opinion concerning this traffic, and are therefore to be regarded as negative signs rather than as positive efforts. These signs were, from one point of view, evidences of moral awakening; they indicated slow, steady development of the idea that to steal even Negroes was wrong. From another point of view, these laws showed the fear of servile insurrection and the desire to ward off danger from the State; again, they often indicated a desire to appear well before the civilized world, and to rid the "land of the free" of the paradox of slavery. Representing such motives, the laws varied all the way from mere regulating acts to absolute prohibitions. On the whole, these acts were poorly conceived, loosely drawn, and wretchedly enforced. The systematic violation of the provisions of many of them led to a widespread belief that enforcement was, in the nature of the case, impossible; and thus, instead of marking ground already won, they were too often sources of distinct moral deterioration. Certainly the carnival of lawlessness that succeeded the Act of 1807, and that which preceded final suppression in 1861, were glaring examples of the failure of the efforts to suppress the slave-trade by mere law.

95. **The Economic Movement.** Economic measures against the trade were those which from the beginning had the best chance of success, but which were least tried. They included tariff measures; efforts to encourage the immigration of free laborers and the emigration of the slaves; measures for changing the character of Southern industry; and, finally, plans to restore the economic balance which slavery destroyed, by raising the condition of the slave to that of complete freedom and responsibility. Like the political efforts, these rested in part on a moral basis; and, as legal enactments, they were also themselves often political measures. They differed, however, from purely moral and political efforts, in having as a main motive the economic gain which a substitution of free for slave labor promised.

The simplest form of such efforts was the revenue duty on slaves that existed in all the colonies. This developed into the prohibitive tariff, and into measures encouraging immigration or industrial improvements. The colonization movement was another form of these efforts; it was inadequately conceived, and not altogether sincere, but it had a sound, although in this case impracticable, economic basis. The one great measure which finally stopped the slave-trade forever was, naturally, the abolition of slavery, i. e., the giving to the Negro the right to sell his labor at a price consistent with his own welfare. The abolition of slavery itself, while due in part to direct moral appeal and political sagacity, was largely the result of the economic collapse of the large-farming slave system.

96. **The Lesson for Americans.** It may be doubted if ever before such political mistakes as the slavery compromises of the Constitutional Convention had such serious results, and yet, by a succession of unexpected accidents, still left a nation in position to work out its destiny. No American can study the connection of slavery with United States history, and not devoutly pray that his country may never have a similar social problem to solve, until it shows more capacity for such work than it has shown in the past. It is neither profitable nor in accordance with scientific truth to consider that whatever the constitutional fathers did was right, or that slavery was a plague sent from God

and fated to be eliminated in due time. We must face the fact that this problem arose principally from the cupidity and carelessness of our ancestors. It was the plain duty of the colonies to crush the trade and the system in its infancy: they preferred to enrich themselves on its profits. It was the plain duty of a Revolution based upon "Liberty" to take steps toward the abolition of slavery: it preferred promises to straightforward action. It was the plain duty of the Constitutional Convention, in founding a new nation, to compromise with a threatening social evil only in case its settlement would thereby be postponed to a more favorable time: this was not the case in the slavery and the slave-trade compromises; there never was a time in the history of America when the system had a slighter economic, political, and moral justification than in 1787; and yet with this real, existent, growing evil before their eyes, a bargain largely of dollars and cents was allowed to open the highway that led straight to the Civil War. Moreover, it was due to no wisdom and foresight on the part of the fathers that fortuitous circumstances made the result of that war what it was, nor was it due to exceptional philanthropy on the part of their descendants that that result included the abolition of slavery.

With the faith of the nation broken at the very outset, the system of slavery untouched, and twenty years' respite given to the slave-trade to feed and foster it, there began, with 1787, that system of bargaining, truckling, and compromising with a moral, political, and economic monstrosity, which makes the history of our dealing with slavery in the first half of the nineteenth century so discreditable to a great people. Each generation sought to shift its load upon the next, and the burden rolled on, until a generation came which was both too weak and too strong to bear it longer. One cannot, to be sure, demand of whole nations exceptional moral foresight and heroism; but a certain hard common-sense in facing the complicated phenomena of political life must be expected in every progressive people. In some respects we as a nation seem to lack this; we have the somewhat inchoate idea that we are not destined to be harassed with great social questions, and that even if we are, and fail to answer them, the fault is with the question and not with us. Consequently we often congratulate ourselves more on getting rid of a problem than on solving it. Such an attitude is dangerous; we have and shall have, as other peoples have had, critical, momentous, and pressing questions to answer. The riddle of the Sphinx may be postponed, it may be evasively answered now; sometime it must be fully answered.

It behooves the United States, therefore, in the interest both of scientific truth and of future social reform, carefully to study such chapters of her history as that of the suppression of the slave-trade. The most obvious question which this study suggests is: How far in a State can a recognized moral wrong safely be compromised? And although this chapter of history can give us no definite answer suited to the ever-varying aspects of political life, yet it would seem to warn any nation from allowing, through carelessness and moral cowardice, any social evil to grow. No persons would have seen the Civil War with more surprise and horror than the Revolutionists of 1776; yet from the small and apparently dying institution of their day arose the walled and castled Slave-Power. From this we may conclude that it behooves nations as well as men to do things at the very moment when they ought to be done.

APPENDIX A.

A CHRONOLOGICAL CONSPECTUS OF COLONIAL AND STATE LEGISLATION RESTRICTING THE AFRICAN SLAVE-TRADE.

1641–1787.

1641. Massachusetts: Limitations on Slavery.

"Liberties of Forreiners & Strangers": 91. "There shall never be any bond slaverie villinage or Captivitie amongst vs, unles it be lawfull Captives taken in iust warres, & such strangers as willingly selle themselves or are sold to us. And those shall have all the liberties & Christian usages w[ch] y[e] law of god established in Jsraell concerning such p/[sons] doeth morally require. This exempts none from servitude who shall be Judged there to by Authoritie."

"Capitall Laws": 10. "If any man stealeth aman or mankinde, he shall surely be put to death" (marginal reference, Exodus xxi. 16). Re-enacted in the codes of 1649, 1660, and 1672. Whitmore, *Reprint of Colonial Laws of 1660*, etc. (1889), pp. 52, 54, 71–117.

1642, April 3. New Netherland: Ten per cent Duty.

"Ordinance of the Director and Council of New Netherland, imposing certain Import and Export Duties." O'Callaghan, *Laws of New Netherland* (1868), p. 31.

1642, Dec. 1. Connecticut: Man-Stealing made a Capital Offence.

"Capitall Lawes," No. 10. Re-enacted in Ludlow's code, 1650. *Colonial Records*, I. 77.

1646, Nov. 4. Massachusetts: Declaration against Man-Stealing.
Testimony of the General Court. For text, see above, page 30. *Colonial Records*, II. 168; III. 84.

1652, April 4. New Netherland: Duty of 15 Guilders.
"Conditions and Regulations" of Trade to Africa. O'Callaghan, *Laws of New Netherland*, pp. 81, 127.

1652, May 18–20. Rhode Island: Perpetual Slavery Prohibited.
For text, see above, page 33. *Colonial Records*, I. 243.

1655, Aug. 6. New Netherland: Ten per cent Export Duty.
"Ordinance of the Director General and Council of New Netherland, imposing a Duty on exported Negroes." O'Callaghan, *Laws of New Netherland*, p. 191.

1664, March 12. Duke of York's Patent: Slavery Regulated.
"Lawes establisht by the Authority of his Majesties Letters patents, granted to his Royall Highnes James Duke of Yorke and Albany; Bearing Date the 12th Day of March in the Sixteenth year of the Raigne of our Soveraigne Lord Kinge Charles the Second." First published at Long Island in 1664.

"Bond slavery": "No Christian shall be kept in Bondslavery villenage or Captivity, Except Such who shall be Judged thereunto by Authority, or such as willingly have sould, or shall sell themselves," etc. Apprenticeship allowed. *Charter to William Penn, and Laws of the Province of Pennsylvania* (1879), pp. 3, 12.

1672, October. Connecticut: Law against Man-Stealing.
"The General Laws and Liberties of Conecticut Colonie."

"Capital Laws": 10. "If any Man stealeth a Man or Man kinde, and selleth him, or if he be found in his hand, he shall be put to death. Exod. 21. 16." *Laws of Connecticut*, 1672 (repr. 1865), p. 9.

1676, March 3. West New Jersey: Slavery Prohibited (?).
"The Concessions and Agreements of the Proprietors, Freeholders and Inhabitants of the Province of West New-Jersey, in America."

Chap. XXIII. "That in all publick Courts of Justice for Tryals of Causes, Civil or Criminal, any Person or Persons, Inhabitants of the said Province, may freely come into, and attend the said Courts, . . . that all and every Person and Persons Inhabiting the said Province, shall, as far as in us lies, be free from Oppression and Slavery." Leaming and Spicer, *Grants, Concessions*, etc., pp. 382, 398.

1688, Feb. 18. Pennsylvania: First Protest of Friends against Slave-Trade.

"At Monthly Meeting of Germantown Friends." For text, see above, page 21. *Fac-simile Copy* (1880).

1695, May. Maryland: 10s. Duty Act.

"An Act for the laying an Imposition upon Negroes, Slaves, and White Persons imported into this Province." Re-enacted in 1696, and included in Acts of 1699 and 1704. Bacon, *Laws*, 1695, ch. ix.; 1696, ch. vii.; 1699, ch. xxiii.; 1704, ch. ix.

1696. Pennsylvania: Protest of Friends.

"That Friends be careful not to encourage the bringing in of any more negroes." Bettle, *Notices of Negro Slavery*, in *Penn. Hist. Soc. Mem.* (1864), I. 383.

1698, Oct. 8. South Carolina: White Servants Encouraged.

"An Act for the Encouragement of the Importation of White Servants."

"Whereas, the great number of negroes which of late have been imported into this Collony may endanger the safety thereof if speedy care be not taken and encouragement given for the importation of white servants."

§ 1. £13 are to be given to any ship master for every male white servant (Irish excepted), between sixteen and forty years, whom he shall bring into Ashley river; and £12 for boys between twelve and sixteen years. Every servant must have at least four years to serve, and every boy seven years.

§ 3. Planters are to take servants in proportion of one to every six male Negroes above sixteen years.

§ 5. Servants are to be distributed by lot.

§ 8. This act to continue three years. Cooper, *Statutes*, II. 153.

1699, April. Virginia: 20s. Duty Act.

"An act for laying an imposition upon servants and slaves imported into this country, towards building the Capitoll." For three years; continued in August, 1701, and April, 1704. Hening, *Statutes*, III. 193, 212, 225.

1703, May 6. South Carolina: Duty Act.

"An Act for the laying an Imposition on Furrs, Skinns, Liquors and other Goods and Merchandize, Imported into and Exported out of this part of this Province, for the raising of a

Fund of Money towards defraying the publick charges and expenses of this Province, and paying the debts due for the Expedition against St. Augustine." 10*s.* on Africans and 20*s.* on others. Cooper, *Statutes*, II. 201.

1704, October. Maryland: 20s. Duty Act.

"An Act imposing Three Pence per Gallon on Rum and Wine, Brandy and Spirits; and Twenty Shillings per Poll for Negroes; for raising a Supply to defray the Public Charge of this Province; and Twenty Shillings per Poll on Irish Servants, to prevent the importing too great a Number of Irish Papists into this Province." Revived in 1708 and 1712. Bacon, *Laws*, 1704, ch. xxxiii.; 1708, ch. xvi.; 1712, ch. xxii.

1705, Jan. 12. Pennsylvania: 10s. Duty Act.

"An Act for Raising a Supply of Two pence half penny per Pound & ten shillings per Head. Also for Granting an Impost & laying on Sundry Liquors & negroes Imported into this Province for the Support of Governmt., & defraying the necessary Publick Charges in the Administration thereof." *Colonial Records* (1852), II. 232, No. 50.

1705, October. Virginia: 6d. Tax on Imported Slaves.

"An act for raising a publick revenue for the better support of the Government," etc. Similar tax by Act of October, 1710. Hening, *Statutes*, III. 344, 490.

1705, October. Virginia: 20s. Duty Act.

"An act for laying an Imposition upon Liquors and Slaves." For two years; re-enacted in October, 1710, for three years, and in October, 1712. *Ibid.*, III. 229, 482; IV. 30.

1705, Dec. 5. Massachusetts: £4 Duty Act.

"An act for the Better Preventing of a Spurious and Mixt Issue," etc.

§ 6. On and after May 1, 1706, every master importing Negroes shall enter his number, name, and sex in the impost office, and insert them in the bill of lading; he shall pay to the commissioner and receiver of the impost £4 per head for every such Negro. Both master and ship are to be security for the payment of the same.

§ 7. If the master neglect to enter the slaves, he shall forfeit £8 for each Negro, one-half to go to the informer and one-half to the government.

§ 8. If any Negro imported shall, within twelve months, be exported and sold in any other plantation, and a receipt from the collector there be shown, a drawback of the whole duty will be allowed. Like drawback will be allowed a purchaser, if any Negro sold die within six weeks after importation. *Mass. Province Laws*, 1705–6, ch. 10.

1708, February. Rhode Island: £3 Duty Act.

No title or text found. Slightly amended by Act of April, 1708; strengthened by Acts of February, 1712, and July 5, 1715; proceeds disposed of by Acts of July, 1715, October, 1717, and June, 1729. *Colonial Records*, IV. 34, 131–5, 138, 143, 191–3, 225, 423–4.

1709, Sept. 24. New York: £3 Duty Act.

"An Act for Laying a Duty on the Tonnage of Vessels and Slaves." A duty of £3 was laid on slaves not imported directly from their native country. Continued by Act of Oct. 30, 1710. *Acts of Assembly*, 1691–1718, pp. 97, 125, 134; Laws of New York, 1691–1773, p. 83.

1710, Dec. 28. Pennsylvania: 40s. Duty Act.

"An impost Act, laying a duty on Negroes, wine, rum and other spirits, cyder and vessels." Repealed by order in Council Feb. 20, 1713. Carey and Bioren, *Laws*, I. 82; Bettle, *Notices of Negro Slavery*, in *Penn. Hist. Soc. Mem.* (1864), I. 415.

1710. Virginia: £5 Duty Act.

"Intended to discourage the importation" of slaves. Title and text not found. Disallowed (?). *Governor Spotswood to the Lords of Trade*, in *Va. Hist. Soc. Coll.*, New Series, I. 52.

1711, July–Aug. New York: Act of 1709 Strengthened.

"An Act for the more effectual putting in Execution an Act of General Assembly, Intituled, An Act for Laying a Duty on the Tonnage of Vessels and Slaves." *Acts of Assembly*, 1691–1718, p. 134.

1711, December. New York: Bill to Increase Duty.

Bill for laying a further duty on slaves. Passed Assembly; lost in Council. *Doc. rel. Col. Hist. New York*, V. 293.

1711. Pennsylvania: Testimony of Quakers.

". . . the Yearly Meeting of Philadelphia, on a representation from the Quarterly Meeting of Chester, that the buying and encouraging the importation of negroes was still practised by some of the members of the society, again repeated and enforced the observance of the advice issued in 1696, and further directed all merchants and factors to write to their correspondents and discourage their sending any more negroes." Bettle, *Notices of Negro Slavery*, in *Penn. Hist. Soc. Mem.* (1864), I. 386.

1712, June 7. Pennsylvania: Prohibitive (?) Duty Act.

"A supplementary Act to an act, entituled, An impost act, laying a duty on Negroes, rum," etc. Disallowed by Great Britain, 1713. Carey and Bioren, *Laws*, I. 87, 88. Cf. *Colonial Records* (1852), II. 553.

1712, June 7. Pennsylvania: Prohibitive Duty Act.

"An act to prevent the Importation of Negroes and Indians into this Province."

"Whereas Divers Plots and Insurrections have frequently happened, not only in the Islands, but on the Main Land of *America*, by Negroes, which have been carried on so far that several of the Inhabitants have been thereby barbarously Murthered, an instance whereof we have lately had in our neighboring Colony of *New York*. And whereas the Importation of Indian Slaves hath given our Neighboring *Indians* in this Province some umbrage of Suspicion and Dis-satisfaction. For Prevention of all which for the future,

"*Be it Enacted* . . . , That from and after the Publication of this Act, upon the Importation of any Negro or Indian, by Land or Water, into this Province, there shall be paid by the Importer, Owner or Possessor thereof, the sum of *Twenty Pounds per head*, for every Negro or Indian so imported or brought in (except Negroes directly brought in from the *West India Islands* before the first Day of the Month called *August* next) unto the proper Officer herein after named, or that shall be appointed according to the Directions of this Act to receive the same," etc. Disallowed by Great Britain, 1713. *Laws of Pennsylvania, collected*, etc. (ed. 1714), p. 165; *Colonial Records* (1852), II. 553; Burge, *Commentaries*, I. 737, note; *Penn. Archives*, I. 162.

1713, March 11. New Jersey: £10 Duty Act.

"An Act for laying a Duty on Negro, Indian and Mulatto Slaves, imported and brought into this Province."

"*Be it Enacted* . . . , That every Person or Persons that shall hereafter Import or bring in, or cause to be imported or brought into this Province, any Negro Indian or Mulatto Slave or Slaves, every such Person or Persons so importing or bringing in, or causing to be imported or brought in, such Slave or Slaves, shall enter with one of the Collectors of her Majestie's Customs of this Province, every such Slave or Slaves, within Twenty Four Hours after such Slave or Slaves is so Imported, and pay the Sum of *Ten Pounds* Money as appointed by her Majesty's Proclamation, for each Slave so imported, or give sufficient Security that the said Sum of *Ten Pounds*, Money aforesaid, shall be well and truly paid within three Months after such Slave or Slaves are so imported, to the Collector or his Deputy of the District into which such Slave or Slaves shall be imported, for the use of her Majesty, her Heirs and Successors, toward the Support of the Government of this Province." For seven years; violations incur forfeiture and sale of slaves at auction; slaves brought from elsewhere than Africa to pay £10, etc. *Laws and Acts of New Jersey*, 1703–1717 (ed. 1717), p. 43; *N. J. Archives*, 1st Series, XIII. 516, 517, 520, 522, 523, 527, 532, 541.

1713, March 26. Great Britain and Spain: The Assiento.

"The Assiento, or Contract for allowing to the Subjects of Great Britain the Liberty of importing Negroes into the Spanish America. Signed by the Catholick King at Madrid, the 26th Day of March, 1713."

Art. I. "First then to procure, by this means, a mutual and reciprocal advantage to the sovereigns and subjects of both crowns, her British majesty does offer and undertake for the persons, whom she shall name and appoint, That they shall oblige and charge themselves with the bringing into the West-Indies of America, belonging to his catholick majesty, in the space of the said 30 years, to commence on the 1st day of May, 1713, and determine on the like day, which will be in the year 1743, *viz.* 144000 negroes, *Piezas de India*, of both sexes, and of all ages, at the rate of 4800 negroes, *Piezas de India*, in each of the said 30 years, with this condition, That the persons who shall go to the West-Indies to take care of the concerns of the assiento, shall avoid giving any offence, for in such case they shall be prosecuted and punished in the same manner, as they would have been in Spain, if the like misdemeanors had been committed there."

Art. II. Assientists to pay a duty of 33 pieces of eight (*Escudos*) for each Negro, which should include all duties.

Art. III. Assientists to advance to his Catholic Majesty 200,000 pieces of eight, which should be returned at the end of the first twenty years, etc. John Almon, *Treaties of Peace, Alliance, and Commerce, between Great-Britain and other Powers* (London, 1772), I. 83–107.

1713, July 13. Great Britain and Spain: Treaty of Utrecht.

"Treaty of Peace and Friendship between the most serene and most potent princess Anne, by the grace of God, Queen of Great Britain, France, and Ireland, Defender of the Faith, &c. and the most serene and most potent Prince Philip V. the Catholick King of Spain, concluded at Utrecht, the $\frac{2}{13}$ Day of July, 1713."

Art. XII. "The Catholick King doth furthermore hereby give and grant to her Britannick majesty, and to the company of her subjects appointed for that purpose, as well the subjects of Spain, as all others, being excluded, the contract for introducing negroes into several parts of the dominions of his Catholick Majesty in America, commonly called *el Pacto de el Assiento de Negros*, for the space of thirty years successively, beginning from the first day of the month of May, in the year 1713, with the same conditions on which the French enjoyed it, or at any time might or ought to enjoy the same, together with a tract or tracts of Land to be allotted by the said Catholick King, and to be granted to the company aforesaid, commonly called *la Compania de el Assiento*, in some convenient place on the river of Plata, (no duties or revenues being payable by the said company on that account, during the time of the abovementioned contract, and no longer) and this settlement of the said society, or those tracts of land, shall be proper and sufficient for planting, and sowing, and for feeding cattle for the subsistence of those who are in the service of the said company, and of their negroes; and that the said negroes may be there kept in safety till they are sold; and moreover, that the ships belonging to the said company may come close to land, and be secure from any danger. But it shall always be lawful for the Catholick King, to appoint an officer in the said place or settlement, who may take care that nothing be done or practised contrary to his royal interests. And all who manage the affairs of the said company there, or belong to it, shall be subject to the inspection of the aforesaid officer, as to all matters relating to the tracts of land abovementioned. But if any doubts, difficulties, or controversies, should arise between the said officer and the managers for the said company, they shall be referred to the determination of the governor of Buenos Ayres. The Catholick King has been likewise pleased to grant to the said company, several other extraordinary advantages, which are more fully and amply explained in the contract of the Assiento, which was made and concluded at Madrid, the 26th day of the month of March, of this present year 1713. Which contract, or *Assiento de Negros*, and all the clauses, conditions, privileges and immunities contained therein, and which are not contrary to this article, are and shall be deemed, and taken to be, part of this treaty, in the same manner as if they had been here inserted word for word." John Almon, *Treaties of Peace, Alliance, and Commerce, between Great-Britain and other Powers*, I. 168–80.

1714, Feb. 18. South Carolina: Duty on American Slaves.

"An Act for laying an additional duty on all Negro Slaves imported into this Province from any part of America." Title quoted in Act of 1719, § 30, *q. v.*

1714, Dec. 18. South Carolina: Prohibitive Duty.

"An additional Act to an Act entitled 'An Act for the better Ordering and Governing Negroes and all other Slaves.'"

§ 9. "And *whereas*, the number of negroes do extremely increase in this Province, and through the afflicting providence of God, the white persons do not proportionably multiply, by reason whereof, the safety of the said Province is greatly endangered; for the prevention of which for the future,

"*Be it further enacted* by the authority aforesaid, That all negro slaves from twelve years old and upwards, imported into this part of this Province from any part of Africa, shall pay such additional duties as is hereafter named, that is to say: — that every merchant or other person whatsoever, who shall, six months after the ratification of this Act, import any negro slaves as aforesaid, shall, for every such slave, pay unto the public receiver for the time being, (within thirty days after such importation,) the sum of two pounds current money of this Province." Cooper, *Statutes*, VII. 365.

1715, Feb. 18. South Carolina: Duty on American Negroes.

"*An additional Act* to an act entitled *an act for raising the sum of*

£2000, *of and from the estates real and personal of the inhabitants of this Province, ratified in open Assembly the* 18*th day of December*, 1714; and for laying an additional duty on all Negroe slaves imported into this Province from any part of America." Title only given. Grimké, *Public Laws*, p. xvi, No. 362.

1715, May 28. Pennsylvania: £5 Duty Act.

"An Act for laying a Duty on *Negroes* imported into this province." Disallowed by Great Britain, 1719. *Acts and Laws of Pennsylvania*, 1715, p. 270; *Colonial Records* (1852), III. 75–6; Chalmers, *Opinions*, II. 118.

1715, June 3. Maryland: 20s. Duty Act.

"An Act laying an Imposition on Negroes . . . ; and also on Irish Servants, to prevent the importing too great a Number of Irish Papists into this Province." Supplemented April 23, 1735, and July 25, 1754. *Compleat Collection of the Laws of Maryland* (ed. 1727), p. 157; Bacon, *Laws*, 1715, ch. xxxvi. § 8; 1735, ch. vi. §§ 1–3; *Acts of Assembly*, 1754, p. 10.

1716, June 30. South Carolina: £3 Duty Act.

"An Act for laying an Imposition on Liquors, Goods and Merchandizes, Imported into and Exported out of this Province, for the raising of a Fund of Money towards the defraying the publick charges and expences of the Government." A duty of £3 was laid on African slaves, and £30 on American slaves. Cooper, *Statutes*, II. 649.

1716. New York: 5 oz. and 10 oz. plate Duty Act.

"An Act to Oblige all Vessels Trading into this Colony (except such as are therein excepted) to pay a certain Duty; and for the further Explanation and rendring more Effectual certain Clauses in an Act of General Assembly of this Colony, Intituled, An Act by which a Duty is laid on Negroes, and other Slaves, imported into this Colony." The act referred to is not to be found. *Acts of Assembly*, 1691–1718, p. 224.

1717, June 8. Maryland: Additional 20s. Duty Act.

"An Act for laying an Additional Duty of Twenty Shillings Current Money per Poll on all Irish Servants, . . . also, the Additional Duty of Twenty Shillings Current Money per Poll on all Negroes, for raising a Fund for the Use of Publick Schools," etc. Continued by Act of 1728. *Compleat Collection of the Laws of Maryland* (ed. 1727), p. 191; Bacon, *Laws*, 1728, ch. viii.

1717, Dec. 11. South Carolina: Prohibitive Duty.

"A further additional Act to an Act entitled An Act for the better ordering and governing of Negroes and all other Slaves; and to an additional Act to an Act entitled An Act for the better ordering and governing of Negroes and all other Slaves."

§ 3. "And *whereas*, the great importation of negroes to this Province, in proportion to the white inhabitants of the same, whereby the future safety of this Province will be greatly endangered; for the prevention whereof,

"*Be it enacted* by the authority aforesaid, That all negro slaves of any age or condition whatsoever, imported or otherwise brought into this Province, from any part of the world, shall pay such additional duties as is hereafter named, that is to say: — that every merchant or other person whatsoever, who shall, eighteen months after the ratification of this Act, import any negro slave as aforesaid, shall, for every such slave, pay unto the public receiver for the time being, at the time of each importation, over and above all the duties already charged on negroes, by any law in force in this Province, the additional sum of forty pounds current money of this Province," etc.

§ 4. This section on duties to be in force for four years after ratification, and thence to the end of the next session of the General Assembly. Cooper, *Statutes*, VII. 368.

1718, Feb. 22. Pennsylvania: Duty Act.

"An Act for continuing a duty on Negroes brought into this province." Carey and Bioren, *Laws*, I. 118.

1719, March 20. South Carolina: £10 Duty Act.

"An Act for laying an Imposition on Negroes, Liquors, and other Goods and Merchandizes, imported, and exported out of this Province, for the raising of a Fund of Money towards the defraying the Publick Charges and Expences of this Government; as also to Repeal several Duty Acts, and Clauses and Paragraphs of Acts, as is herein mentioned." This repeals former duty acts (e. g. that of 1714), and lays a duty of £10 on African slaves, and £30 on American slaves. Cooper, *Statutes*, III. 56.

1721, Sept. 21. South Carolina: £10 Duty Act.

"An Act for granting to His Majesty a Duty and Imposition on Negroes, Liquors, and other Goods and Merchandize, imported into and exported out of this Province." This was a continuation of the Act of 1719. *Ibid.*, III. 159.

1722, Feb. 23. South Carolina: £10 Duty Act.

"An Act for Granting to His Majesty a Duty and Imposition on Negroes, Liquors, and other Goods and Merchandizes, for the use of the Publick of this Province."

§ 1. ". . . on all negro slaves imported from Africa directly, or any other place whatsoever, Spanish negroes excepted, if above ten years of age, ten pounds; on all negroes under ten years of age, (sucking children excepted) five pounds," etc.

§ 3. "And whereas, it has proved to the detriment of some of the inhabitants of this Province, who have purchased negroes imported here from the Colonies of America, that they were either transported thence by the Courts of justice, or sent off by private persons for their ill behaviour and misdemeanours, to prevent which for the future,

"*Be it enacted* by the authority aforesaid, That all negroes imported in this Province from any part of America, after the ratification of this Act, above ten years of age, shall pay unto the Publick Receiver as a duty, the sum of fifty pounds, and all such negroes under the age of ten years, (sucking children excepted) the sum of five pounds of like current money, unless the owner or agent shall produce a testimonial under the hand and seal of any Notary Publick of the Colonies or plantations from whence such negroes came last, before whom it was proved upon oath, that the same are new negroes, and have not been six months on shoar in any part of America," etc.

§ 4. "And whereas, the importation of Spanish Indians, mustees, negroes, and mulattoes, may be of dangerous consequence by inticing the slaves belonging to the inhabitants of this Province to desert with them to the Spanish settlements near us,

"*Be it therefore enacted* That all such Spanish negroes, Indians, mustees, or mulattoes, so imported into this Province, shall pay unto the Publick Receiver, for the use of this Province, a duty of one hundred and fifty pounds, current money of this Province."

§ 19. Rebate of three-fourths of the duty allowed in case of re-exportation in six months.

§ 31. Act of 1721 repealed.

§ 36. This act to continue in force for three years, and thence to the end of the next session of the General Assembly, and no longer. Cooper, *Statutes*, III. 193.

1722, May 12. Pennsylvania: Duty Act.

"An Act for laying a duty on Negroes imported into this province." Carey and Bioren, *Laws*, I. 165.

1723, May. Virginia: Duty Act.

"An Act for laying a Duty on Liquors and Slaves." Title only; repealed by proclamation Oct. 27, 1724. Hening, *Statutes*, IV. 118.

1723, June 18. Rhode Island: Back Duties Collected.

Resolve appointing the attorney-general to collect back duties on Negroes. *Colonial Records*, IV. 330.

1726, March 5. Pennsylvania: £10 Duty Act.

"An Act for the better regulating of Negroes in this province." Carey and Bioren, *Laws*, I. 214; Bettle, *Notices of Negro Slavery*, in *Penn. Hist. Soc. Mem.* (1864), I. 388.

1726, March 5. Pennsylvania: Duty Act.

"An Act for laying a duty on Negroes imported into this province." Carey and Bioren, *Laws*, I. 213.

1727, February. Virginia: Prohibitive Duty Act (?).

"An Act for laying a Duty on Slaves imported; and for appointing a Treasurer." Title only found; the duty was probably prohibitive; it was enacted with a suspending clause, and was not assented to by the king. Hening, *Statutes*, IV. 182.

1728, Aug. 31. New York: £2 and £4 Duty Act.

"An Act to repeal some Parts and to continue and enforce other Parts of the Act therein mentioned, and for granting several Duties to His Majesty, for supporting His Government in the Colony of New York" from Sept. 1, 1728, to Sept. 1, 1733. Same duty continued by Act of 1732. *Laws of New York*, 1691–1773, pp. 148, 171; *Doc. rel. Col. Hist. New York*, VI. 32, 33, 34, 37, 38.

1728, Sept. 14. Massachusetts: Act of 1705 Strengthened.

"An Act more effectually to secure the Duty on the Importation of Negros." For seven years; substantially the same law re-enacted Jan. 26, 1738, for ten years. *Mass. Province Laws*, 1728–9, ch. 16; 1738–9, ch. 27.

1729, May 10. Pennsylvania: 40s. Duty Act.

"An Act for laying a Duty on Negroes imported into this Province." *Laws of Pennsylvania* (ed. 1742), p. 354, ch. 287.

1732, May. Rhode Island: Repeal of Act of 1712.

"Whereas, there was an act made and passed by the General Assembly, at their session, held at Newport, the 27th day of February, 1711 [O. S., N. S. = 1712], entitled 'An Act for laying a duty on negro slaves that shall be imported into this colony,' and this Assembly being directed by His Majesty's instructions to repeal the same; —

"Therefore, be it enacted by the General Assembly . . . that the said act . . . be, and it is hereby repealed, made null and void, and of none effect for the future." If this is the act mentioned under Act of 1708, the title is wrongly cited; if not, the act is lost. *Colonial Records*, IV. 471.

1732, May. Virginia: Five per cent Duty Act.

"An Act for laying a Duty upon Slaves, to be paid by the Buyers." For four years; continued and slightly amended by Acts of 1734, 1736, 1738, 1742, and 1745; revived February, 1752, and continued by Acts of November, 1753, February, 1759, November, 1766, and 1769; revived (or continued ?) by Act of February, 1772, until 1778. Hening, *Statutes*, IV. 317, 394, 469; V. 28, 160, 318; VI. 217, 353; VII. 281; VIII. 190, 336, 530.

1734, November. New York: Duty Act.

"An act to lay a duty on Negroes & a tax on the Slaves therein mentioned during the time and for the uses within mentioned." The tax was 1*s*. yearly per slave. *Doc. rel. Col. Hist. New York*, VI. 38.

1734, Nov. 28. New York: £2 and £4 (?) Duty Act.

"An Act to lay a Duty on the Goods, and a Tax on the Slaves therein mentioned, during the Time, and for the Uses mentioned in the same." Possibly there were two acts this year. *Laws of New York*, 1691–1773, p. 186; *Doc. rel. Col. Hist. New York*, VI. 27.

1735. Georgia: Prohibitive Act.

An "act for rendering the colony of Georgia more defensible by prohibiting the importation and use of black slaves or negroes into the same." W. B. Stevens, *History of Georgia*, I. 311; [B. Martyn], *Account of the Progress of Georgia* (1741), pp. 9–10; Prince Hoare, *Memoirs of Granville Sharp* (London, 1820), p. 157.

1740, April 5. South Carolina: £100 Prohibitive Duty Act.

"An Act for the better strengthening of this Province, by granting to His Majesty certain taxes and impositions on the purchasers of Negroes imported," etc. The duty on slaves from America was £150. Continued to 1744. Cooper, *Statutes*, III. 556. Cf. *Abstract Evidence on Slave-Trade before Committee of House of Commons*, 1790–91 (London, 1791), p. 150.

1740, May. Virginia: Additional Five per cent Duty Act.

"An Act, for laying an additional Duty upon Slaves, to be paid by the Buyer, for encouraging persons to enlist in his Majesty's service: And for preventing desertion." To continue until July 1, 1744. Hening, *Statutes*, V. 92.

1751, June 14. South Carolina: White Servants Encouraged.

"An Act for the better strengthening of this Province, by granting to His Majesty certain Taxes and Impositions on the purchasers of Negroes and other slaves imported, and for appropriating the same to the uses therein mentioned, and for granting to His Majesty a duty on Liquors and other Goods and Merchandize, for the uses therein mentioned, and for exempting the purchasers of Negroes and other slaves imported from payment of the Tax, and the Liquors and other Goods and Merchandize from the duties imposed by any former Act or Acts of the General Assembly of this Province."

"Whereas, the best way to prevent the mischiefs that may be attended by the great importation of negroes into this Province, will be to establish a method by which such importation should be made a necessary means of introducing a proportionable number of white inhabitants into the same; therefore for the effectual raising and appropriating a fund sufficient for the better settling of this Province with white inhabitants, we, his Majesty's most dutiful and loyal subjects, the House of Assembly now met in General Assembly, do cheerfully give and grant unto the King's most excellent Majesty, his heirs and successors, the several taxes and impositions hereinafter mentioned, for the uses and to be raised, appropriated, paid and applied as is hereinafter directed and appointed, and not otherwise, and do humbly pray his most sacred Majesty that it may be enacted,

§ 1. "*And be it enacted*, by his Excellency James Glen, Esquire, Governor in chief and Captain General in and over the Province of South Carolina, by and with the advice and consent of his Majesty's honorable Council, and the House of Assembly of the said Province, and by the authority of the same, That from and immediately after the passing of this Act, there shall be imposed on and paid by all and every the inhabitants of this Province, and other person and persons whosoever, first purchasing any negro or other slave, hereafter to be imported, a certain tax or sum of ten pounds current money for every such negro and other slave of the height of four feet two inches and upwards; and for every one under that height, and above three feet two inches, the sum of five pounds like money; and for all under three feet two inches, (sucking children excepted) two pounds and ten shillings like money, which every such inhabitant of this Province, and other person and persons whosoever shall so purchase or buy as aforesaid, which said sums of ten pounds and five pounds and two pounds and ten shillings respectively, shall be paid by such purchaser for every such slave, at the time of his, her or their purchasing of the same, to the public treasurer of this Province for the time being, for the uses hereinafter mentioned, set down and appointed, under pain of forfeiting all and every such negroes and slaves, for which the said taxes or impositions shall not be paid, pursuant to the directions of this Act, to be sued for, recovered and applied in the manner hereinafter directed."

§ 6. "*And be it further enacted* by the authority aforesaid, That the said tax hereby imposed on negroes and other slaves, paid or to be paid by or on the behalf of the purchasers as aforesaid, by virtue of this Act, shall be applied and appropriated as followeth, and to no other use, or in any other manner whatever, (that is to say) that three-fifth parts (the whole into five equal parts to be divided) of the net sum arising by the said tax, for and during the term of five years from the time of passing this Act, be applied and the same is hereby applied for payment of the sum of six pounds proclamation money to every poor foreign protestant whatever from Europe, or other poor protestant (his Majesty's subject) who shall produce a certificate under the seal of any corporation, or a certificate under the hands of the minister and church-wardens of any parish, or the minister and elders of any church, meeting or congregation in Great

Britain or Ireland, of the good character of such poor protestant, above the age of twelve and under the age of fifty years, and for payment of the sum of three pounds like money, to every such poor protestant under the age of twelve and above the age of two years; who shall come into this Province within the first three years of the said term of five years, and settle on any part of the southern frontier lying between Pon Pon and Savannah rivers, or in the central parts of this Province," etc. For the last two years the bounty is £4 and £2.

§ 7. After the expiration of this term of five years, the sum is appropriated to the protestants settling anywhere in the State, and the bounty is £2 13*s*. 4*d*., and £1 6*s*. 8*d*.

§ 8. One other fifth of the tax is appropriated to survey lands, and the remaining fifth as a bounty for ship-building, and for encouraging the settlement of ship-builders.

§ 14. Rebate of three-fourths of the tax allowed in case of re-exportation of the slaves in six months.

§ 16. "*And be it further enacted* by the authority aforesaid, That every person or persons who after the passing this Act shall purchase any slave or slaves which shall be brought or imported into this Province, either by land or water, from any of his Majesty's plantations or colonies in America, that have been in any such colony or plantation for the space of six months; and if such slave or slaves have not been so long in such colony or plantation, the importer shall be obliged to make oath or produce a proper certificate thereof, or otherwise every such importer shall pay a further tax or imposition of fifty pounds, over and besides the tax hereby imposed for every such slave which he or they shall purchase as aforesaid." Actual settlers bringing slaves are excepted.

§ 41. This act to continue in force ten years from its passage, and thence to the end of the next session of the General Assembly, and no longer. Cooper, *Statutes*, III. 739.

1753, Dec. 12. New York: 5 oz. and 10 oz. plate Duty Act.

"An Act for granting to His Majesty the several Duties and Impositions, on Goods, Wares and Merchandizes imported into this Colony, therein mentioned." Annually continued until 1767, or perhaps until 1774. *Laws of New York*, 1752–62, p. 21, ch. xxvii.; *Doc. rel. Col. Hist. New York*, VII. 907; VIII. 452.

1754, February. Virginia: Additional Five per cent Duty Act.

"An Act for the encouragement and protection of the settlers upon the waters of the Mississippi." For three years; continued in 1755 and 1763; revived in 1772, and continued until 1778. Hening, *Statutes*, VI. 417, 468; VII. 639; VIII. 530.

1754, July 25. Maryland: Additional 10s. Duty Act.

"An Act for his Majesty's Service." Bacon, *Laws*, 1754, ch. ix.

1755, May. Virginia: Additional Ten per cent Duty Act.

"An act to explain an act, intituled, An act for raising the sum of twenty thousand pounds, for the protection of his majesty's subjects, against the insults and encroachments of the French; and for other purposes therein mentioned."

§ 10. ". . . from and after the passing of this act, there shall be levied and paid to our sovereign lord the king, his heirs and successors, for all slaves imported, or brought into this colony and dominion for sale, either by land or water, from any part [port] or place whatsoever, by the buyer, or purchaser, after the rate of ten per centum, on the amount of each respective purchase, over and above the several duties already laid on slaves, imported as aforesaid, by an act or acts of Assembly, now subsisting, and also over and above the duty laid by" the Act of 1754. Repealed by Act of May, 1760, § 11, ". . . inasmuch as the same prevents the importation of slaves, and thereby lessens the fund arising from the duties upon slaves." Hening, *Statutes*, VI. 461; VII. 363. Cf. *Dinwiddie Papers*, II. 86.

1756, March 22. Maryland: Additional 20s. Duty Act.

"An Act for granting a Supply of Forty Thousand Pounds, for his Majesty's Service," etc. For five years. Bacon, *Laws*, 1756, ch. v.

1757, April. Virginia: Additional Ten per cent Duty Act.

"An Act for granting an aid to his majesty for the better protection of this colony, and for other purposes therein mentioned."

§ 22. ". . . from and after the ninth day of July, one thousand seven hundred and fifty-eight, during the term of seven years, there shall be paid for all slaves imported into this colony, for sale, either by land or water, from any port or place whatsoever, by the buyer or purchaser thereof, after the rate of ten per centum on the amount of each respective purchase, over and above the several duties already laid upon slaves imported, as aforesaid, by any act or acts of Assembly now subsisting in this colony," etc. Repealed by Act of March, 1761, § 6, as being "found very inconvenient." Hening, *Statutes*, VII. 69, 383.

1759, November. Virginia: Twenty per cent Duty Act.

"An Act to oblige the persons bringing slaves into this colony from Maryland, Carolina, and the West-Indies, for their own use, to pay a duty."

§ 1. ". . . from and after the passing of this act, there shall be paid . . . for all slaves imported or brought into this colony and dominion from Maryland, North-Carolina, or any other place in America, by the owner or importer thereof, after the rate of twenty per centum on the amount of each respective purchase," etc. This act to continue until April 20, 1767; continued in 1766 and 1769, until 1773; altered by Act of 1772, *q. v.* *Ibid.*, VII. 338; VIII. 191, 336.

1760. South Carolina: Total Prohibition.

Text not found; act disallowed by Great Britain. Cf. Burge, *Commentaries*, I. 737, note; W. B. Stevens, *History of Georgia*, I. 286.

1761, March 14. Pennsylvania: £10 Duty Act.

"An Act for laying a duty on Negroes and Mulattoe slaves, imported into this province." Continued in 1768; repealed (or disallowed) in 1780. Carey and Bioren, *Laws*, I. 371, 451; *Acts of Assembly* (ed. 1782), p. 149; *Colonial Records* (1852), VIII. 576.

1761, April 22. Pennsylvania: Prohibitive Duty Act.

"A Supplement to an act, entituled An Act for laying a duty on Negroes and Mulattoe slaves, imported into this province." Continued in 1768. Carey and Bioren, *Laws*, I. 371, 451; Bettle, *Notices of Negro Slavery*, in *Penn. Hist. Soc. Mem.* (1864), I. 388–9.

1763, Nov. 26. Maryland: Additional £2 Duty Act.

"An Act for imposing an additional Duty of Two Pounds per Poll on all Negroes Imported into this Province."

§ 1. All persons importing Negroes by land or water into this province, shall at the time of entry pay to the naval officer the sum of two pounds, current money, over and above the duties now payable by law, for every Negro so imported or brought in, on forfeiture of £10 current money for every Negro so brought in and not paid for. One half of the penalty is to go to the informer, the other half to the use of the county schools. The duty shall be collected, accounted for, and paid by the naval officers, in the same manner as former duties on Negroes.

§ 2. But persons removing from any other of his Majesty's dominions in order to settle and reside within this province, may import their slaves for carrying on their proper occupations at the time of removal, duty free.

§ 3. Importers of Negroes, exporting the same within two months of the time of their importation, on application to the naval officer shall be paid the aforesaid duty. Bacon, *Laws*, 1763, ch. xxviii.

1763 (circa). New Jersey: Prohibitive Duty Act.

"An Act for laying a duty on Negroes and Mulatto Slaves Imported into this Province." Disallowed (?) by Great Britain. *N. J. Archives*, IX. 345–6, 383, 447, 458.

1764, Aug. 25. South Carolina: Additional £100 Duty Act.

"An Act for laying an additional duty upon all Negroes hereafter to be imported into this Province, for the time therein mentioned, to be paid by the first purchasers of such Negroes." Cooper, *Statutes*, IV. 187.

1766, November. Virginia: Proposed Duty Act.

"An act for laying an additional duty upon slaves imported into this colony."

§ 1. "... from and after the passing of this act there shall be levied and paid ... for all slaves imported or brought into this colony for sale, either by land or water from any port or place whatsoever, by the buyer or purchaser, after the rate of ten per centum on the amount of each respective purchase over and above the several duties already laid upon slaves imported or brought into this colony as aforesaid," etc. To be suspended until the king's consent is given, and then to continue seven years. The same act was passed again in 1769. Hening, *Statutes*, VIII. 237, 337.

1766. Rhode Island: Restrictive Measure (?).

Title and text not found. Cf. *Digest* of 1798, under "Slave Trade;" *Public Laws of Rhode Island* (revision of 1822), p. 441.

1768, Feb. 20. Pennsylvania: Re-enactment of Acts of 1761.

Titles only found. Dallas, *Laws*, I. 490; *Colonial Records* (1852), IX. 472, 637, 641.

1769, Nov. 16. New Jersey: £15 Duty Act.

"An Act for laying a Duty on the Purchasers of Slaves imported into this Colony."

"Whereas Duties on the Importation of Negroes in several of the neighbouring Colonies hath, on Experience, been found beneficial in the Introduction of sober, industrious Foreigners, to settle under His Majesty's Allegiance, and the promoting a Spirit of Industry among the Inhabitants in general: *In order therefore* to promote the same good Designs in this Government, and that such as choose to purchase Slaves may contribute some equitable Proportion of the publick Burdens," etc. A duty of "*Fifteen Pounds*, Proclamation Money, is laid." *Acts of Assembly* (Allinson, 1776), p. 315.

1769 (circa). Connecticut: Importation Prohibited(?).

Title and text not found. "Whereas, the increase of slaves is injurious to the poor, and inconvenient, therefore," etc. Fowler, *Historical Status of the Negro in Connecticut*, in *Local Law*, etc., p. 125.

1770. Rhode Island: Bill to Prohibit Importation.

Bill to prohibit importation of slaves fails. Arnold, *History of Rhode Island* (1859), II. 304, 321, 337.

1771, April 12. Massachusetts: Bill to Prevent Importation.

Bill passes both houses and fails of Governor Hutchinson's assent. *House Journal*, pp. 211, 215, 219, 228, 234, 236, 240, 242–3.

1771. Maryland: Additional £5 Duty Act.

"An Act for imposing a further additional duty of five pounds current money per poll on all negroes imported into this province." For seven years. *Laws of Maryland since* 1763: 1771, ch. vii.; cf. 1773, sess. Nov.–Dec., ch. xiv.

1772, April 1. Virginia: Address to the King.

". . . The importation of slaves into the colonies from the coast of Africa hath long been considered as a trade of great inhumanity, and under its *present encouragement*, we have too much reason to fear *will endanger the very existence* of your majesty's American dominions. . . .

"Deeply impressed with these sentiments, we most humbly beseech your majesty to *remove all those restraints* on your majesty's governors of this colony, *which inhibit their assenting to such laws as might check so very pernicious a commerce.*" *Journals of the House of Burgesses*, p. 131; quoted in Tucker, *Dissertation on Slavery* (repr. 1861), p. 43.

1773, Feb. 26. Pennsylvania: Additional £10 Duty Act.

"An Act for making perpetual the act . . . [of 1761] . . . and laying an additional duty on the said slaves." Dallas, *Laws*, I. 671; *Acts of Assembly* (ed. 1782), p. 149.

1774, March, June. Massachusetts: Bills to Prohibit Importation.

Two bills designed to prohibit the importation of slaves fail of the governor's assent. First bill: *General Court Records*, XXX. 248, 264; *Mass. Archives, Domestic Relations*, 1643–1774, IX. 457. Second bill: *General Court Records*, XXX. 308, 322.

1774, June. Rhode Island: Importation Restricted.

"An Act prohibiting the importation of Negroes into this Colony."

"Whereas, the inhabitants of America are generally engaged in the preservation of their own rights and liberties, among which, that of personal freedom must be considered as the greatest; as those who are desirous of enjoying all the advantages of liberty themselves, should be willing to extend personal liberty to others; —

"Therefore, be it enacted . . . that for the future, no negro or mulatto slave shall be brought into this colony; and in case any slave shall hereafter be brought in, he or she shall be, and are hereby, rendered immediately free, so far as respects personal freedom, and the enjoyment of private property, in the same manner as the native Indians."

Provided that the slaves of settlers and travellers be excepted.

"Provided, also, that nothing in this act shall extend, or be deemed to extend, to any negro or mulatto slave brought from the coast of Africa, into the West Indies, on board any vessel belonging to this colony, and which negro or mulatto slave could not be disposed of in the West Indies, but shall be brought into this colony.

"Provided, that the owner of such negro or mulatto slave give bond to the general treasurer of the said colony, within ten days after such arrival in the sum of £100, lawful money, for each and every such negro or mulatto slave so brought in, that such negro or mulatto slave shall be exported out of the colony, within one year from the date of such bond; if such negro or mulatto be alive, and in a condition to be removed."

"Provided, also, that nothing in this act shall extend, or be deemed to extend, to any negro or mulatto slave that may be on board any vessel belonging to this colony, now at sea, in her present voyage." Heavy penalties are laid for bringing in Negroes in order to free them. *Colonial Records*, VII. 251–3.

[1784, February: "It is voted and resolved, that the whole of the clause contained in an act of this Assembly, passed at June session, A.D. 1774, permitting slaves brought from the coast of Africa into the West Indies, on board any vessel belonging to this (then colony, now) state, and who could not be disposed of in the West Indies, &c., be, and the same is, hereby repealed." *Colonial Records*, X. 8.]

1774, October. Connecticut: Importation Prohibited.

"An Act for prohibiting the Importation of Indian, Negro or Molatto Slaves."

". . . no indian, negro or molatto Slave shall at any time hereafter be brought or imported into this Colony, by sea or land, from any place or places whatsoever, to be disposed of, left or sold within this Colony." This was re-enacted in the revision of 1784, and slaves born after 1784 were ordered to be emancipated at the age of twenty-five. *Colonial Records*, XIV. 329; *Acts and Laws of Connecticut* (ed. 1784), pp. 233–4.

1774. New Jersey: Proposed Prohibitive Duty.

"A Bill for laying a Duty on Indian, Negroe and Molatto Slaves, imported into this Colony." Passed the Assembly, and was rejected by the Council as "plainly" intending "an intire Prohibition," etc. *N. J. Archives*, 1st Series, VI. 222.

1775, March 27. Delaware: Bill to Prohibit Importation.

Passed the Assembly and was vetoed by the governor. Force, *American Archives*, 4th Series, II. 128–9.

1775, Nov. 23. Virginia: On Lord Dunmore's Proclamation.

Williamsburg Convention to the public: "Our Assemblies have repeatedly passed acts, laying heavy duties upon imported Negroes, by which they meant altogether to prevent the horrid traffick; but their humane intentions have been as often frustrated by the cruelty and covetousness of a set of *English* merchants." . . . The Americans would, if possible, "not only prevent any more Negroes from losing their freedom, but restore it to such as have already unhappily lost it." This is evidently addressed in part to Negroes, to keep them from joining the British. *Ibid.*, III. 1387.

1776, June 2. Virginia: Preamble to Frame of Government.

Blame for the slave-trade thrown on the king. See above, page 13. Hening, *Statutes*, IX. 112–3.

1776, Aug.–Sept. Delaware: Constitution.

"The Constitution or system of Government agreed to and resolved upon by the Representatives in full Convention of the Delaware State," etc.

§ 26. "No person hereafter imported into this State from *Africa* ought to be held in slavery on any pretence whatever; and no Negro, Indian, or Mulatto slave ought to be brought into this State, for sale, from any part of the world." Force, *American Archives*, 5th Series, I. 1174–9.

1777, July 2. Vermont: Slavery Condemned.

The first Constitution declares slavery a violation of "natural, inherent and unalienable rights." *Vermont State Papers*, 1779–86, p. 244.

1777. Maryland: Negro Duty Maintained

"An Act concerning duties."

". . . no duties imposed by act of assembly on any article or thing imported into or exported out of this state (except duties imposed on the importation of negroes), shall be taken or received within two years from the end of the present session of the general assembly." *Laws of Maryland since* 1763: 1777, sess. Feb.–Apr., ch. xviii.

1778, Sept. 7. Pennsylvania: Act to Collect Back Duties.

"An Act for the recovery of the duties on Negroes and Mulattoe slaves, which on the fourth day of July, one thousand seven hundred and seventy-six, were due to this state," etc. Dallas, *Laws*, I. 782.

1778, October. Virginia: Importation Prohibited.

"An act for preventing the farther importation of Slaves.

§ 1. "For preventing the farther importation of slaves into this commonwealth, *Be it enacted by the General Assembly*, That from and after the passing of this act no slave or slaves shall hereafter be imported into this commonwealth by sea or land, nor shall any slaves so imported be sold or bought by any person whatsoever.

§ 2. "Every person hereafter importing slaves into this commonwealth contrary to this act shall forfeit and pay the sum of one thousand pounds for every slave so imported, and every person selling or buying any such slaves shall in like manner forfeit and pay the sum of five hundred pounds for every slave so sold or bought," etc.

§ 3. "*And be it farther enacted*, That every slave imported into this commonwealth, contrary to the true intent and meaning of this act, shall, upon such importation become free."

§ 4. Exceptions are *bona fide* settlers with slaves not imported later than Nov. 1, 1778, nor intended to be sold; and transient travellers. Re-enacted in substance in the revision of October, 1785. For a temporary exception to this act, as concerns citizens of Georgia and South Carolina during the war, see Act of May, 1780. Hening, *Statutes*, IX. 471; X. 307; XII. 182.

1779, October. Rhode Island: Slave-Trade Restricted.

"An Act prohibiting slaves being sold out of the state, against their consent." Title only found. *Colonial Records*, VIII. 618; Arnold, *History of Rhode Island*, II. 449.

1779, Vermont: Importation Prohibited.

"An Act for securing the general privileges of the people," etc. The act abolished slavery. *Vermont State Papers*, 1779–86, p. 287.

1780. Massachusetts: Slavery Abolished.

Passage in the Constitution which was held by the courts to abolish slavery: "Art. I. All men are born free and equal, and have certain, natural, essential, and unalienable rights; among which may be reckoned the right of enjoying and defending their lives and liberties," etc. *Constitution of Massachusetts*, Part I., Art. 1; prefixed to *Perpetual Laws* (1789).

1780, March 1. Pennsylvania: Slavery Abolished.

"An Act for the gradual abolition of slavery."

§ 5. All slaves to be registered before Nov. 1.

§ 10. None but slaves "registered as aforesaid, shall, at any time hereafter, be deemed, adjudged, or holden, within the territories of this commonwealth, as slaves or servants for life, but as free men and free women; except the domestic slaves attending upon Delegates in Congress from the other American States," and those of travellers not remaining over six months, foreign ministers, etc., "provided such domestic slaves be not aliened or sold to any inhabitant," etc.

§ 11. Fugitive slaves from other states may be taken back.

§ 14. Former duty acts, etc., repealed. Dallas, *Laws*, I. 838. Cf. *Penn. Archives*, VII. 79; VIII. 720.

1783, April. Confederation: Slave-Trade in Treaty of 1783.

"To the earnest wish of Jay that British ships should have no right under the convention to carry into the states any slaves from any part of the world, it being the intention o the United States entirely to prohibit their importation, Fox answered promptly: 'If that be their policy, it never can be competent to us to dispute with them their own regulations.'" Fox to Hartley, June 10, 1783, in Bancroft, *History of the Constitution*, I. 61. Cf. Sparks, *Diplomatic Correspondence*, X. 154, June, 1783.

1783. Maryland: Importation Prohibited.

"An Act to prohibit the bringing slaves into this state."

". . . it shall not be lawful, after the passing this act, to import or bring into this state, by land or water, any negro, mulatto, or other slave, for sale, or to reside within this state; and any person brought into this state as a slave contrary to this act, if a slave before, shall thereupon immediately cease to be a slave, and shall be free; provided that this act shall not prohibit any person, being a citizen of some one of the United States, coming into this state, with a *bona fide* intention of settling therein, and who shall actually reside within this state for one year at least, . . . to import or bring in any slave or slaves which before belonged to such person, and which slave or slaves had been an inhabitant of some one of the United States, for the space of three whole years next preceding such importation," etc. *Laws of Maryland since* 1763: 1783, sess. April–June, ch. xxiii.

1783, Aug. 13. South Carolina: £3 and £20 Duty Act.

"An Act for levying and collecting certain duties and imposts therein mentioned, in aid of the public revenue." Cooper, *Statutes*, IV. 576.

1784, February. Rhode Island: Manumission.

"An Act authorizing the manumission of negroes, mulattoes, and others, and for the gradual abolition of slavery." Persons born after March, 1784, to be free. Bill framed pursuant to a petition of Quakers. *Colonial Records*, X. 7–8; Arnold, *History of Rhode Island*, II. 503.

1784, March 26. South Carolina: £3 and £5 Duty Act.

"An Act for levying and collecting certain Duties," etc. Cooper, *Statutes*, IV. 607.

1785, April 12. New York: Partial Prohibition.

"An Act granting a bounty on hemp to be raised within this State, and imposing an additional duty on sundry articles of merchandise, and for other purposes therein mentioned."

". . . *And be it further enacted by the authority aforesaid,* That if any negro or other person to be imported or brought into this State from any of the United States or from any other place or country after the first day of June next, shall be sold as a slave or slaves within this State, the seller or his or her factor or agent, shall be deemed guilty of a public offence, and shall for every such offence forfeit the sum of one hundred pounds lawful money of New York, to be recovered by any person," etc.

"*And be it further enacted* . . . That every such person imported or brought into this State and sold contrary to the true intent and meaning of this act shall be freed." *Laws of New York,* 1785–88 (ed. 1886), pp. 120–21.

1785. Rhode Island: Restrictive Measure (?).

Title and text not found. Cf. *Public Laws of Rhode Island* (revision of 1822), p. 441.

1786, March 2. New Jersey: Importation Prohibited.

"An Act to prevent the importation of Slaves into the State of New Jersey, and to authorize the Manumission of them under certain restrictions, and to prevent the Abuse of Slaves."

"Whereas the Principles of Justice and Humanity require that the barbarous Custom of bringing the unoffending African from his native Country and Connections into a State of Slavery ought to be discountenanced, and as soon as possible prevented; and sound Policy also requires, in order to afford ample Support to such of the Community as depend upon their Labour for their daily Subsistence, that the Importation of Slaves into this State from any other State or Country whatsoever, ought to be prohibited under certain Restrictions; and that such as are under Servitude in the State ought to be protected by Law from those Exercises of wanton Cruelty too often practiced upon them; and that every unnecessary Obstruction in the Way of freeing Slaves should be removed; therefore,

§ 1. "*Be it Enacted by the Council and General Assembly of this State, and it is hereby Enacted by the Authority of the same*, That from and after the Publication of this Act, it shall not be lawful for any Person or Persons whatsoever to bring into this State, either for Sale or for Servitude, any Negro Slave brought from Africa since the Year Seventeen Hundred and Seventy-six; and every Person offending by bringing into this State any such Negro Slave shall, for each Slave, forfeit and Pay the Sum of Fifty Pounds, to be sued for and recovered with Costs by the Collector of the Township into which such Slave shall be brought, to be applied when recovered to the Use of the State.

§ 2. "*And be it further Enacted by the Authority aforesaid*, That if any Person shall either bring or procure to be brought into this State, any Negro or Mulatto Slave, who shall not have been born in or brought from Africa since the Year above mentioned, and either sell or buy, or cause such Negro or Mulatto Slave to be sold or remain in this State, for the Space of six Months, every such Person so bringing or procuring to be brought or selling or purchasing such Slave, not born in or brought from Africa since the Year aforesaid, shall for every such Slave, forfeit and pay the Sum of Twenty Pounds, to be sued for and recovered with Costs by the Collector of the Township into which such Slave shall be brought or remain after the Time limited for that Purpose, the Forfeiture to be applied to the Use of the State as aforesaid.

§ 3. "*Provided always, and be it further Enacted by the Authority aforesaid*, That Nothing in this Act contained shall be construed to prevent any Person who shall remove into the State, to take a settled Residence here, from bringing all his or her Slaves without incurring the Penalties aforesaid, excepting such Slaves as shall have been brought from Africa since the Year first above mentioned, or to prevent any Foreigners or others having only a temporary Residence in this State, for the Purpose of transacting any particular Business, or on their Travels, from bringing and employing such Slaves as Servants, during the Time of his or her Stay here, provided such Slaves shall not be sold or disposed of in this State." *Acts of the Tenth General Assembly* (Tower Collection of Laws).

1786, Oct. 30. Vermont: External Trade Prohibited.

"An act to prevent the sale and transportation of Negroes and Molattoes out of this State." £100 penalty. *Statutes of Vermont* (ed. 1787), p. 105.

1786. North Carolina: Prohibitive Duty.

"An act to impose a duty on all slaves brought into this state by land or water."

"Whereas the importation of slaves into this state is productive of evil consequences, and highly impolitic," etc. A prohibitive duty is imposed. The exact text was not found.

§ 6. Slaves introduced from States which have passed emancipation acts are to be returned in three months; if not, a bond of £50 is to be forfeited, and a fine of £100 imposed.

§ 8. Act to take effect next Feb. 1; repealed by Act of 1790, ch. 18. Martin, *Iredell's Acts of Assembly*, I. 413, 492.

1787, Feb. 3. Delaware: Exportation Prohibited.

"An Act to prevent the exportation of slaves, and for other purposes." *Laws of Delaware* (ed. 1797), p. 884, ch. 145 b.

1787, March 28. South Carolina: Total Prohibition.

"An Act to regulate the recovery and payment of debts and for prohibiting the importation of negroes for the time therein mentioned." Title only given. Grimké, *Public Laws*, p. lxviii, No. 1485.

1787, March 28. South Carolina: Importation Prohibited.

"An Ordinance to impose a Penalty on any person who shall import into this State any Negroes, contrary to the Instalment Act."

1. "*Be it ordained*, by the honorable the Senate and House of Representatives, met in General Assembly, and by the authority of the same, That any person importing or bringing into this State a negro slave, contrary to the Act to regulate the recovery of debts and prohibiting the importation of negroes, shall, besides the forfeiture of such negro or slave, be liable to a penalty of one hundred pounds, to the use of the State, for every such negro or slave so imported and brought in, in addition to the forfeiture in and by the said Act prescribed." Cooper, *Statutes*, VII. 430.

1787, October. Rhode Island: Importation Prohibited.

"An act to prevent the slave trade and to encourage the abolition of slavery." This act prohibited and censured trade under penalty of £100 for each person and £1,000 for each vessel. Bartlett, *Index to the Printed Acts and Resolves*, p. 333; *Narragansett Historical Register*, II. 298–9.

APPENDIX B.

A CHRONOLOGICAL CONSPECTUS OF STATE, NATIONAL, AND INTERNATIONAL LEGISLATION.

1788–1871.

As the State statutes and Congressional reports and bills are difficult to find, the significant parts of such documents are printed in full. In the case of national statutes and treaties, the texts may easily be found through the references.

1788, Feb. 22. New York: Slave-Trade Prohibited.

"An Act concerning slaves."

"Whereas in consequence of the act directing a revision of the laws of this State, it is expedient that the several existing laws relative to slaves, should be revised, and comprized in one. Therefore, *Be it enacted*," etc.

"And to prevent the further importation of slaves into this State, *Be it further enacted by the authority aforesaid*, That if any person shall sell as a slave within this State any negro, or other person, who has been imported or brought into this State, after" June 1, 1785, "such seller, or his or her factor or agent, making such sale, shall be deemed guilty of a public offence, and shall for every such offence, forfeit the sum of one hundred pounds. . . . *And further*, That every person so imported . . . shall be free." The purchase of slaves for removal to another State is prohibited under penalty of £100. *Laws of New York*, 1785–88 (ed. 1886), pp. 675–6.

1788, March 25. Massachusetts: Slave-Trade Prohibited.

"An Act to prevent the Slave-Trade, and for granting Relief to the Families of such unhappy Persons as may be kidnapped or decoyed away from this Commonwealth."

"Whereas by the African trade for slaves, the lives and liberties of many innocent persons have been from time to time sacrificed to the lust of gain: And whereas some persons residing in this Commonwealth may be so regardless of the rights of human kind, as to be concerned in that unrighteous commerce:

§ 1. "Be it therefore enacted by the Senate and House of Representatives, in General Court assembled, and by the authority of the same, That no citizen of this Commonwealth, or other person residing within the same, shall for himself, or any other person whatsoever, either as master, factor, supercargo, owner or hirer, in whole or in part, of any vessel, directly or indirectly, import or transport, or buy or sell, or receive on board, his or their vessel, with intent to cause to be imported or transported, any of the inhabitants of any State or Kingdom, in that part of the world called *Africa*, as slaves, or as servants for term of years." Any person convicted of doing this shall forfeit and pay the sum of £50 for every person received on board, and the sum of £200 for every vessel fitted out for the trade, "to be recovered by action of debt, in any Court within this Commonwealth, proper to try the same; the one moiety thereof to the use of this Commonwealth, and the other moiety to the person who shall prosecute for and recover the same."

§ 2. All insurance on said vessels and cargo shall be null and void; "and this act may be given in evidence under the general issue, in any suit or action commenced for the recovery of insurance so made," etc.

§ 4. "*Provided* . . . That this act do not extend to vessels which have already sailed, their owners, factors, or commanders, for and during their present voyage, or to any insurance that shall have been made, previous to the passing of the same." *Perpetual Laws of Massachusetts*, 1780–89 (ed. 1789), p. 235.

1788, March 29. Pennsylvania: Slave-Trade Prohibited.

"An Act to explain and amend an act, entituled, 'An Act for the gradual abolition of slavery.'"

§ 2. Slaves brought in by persons intending to settle shall be free.

§ 3. ". . . no negro or mulatto slave, or servant for term of years," except servants of congressmen, consuls, etc., "shall be removed out of this state, with the design and intention that the place of abode or residence of such slave or servant shall be thereby altered or changed, or with the design and intention that such slave or servant, if a female, and pregnant, shall be detained and kept out of this state till her delivery of the child of which she is or shall be pregnant, or with the design and intention that such slave or servant shall be brought again into this state, after the expiration of six months from the time of such slave or servant having been first brought into this state, without his or her consent, if of full age, testified upon a private examination, before two Justices of the peace of the city or county in which he or she shall reside, or, being under the age of twenty-one years, without his or her consent, testified in manner aforesaid, and also without the consent of his or her parents," etc. Penalty for every such offence, £75.

§ 5. ". . . if any person or persons shall build, fit, equip, man, or otherwise prepare any ship or vessel, within any port of this state, or shall cause any ship or other vessel to sail from any port of this state, for the purpose of carrying on a trade or traffic in slaves, to, from, or between Europe, Asia, Africa or America, or any places or countries whatever, or of transporting slaves to or from one port or place to another, in any part or parts of the world, such ship or vessel, her tackle, furniture, apparel, and other appurtenances, shall be forfeited to the commonwealth. . . . And, moreover, all and every person and persons so building, fitting out," etc., shall forfeit £1000. Dallas, *Laws*, II. 586.

1788, October. Connecticut: Slave-Trade Prohibited.

"An Act to prevent the Slave-Trade."

"*Be it enacted by the Governor, Council and Representatives in General Court assembled, and by the Authority of the same,* That no Citizen or Inhabitant of this State, shall for himself, or any other Person, either as Master, Factor, Supercargo, Owner or Hirer, in Whole, or in Part, of any Vessel, directly or indirectly, import or transport, or buy or sell, or receive on board his or her Vessel, with Intent to cause to be imported or transported, any of the Inhabitants of any Country in Africa, as Slaves or Servants, for Term of Years; upon Penalty of *Fifty Pounds*, for every Person so received on board, as aforesaid; and of *Five Hundred Pounds* for every such Vessel employed in the Importation or

Transportation aforesaid; to be recovered by Action, Bill, Plaint or Information; the one Half to the Plaintiff, and the other Half to the Use of this State." And all insurance on vessels and slaves shall be void. This act to be given as evidence under general issue, in any suit commenced for recovery of such insurance.

". . . if any Person shall kidnap . . . any free Negro," etc., inhabitant of this State, he shall forfeit £100. Every vessel clearing for the coast of Africa or any other part of the world, and suspected to be in the slave-trade, must give bond in £1000. Slightly amended in 1789. *Acts and Laws of Connecticut* (ed. 1784), pp. 368–9, 388.

1788, Nov. 4. South Carolina: Temporary Prohibition.

"An Act to regulate the Payment and Recovery of Debts, and to prohibit the Importation of Negroes, for the Time therein limited."

§ 16. "No negro or other slave shall be imported or brought into this State either by land or water on or before the first of January, 1793, under the penalty of forfeiting every such slave or slaves to any person who will sue or inform for the same; and under further penalty of paying £100 to the use of the State for every such negro or slave so imported or brought in: *Provided*, That nothing in this prohibition contained shall extend to such slaves as are now the property of citizens of the United States, and at the time of passing this act shall be within the limits of the said United States.

§ 17. "All former instalment laws, and an ordinance imposing a penalty on persons importing negroes into this State, passed the 28th day of March 1787, are hereby repealed." Grimké, *Public Laws*, p. 466.

1789, Feb. 3. Delaware: Slave-Trade Prohibited.

"*An additional Supplementary* ACT *to an act, intituled*, An act to prevent the exportation of slaves, and for other purposes."

"Whereas it is inconsistent with that spirit of general liberty which pervades the constitution of this state, that vessels should be fitted out, or equipped, in any of the ports thereof, for the purpose of receiving and transporting the natives of Africa to places where they are held in slavery; or that any acts should be deemed lawful, which tend to encourage or promote such iniquitous traffic among us:

§ 1. "*Be it therefore enacted by the General Assembly of Delaware*, That if any owner or owners, master, agent, or factor, shall fit out, equip, man, or otherwise prepare, any ship or vessel within any port or place in this state, or shall cause any ship, or other vessel, to sail from any port or place in this state, for the purpose of carrying on a trade or traffic in slaves, to, from, or between, Europe, Asia, Africa, or America, or any places or countries whatever, or of transporting slaves to, or from, one port or place to another, in any part or parts of the world; such ship or vessel, her tackle, furniture, apparel, and other appurtenances, shall be forfeited to this state. . . . And moreover, all and every person and persons so fitting out . . . any ship or vessel . . . shall severally forfeit and pay the sum of Five Hundred Pounds;" one-half to the state, and one-half to the informer.

§ 2. "*And whereas* it has been found by experience, that the act, intituled, *An act to prevent the exportation of slaves, and for other purposes*, has not produced all the good effects expected therefrom," any one exporting a slave to Maryland, Virginia, North Carolina, South Carolina, Georgia, or the West Indies, without license, shall forfeit £100 for each slave exported and £20 for each attempt.

§ 3. Slaves to be tried by jury for capital offences. *Laws of Delaware* (ed. 1797), p. 942, ch. 194 b.

1789, May 13. Congress (House): Proposed Duty on Slaves Imported.

A tax of $10 per head on slaves imported, moved by Parker of Virginia. After debate, withdrawn. *Annals of Cong.*, 1 Cong. 1 sess. pp. 336–42.

1789, Sept. 19. Congress (House): Bill to Tax Slaves Imported.

A committee under Parker of Virginia reports, "a bill concerning the importation of certain persons prior to the year 1808." Read once and postponed until next session. *House Journal* (repr. 1826), 1 Cong. 1 sess. I. 37, 114; *Annals of Cong.*, 1 Cong. 1 sess., pp. 366, 903.

1790, March 22. Congress (House): Declaration of Powers.

See above, page 78.

1790, March 22. New York: Amendment of Act of 1788.

"An Act to amend the act entitled 'An act concerning slaves.'"

"Whereas many inconveniences have arisen from the prohibiting the exporting of slaves from this State. Therefore

Be it enacted . . ., That where any slave shall hereafter be convicted of a crime under the degree of a capital offence, in the supreme court, or the court of oyer and terminer, and general gaol delivery, or a court of general sessions of the peace within this State, it shall and may be lawful to and for the master or mistress to cause such slave to be transported out of this State," etc. *Laws of New York*, 1789–96 (ed. 1886), p. 151.

1792, May. Connecticut: Act of 1788 Strengthened.

"An Act in addition to an Act, entitled 'An Act to prevent the Slave Trade.'"

This provided that persons directly or indirectly aiding or assisting in slave-trading should be fined £100. All notes, bonds, mortgages, etc., of any kind, made or executed in payment for any slave imported contrary to this act, are declared null and void. Persons removing from the State might carry away their slaves. *Acts and Laws of Connecticut* (ed. 1784), pp. 412–3.

1792, Dec. 17. Virginia: Revision of Acts.

"An Act to reduce into one, the several acts concerning slaves, free negroes, and mulattoes."

§ 1. "*Be it enacted* . . ., That no persons shall henceforth be slaves within this commonwealth, except such as were so on the seventeenth day of October," 1785, "and the descendants of the females of them.

§ 2. "Slaves which shall hereafter be brought into this commonwealth, and kept therein one whole year together, or so long at different times as shall amount to one year, shall be free."

§ 4. "*Provided*, That nothing in this act contained, shall be construed to extend to those who may incline to remove from any of the United States and become citizens of this, if within sixty days after such removal, he or she shall take the following oath before some justice of the peace of this commonwealth: '*I, A. B., do swear, that my removal into the state of Virginia, was with no intent of evading the laws for preventing the further importation of slaves, nor have I brought with me any slaves, with an intention of selling them, nor have any of the slaves which I have brought with me, been imported from Africa, or any of the West India islands, since the first day of November*,'" 1778, etc.

§ 53. This act to be in force immediately. *Statutes at Large of Virginia, New Series*, I. 122.

1792, Dec. 21. South Carolina: Importation Prohibited until 1795.

"An Act to prohibit the importation of Slaves from Africa, or other places beyond sea, into this State, for two years; and also to prohibit the importation or bringing in Slaves, or Negroes, Mulattoes, Indians, Moors or Mestizoes, bound for a term of years, from any of the United States, by land or by water."

"Whereas, it is deemed inexpedient to increase the number of slaves within this State, in our present circumstances and situation;

§ 1. "*Be it therefore enacted* . . ., That no slave shall be imported into this State from Africa, the West India Islands, or other place beyond sea, for and during the term of two years, commencing from the first day of January next, which will be in the year of our Lord one thousand seven hundred and ninety-three."

§ 2. No slaves, Negroes, Indians, etc., bound for a term of years, to be brought in from any of the United States or bordering countries. Settlers may bring their slaves. Cooper, *Statutes*, VII. 431.

1793, Dec. 19. Georgia: Importation Prohibited.

"An act to prevent the importation of negroes into this state from the places herein mentioned." Title only. Re-enacted (?) by the Constitution of 1798. Marbury and Crawford, *Digest*, p. 442; Prince, *Digest*, p. 786.

1794. North Carolina: Importation Prohibited.

"An act to prevent the further importation and bringing of slaves and indented servants of colour into this state."

§ 1. "*Be it enacted* . . ., That from and after the first day of May next, no slave or indented servant of colour shall be imported or brought into this state by land or water; nor shall any slave or indented servant of colour, who may be imported or brought contrary to the intent and meaning of this act, be bought, sold or hired by any person whatever."

§ 2. Penalty for importing, £100 per slave; for buying or selling, the same.

§ 4. Persons removing, travelling, etc., are excepted. The act was amended slightly in 1796. Martin, *Iredell's Acts of Assembly*, II. 53, 94.

1794, March 22. United States Statute: Export Slave-Trade Forbidden.

"An Act to prohibit the carrying on the Slave Trade from the United States to any foreign place or country." *Statutes at Large*, I. 347. For proceedings in Congress, see *Senate Journal* (repr. 1820), 3 Cong. 1 sess. II. 51; *House Journal* (repr. 1826), 3 Cong. 1 sess. II. 76, 84, 85, 96, 98, 99, 100; *Annals of Cong.*, 3 Cong. 1 sess. pp. 64, 70, 72.

1794, Dec. 20. South Carolina: Act of 1792 Extended.

"An Act to revive and extend an Act entitled 'An Act to prohibit the importation of Slaves from Africa, or other places beyond Sea, into this State, for two years; and also, to prohibit the importation or bringing in of Negro Slaves, Mulattoes, Indians, Moors or Mestizoes, bound for a term of years, from any of the United States, by Land or Water.'"

§ 1. Act of 1792 extended until Jan. 1, 1797.

§ 2. It shall not be lawful hereafter to import slaves, free Negroes, etc., from the West Indies, any part of America outside the United States, "or from other parts beyond sea." Such slaves are to be forfeited and sold; the importer to be fined £50; free Negroes to be re-transported. Cooper, *Statutes*, VII. 433.

1795. North Carolina: Act against West Indian Slaves.

"An act to prevent any person who may emigrate from any of the West India or Bahama islands, or the French, Dutch or Spanish settlements on the southern coast of America, from bringing slaves into this state, and also for imposing certain restrictions on free persons of colour who may hereafter come into this state." Penalty, £100 for each slave over 15 years of age. *Laws of North Carolina* (revision of 1819), I. 786.

1796. Maryland: Importation Prohibited.

"An Act relating to Negroes, and to repeal the acts of assembly therein mentioned."

"*Be it enacted* . . ., That it shall not be lawful, from and after the passing of this act, to import or bring into this state, by land or water, any negro, mulatto or other slave, for sale, or to reside within this state; and any person brought into this state as a slave contrary to this act, if a slave before, shall thereupon immediately cease to be the property of the person or persons so importing or bringing such slave within this state, and shall be free."

§ 2. Any citizen of the United States, coming into the State to take up *bona fide* residence, may bring with him, or within one year import, any slave which was his property at the time of removal, "which slaves, or the mother of which slaves, shall have been a resident of the United States, or some one of them, three whole years next preceding such removal."

§ 3. Such slaves cannot be sold within three years, except by will, etc. In 1797, "A Supplementary Act," etc., slightly amended the preceding, allowing guardians, executors, etc., to import the slaves of the estate. Dorsey, *Laws*, I. 334, 344.

1796, Dec. 19. South Carolina: Importation Prohibited until 1799.

"An Act to prohibit the importation of Negroes, until the first day of January, one thousand seven hundred and ninety-nine."

"Whereas, it appears to be highly impolitic to import negroes from Africa, or other places beyond seas," etc. Extended by acts of Dec. 21, 1798, and Dec. 20, 1800, until Jan. 1, 1803. Cooper, *Statutes*, VII. 434, 436.

1797, Jan. 18. Delaware: Codification of Acts.

"An Act concerning Negro and Mulatto slaves."

§ 5. ". . . any Negro or Mulatto slave, who hath been or shall be brought into this state contrary to the intent and meaning of [the act of 1787]; and any Negro or Mulatto slave who hath been or shall be exported, or sold with an intention for exportation, or carried out for sale from this state, contrary to the intent and meaning of [the act of 1793], shall be, and are hereby declared free; any thing in this act to the contrary notwithstanding." *Laws of Delaware* (ed. 1797), p. 1321, ch. 124 c.

1798, Jan. 31. Georgia: Importation Prohibited.

"An act to prohibit the further importation of slaves into this state."

§ 1. ". . . six months after the passing of this act, it shall be unlawful for any person or persons to import into this state, from Africa or elsewhere, any negro or negroes of any age or sex." Every person so offending shall forfeit for the first offence the sum of $1,000 for every negro so imported, and for every subsequent offence the sum of $1,000, one half for the use of the informer, and one half for the use of the State.

§ 2. Slaves not to be brought from other States for sale after three months.

§ 3. Persons convicted of bringing slaves into this State with a view to sell them, are subject to the same penalties as if they had sold them. Marbury and Crawford, *Digest*, p. 440.

1798, March 14. New Jersey: Slave-Trade Prohibited.

"An Act respecting slaves."

§ 12. "*And be it enacted*, That from and after the passing of this act, it shall not be lawful for any person or persons whatsoever, to bring into this state, either for sale or for servitude, any negro or other slave whatsoever." Penalty, $140 for each slave; travellers and temporary residents excepted.

§ 17. Any persons fitting out vessels for the slave-trade shall forfeit them. Paterson, *Digest*, p. 307.

1798, April 7. United States Statute: Importation into Mississippi Territory Prohibited.

"An Act for an amicable settlement of limits with the state of Georgia, and authorizing the establishment of a government in the Mississippi territory." *Statutes at Large*, I. 549. For proceedings in Congress, see *Annals of Cong.*, 5 Cong. 2 sess. pp. 511, 512, 513, 514, 515, 532, 533, 1235, 1249, 1277–84, 1296, 1298–1312, 1313, 1318.

1798, May 30. Georgia: Constitutional Prohibition.

Constitution of Georgia: —

Art. IV. § 11. "There shall be no future importation of slaves into this state from Africa, or any foreign place, after the first day of October next. The legislature shall have no power to pass laws for the emancipation of slaves, without the consent of each of their respective owners previous to such emancipation. They shall have no power to prevent emigrants, from either of the United States to this state, from bringing with them such persons as may be deemed slaves, by the laws of any one of the United States." Marbury and Crawford, *Digest*, p. 30.

1800, May 10. United States Statute: Americans Forbidden to Trade from one Foreign Country to Another.

"An Act in addition to the act intituled 'An act to prohibit the carrying on the Slave Trade from the United States to any foreign place or country.'" *Statutes at Large*, II. 70. For proceedings in Congress, see *Senate Journal* (repr. 1821), 6 Cong. 1 sess. III. 72, 77, 88, 92.

1800, Dec. 20. South Carolina: Slaves and Free Negroes Prohibited.

"An Act to prevent Negro Slaves and other persons of Colour, from being brought into or entering this State." Supplemented Dec. 19, 1801, and amended Dec. 18, 1802. Cooper, *Statutes*, VII. 436, 444, 447.

1801, April 8. New York: Slave-Trade Prohibited.

"An Act concerning slaves and servants."

". . . *And be it further enacted*, That no slave shall hereafter be imported or brought into this State, unless the person importing or bringing such slave shall be coming into this State with intent to reside permanently therein and shall have resided without this State, and also have owned such slave at least during one year next preceding the importing or bringing in of such slave," etc. A certificate, sworn to, must be obtained; any violation of this act or neglect to take out such certificate will result in freedom to the slave. Any sale or limited transfer of any person hereafter imported to be a public offence, under penalty of $250, and freedom to the slave transferred. The export of slaves or of any person freed by this act is forbidden, under penalty of $250 and freedom to the slave. Transportation for crime is permitted. Re-enacted with amendments March 31, 1817. *Laws of New York*, 1801 (ed. 1887), pp. 547–52; *Laws of New York*, 1817 (ed. 1817), p. 136.

1803, Feb. 28. United States Statute: Importation into States Prohibiting Forbidden.

"An Act to prevent the importation of certain persons into certain states, where, by the laws thereof, their admission is prohibited." *Statutes at Large*, II. 205. For copy of the proposed bill which this replaced, see *Annals of Cong.*, 7 Cong. 2 sess. p. 467. For proceedings in Congress, see *House Journal* (repr. 1826), 7 Cong. 2 sess. IV. 304, 324, 347; *Senate Journal* (repr. 1821), 7 Cong. 2 sess. III. 267, 268, 269–70, 273, 275, 276, 279.

1803. Dec. 17. South Carolina: African Slaves Admitted.

"An Act to alter and amend the several Acts respecting the importation or bringing into this State, from beyond seas, or elsewhere, Negroes and other persons of colour; and for other purposes therein mentioned."

§ 1. Acts of 1792, 1794, 1796, 1798, 1800, 1802, hereby repealed.

§ 2. Importation of Negroes from the West Indies prohibited.

§ 3. No Negro over fifteen years of age to be imported from the United States except under certificate of good character.

§ 5. Negroes illegally imported to be forfeited and sold, etc. Cooper, *Statutes*, VII. 449.

1804. [**Denmark.**

Act of 1792 abolishing the slave-trade goes into effect.]

1804, Feb. 14. Congress (House): Proposed Censure of South Carolina.

Representative Moore of South Carolina offered the following resolution, as a substitute to Mr. Bard's taxing proposition of Jan. 6:—

"*Resolved*, That this House receive with painful sensibility information that one of the Southern States, by a repeal of certain prohibitory laws, have permitted a traffic unjust in its nature, and highly impolitic in free Governments." Ruled out of order by the chairman of the Committee of the Whole. *Annals of Cong.*, 8 Cong. 1 sess. p. 1004.

1804, Feb. 15. Congress (House): Proposed Duty.

"*Resolved*, That a tax of ten dollars be imposed on every slave imported into any part of the United States."

"*Ordered*, That a bill, or bills, be brought in, pursuant to the said resolution," etc. Feb. 16 "a bill laying a duty on slaves imported into the United States" was read, but was never considered. *House Journal* (repr. 1826), 8 Cong. 1 sess. IV. 523, 578, 580, 581–2, 585; *Annals of Cong.*, 8 Cong. 1 sess. pp. 820, 876, 991, 1012, 1020, 1024–36.

1804, March 26. United States Statute: Slave-Trade Limited.

"An Act erecting Louisiana into two territories," etc. Acts of 1794 and 1803 extended to Louisiana. *Statutes at Large*, II. 283. For proceedings in Congress, see *Annals of Cong.*, 8 Cong. 1 sess. pp. 106, 211, 223, 231, 233–4, 238, 255, 1038, 1054–68, 1069–79, 1128–30, 1185–9.

1805, Feb. 15. Massachusetts: Proposed Amendment.

"*Resolve requesting the Governor to transmit to the Senators and Representatives in Congress, and the Executives of the several States this Resolution, as an amendment to the Constitution of the United States, respecting Slaves.*" June 8, Governor's message; Connecticut answers that it is inexpedient; Maryland opposes the proposition. *Massachusetts Resolves*, February, 1805, p. 55; June, 1805, p. 18. See below, March 3, 1805.

1805, March 2. United States Statute: Slave-Trade to Orleans Territory Permitted.

"An Act further providing for the government of the territory of Orleans."

§ 1. A territorial government erected similar to Mississippi, with same rights and privileges.

§ 5. 6th Article of Ordinance of 1787, on slaves, not to extend to this territory.

Statutes at Large, II. 322. For proceedings in Congress, see *Annals of Cong.*, 8 Cong. 2 sess. pp. 28, 30, 45–6, 47, 48, 54, 59–61, 69, 727–8, 871–2, 957, 1016–9, 1020–1, 1201, 1209–10, 1211. Cf. *Statutes at Large*, II. 331; *Annals of Cong.*, 8 Cong. 2 sess., pp. 50, 51, 52, 57, 68, 69, 1213, 1215. In *Journals*, see Index, Senate Bills Nos. 8, 11.

1805, March 3. Congress (House): Massachusetts Proposition to Amend Constitution.

Mr. Varnum of Massachusetts presented the resolution of the Legislature of Massachusetts, "instructing the Senators, and requesting the Representatives in Congress, from the said State, to take all legal and necessary steps, to use their utmost exertions, as soon as the same is practicable, to obtain an amendment to the Federal Constitution, so as to authorize and empower the Congress of the United States to pass a law, whenever they may deem it expedient, to prevent the further importation of slaves from any of the West India Islands, from the coast of Africa, or elsewhere, into the United States, or any part thereof." A motion was made that Congress have power to prevent further importation; it was read and ordered to lie on the table. *House Journal* (repr. 1826), 8 Cong. 2 sess. V. 171; *Annals of Cong.*, 8 Cong. 2 sess. pp. 1221–2. For the original resolution, see *Massachusetts Resolves*, May, 1802, to March, 1806, Vol. II. A. (State House ed., p. 239.)

1805, Dec. 17. Congress (Senate): Proposition to Prohibit Importation.

A "bill to prohibit the importation of certain persons therein described into any port or place within the jurisdiction of the United States, from and after" Jan. 1, 1808, was read twice and postponed. *Senate Journal* (repr. 1821), 9 Cong. 1 sess. IV. 10–11; *Annals of Cong.*, 9 Cong. 1 sess. pp. 20–1.

1806, Jan. 20. Congress (House): Vermont Proposed Amendment.

"Mr. Olin, one of the Representatives from the State of Vermont, presented to the House certain resolutions of the General Assembly of the said State, proposing an article of amendment to the Constitution of the United States, to prevent the further importation of slaves, or people of color, from any of the West India Islands, from the coast of Africa, or elsewhere, into the United States, or any part thereof; which were read, and ordered to lie on the table." No further mention found. *House Journal* (repr. 1826), 9 Cong. 1 sess. V. 238; *Annals of Cong.*, 9 Cong. 1 sess. pp. 343–4.

1806, Jan. 25. Virginia: Imported Slaves to be Sold.

"An Act to amend the several laws concerning slaves."

§ 5. If the jury before whom the importer is brought "shall find that the said slave or slaves were brought into this commonwealth, and have remained therein, contrary to the provisions of this act, the court shall make an order, directing him, her or them to be delivered to the overseers of the poor, to be by them sold for cash and applied as herein directed."

§ 8. Penalty for bringing slaves, $400 per slave; the same for buying or hiring, knowingly, such a slave.

§ 16. This act to take effect May 1, 1806. *Statutes at Large of Virginia*, New Series, III. 251.

1806, Jan. 27. Congress (House): Bill to Tax Slaves Imported.

"A Bill laying a duty on slaves imported into any of the United States." Finally dropped. *House Journal* (repr. 1826), 8 Cong. 2 sess. V. 129; *Ibid.*, 9 Cong. 1 sess. V. 195, 223, 240, 242, 243–4, 248, 260, 262, 264, 276–7, 287, 294, 305, 309, 338; *Annals of Cong.*, 9 Cong. 1 sess. pp. 273, 274, 346, 358, 372, 434, 442–4, 533.

1806, Feb. 4. Congress (House): Proposition to Prohibit Slave-Trade after 1807.

Mr. Bidwell moved that the following section be added to the bill for taxing slaves imported, — that any ship so engaged be forfeited. The proposition was rejected, yeas, 17, nays, 86 (?). *Annals of Cong.*, 9 Cong. 1 sess. p. 438.

1806, Feb. 10. Congress (House): New Hampshire Proposed Amendment.

"Mr. Tenney . . . presented to the House certain resolutions of the Legislature of the State of New Hampshire, 'proposing an amendment to the Constitution of the United States, so as to authorize and empower Congress to pass a law, whenever they may deem it expedient, to prevent the further importation of slaves,' or people of color, into the United States, or any part thereof." Read and laid on the table. *House Journal* (repr. 1826), 9 Cong. 1 sess. V. 266; *Annals of Cong.*, 9 Cong. 1 sess. p. 448.

1806, Feb. 17. Congress (House): Proposition on Slave-Trade.

The committee on the slave-trade reported a resolution: —

"*Resolved*, That it shall not be lawful for any person or persons, to import or bring into any of the Territories of the United States, any slave or slaves that may hereafter be imported into the United States." *House Journal*, 9 Cong. 1 sess. V. 264, 278, 308, 345–6; *House Reports*, 9 Cong. 1 sess. II. Feb. 17, 1806; *Annals of Cong.*, 9 Cong. 1 sess. pp. 472–3.

1806, April 7. Congress (Senate): Maryland Proposed Amendment.

"Mr. Wright communicated a resolution of the legislature of the state of Maryland instructing their Senators and Representatives in Congress to use their utmost exertions to obtain an amendment to the constitution of the United States to prevent the further importation of slaves; whereupon, Mr. Wright submitted the following resolutions for the consideration of the Senate. . . .

"*Resolved*, That the migration or importation of slaves into the United States, or any territory thereof, be prohibited after the first day of January, 1808." Considered April 10, and further consideration postponed until the first Monday in December next. *Senate Journal* (repr. 1821), 9 Cong. 1 sess. IV. 76–7, 79; *Annals of Cong.*, 9 Cong. 1 sess. pp. 229, 232.

1806, Dec. 2. President Jefferson's Message.

See above, page 95. *House Journal* (repr. 1826), 9 Cong. 2 sess. V. 468.

1806, Dec. 15. Congress (House): Proposition on Slave-Trade.

"A bill to prohibit the importation or bringing of slaves into the United States, etc.," after Dec. 31, 1807. Finally merged into Senate bill. *Ibid.*, House Bill No. 148.

1806, Dec. 17. Congress (House): Sloan's Proposition.

Proposition to amend the House bill by inserting after the article declaring the forfeiture of an illegally imported slave, "And such person or slave shall be entitled to his freedom." Lost. *Annals of Cong.*, 9 Cong. 2 sess. pp. 167–77, 180–89.

1806, Dec. 29. Congress (House): Sloan's Second Proposition.

Illegally imported Africans to be either freed, apprenticed, or returned to Africa. Lost; Jan. 5, 1807, a somewhat similar proposition was also lost. *Ibid.*, pp. 226–8, 254.

1806, Dec. 31. Great Britain: Rejected Treaty.

"Treaty of amity, commerce, and navigation, between His Britannic Majesty and the United States of America."

"Art. XXIV. The high contracting parties engage to communicate to each other, without delay, all such laws as have been or shall be hereafter enacted by their respective Legislatures, as also all measures which shall have been taken for the abolition or limitation of the African slave trade; and they further agree to use their best endeavors to procure the co-operation of other Powers for the final and complete abolition of a trade so repugnant to the principles of justice and humanity." *Amer. State Papers*, *Foreign*, III. 147, 151.

1807, March 25. [England: Slave-Trade Abolished.

"An Act for the Abolition of the Slave Trade." *Statute* 47 *George III.*, 1 sess. ch. 36.]

1807, Jan. 7. Congress (House): Bidwell's Proposition.

"Provided, that no person shall be sold as a slave by virtue of this act." Offered as an amendment to § 3 of House bill; defeated 60 to 61, Speaker voting. A similar proposition was made Dec. 23, 1806. *House Journal* (repr. 1826), 9 Cong. 2 sess. V. 513–6. Cf. *Annals of Cong.*, 9 Cong. 2 sess. pp. 199–203, 265–7.

1807, Feb. 9. Congress (House): Section Seven of House Bill.

§ 7 of the bill reported to the House by the committee provided that all Negroes imported should be conveyed whither the President might direct and there be indentured as apprentices, or employed in whatever way the President might deem best for them and the country; provided that no such Negroes should be indentured or employed except in some State in which provision is now made for the gradual abolition of slavery. Blank spaces were left for limiting the term of indenture. The report was never acted on. *Annals of Cong.*, 9 Cong. 2 sess. pp. 477–8.

1807, March 2. United States Statute: Importation Prohibited.

"An Act to prohibit the importation of Slaves into any port or place within the jurisdiction of the United States, from and after the first day of January, in the year of our Lord one thousand eight hundred and eight." Bills to amend § 8, so as to make less ambiguous the permit given to the internal traffic, were introduced Feb. 27 and Nov. 27. *Statutes at Large*, II. 426. For proceedings in Senate, see *Senate Journal* (repr. 1821), 9 Cong. 1–2 sess. IV. 11, 112, 123, 124, 132, 133, 150, 158, 164, 165, 167, 168; *Annals of Cong.*, 9 Cong. 2 sess. pp. 16, 19, 23, 33, 36, 45, 47, 68, 69, 70, 71, 79, 87, 93. For proceedings in House, see *House Journal* (repr. 1826), 9 Cong. 2 sess. V. 470, 482, 488, 490, 491, 496, 500, 504, 510, 513–6, 517, 540, 557, 575, 579, 581, 583–4, 585, 592, 594, 610, 613–4, 616, 623, 638, 640; 10 Cong. 1 sess. VI. 27, 50; *Annals of Cong.*, 9 Cong. 2 sess. pp. 167, 180, 200, 220, 231, 254, 264, 270.

1808, Feb. 23. Congress (Senate): Proposition to Amend Constitution.

"Agreeably to instructions from the legislature of the state of Pennsylvania to their Senators in Congress, Mr. Maclay submitted the following resolution, which was read for consideration: —

"*Resolved* . . ., That the Constitution of the United States be so altered and amended, as to prevent the Congress of the United States, and the legislatures of any state in the Union, from authorizing the importation of slaves." No further mention. *Senate Journal* (repr. 1821), 10 Cong. 1 sess. IV. 235; *Annals of Cong.*, 10 Cong. 1 sess. p. 134. For the full text of the instructions, see *Amer. State Papers, Miscellaneous*, I. 716.

1810, Dec. 5. President Madison's Message.

"Among the commercial abuses still committed under the American flag, . . . it appears that American citizens are instrumental in carrying on a traffic in enslaved Africans, equally in violation of the laws of humanity, and in defiance of those of their own country. The same just and benevolent motives which produced the interdiction in force against this criminal conduct, will doubtless be felt by Congress, in devising further means of suppressing the evil." *House Journal* (repr. 1826), 11 Cong. 3 sess. VII. 435.

1811, Jan. 15. United States Statute: Secret Act and Joint Resolution against Amelia Island Smugglers.

Statutes at Large, III. 471 ff.

1815, March 29. [France: Abolition of Slave-Trade.

Napoleon on his return from Elba decrees the abolition of the slave-trade. Decree re-enacted in 1818 by the Bourbon dynasty. *British and Foreign State Papers*, 1815–16, p. 196, note; 1817–18, p. 1025.]

1815, Feb. 18. Great Britain: Treaty of Ghent.

"Treaty of peace and amity. Concluded December 24, 1814; Ratifications exchanged at Washington February 17, 1815; Proclaimed February 18, 1815."

Art. X. "Whereas the traffic in slaves is irreconcilable with the principles of humanity and justice, and whereas both His Majesty and the United States are desirous of continuing their efforts to promote its entire abolition, it is hereby agreed that both the contracting parties shall use their best endeavors to accomplish so desirable an object." *U. S. Treaties and Conventions* (ed. 1889), p. 405.

1815, Dec. 8. Alabama and Mississippi Territory: Act to Dispose of Illegally Imported Slaves.

"An Act concerning Slaves brought into this Territory, contrary to the Laws of the United States." Slaves to be sold at auction, and the proceeds to be divided between the territorial treasury and the collector or informer. Toulmin, *Digest of the Laws of Alabama*, p. 637; *Statutes of Mississippi digested*, etc. (ed. 1816), p. 389.

1816, Nov. 18. North Carolina: Act to Dispose of Illegally Imported Slaves.

"An act to direct the disposal of negroes, mulattoes and persons of colour, imported into this state, contrary to the provisions of an act of the Congress of the United States, entitled 'an act to prohibit the importation of slaves into any port or place, within the jurisdiction of the United States, from and after the first day of January, in the year of our Lord one thousand eight hundred and eight.'"

§ 1. Every slave illegally imported after 1808 shall be sold for the use of the State.

§ 2. The sheriff shall seize and sell such slave, and pay the proceeds to the treasurer of the State.

§ 3. If the slave abscond, the sheriff may offer a reward not exceeding one-fifth of the value of the slave. *Laws of North Carolina*, 1816, ch. xii. p. 9; *Laws of North Carolina* (revision of 1819), II. 1350.

1816, Dec. 3. President Madison's Message.

"The United States having been the first to abolish, within the extent of their authority, the transportation of the natives of Africa into slavery, by prohibiting the introduction of slaves, and by punishing their citizens participating in the traffick, cannot but be gratified at the progress, made by concurrent efforts of other nations, towards a general suppression of so great an evil. They must feel, at the same time, the greater solicitude to give the fullest efficacy to their own regulations. With that view, the interposition of Congress appears to be required by the violations and evasions which, it is suggested, are chargeable on unworthy citizens, who mingle in the slave trade under foreign flags, and with foreign ports; and by collusive importations of slaves into the United States, through adjoining ports and territories. I present the subject to Congress, with a full assurance of their disposition to apply all the remedy which can be afforded by an amendment of the law. The regulations which were intended to guard against abuses of a kindred character, in the trade between the several States, ought also to be rendered more effectual for their humane object." *House Journal*, 14 Cong. 2 sess. pp. 15–6.

1817, Feb. 11. Congress (House): Proposed Joint Resolution.

"Joint Resolution for abolishing the traffick in Slaves, and the Colinization [*sic*] of the Free People of Colour of the United States."

"*Resolved*, . . . That the President be, and he is hereby authorized to consult and negotiate with all the governments where ministers of the United States are, or shall be accredited, on the means of effecting an entire and immediate abolition of the traffick in slaves. And, also, to enter into a convention with the government of Great Britain, for receiving into the colony of Sierra Leone, such of the free people of colour of the United States as, with their own consent, shall be carried thither. . . .

"*Resolved*, That adequate provision shall hereafter be made to defray any necessary expenses which may be incurred in carrying the preceding resolution into effect." Reported on petition of the Colonization Society by the committee on the President's Message. No further record. *House Journal*, 14 Cong. 2 sess. pp. 25–7, 380; *House Doc.*, 14 Cong. 2 sess. No. 77.

1817, July 28. [**Great Britain and Portugal: First Concession of Right of Search.**

"By this treaty, ships of war of each of the nations might visit merchant vessels of both, if suspected of having slaves on board, acquired by illicit traffic." This "related only to the trade north of the equator; for the slave-trade of Portugal within the regions of western Africa, to the south of the equator, continued long after this to be carried on with great vigor." Woolsey, *International Law* (1874), § 197, pp. 331–2; *British and Foreign State Papers*, 1816–17, pp. 85–118.]

1817, Sept. 23. [**Great Britain and Spain: Abolition of Trade North of Equator.**

"By the treaty of Madrid, . . . Great Britain obtained from Spain, for the sum of four hundred thousand pounds, the immediate abolition of the trade north of the equator, its entire abolition after 1820, and the concession of the same mutual right of search, which the treaty with Portugal had just established." Woolsey, *International Law* (1874), § 197, p. 332; *British and Foreign State Papers*, 1816–17, pp. 33–74.]

1817, Dec. 2. President Monroe's Message on Amelia Island, etc.

"A just regard for the rights and interests of the United States required that they [i. e., the Amelia Island and Galveston pirates] should be suppressed, and orders have been accordingly issued to that effect. The imperious considerations which produced this measure will be explained to the parties whom it may, in any degree, concern." *House Journal*, 15 Cong. 1 sess. p. 11.

1817, Dec. 19. Georgia: Act to Dispose of Illegally Imported Slaves.

"An Act for disposing of any such negro, mulatto, or person of color, who has been or may hereafter be imported or brought into this State in violation of an act of the United States, entitled an act to prohibit the importation of slaves," etc.

§ 1. The governor by agent shall receive such Negroes, and,

§ 2. sell them, or,

§ 3. give them to the Colonization Society to be transported, on condition that the Society reimburse the State for all expense, and transport them at their own cost. Prince, *Digest*, p. 793.

1818, Jan. 10. Congress (House): Bill to Supplement Act of 1807.

Mr. Middleton, from the committee on so much of the President's Message as related to the illicit introduction of slaves into the

United States from Amelia Island, reported a bill in addition to former acts prohibiting the introduction of slaves into the United States. This was read twice and committed; April 1 it was considered in Committee of the Whole; Mr. Middleton offered a substitute, which was ordered to be laid on table and to be printed; it became the Act of 1819. See below, March 3, 1819. *House Journal*, 15 Cong. 1 sess. pp. 131, 410.

1818, Jan. 13. President Monroe's Special Message.

"I have the satisfaction to inform Congress, that the establishment at Amelia Island has been suppressed, and without the effusion of blood. The papers which explain this transaction, I now lay before Congress," etc. *Ibid.*, pp. 137–9.

1818, Feb. 9. Congress (Senate): Bill to Register (?) Slaves.

"A bill respecting the transportation of persons of color, for sale, or to be held to labor." Passed Senate, dropped in House; similar bill Dec. 9, 1818, also dropped in House. *Senate Journal*, 15 Cong. 1 sess. pp. 147, 152, 157, 165, 170, 188, 201, 203, 232, 237; 15 Cong. 2 sess. pp. 63, 74, 77, 202, 207, 285, 291, 297; *House Journal*, 15 Cong. 1 sess. p. 332; 15 Cong. 2 sess. pp. 303, 305, 316.

1818, April 4. Congress (House): Proposition to Amend Constitution.

Mr. Livermore's resolution:—

"No person shall be held to service or labour as a slave, nor shall slavery be tolerated in any state hereafter admitted into the Union, or made one of the United States of America." Read, and on the question, "Will the House consider the same?" it was determined in the negative. *House Journal*, 15 Cong. 1 sess. pp. 420–1; *Annals of Cong.*, 15 Cong. 1 sess. pp. 1675–6.

1818, April 20. United States Statute: Act in Addition to Act of 1807.

"An Act in addition to 'An act to prohibit the introduction [importation] of slaves into any port or place within the jurisdiction of the United States, from and after the first day of January, in the year of our Lord one thousand eight hundred and eight,' and to repeal certain parts of the same." *Statutes at Large*, III. 450. For proceedings in Congress, see *Senate Journal*, 15 Cong. 1 sess. pp. 243, 304, 315, 333, 338, 340, 348, 377, 386, 388, 391, 403, 406; *House Journal*, 15 Cong. 1 sess. pp. 450, 452, 456, 468, 479, 484, 492, 505.

1818, May 4. [Great Britain and Netherlands: Treaty.

Right of Search granted for the suppression of the slave-trade. *British and Foreign State Papers*, 1817–18, pp. 125–43.]

1818, Dec. 19. Georgia: Act of 1817 Reinforced.

No title found. "*Whereas* numbers of African slaves have been illegally introduced into the State, in direct violation of the laws of the United States and of this State, *Be it therefore enacted*," etc. Informers are to receive one-tenth of the net proceeds from the sale of illegally imported Africans, "*Provided*, nothing herein contained shall be so construed as to extend farther back than the year 1817." Prince, *Digest*, p. 798.

1819, Feb. 8. Congress (Senate): Bill in Addition to Former Acts.

"A bill supplementary to an act, passed the 2d day of March, 1807, entitled," etc. Postponed. *Senate Journal*, 15 Cong. 2 sess. pp. 234, 244, 311–2, 347.

1819, March 3. United States Statute: Cruisers Authorized, etc.

"An Act in addition to the Acts prohibiting the slave trade." *Statutes at Large*, III. 532. For proceedings in Congress, see *Senate Journal*, 15 Cong. 2 sess. pp. 338, 339, 343, 345, 350, 362; *House Journal*, 15 Cong. 2 sess. pp. 9–19, 42–3, 150, 179, 330, 334, 341, 343, 352.

1819, Dec. 7. President Monroe's Message.

"Due attention has likewise been paid to the suppression of the slave trade, in compliance with a law of the last session. Orders have been given to the commanders of all our public ships to seize all vessels navigated under our flag, engaged in that trade, and to bring them in, to be proceeded against, in the manner prescribed by that law. It is hoped that these vigorous measures, supported by like acts by other nations, will soon terminate a commerce so disgraceful to the civilized world." *House Journal*, 16 Cong. 1 sess. p. 18.

1820, Jan. 19. Congress (House): Proposed Registry of Slaves.

"On motion of Mr. Cuthbert,

'Resolved, That the Committee on the Slave Trade be instructed to enquire into the expediency of establishing a registry of slaves, more effectually to prevent the importation of slaves into the United States, or the territories thereof." No further mention. *Ibid.*, p. 150.

1820, Feb. 5. Congress (House): Proposition on Slave-Trade.

"Mr. Meigs submitted the following preamble and resolution:

"Whereas, slavery in the United States is an evil of great and increasing magnitude; one which merits the greatest efforts of this nation to remedy: Therefore,

"Resolved, That a committee be appointed to enquire into the expediency of devoting the public lands as a fund for the purpose of,

"1st, Employing a naval force competent to the annihilation of the slave trade;

"2dly, The emancipation of slaves in the United States; and,

"3dly, Colonizing them in such way as shall be conducive to their comfort and happiness, in Africa, their mother country." Read, and, on motion of Walker of North Carolina, ordered to lie on the table. Feb. 7, Mr. Meigs moved that the House now consider the above-mentioned resolution, but it was decided in the negative. Feb. 18, he made a similar motion and proceeded to discussion, but was ruled out of order by the Speaker. He appealed, but the Speaker was sustained, and the House refused to take up the resolution. No further record appears. *Ibid.*, pp. 196, 200, 227.

1820, Feb. 23. Massachusetts: Slavery in Western Territory.

"*Resolve respecting Slavery*":—

"The Committee of both Houses, who were appointed to consider 'what measures it may be proper for the Legislature of this Commonwealth to adopt, in the expression of their sentiments and views, relative to the interesting subject, now before Congress, of interdicting slavery in the New States, which may be admitted into the Union, beyond the River Mississippi,' respectfully submit the following report: . . .

"Nor has this question less importance as to its influence on the slave trade. Should slavery be further permitted, an immense new market for slaves would be opened. It is well known that notwithstanding the strictness of our laws, and the vigilance of the government, thousands are now annually imported from Africa," etc. *Massachusetts Resolves*, May, 1819, to February, 1824, pp. 147–51.

1820, May 12. Congress (House): Resolution for Negotiation.

"Resolved by the Senate and House of Representatives of the United States of America in Congress assembled, That the

President of the United States be requested to negociate with all the governments where ministers of the United States are or shall be accredited, on the means of effecting an entire and immediate abolition of the slave trade." Passed House, May 12, 1820; lost in Senate, May 15, 1820. *House Journal*, 16 Cong. 1 sess. pp. 497, 518, 520–21, 526; *Annals of Cong.*, 16 Cong. 1 sess. pp. 697–700.

1820, May 15. United States Statute: Slave-Trade made Piracy.

"An act to continue in force 'An act to protect the commerce of the United States, and punish the crime of piracy,' and also to make further provisions for punishing the crime of piracy." Continued by several statutes until passage of the Act of 1823, *q. v.* *Statutes at Large*, III. 600. For proceedings in Congress, see *Senate Journal*, 16 Cong. 1 sess. pp. 238, 241, 268, 286–7, 314, 331, 346, 350, 409, 412, 417, 422, 424, 425; *House Journal*, 16 Cong. 1 sess. pp. 453, 454, 494, 518, 520, 522, 537, 539, 540, 542. There was also a House bill, which was dropped: cf. *House Journal*, 16 Cong. 1 sess. pp. 21, 113, 280, 453, 494.

1820, Nov. 14. President Monroe's Message.

"In execution of the law of the last session, for the suppression of the slave trade, some of our public ships have also been employed on the coast of Africa, where several captures have already been made of vessels engaged in that disgraceful traffic." *Senate Journal*, 16 Cong. 2 sess. pp. 16–7.

1821, Feb. 15. Congress (House): Meigs's Resolution.

Mr. Meigs offered in modified form the resolutions submitted at the last session: —

"Whereas slavery, in the United States, is an evil, acknowledged to be of great and increasing magnitude, . . . therefore,

"Resolved, That a committee be appointed to inquire into the expediency of devoting five hundred million acres of the public lands, next west of the Mississippi, as a fund for the purpose of, in the

"*First place;* Employing a naval force, competent to the annihilation of the slave trade," etc. Question to consider decided in the affirmative, 63 to 50; laid on the table, 66 to 55. *House Journal*, 16 Cong. 2 sess. p. 238; *Annals of Cong.*, 16 Cong. 2 sess. pp. 1168–70.

1821, Dec. 3. President Monroe's Message.

"Like success has attended our efforts to suppress the slave trade. Under the flag of the United States, and the sanction of their papers, the trade may be considered as entirely suppressed; and, if any of our citizens are engaged in it, under the flag and papers of other powers, it is only from a respect to the rights of those powers, that these offenders are not seized and brought home, to receive the punishment which the laws inflict. If every other power should adopt the same policy, and pursue the same vigorous means for carrying it into effect, the trade could no longer exist." *House Journal*, 17 Cong. 1 sess. p. 22.

1822, April 12. Congress (House): Proposed Resolution.

"*Resolved*, That the President of the United States be requested to enter into such arrangements as he may deem suitable and proper, with one or more of the maritime powers of Europe, for the effectual abolition of the slave trade." *House Reports*, 17 Cong. 1 sess. II. No. 92, p. 4; *Annals of Cong.*, 17 Cong. 1 sess. p. 1538.

1822, June 18. Mississippi: Act on Importation, etc.

"An act, to reduce into one, the several acts, concerning slaves, free negroes, and mulattoes."

§ 2. Slaves born and resident in the United States, and not criminals, may be imported.

§ 3. No slave born or resident outside the United States shall be brought in, under penalty of $1,000 per slave. Travellers are excepted. *Revised Code of the Laws of Mississippi* (Natchez, 1824), p. 369.

1822, Dec. 3. President Monroe's Message.

"A cruise has also been maintained on the coast of Africa, when the season would permit, for the suppression of the slave-trade; and orders have been given to the commanders of all our public ships to seize our own vessels, should they find any engaged in that trade, and to bring them in for adjudication." *House Journal*, 17 Cong. 2 sess. pp. 12, 21.

1823, Jan. 1. Alabama: Act to Dispose of Illegally Imported Slaves.

"An Act to carry into effect the laws of the United States prohibiting the slave trade."

§ 1. "*Be it enacted*, . . . That the Governor of this state be . . . authorized and required to appoint some suitable person, as the agent of the state, to receive all and every slave or slaves or persons of colour, who may have been brought into this state in violation of the laws of the United States, prohibiting the slave trade: *Provided*, that the authority of the said agent is not to extend to slaves who have been condemned and sold."

§ 2. The agent must give bonds.

§ 3. "*And be it further enacted*, That the said slaves, when so placed in the possession of the state, as aforesaid, shall be employed on such public work or works, as shall be deemed by the Governor of most value and utility to the public interest."

§ 4. A part may be hired out to support those employed in public work.

§ 5. "*And be it further enacted*, That in all cases in which a decree of any court having competent authority, shall be in favor of any or claimant or claimants, the said slaves shall be truly and faithfully, by said agent, delivered to such claimant or claimants: but in case of their condemnation, they shall be sold by such agent for cash to the highest bidder, by giving sixty days notice," etc. *Acts of the Assembly of Alabama*, 1822 (Cahawba, 1823), p. 62.

1823, Jan. 30. United States Statute: Piracy Act made Perpetual.

"An Act in addition to 'An act to continue in force "An act to protect the commerce of the United States, and punish the crime of piracy,"'" etc. *Statutes at Large*, III. 510–14, 721, 789. For proceedings in Congress, see *Senate Journal*, 17 Cong. 2 sess. pp. 61, 64, 70, 83, 98, 101, 106, 110, 111, 122, 137; *House Journal*, 17 Cong. 2 sess. pp. 73, 76, 156, 183, 189.

1823, Feb. 10. Congress (House): Resolution on Slave-Trade.

Mr. Mercer offered the following resolution: —

"*Resolved*, That the President of the United States be requested to enter upon, and to prosecute, from time to time, such negotiations with the several maritime powers of Europe and America, as he may deem expedient, for the effectual abolition of the African slave trade, and its ultimate denunciation as piracy, under the law of nations, by the consent of the civilized world." Agreed to Feb. 28; passed Senate. *House Journal*, 17 Cong. 2 sess. pp. 212, 280–82; *Annals of Cong.*, 17 Cong. 2 sess. pp. 928, 1147–55.

1823, March 3. United States Statute: Appropriation.

"An Act making appropriations for the support of the navy," etc.

"To enable the President of the United States to carry into effect the act" of 1819, $50,000. *Statutes at Large*, III. 763, 764.

1823. President: Proposed Treaties.

Letters to various governments in accordance with the resolution of 1823: April 28, to Spain; May 17, to Buenos Ayres; May 27, to United States of Colombia; Aug. 14, to Portugal. See above, Feb. 10, 1823. *House Doc.*, 18 Cong. 1 sess. VI. No. 119.

1823, June 24. Great Britain: Proposed Treaty.

Adams, March 31, proposes that the trade be made piracy. Canning, April 8, reminds Adams of the treaty of Ghent and asks for the granting of a mutual Right of Search to suppress the slave-trade. The matter is further discussed until June 24. Minister Rush is empowered to propose a treaty involving the Right of Search, etc. This treaty was substantially the one signed (see below, March 13, 1824), differing principally in the first article.

"Article I. The two high contracting Powers, having each separately, by its own laws, subjected their subjects and citizens, who may be convicted of carrying on the illicit traffic in slaves on the coast of Africa, to the penalties of piracy, do hereby agree to use their influence, respectively, with the other maritime and civilized nations of the world, to the end that the said African slave trade may be recognized, and declared to be, piracy, under the law of nations." *House Doc.*, 18 Cong. 1 sess. VI. No. 119.

1824, Feb. 6. Congress (House): Proposition to Amend Constitution.

Mr. Abbot's resolution on persons of color:—

"That no part of the constitution of the United States ought to be construed, or shall be construed to authorize the importation or ingress of any person of color into any one of the United States, contrary to the laws of such state." Read first and second time and committed to the Committee of the Whole. *House Journal*, 18 Cong. 1 sess. p. 208; *Annals of Cong.*, 18 Cong. 1 sess. p. 1399.

1824, March 13. Great Britain: Proposed Treaty of 1824.

"The Convention:"—

Art. I. "The commanders and commissioned officers of each of the two high contracting parties, duly authorized, under the regulations and instructions of their respective Governments, to cruize on the coasts of Africa, of America, and of the West

Indies, for the suppression of the slave trade," shall have the power to seize and bring into port any vessel owned by subjects of the two contracting parties, found engaging in the slave-trade. The vessel shall be taken for trial to the country where she belongs.

Art. II. Provides that even if the vessel seized does not belong to a citizen or citizens of either of the two contracting parties, but is chartered by them, she may be seized in the same way as if she belonged to them.

Art. III. Requires that in all cases where any vessel of either party shall be boarded by any naval officer of the other party, on suspicion of being concerned in the slave-trade, the officer shall deliver to the captain of the vessel so boarded a certificate in writing, signed by the naval officer, specifying his rank, etc., and the object of his visit. Provision is made for the delivery of ships and papers to the tribunal before which they are brought.

Art. IV. Limits the Right of Search, recognized by the Convention, to such investigation as shall be necessary to ascertain the fact whether the said vessel is or is not engaged in the slave-trade. No person shall be taken out of the vessel so visited unless for reasons of health.

Art. V. Makes it the duty of the commander of either nation, having captured a vessel of the other under the treaty, to receive unto his custody the vessel captured, and send or carry it into some port of the vessel's own country for adjudication, in which case triplicate declarations are to be signed, etc.

Art. VI. Provides that in cases of capture by the officer of either party, on a station where no national vessel is cruising, the captor shall either send or carry his prize to some convenient port of its own country for adjudication, etc.

Art. VII. Provides that the commander and crew of the captured vessel shall be proceeded against as pirates, in the ports to which they are brought, etc.

Art. VIII. Confines the Right of Search, under this treaty, to such officers of both parties as are especially authorized to execute the laws of their countries in regard to the slave-trade. For every abusive exercise of this right, officers are to be personally liable in costs and damages, etc.

Art. IX. Provides that the government of either nation shall inquire into abuses of this Convention and of the laws of the two coun tries, and inflict on guilty officers the proper punishment.

Art. X. Declares that the right, reciprocally conceded by this treaty, is wholly and exclusively founded on the consideration that the two nations have by their laws made the slave-trade piracy, and is not to be taken to affect in any other way the rights of the parties, etc.; it further engages that each power shall use its influence with all other civilized powers, to procure from them the acknowledgment that the slave-trade is piracy under the law of nations.

Art. XI. Provides that the ratifications of the treaty shall be exchanged at London within twelve months, or as much sooner as possible. Signed by Mr. Rush, Minister to the Court of St. James, March 13, 1824.

The above is a synopsis of the treaty as it was laid before the Senate. It was ratified by the Senate with certain conditions, one of which was that the duration of this treaty should be limited to the pleasure of the two parties on six months' notice; another was that the Right of Search should be limited to the African and West Indian seas: i. e., the word "America" was struck out. This treaty as amended and passed by the Senate (cf. above, p. 139) was rejected by Great Britain. A counter project was suggested by her, but not accepted (cf. above, p. 142). The striking out of the word "America" was declared to be the insuperable objection. *Senate Doc.*, 18 Cong. 2 sess. I. No. 1, pp. 15–20; *Niles's Register*, 3rd Series, XXVI. 230–2. For proceedings in Senate, see *Amer. State Papers, Foreign*, V. 360–2.

1824, March 31. [**Great Britain: Slave-Trade made Piracy.**

"An Act for the more effectual Suppression of the *African* Slave Trade."

Any person engaging in the slave-trade "shall be deemed and adjudged guilty of Piracy, Felony and Robbery, and being convicted thereof shall suffer Death without Benefit of Clergy, and Loss of Lands, Goods and Chattels, as Pirates, Felons and Robbers upon the Seas ought to suffer," etc. *Statute* 5 *George IV.*, ch. 17; *Amer. State Papers, Foreign*, V. 342.]

1824, April 16. Congress (House): Bill to Suppress Slave-Trade.

"Mr. Govan, from the committee to which was referred so much of the President's Message as relates to the suppression of the

Slave Trade, reported a bill respecting the slave trade; which was read twice, and committed to a Committee of the Whole." § 1. Provided a fine not exceeding $5,000, imprisonment not exceeding 7 years, and forfeiture of ship, for equipping a slaver even for the foreign trade; and a fine not exceeding $3,000, and imprisonment not exceeding 5 years, for serving on board any slaver. *Annals of Cong.*, 18 Cong. 1 sess. pp. 2397–8; *House Journal*, 18 Cong. 1 sess. pp. 26, 180, 181, 323, 329, 356, 423.

1824, May 21. President Monroe's Message on Treaty of 1824.

Amer. State Papers, Foreign, V. 344–6.

1824, Nov. 6. [**Great Britain and Sweden: Treaty.**

Right of Search granted for the suppression of the slave-trade. *British and Foreign State Papers*, 1824–5, pp. 3–28.]

1824, Nov. 6. Great Britain: Counter Project of 1825.

Great Britain proposes to conclude the treaty as amended by the Senate, if the word "America" is reinstated in Art. I. (Cf. above, March 13, 1824.) February 16, 1825, the House Committee favors this project; March 2, Addington reminds Adams of this counter proposal; April 6, Clay refuses to reopen negotiations on account of the failure of the Colombian treaty. *Amer. State Papers, Foreign*, V. 367; *House Reports*, 18 Cong. 2 sess. I. No. 70; *House Doc.*, 19 Cong. 1 sess. I. No. 16.

1824, Dec. 7. President Monroe's Message.

"It is a cause of serious regret, that no arrangement has yet been finally concluded between the two Governments, to secure, by joint co-operation, the suppression of the slave trade. It was the object of the British Government, in the early stages of the negotiation, to adopt a plan for the suppression, which should include the concession of the mutual right of search by the ships of war of each party, of the vessels of the other, for suspected offenders. This was objected to by this Government, on the principle that, as the right of search was a right of war of a belligerant towards a neutral power, it might have an ill effect to extend it, by treaty, to an offence which had been made comparatively mild, to a time of peace. Anxious, however, for the suppression of this trade, it was thought adviseable, in compliance with a resolution of the House of Representatives, founded on an act of Congress, to propose to the British Government an expedient, which should be free from that objection, and more effectual for the object, by making it piratical. . . . A convention to this effect was concluded and signed, in London," on the 13th of March, 1824, "by plenipotentiaries duly authorized by both Governments, to the ratification of which certain obstacles have arisen, which are not yet entirely removed." [For the removal of which, the documents relating to the negotiation are submitted for the action of Congress]. . . .

"In execution of the laws for the suppression of the slave trade, a vessel has been occasionally sent from that squadron to the coast of Africa, with orders to return thence by the usual track of the slave ships, and to seize any of our vessels which might be engaged in that trade. None have been found, and, it is believed, that none are thus employed. It is well known, however, that the trade still exists under other flags." *House Journal*, 18 Cong. 2 sess. pp. 11, 12, 19, 27, 241; *House Reports*, 18 Cong. 2 sess. I. No. 70; Gales and Seaton, *Register of Debates*, I. 625–8, and Appendix, p. 2 ff.

1825, Feb. 21. United States of Colombia: Proposed Treaty.

The President sends to the Senate a treaty with the United States of Colombia drawn, as United States Minister Anderson said, similar to that signed at London, with the alterations made by the Senate. March 9, 1825, the Senate rejects this treaty. *Amer. State Papers, Foreign*, V. 729–35.

1825, Feb. 28. Congress (House): Proposed Resolution on Slave-Trade.

Mr. Mercer laid on the table the following resolution: —

"*Resolved*, That the President of the United States be requested to enter upon, and prosecute from time to time, such negotiations with the several maritime powers of Europe and America, as he may deem expedient for the effectual abolition of the slave trade, and its ultimate denunciation, as piracy, under the law of nations, by the consent of the civilized world." The House refused to consider the resolution. *House Journal*, 18 Cong. 2 sess. p. 280; Gales and Seaton, *Register of Debates*, I. 697, 736.

1825, March 3. Congress (House): Proposed Resolution against Right of Search.

"Mr. Forsyth submitted the following resolution:

"*Resolved*, That while this House anxiously desires that the Slave

Trade should be, universally, denounced as Piracy, and, as such, should be detected and punished under the law of nations, it considers that it would be highly inexpedient to enter into engagements with any foreign power, by which *all* the merchant vessels of the United States would be exposed to the inconveniences of any regulation of search, from which any merchant vessels of that foreign power would be exempted." Resolution laid on the table. *House Journal*, 18 Cong. 2 sess. pp. 308–9; Gales and Seaton, *Register of Debates*, I. 739.

1825, Dec. 6. President Adams's Message.

"The objects of the West India Squadron have been, to carry into execution the laws for the suppression of the African Slave Trade: for the protection of our commerce against vessels of piratical character. . . . These objects, during the present year, have been accomplished more effectually than at any former period. The African Slave Trade has long been excluded from the use of our flag; and if some few citizens of our country have continued to set the laws of the Union, as well as those of nature and humanity, at defiance, by persevering in that abominable traffic, it has been only by sheltering themselves under the banners of other nations, less earnest for the total extinction of the trade than ours." *House Journal*, 19 Cong. 1 sess. pp. 20, 96, 296–7, 305, 323, 329, 394–5, 399, 410, 414, 421, 451, 640.

1826, Feb. 14. Congress (House): Proposition to Repeal Parts of Act of 1819.

"Mr. Forsyth submitted the following resolutions, viz.:

1. "*Resolved*, That it is expedient to repeal so much of the act of the 3d March, 1819, entitled, 'An act in addition to the acts prohibiting the slave trade,' as provides for the appointment of agents on the coast of Africa.
2. "*Resolved*, That it is expedient so to modify the said act of the 3d of March, 1819, as to release the United States from all obligation to support the negroes already removed to the coast of Africa, and to provide for such a disposition of those taken in slave ships who now are in, or who may be, hereafter, brought into the United States, as shall secure to them a fair opportunity of obtaining a comfortable subsistence, without any aid from the public treasury." Read and laid on the table. *Ibid.*, p. 258.

1826, March 14. United States Statute: Appropriation.

"An Act making appropriations for the support of the navy," etc.

"For the agency on the coast of Africa, for receiving the negroes," etc., $32,000. *Statutes at Large*, IV. 140, 141.

1827, March 2. United States Statute: Appropriation.

"An Act making appropriations for the support of the Navy," etc.

"For the agency on the coast of Africa," etc., $56,710. *Ibid.*, IV. 206, 208.

1827, March 11. Texas: Introduction of Slaves Prohibited.

Constitution of the State of Coahuila and Texas. Preliminary Provisions: —

Art. 13. "From and after the promulgation of the constitution in the capital of each district, no one shall be born a slave in the state, and after six months the introduction of slaves under any pretext shall not be permitted." *Laws and Decrees of Coahuila and Texas* (Houston, 1839), p. 314.

1827, Sept. 15. Texas: Decree against Slave-Trade.

"The Congress of the State of Coahuila and Texas decrees as follows:"

Art. 1. All slaves to be registered.

Art. 2, 3. Births and deaths to be recorded.

Art. 4. "Those who introduce slaves, after the expiration of the term specified in article 13 of the Constitution, shall be subject to the penalties established by the general law of the 13th of July, 1824." *Ibid.*, pp. 78–9.

1828, Feb. 25. Congress (House): Proposed Bill to Abolish African Agency, etc.

"Mr. McDuffie, from the Committee of Ways and Means, . . . reported the following bill:

"A bill to abolish the Agency of the United States on the Coast of Africa, to provide other means of carrying into effect the laws prohibiting the slave trade, and for other purposes." This bill was amended so as to become the act of May 24, 1828 (see below). *House Reports*, 21 Cong. 1 sess. III. No. 348, p. 278.

1828, May 24. United States Statute: Appropriation.

"An Act making an appropriation for the suppression of the slave trade." *Statutes at Large*, IV. 302; *House Journal*, 20 Cong. 1 sess., House Bill No. 190.

1829, Jan. 28. Congress (House): Bill to Amend Act of 1807.

The Committee on Commerce reported "a bill (No. 399) to

amend an act, entitled 'An act to prohibit the importation of slaves,'" etc. Referred to Committee of the Whole. *House Journal*, 20 Cong. 2 sess. pp. 58, 84, 215. Cf. *Ibid.*, 20 Cong. 1 sess. pp. 121, 135.

1829, March 2. United States Statute: Appropriation.

"An Act making additional appropriations for the support of the navy," etc.

"For the reimbursement of the marshal of Florida for expenses incurred in the case of certain Africans who were wrecked on the coast of the United States, and for the expense of exporting them to Africa," $16,000. *Statutes at Large*, IV. 353, 354.

1830, April 7. Congress (House): Resolution against Slave-Trade.

Mr. Mercer reported the following resolution: —

"*Resolved*, That the President of the United States be requested to consult and negotiate with all the Governments where Ministers of the United States are, or shall be accredited, on the means of effecting an entire and immediate abolition of the African slave trade; and especially, on the expediency, with that view, of causing it to be universally denounced as piratical." Referred to Committee of the Whole; no further action recorded. *House Journal*, 21 Cong. 1 sess. p. 512.

1830, April 7. Congress (House): Proposition to Amend Act of March 3, 1819.

Mr. Mercer, from the committee to which was referred the memorial of the American Colonization Society, and also memorials, from the inhabitants of Kentucky and Ohio, reported with a bill (No. 412) to amend "An act in addition to the acts prohibiting the slave trade," passed March 3, 1819. Read twice and referred to Committee of the Whole. *Ibid.*

1830, May 31. Congress (Statute): Appropriation.

"An Act making a re-appropriation of a sum heretofore appropriated for the suppression of the slave trade." *Statutes at Large*, IV. 425; *Senate Journal*, 21 Cong. 1 sess. pp. 359, 360, 383; *House Journal*, 21 Cong. 1 sess. pp. 624, 808–11.

1830. [Brazil: Prohibition of Slave-Trade.

Slave-trade prohibited under severe penalties.]

1831, 1833. [Great Britain and France: Treaty Granting Right of Search.

Convention between Great Britain and France granting a mutual limited Right of Search on the East and West coasts of

Africa, and on the coasts of the West Indies and Brazil. *British and Foreign State Papers*, 1830–1, p. 641 ff; 1832–3, p. 286 ff.]

1831, Feb. 16. Congress (House): Proposed Resolution on Slave-Trade.

"Mr. Mercer moved to suspend the rule of the House in regard to motions, for the purpose of enabling himself to submit a resolution requesting the Executive to enter into negotiations with the maritime Powers of Europe, to induce them to enact laws declaring the African slave trade piracy, and punishing it as such." The motion was lost. Gales and Seaton, *Register of Debates*, VII. 726.

1831, March 2. United States Statute: Appropriation.

"An Act making appropriations for the naval service," etc.

"For carrying into effect the acts for the suppression of the slave trade," etc., $16,000. *Statutes at Large*, IV. 460, 462.

1831, March 3. Congress (House): Resolution as to Treaties.

"Mr. Mercer moved to suspend the rule to enable him to submit the following resolution:

"*Resolved*, That the President of the United States be requested to renew, and to prosecute from time to time, such negotiations with the several maritime powers of Europe and America as he may deem expedient for the effectual abolition of the African slave trade, and its ultimate denunciation as piracy, under the laws of nations, by the consent of the civilized world." The rule was suspended by a vote of 108 to 36, and the resolution passed, 118 to 32. *House Journal*, 21 Cong. 2 sess. pp. 426–8.

1833, Feb. 20. United States Statute: Appropriation.

"An Act making appropriations for the naval service," etc.

" . . . for carrying into effect the acts for the suppression of the slave trade," etc., $5,000. *Statutes at Large*, IV. 614, 615.

1833, August. Great Britain and France: Proposed Treaty with the United States.

British and French ministers simultaneously invited the United States to accede to the Convention just concluded between them for the suppression of the slave-trade. The Secretary of State, Mr. M'Lane, deferred answer until the meeting of Congress, and then postponed negotiations on account of the irritable state of the country on the slave question. Great

Britain had proposed that "A reciprocal right of search . . . be conceded by the United States, limited as to place, and subject to specified restrictions. It is to be employed only in repressing the Slave Trade, and to be exercised under a written and specific authority, conferred on the Commander of the visiting ship." In the act of accession, "it will be necessary that the right of search should be extended to the coasts of the United States," and Great Britain will in turn extend it to the British West Indies. This proposal was finally refused, March 24, 1834, chiefly, as stated, because of the extension of the Right of Search to the coasts of the United States. This part was waived by Great Britain, July 7, 1834. On Sept. 12 the French Minister joined in urging accession. On Oct. 4, 1834, Forsyth states that the determination has "been definitely formed, not to make the United States a party to any Convention on the subject of the Slave Trade." *Parliamentary Papers*, 1835, Vol. LI., *Slave Trade*, Class B., pp. 84–92.

1833, Dec. 23. Georgia: Slave-Trade Acts Amended.

"An Act to reform, amend, and consolidate the penal laws of the State of Georgia."

13th Division. "Offences relative to Slaves": —

§ 1. "If any person or persons shall bring, import, or introduce into this State, or aid or assist, or knowingly become concerned or interested, in bringing, importing, or intro ducing into this State, either by land or by water, or in any manner whatever, any slave or slaves, each and every such person or persons so offending, shall be deemed principals in law, and guilty of a high misdemeanor, and . . . on conviction, shall be punished by a fine not exceeding five hundred dollars each, for each and every slave, . . . and imprisonment and labor in the penitentiary for any time not less than one year, nor longer than four years." Residents, however, may bring slaves for their own use, but must register and swear they are not for sale, hire, mortgage, etc.

§ 6. Penalty for knowingly receiving such slaves, $500. Slightly amended Dec. 23, 1836, e. g., emigrants were allowed to hire slaves out, etc.; amended Dec. 19, 1849, so as to allow importation of slaves from "any other slave holding State of this Union." Prince, *Digest*, pp. 619, 653, 812; Cobb, *Digest*, II. 1018.

1834, Jan. 24. United States Statute: Appropriation.

"An Act making appropriations for the naval service," etc.

"For carrying into effect the acts for the suppression of the slave trade," etc., $5,000. *Statutes at Large*, IV. 670, 671.

1836, March 17. Texas: African Slave-Trade Prohibited.

Constitution of the Republic of Texas: General Provisions: —

§ 9. All persons of color who were slaves for life before coming to Texas shall remain so. "Congress shall pass no laws to prohibit emigrants from bringing their slaves into the republic with them, and holding them by the same tenure by which such slaves were held in the United States; . . . the importation or admission of Africans or negroes into this republic, excepting from the United States of America, is forever prohibited, and declared to be piracy." *Laws of the Republic of Texas* (Houston, 1838), I. 19.

1836, Dec. 21. Texas: Slave-Trade made Piracy.

"An Act supplementary to an act, for the punishment of Crimes and Misdemeanors."

§ 1. "*Be it enacted* . . . , That if any person or persons shall introduce any African negro or negroes, contrary to the true intent and meaning of the ninth section of the general provisions of the constitution, . . . except such as are from the United States of America, and had been held as slaves therein, be considered guilty of piracy; and upon conviction thereof, before any court having cognizance of the same, shall suffer death, without the benefit of clergy."

2. The introduction of Negroes from the United States of America, except of those legally held as slaves there, shall be piracy. *Ibid.*, I. 197. Cf. *House Doc.*, 27 Cong. 1 sess. No. 34, p. 42.

1837, March 3. United States Statute: Appropriation.

"An Act making appropriations for the naval service," etc.

"For carrying into effect the acts for the suppression of the slave trade," etc., $11,413.57. *Statutes at Large*, V. 155, 157.

1838, March 19. Congress (Senate): Slave-Trade with Texas, etc.

"Mr. Morris submitted the following motion for consideration:

"*Resolved*, That the Committee on the Judiciary be instructed to inquire whether the present laws of the United States, on the subject of the slave trade, will prohibit that trade being carried on between citizens of the United States and citizens of the

Republic of Texas, either by land or by sea; and whether it would be lawful in vessels owned by citizens of that Republic, and not lawful in vessels owned by citizens of this, or lawful in both, and by citizens of both countries; and also whether a slave carried from the United States into a foreign country, and brought back, on returning into the United States, is considered a free person, or is liable to be sent back, if demanded, as a slave, into that country from which he or she last came; and also whether any additional legislation by Congress is necessary on any of these subjects." March 20, the motion of Mr. Walker that this resolution "lie on the table," was determined in the affirmative, 32 to 9. *Senate Journal,* 25 Cong. 2 sess. pp. 297–8, 300.

1839, Feb. 5. Congress (Senate): Bill to Amend Slave-Trade Acts.

"Mr. Strange, on leave, and in pursuance of notice given, introduced a bill to amend an act entitled an act to prohibit the importation of slaves into any port in the jurisdiction of the United States; which was read twice, and referred to the Committee on Commerce." March 1, the Committee was discharged from further consideration of the bill. *Congressional Globe,* 25 Cong. 3 sess. p. 172; *Senate Journal,* 25 Cong. 3 sess. pp. 200, 313.

1839, Dec. 24. President Van Buren's Message.

"It will be seen by the report of the Secretary of the navy respecting the disposition of our ships of war, that it has been deemed necessary to station a competent force on the coast of Africa, to prevent a fraudulent use of our flag by foreigners.

"Recent experience has shown that the provisions in our existing laws which relate to the sale and transfer of American vessels while abroad, are extremely defective. Advantage has been taken of these defects to give to vessels wholly belonging to foreigners, and navigating the ocean, an apparent American ownership. This character has been so well simulated as to afford them comparative security in prosecuting the slave trade, a traffic emphatically denounced in our statutes, regarded with abhorrence by our citizens, and of which the effectual suppression is nowhere more sincerely desired than in the United States. These circumstances make it proper to recommend to your early attention a careful revision of these laws, so that . . .

the integrity and honor of our flag may be carefully preserved." *House Journal*, 26 Cong. 1 sess. pp. 117–8.

1840, Jan. 3. Congress (Senate): Bill to Amend Act of 1807.

"Agreeably to notice, Mr. Strange asked and obtained leave to bring in a bill (Senate, No. 123) to amend an act entitled 'An act to prohibit the importation of slaves into any port or place within the jurisdiction of the United States from and after the 1st day of January, in the year 1808,' approved the 2d day of March, 1807; which was read the first and second times, by unanimous consent, and referred to the Committee on the Judiciary." Jan. 8, it was reported without amendment; May 11, it was considered, and, on motion by Mr. King, "*Ordered*, That it lie on the table." *Senate Journal*, 26 Cong. 1 sess. pp. 73, 87, 363.

1840, May 4. Congress (Senate): Bill on Slave-Trade.

"Mr. Davis, from the Committee on Commerce, reported a bill (Senate, No. 335) making further provision to prevent the abuse of the flag of the United States, and the use of unauthorized papers in the foreign slavetrade, and for other purposes." This passed the Senate, but was dropped in the House. *Ibid.*, pp. 356, 359, 440, 442; *House Journal*, 26 Cong. 1 sess. pp. 1138, 1228, 1257.

1841, June 1. Congress (House): President Tyler's Message.

"I shall also, at the proper season, invite your attention to the statutory enactments for the suppression of the slave trade, which may require to be rendered more efficient in their provisions. There is reason to believe that the traffic is on the increase. Whether such increase is to be ascribed to the abolition of slave labor in the British possessions in our vicinity, and an attendant diminution in the supply of those articles which enter into the general consumption of the world, thereby augmenting the demand from other quarters, . . . it were needless to inquire. The highest considerations of public honor, as well as the strongest promptings of humanity, require a resort to the most vigorous efforts to suppress the trade." *House Journal*, 27 Cong. 1 sess. pp. 31, 184.

1841, Dec. 7. President Tyler's Message.

Though the United States is desirous to suppress the slave-trade, she will not submit to interpolations into the maritime code at will by other nations. This government has expressed its repugnance to the trade by several laws. It is a matter for deliberation whether we will enter upon treaties containing mutual stipulations upon the subject with other governments. The United States will demand indemnity for all depredations by Great Britain.

"I invite your attention to existing laws for the suppression of the African slave trade, and recommend all such alterations as may give to them greater force and efficacy. That the American flag is grossly abused by the abandoned and profligate of other nations is but too probable. Congress has, not long since, had this subject under its consideration, and its importance well justifies renewed and anxious attention." *House Journal*, 27 Cong. 2 sess. pp. 14–5, 86, 113.

1841, Dec. 20. [**Great Britain, Austria, Russia, Prussia, and France: Quintuple Treaty**.] *British and Foreign State Papers*, 1841–2, p. 269 ff.

1842, Feb. 15. Right of Search: Cass's Protest.

Cass writes to Webster, that, considering the fact that the signing of the Quintuple Treaty would oblige the participants to exercise the Right of Search denied by the United States, or to make a change in the hitherto recognized law of nations, he, on his own responsibility, addressed the following protest to the French Minister of Foreign Affairs, M. Guizot: —

"LEGATION OF THE UNITED STATES,
"PARIS, February 13, 1842.

"SIR: The recent signature of a treaty, having for its object the suppression of the African slave trade, by five of the powers of Europe, and to which France is a party, is a fact of such general notoriety that it may be assumed as the basis of any diplomatic representations which the subject may fairly require."

The United States is no party to this treaty. She denies the Right of Visitation which England asserts. [Quotes from the presidential message of Dec. 7, 1841.] This principle is asserted by the treaty.

". . . The moral effect which such a union of five great powers, two of which are eminently maritime, but three of which have perhaps never had a vessel engaged in that traffic, is calculated to produce upon the United States, and upon other nations who, like them, may be indisposed to these combined movements, though it may be regretted, yet furnishes no just cause of complaint. But the subject assumes another aspect when they are told by one of the parties that their vessels are to be forcibly entered and examined, in order to carry into effect these stipulations. Certainly the American Government does not believe that the high powers, contracting parties to this treaty, have any wish to compel the United States, by force, to adopt their measures to its provisions, or to adopt its stipulations . . . ; and they will see with pleasure the prompt disavowal made by yourself, sir, in the name of your country, . . . of any intentions of this nature. But were it otherwise, . . . They would prepare themselves with apprehension, indeed, but without dismay — with regret, but with firmness — for one of those desperate struggles which have sometimes occurred in the history of the world."

If, as England says, these treaties cannot be executed without visiting United States ships, then France must pursue the same course. It is hoped, therefore, that his Majesty will, before signing this treaty, carefully examine the pretensions of England and their compatibility with the law of nations and the honor of the United States. *Senate Doc.*, 27 Cong. 3 sess. II. No. 52, and IV. No. 223; 29 Cong. 1 sess. VIII. No. 377, pp. 192–5.

1842, Feb. 26. Mississippi: Resolutions on Creole Case.

The following resolutions were referred to the Committee on Foreign Affairs in the United States Congress, House of Representatives, May 10, 1842:

"Whereas, the right of search has never been yielded to Great Britain," and the brig Creole has not been surrendered by the British authorities, etc., therefore,

§ 1. "*Be it resolved by the Legislature of the State of Mississippi*, That . . . the right of search cannot be conceded to Great Britain without a manifest servile submission, unworthy a free nation. . . .

§ 2. "*Resolved*, That any attempt to detain and search our vessels, by British cruisers, should be held and esteemed an unjustifiable outrage on the part of the Queen's Government; and that any such outrage, which may have occurred since Lord Aberdeen's note to our envoy at the Court of St. James, of date October thirteen, eighteen hundred and forty-one, (if any,) may well be deemed, by our Government, just cause of war."

§ 3. "*Resolved*, That the Legislature of the State, in view of the late murderous insurrection of the slaves on board the Creole, their reception in a British port, the absolute connivance at their crimes, manifest in the protection extended to them by the British authorities, most solemnly declare their firm conviction that, if the conduct of those authorities be submitted to, compounded for by the payment of money, or in any other manner, or atoned for in any mode except by the surrender of the actual criminals to the Federal Government, and the delivery of the other identical slaves to their rightful owner or owners, or his or their agents, the slaveholding States would have most just cause to apprehend that the American flag is powerless to protect American property; that the Federal Government is not sufficiently energetic in the maintenance and preservation of their peculiar rights; and that these rights, therefore, are in imminent danger."

§ 4. *Resolved*, That restitution should be demanded "at all hazards." *House Doc.*, 27 Cong. 2 sess. IV. No. 215.

1842, March 21. Congress (House): Giddings's Resolutions.

Mr. Giddings moved the following resolutions:—

§ 5. "*Resolved*, That when a ship belonging to the citizens of any State of this Union leaves the waters and territory of such State, and enters upon the high seas, the persons on board cease to be subject to the slave laws of such State, and therefore are governed in their relations to each other by, and are amenable to, the laws of the United States."

§ 6. *Resolved*, That the slaves in the brig Creole are amenable only to the laws of the United States.

§ 7. *Resolved*, That those slaves by resuming their natural liberty violated no laws of the United States.

§ 8. *Resolved*, That all attempts to re-enslave them are unconstitutional, etc.

Moved that these resolutions lie on the table; defeated, 53 to 125. Mr. Giddings withdrew the resolutions. Moved to censure Mr. Giddings, and he was finally censured. *House Journal*, 27 Cong. 2 sess. pp. 567–80.

1842, May 10. Congress (House): Remonstrance of Mississippi against Right of Search.

"Mr. Gwin presented resolutions of the Legislature of the State of Mississippi, against granting the right of search to Great Britain for the purpose of suppressing the African slave trade; urging the Government to demand of the British Government redress and restitution in relation to the case of the brig Creole and the slaves on board." Referred to the Committee on Foreign Affairs. *House Journal*, 27 Cong. 2 sess. p. 800.

1842, Aug. 4. United States Statute: Appropriation.

"An Act making appropriations for the naval service," etc.

"For carrying into effect the acts for the suppression of the slave trade," etc. $10,543.42. *Statutes at Large*, V. 500, 501.

1842, Nov. 10. Joint-Cruising Treaty with Great Britain.

"Treaty to settle and define boundaries; for the final suppression of the African slave-trade; and for the giving up of criminals fugitive from justice. Concluded August 9, 1842; ratifications exchanged at London October 13, 1842; proclaimed November 10, 1842." Articles VIII., and IX. Ratified by the Senate by a vote of 39 to 9, after several unsuccessful attempts to amend it. *U. S. Treaties and Conventions* (1889), pp. 436–7; *Senate Exec. Journal*, VI. 118–32.

1842, Dec. 7. President Tyler's Message.

The treaty of Ghent binds the United States and Great Britain to the suppression of the slave-trade. The Right of Search was refused by the United States, and our Minister in France for that reason protested against the Quintuple Treaty; his conduct had the approval of the administration. On this account the eighth article was inserted, causing each government to keep a flotilla in African waters to enforce the laws. If this should be done by all the powers, the trade would be swept from the ocean. *House Journal*, 27 Cong. 3 sess. pp. 16–7.

1843, Feb. 22. Congress (Senate): Appropriation Opposed.

Motion by Mr. Benton, during debate on naval appropriations, to strike out appropriation "for the support of Africans recaptured on the coast of Africa or elsewhere, and returned to Africa by the armed vessels of the United States, $5,000." Lost; similar proposition by Bagby, lost. Proposition to strike out appropriation for squadron, lost. March 3, bill becomes a law, with appropriation for Africans, but without that for squadron. *Congressional Globe*, 27 Cong. 3 sess. pp. 328, 331–6; *Statutes at Large*, V. 615.

1845, Feb. 20. President Tyler's Special Message to Congress.

Message on violations of Brazilian slave-trade laws by Americans. *House Journal*, 28 Cong. 2 sess. pp. 425, 463; *House Doc.*, 28 Cong. 2 sess. IV. No. 148. Cf. *Ibid.*, 29 Cong. 1 sess. III. No. 43.

1846, Aug. 10. United States Statute: Appropriation.

"For carrying into effect the acts for the suppression of the slave trade, including the support of recaptured Africans, and their removal to their country, twenty-five thousand dollars." *Statutes at Large*, IX. 96.

1849, Dec. 4. President Taylor's Message.

"Your attention is earnestly invited to an amendment of our existing laws relating to the African slave-trade, with a view to the effectual suppression of that barbarous traffic. It is not to be denied that this trade is still, in part, carried on by means of vessels built in the United States, and owned or navigated by some of our citizens." *House Exec. Doc.*, 31 Cong. 1 sess. III. No. 5, pp. 7–8.

1850, Aug. 1. Congress (House): Bill for War Steamers.

"A bill (House, No. 367) to establish a line of war steamers to the coast of Africa for the suppression of the slave trade and the promotion of commerce and colonization." Read twice, and referred to Committee of the Whole. *House Journal*, 31 Cong. 1 sess. pp. 1022, 1158, 1217.

1850, Dec. 16. Congress (House): Treaty of Washington.

"Mr. Burt, by unanimous consent, introduced a joint resolution (No. 28) 'to terminate the eighth article of the treaty between the United States and Great Britain concluded at Washington the ninth day of August, 1842.'" Read twice, and referred to the Committee on Naval Affairs. *Ibid.*, 31 Cong. 2 sess. p. 64.

1851, Jan. 22. Congress (Senate): Resolution on Sea Letters.

"The following resolution, submitted by Mr. Clay the 20th instant, came up for consideration: —

"*Resolved*, That the Committee on Commerce be instructed to inquire into the expediency of making more effectual provision by law to prevent the employment of American vessels and American seamen in the African slave trade, and especially as to the expediency of granting sea letters or other evidence of national character to American vessels clearing out of the ports of the empire of Brazil for the western coast of Africa." Agreed to. *Congressional Globe*, 31 Cong. 2 sess. pp. 304–9; *Senate Journal*, 31 Cong. 2 sess. pp. 95, 102–3.

1851, Feb. 19. Congress (Senate): Bill on Slave-Trade.

"A bill (Senate, No. 472) concerning the intercourse and trade of vessels of the United States with certain places on the eastern and western coasts of Africa, and for other purposes." Read once. *Senate Journal*, 31 Cong. 2 sess. pp. 42, 45, 84, 94, 159, 193–4; *Congressional Globe*, 31 Cong. 2 sess. pp. 246–7.

1851, Dec. 3. Congress (House): Bill to Amend Act of 1807.

Mr. Giddings gave notice of a bill to repeal §§ 9 and 10 of the act to prohibit the importation of slaves, etc. from and after Jan. 1, 1808. *House Journal*, 32 Cong. 1 sess. p. 42. Cf. *Ibid.*, 33 Cong. 1 sess. p. 147.

1852, Feb. 5. Alabama: Illegal Importations.

By code approved on this date: —

§§ 2058–2062. If slaves have been imported contrary to law, they are to be sold, and one fourth paid to the agent or informer and the residue to the treasury. An agent is to be appointed to take charge of such slaves, who is to give bond. Pending controversy, he may hire the slaves out. Ormond, *Code of Alabama*, pp. 392–3.

1853, March 3. Congress (Senate): Appropriation Proposed.

A bill making appropriations for the naval service for the year ending June 30, 1854. Mr. Underwood offered the following amendment: —

"For executing the provisions of the act approved 3d of March, 1819, entitled 'An act in addition to the acts prohibiting the slave trade,' $20,000." Amendment agreed to, and bill passed. It appears, however, to have been subsequently amended in the House, and the appropriation does not stand in the final act. *Congressional Globe*, 32 Cong. 2 sess. p. 1072; *Statutes at Large*, X. 214.

1854, May 22. Congress (Senate): West India Slave-Trade.

Mr. Clayton presented the following resolution, which was unanimously agreed to: —

"*Resolved*, That the Committee on Foreign Relations be instructed to inquire into the expediency of providing by law for such restrictions on the power of American consuls residing in the

Spanish West India islands to issue sea letters on the transfer of American vessels in those islands, as will prevent the abuse of the American flag in protecting persons engaged in the African slave trade." June 26, 1854, this committee reported "a bill (Senate, No. 416) for the more effectual suppression of the slave-trade in American built vessels." Passed Senate, postponed in House. *Senate Journal*, 33 Cong. 1 sess. pp. 404, 457–8, 472–3, 476; *House Journal*, 33 Cong. 1 sess. pp. 1093, 1332–3; *Congressional Globe*, 33 Cong. 1 sess. pp. 1257–61, 1511–3, 1591–3, 2139.

1854, May 29. Congress (Senate): Treaty of Washington.

Resolved, "that, in the opinion of the Senate, it is expedient, and in conformity with the interests and sound policy of the United States, that the eighth article of the treaty between this government and Great Britain, of the 9th of August, 1842, should be abrogated." Introduced by Slidell, and favorably reported from Committee on Foreign Relations in Executive Session, June 13, 1854. *Senate Journal*, 34 Cong. 1–2 sess. pp. 396, 695–8; *Senate Reports*, 34 Cong. 1 sess. I. No. 195.

1854, June 21. Congress (Senate): Bill Regulating Navigation.

"Mr. Seward asked and obtained leave to bring in a bill (Senate, No. 407) to regulate navigation to the coast of Africa in vessels owned by citizens of the United States, in certain cases; which was read and passed to a second reading." June 22, ordered to be printed. *Senate Journal*, 33 Cong. 1 sess. pp. 448, 451; *Congressional Globe*, 33 Cong. 1 sess. pp. 1456, 1461, 1472.

1854, June 26. Congress (Senate): Bill to Suppress Slave-Trade.

"A bill for the more effectual suppression of the slave trade in American built vessels." See references to May 22, 1854, above.

1856, June 23. Congress (House): Proposition to Amend Act of 1818.

Notice given of a bill to amend the Act of April 20, 1818. *House Journal*, 34 Cong. 1 sess. II. 1101.

1856, Aug. 18. United States Statute: Appropriation.

To carry out the Act of March 3, 1819, and subsequent acts, $8,000. *Statutes at Large*, XI. 90.

1856, Nov. 24. South Carolina: Governor's Message.

Governor Adams, in his annual message to the legislature, said:—

"It is apprehended that the opening of this trade [*i. e.*, the slave-trade] will lessen the value of slaves, and ultimately destroy the institution. It is a sufficient answer to point to the fact, that unrestricted immigration has not diminished the value of labor in the Northwestern section of the confederacy. The cry there is, want of labor, notwithstanding capital has the pauperism of the old world to press into its grinding service. If we cannot supply the demand for slave labor, then we must expect to be supplied with a species of labor we do not want, and which is, from the very nature of things, antagonistic to our institutions. It is much better that our drays should be driven by slaves — that our factories should be worked by slaves — that our hotels should be served by slaves — that our locomotives should be manned by slaves, than that we should be exposed to the introduction, from any quarter, of a population alien to us by birth, training, and education, and which, in the process of time, must lead to that conflict between capital and labor, 'which makes it so difficult to maintain free institutions in all wealthy and highly civilized nations where such institutions as ours do not exist.' In all slaveholding States, true policy dictates that the superior race should direct, and the inferior perform all menial service. Competition between the white and black man for this service, may not disturb Northern sensibility, but it does not exactly suit our latitude." *South Carolina House Journal*, 1856, p. 36; Cluskey, *Political Text-Book*, 14 edition, p. 585.

1856, Dec. 15. Congress (House): Reopening of Slave-Trade.

"*Resolved*, That this House of Representatives regards all suggestions and propositions of every kind, by whomsoever made, for a revival of the African slave trade, as shocking to the moral sentiment of the enlightened portion of mankind; and that any action on the part of Congress conniving at or legalizing that horrid and inhuman traffic would justly subject the government and citizens of the United States to the reproach and execration of all civilized and Christian people throughout the world." Offered by Mr. Etheridge; agreed to, 152 to 57. *House Journal*, 34 Cong. 3 sess. pp. 105–11; *Congressional Globe*, 34 Cong. 3 sess. pp. 123–5, and Appendix, pp. 364–70.

1856, Dec. 15. Congress (House): Reopening of Slave-Trade.

"*Resolved*, That it is inexpedient to repeal the laws prohibiting the African slave trade." Offered by Mr. Orr; not voted upon. *Congressional Globe*, 34 Cong. 3 sess. p. 123.

1856, Dec. 15. Congress (House): Reopening of Slave-Trade.

"*Resolved,* That it is inexpedient, unwise, and contrary to the settled policy of the United States, to repeal the laws prohibiting the African slave trade." Offered by Mr. Orr; agreed to, 183 to 8. *House Journal,* 34 Cong. 3 sess. pp. 111–3; *Congressional Globe,* 34 Cong. 3 sess. pp. 125–6.

1856, Dec. 15. Congress (House): Reopening of Slave-Trade.

"*Resolved,* That the House of Representatives, expressing, as they believe, public opinion both North and South, are utterly opposed to the reopening of the slave trade." Offered by Mr. Boyce; not voted upon. *Congressional Globe,* 34 Cong. 3 sess. p. 125.

1857. South Carolina: Report of Legislative Committee.

Special committee of seven on the slave-trade clause in the Governor's message report: majority report of six members, favoring the reopening of the African slave-trade; minority report of Pettigrew, opposing it. *Report of the Special Committee,* etc., published in 1857.

1857, March 3. United States Statute: Appropriation.

To carry out the Act of March 3, 1819, and subsequent acts, $8,000. *Statutes at Large,* XI. 227; *House Journal,* 34 Cong. 3 sess. p. 397. Cf. *House Exec. Doc.,* 34 Cong. 3 sess. IX. No. 70.

1858, March (?). Louisiana: Bill to Import Africans.

Passed House; lost in Senate by two votes. Cf. *Congressional Globe,* 35 Cong. 1 sess. p. 1362.

1858, Dec. 6. President Buchanan's Message.

"The truth is, that Cuba in its existing colonial condition, is a constant source of injury and annoyance to the American people. It is the only spot in the civilized world where the African slave trade is tolerated; and we are bound by treaty with Great Britain to maintain a naval force on the coast of Africa, at much expense both of life and treasure, solely for the purpose of arresting slavers bound to that island. The late serious difficulties between the United States and Great Britain respecting the right of search, now so happily terminated, could never have arisen if Cuba had not afforded a market for slaves. As long as this market shall remain open, there can be no hope for the civilization of benighted Africa. . . .

"It has been made known to the world by my predecessors that the United States have, on several occasions, endeavored to acquire Cuba from Spain by honorable negotiation. If this were accomplished, the last relic of the African slave trade would instantly disappear. We would not, if we could, acquire Cuba in any other manner. This is due to our national character. . . . This course we shall ever pursue, unless circumstances should occur, which we do not now anticipate, rendering a departure from it clearly justifiable, under the imperative and overruling law of self-preservation." *House Exec. Doc.*, 35 Cong. 2 sess. II. No. 2, pp. 14–5. See also *Ibid.*, pp. 31–3.

1858, Dec. 23. Congress (House): Resolution on Slave-Trade.

On motion of Mr. Farnsworth,

"*Resolved*, That the Committee on Naval Affairs be requested to inquire and report to this House if any, and what, further legislation is necessary on the part of the United States to fully carry out and perform the stipulations contained in the eighth article of the treaty with Great Britain (known as the 'Ashburton treaty') for the suppression of the slave trade." *House Journal*, 35 Cong. 2 sess. pp. 115–6.

1859, Jan. 5. Congress (Senate): Resolution on Slave-Trade.

On motion of Mr. Seward, Dec. 21, 1858,

"*Resolved*, That the Committee on the Judiciary inquire whether any amendments to existing laws ought to be made for the suppression of the African slave trade." *Senate Journal*, 35 Cong. 2 sess. pp. 80, 108, 115.

1859, Jan. 13. Congress (Senate): Bill on Slave-Trade.

Mr. Seward introduced "a bill (Senate, No. 510) in addition to the acts which prohibit the slave trade." Referred to committee, reported, and dropped. *Ibid.*, pp. 134, 321.

1859, Jan. 31. Congress (House): Reopening of Slave-Trade.

"Mr. Kilgore moved that the rules be suspended, so as to enable him to submit the following preamble and resolutions, viz:

"Whereas the laws prohibiting the African slave trade have become a topic of discussion with newspaper writers and political agitators, many of them boldly denouncing these laws as unwise in policy and disgraceful in their provisions, and insisting on the justice and propriety of their repeal, and the revival of the odious traffic in African slaves; and whereas recent demonstrations afford strong reasons to apprehend that said laws are to be set at defiance, and their violation openly countenanced and encouraged by a portion of the citizens of some of the States of this Union; and whereas it is proper in view of said facts that the sentiments of the people's representatives in Congress should be made public in relation thereto: Therefore—

"*Resolved*, That while we recognize no right on the part of the federal government, or any other law-making power, save that of the States wherein it exists, to interfere with or disturb the institution of domestic slavery where it is established or protected by State legislation, we do hold that Congress has power to prohibit the foreign traffic, and that no legislation can be too thorough in its measures, nor can any penalty known to the catalogue of modern punishment for crime be too severe against a traffic so inhuman and unchristian.

"*Resolved*, That the laws in force against said traffic are founded upon the broadest principles of philanthropy, religion, and humanity; that they should remain unchanged, except so far as legislation may be needed to render them more efficient; that they should be faithfully and promptly executed by our government, and respected by all good citizens.

"*Resolved*, That the Executive should be sustained and commended for any proper efforts whenever and wherever made to enforce said laws, and to bring to speedy punishment the wicked violators thereof, and all their aiders and abettors."

Failed of the two-thirds vote necessary to suspend the rules—the vote being 115 to 84—and was dropped. *House Journal*, 35 Cong. 2 sess. pp. 298–9.

1859, March 3. United States Statute: Appropriation.

To carry out the Act of March 3, 1819, and subsequent acts, and to pay expenses already incurred, $75,000. *Statutes at Large*, XI. 404.

1859, Dec. 19. President Buchanan's Message.

"All lawful means at my command have been employed, and shall continue to be employed, to execute the laws against the African slave trade. After a most careful and rigorous examination of our coasts, and a thorough investigation of the subject, we have not been able to discover that any slaves have been imported into the United States except the cargo by the Wanderer, numbering between three and four hundred. Those engaged in this unlawful enterprise have been rigorously prosecuted, but not with as much success as their crimes have deserved. A number of them are still under prosecution. [Here follows a history of our slave-trade legislation.]

"These acts of Congress, it is believed, have, with very rare and insignificant exceptions, accomplished their purpose. For a period of more than half a century there has been no perceptible addition to the number of our domestic slaves. . . . Reopen the trade, and it would be difficult to determine whether the effect would be more deleterious on the interests of the master, or on those of the native born slave, . . . " *Senate Exec. Doc.*, 36 Cong. 1 sess. I. No. 2, pp. 5–8.

1860, March 20. Congress (Senate): Proposed Resolution.

"Mr. Wilson submitted the following resolution; which was considered, by unanimous consent, and agreed to: —

"*Resolved*, That the Committee on the Judiciary be instructed to inquire into the expediency of so amending the laws of the United States in relation to the suppression of the African slave trade as to provide a penalty of imprisonment for life for a participation in such trade, instead of the penalty of forfeiture of life, as now provided; and also an amendment of such laws as will include in the punishment for said offense all persons who fit out or are in any way connected with or interested in fitting out expeditions or vessels for the purpose of engaging in such slave trade." *Senate Journal*, 36 Cong. 1 sess. p. 274.

1860, March 20. Congress (Senate): Right of Search.

"Mr. Wilson asked, and by unanimous consent obtained, leave to bring in a joint resolution (Senate, No. 20) to secure the right of search on the coast of Africa, for the more effectual suppression of the African slave trade." Read twice, and referred to Committee on Foreign Relations. *Ibid.*

1860, March 20. Congress (Senate): Steam Vessels for Slave-Trade.

"Mr. Wilson asked, and by unanimous consent obtained, leave to bring in a bill (Senate, No. 296) for the construction of five steam screw sloops-of-war, for service on the African coast." Read twice, and referred to Committee on Naval Affairs; May 23, reported with an amendment. *Ibid.*, pp. 274, 494–5.

1860, March 26. Congress (House): Proposed Resolutions.

"Mr. Morse submitted . . . the following resolutions; which were read and committed to the Committee of the Whole House on the state of the Union, viz:

"*Resolved*, That for the more effectual suppression of the African slave trade the treaty of 1842 . . . , requiring each country to keep *eighty* guns on the coast of Africa for that purpose, should be so changed as to require a specified and sufficient number of small steamers and fast sailing brigs or schooners to be kept on said coast. . . .

"*Resolved*, That as the African slave trade appears to be rapidly increasing, some effective mode of identifying the nationality of a vessel on the coast of Africa suspected of being in the slave trade or of wearing false colors should be immediately adopted and carried into effect by the leading maritime nations of the earth; and that the government of the United States has thus far, by refusing to aid in establishing such a system, shown a strange neglect of one of the best means of suppressing said trade.

"*Resolved*, That the African slave trade is against the moral sentiment of mankind and a crime against human nature; and that as the most highly civilized nations have made it a criminal offence or piracy under their own municipal laws, it ought at once and without hesitation to be declared a crime by the code of international law; and that . . . the President be requested to open negotiations on this subject with the leading powers of Europe." . . . *House Journal*, 36 Cong. 1 sess. I. 588–9.

1860, April 16. Congress (Senate): Bill on Slave-Trade.

"Mr. Wilson asked, and by unanimous consent obtained, leave to bring in a bill (Senate, No. 408) for the more effectual suppression of the slave trade." Bill read twice, and ordered to lie on the table; May 21, referred to Committee on the Judiciary, and printed. *Senate Journal*, 36 Cong. 1 sess. pp. 394, 485; *Congressional Globe*, 36 Cong. 1 sess. pp. 1721, 2207–11.

1860, May 21. Congress (House): Buyers of Imported Negroes.

"Mr. Wells submitted the following resolution, and debate arising thereon, it lies over under the rule, viz:

"*Resolved*, That the Committee on the Judiciary be instructed to report forthwith a bill providing that any person purchasing any negro or other person imported into this country in violation of the laws for suppressing the slave trade, shall not by reason of said purchase acquire any title to said negro or person; and where such purchase is made with a knowledge that such negro or other person has been so imported, shall forfeit not less than one thousand dollars, and be punished by imprisonment for a term not less than six months." *House Journal*, 36 Cong. 1 sess. II. 880.

1860, May 26. United States Statute: Appropriation.

To carry out the Act of March 3, 1819, and subsequent acts, $40,000. *Statutes at Large*, XII. 21.

1860, June 16. United States Statute: Additional Act to Act of 1819.

"An Act to amend an Act entitled 'An Act in addition to the Acts Prohibiting the Slave Trade.'" *Ibid.*, XII. 40–1; *Senate Journal*, 36 Cong. 1 sess., Senate Bill No. 464.

1860, July 11. Great Britain: Proposed Co-operation.

Lord John Russell suggested for the suppression of the trade:—

"1st. A systematic plan of cruising on the coast of Cuba by the vessels of Great Britain, Spain, and the United States.

"2d. Laws of registration and inspection in the Island of Cuba, by which the employment of slaves, imported contrary to law, might be detected by the Spanish authorities.

"3d. A plan of emigration from China, regulated by the agents of European nations, in conjunction with the Chinese authorities." President Buchanan refused to co-operate on this plan. *House Exec. Doc.*, 36 Cong. 2 sess. IV. No. 7, pp. 441–3, 446–8.

1860, Dec. 3. President Buchanan's Message.

"It is with great satisfaction I communicate the fact that since the date of my last annual message not a single slave has been imported into the United States in violation of the laws prohibiting the African slave trade. This statement is founded upon a thorough examination and investigation of the subject. Indeed, the spirit which prevailed some time since among a portion of our fellow-citizens in favor of this trade seems to have entirely subsided." *Senate Exec. Doc.*, 36 Cong. 2 sess. I. No. 1, p. 24.

1860, Dec. 12. Congress (House): Proposition to Amend Constitution.

Mr. John Cochrane's resolution:—

"The migration or importation of slaves into the United States or any of the Territories thereof, from any foreign country, is hereby prohibited." *House Journal*, 36 Cong. 2 sess. pp. 61–2; *Congressional Globe*, 36 Cong. 2 sess. p. 77.

1860, Dec. 24. Congress (Senate): Bill on Slave-Trade.

"Mr. Wilson asked, and by unanimous consent obtained, leave to bring in a bill (Senate, No. 529) for the more effectual suppression of the slave trade." Read twice, and referred to Committee on the Judiciary; not mentioned again. *Senate Journal*, 36 Cong. 2 sess. p. 62; *Congressional Globe*, 36 Cong. 2 sess. p. 182.

1861, Jan. 7. Congress (House): Proposition to Amend Constitution.

Mr. Etheridge's resolution:—

§ 5. "The migration or importation of persons held to service or labor for life, or a term of years, into any of the States, or the Territories belonging to the United States, is perpetually prohibited; and Congress shall pass all laws necessary to make said prohibition effective." *Congressional Globe*, 36 Cong. 2 sess. p. 279.

1861, Jan. 23. Congress (House): Proposition to Amend Constitution.

Resolution of Mr. Morris of Pennsylvania:—

"Neither Congress nor a Territorial Legislature shall make any law respecting slavery or involuntary servitude, except as a punishment for crime; but Congress may pass laws for the suppression of the African slave trade, and the rendition of fugitives from service or labor in the States." Mr. Morris asked to have it printed, that he might at the proper time move it as an amendment to the report of the select committee of thirty-three. It was ordered to be printed. *Ibid.*, p. 527.

1861, Feb. 1. Congress (House): Proposition to Amend Constitution.

Resolution of Mr. Kellogg of Illinois:—

§ 16. "The migration or importation of persons held to service or involuntary servitude into any State, Territory, or place within the United States, from any place or country beyond the limits of the United States or Territories thereof, is forever prohibited." Considered Feb. 27, 1861, and lost. *Ibid.*, pp. 690, 1243, 1259–60.

1861, Feb. 8. Confederate States of America: Importation Prohibited.

Constitution for the Provisional Government of the Confederate States of America, Article I. Section 7:—

"1. The importation of African negroes from any foreign country other than the slave-holding States of the United States, is hereby forbidden; and Congress are required to pass such laws as shall effectually prevent the same.

"2. The Congress shall also have power to prohibit the introduction of slaves from any State not a member of this Confederacy." March 11, 1861, this article was placed in the permanent Constitution. The first line was changed so as to read "negroes of the African race." *C. S. A. Statutes at Large*, 1861–2, pp. 3, 15.

1861, Feb. 9. Confederate States of America: Statutory Prohibition.

Be it enacted by the Confederate States of America in Congress assembled, That all the laws of the United States of America in force and in use in the Confederate States of America on the first day of November last, and not inconsistent with the Constitution of the Confederate States, be and the same are hereby continued in force until altered or repealed by the Congress." *Ibid.*, p. 27.

1861, Feb. 19. United States Statute: Appropriation.

To supply deficiencies in the fund hitherto appropriated to carry out the Act of March 3, 1819, and subsequent acts, $900,000. *Statutes at Large*, XII. 132.

1861, March 2. United States Statute: Appropriation.

To carry out the Act of March 3, 1819, and subsequent acts, and to provide compensation for district attorneys and marshals, $900,000. *Ibid.*, XII. 218–9.

1861, Dec. 3. President Lincoln's Message.

"The execution of the laws for the suppression of the African slave trade has been confided to the Department of the Interior. It is a subject of gratulation that the efforts which have been made for the suppression of this inhuman traffic have been recently attended with unusual success. Five vessels being fitted out for the slave trade have been seized and condemned. Two mates of vessels engaged in the trade, and one person in equipping a vessel as a slaver, have been convicted and subjected to the penalty of fine and imprisonment, and one captain, taken with a cargo of Africans on board his vessel, has been convicted of the highest grade of offence under our laws, the punishment of which is death." *Senate Exec. Doc.*, 37 Cong. 2 sess. I. No. 1, p. 13.

1862, Jan. 27. Congress (Senate): Bill on Slave-Trade.

"Agreeably to notice Mr. Wilson, of Massachusetts, asked and obtained leave to bring in a bill (Senate, No. 173), for the more effectual suppression of the slave trade." Read twice, and referred to Committee on the Judiciary; Feb. 11, 1863, reported adversely, and postponed indefinitely. *Senate Journal*, 37 Cong. 2 sess. p. 143; 37 Cong. 3 sess. pp. 231–2.

1862, March 14. United States Statute: Appropriation.

For compensation to United States marshals, district attorneys, etc., for services in the suppression of the slave-trade, so much of the appropriation of March 2, 1861, as may be expedient and proper, not exceeding in all $10,000. *Statutes at Large*, XII. 368–9.

1862, March 25. United States Statute: Prize Law.

"An Act to facilitate Judicial Proceedings in Adjudications upon Captured Property, and for the better Administration of the Law of Prize." Applied to captures under the slave-trade law. *Ibid.*, XII. 374–5; *Congressional Globe*, 37 Cong. 2 sess., Appendix, pp. 346–7.

1862, June 7. Great Britain: Treaty of 1862.

"Treaty for the suppression of the African slave trade. Concluded at Washington April 7, 1862; ratifications exchanged at London May 20, 1862; proclaimed June 7, 1862." Ratified unanimously by the Senate. *U. S. Treaties and Conventions* (1889), pp. 454–66. See also *Senate Exec. Journal*, XII. pp. 230, 231, 240, 254, 391, 400, 403.

1862, July 11. United States Statute: Treaty of 1862 Carried into Effect.

"An Act to carry into Effect the Treaty between the United States and her Britannic Majesty for the Suppression of the African Slave-Trade." *Statutes at Large*, XII. 531; *Senate Journal* and *House Journal*, 37 Cong. 2 sess., Senate Bill No. 352.

1862, July 17. United States Statute: Former Acts Amended.

"An Act to amend an Act entitled 'An Act to amend an Act entitled "An Act in Addition to the Acts prohibiting the Slave Trade."'" *Statutes at Large*, XII. 592–3; *Senate Journal* and *House Journal*, 37 Cong. 2 sess., Senate Bill No. 385.

1863, Feb. 4. United States Statute: Appropriation.

To carry out the treaty with Great Britain, proclaimed July 11, 1862, $17,000. *Statutes at Large*, XII. 639.

1863, March 3. Congress: Joint Resolution.

"Joint Resolution respecting the Compensation of the Judges and so forth, under the Treaty with Great Britain and other Persons employed in the Suppression of the Slave Trade." *Statutes at Large*, XII. 829.

1863, April 22. Great Britain: Treaty of 1862 Amended.

"Additional article to the treaty for the suppression of the African slave trade of April 7, 1862." Concluded February 17, 1863; ratifications exchanged at London April 1, 1863; proclaimed April 22, 1863.

Right of Search extended. *U. S. Treaties and Conventions* (1889), pp. 466–7.

1863, Dec. 17. Congress (House): Resolution on Coastwise Slave-Trade.

Mr. Julian introduced a bill to repeal portions of the Act of March 2, 1807, relative to the coastwise slave-trade. Read twice, and referred to Committee on the Judiciary. *Congressional Globe*, 38 Cong. 1 sess. p. 46.

1864, July 2. United States Statute: Coastwise Slave-Trade Prohibited Forever.

§ 9 of Appropriation Act repeals §§ 8 and 9 of Act of 1807. *Statutes at Large*, XIII. 353.

1864, Dec. 7. Great Britain: International Proposition.

"The crime of trading in human beings has been for many years branded by the reprobation of all civilized nations. Still the atrocious traffic subsists, and many persons flourish on the gains they have derived from that polluted source.

"Her Majesty's government, contemplating, on the one hand, with satisfaction the unanimous abhorrence which the crime inspires, and, on the other hand, with pain and disgust the slave-trading speculations which still subist [*sic*], have come to the conclusion that no measure would be so effectual to put a stop to these wicked acts as the punishment of all persons who can be proved to be guilty of carrying slaves across the sea. Her Majesty's government, therefore, invite the government of the United States to consider whether it would not be practicable, honorable, and humane ——

"1st. To make a general declaration, that the governments who are parties to it denounce the slave trade as piracy.

"2d. That the aforesaid governments should propose to their legislatures to affix the penalties of piracy already existing in their laws — provided, only, that the penalty in this case be that of death — to all persons, being subjects or citizens of one of the contracting powers, who shall be convicted in a court which takes cognizance of piracy, of being concerned in carrying human beings across the sea for the purpose of sale, or for the purpose of serving as slaves, in any country or colony in the world." Signed,

"RUSSELL."

Similar letters were addressed to France, Spain, Portugal, Austria, Prussia, Italy, Netherlands, and Russia. *Diplomatic Correspondence*, 1865, pt. ii. pp. 4, 58–9, etc.

1865, Jan. 24. United States Statute: Appropriation.

To carry out the treaty with Great Britain, proclaimed July 11, 1862, $17,000. *Statutes at Large*, XIII. 424.

1866, April 7. United States Statute: Compensation to Marshals, etc.

For additional compensation to United States marshals, district attorneys, etc., for services in the suppression of the slave-trade, so much of the appropriation of March 2, 1861, as may be expedient and proper, not exceeding in all $10,000; and also so much as may be necessary to pay the salaries of judges and the expenses of mixed courts. *Ibid.*, XIV. 23.

1866, July 25. United States Statute: Appropriation.

To carry out the treaty with Great Britain, proclaimed July 11, 1862, $17,000. *Ibid.*, XIV. 226.

1867, Feb. 28. United States Statute: Appropriation.

To carry out the treaty with Great Britain, proclaimed July 11, 1862, $17,000. *Ibid.*, XIV. 414–5.

1868, March 30. United States Statute: Appropriation.

To carry out the treaty with Great Britain, proclaimed July 11, 1862, $12,500. *Ibid.*, XV. 58.

1869, Jan. 6. Congress (House): Abrogation of Treaty of 1862.

Mr. Kelsey asked unanimous consent to introduce the following resolution: —

"Whereas the slave trade has been practically suppressed; and whereas by our treaty with Great Britain for the suppression of the slave trade large appropriations are annually required to carry out the provisions thereof: Therefore,

"*Resolved*, That the Committee on Foreign Affairs are hereby instructed to inquire into the expediency of taking proper steps to secure the abrogation or modification of the treaty with Great Britain for the suppression of the slave trade." Mr. Arnell objected. *Congressional Globe*, 40 Cong. 3 sess. p. 224.

1869, March 3. United States Statute: Appropriation.

To carry out the treaty with Great Britain, proclaimed July 11, 1862, $12,500; provided that the salaries of judges be paid only on condition that they reside where the courts are held, and that Great Britain be asked to consent to abolish mixed courts. *Statutes at Large*, XV. 321.

1870, April 22. Congress (Senate): Bill to Repeal Act of 1803.

Senate Bill No. 251, to repeal an act entitled "An act to prevent the importation of certain persons into certain States where by the laws thereof their admission is prohibited." Mr. Sumner said that the bill had passed the Senate once, and that he hoped it would now pass. Passed; title amended by adding "approved February 28, 1803;" June 29, bill passed over in House; July 14, consideration again postponed on Mr. Woodward's objection. *Congressional Globe*, 41 Cong. 2 sess. pp. 2894, 2932, 4953, 5594.

1870, Sept. 16. Great Britain: Additional Treaty.

"Additional convention to the treaty of April 7, 1862, respecting the African slave trade." Concluded June 3, 1870; ratifications exchanged at London August 10, 1870; proclaimed September 16, 1870. *U. S. Treaties and Conventions* (1889), pp. 472–6.

1871, Dec. 11. Congress (House): Bill on Slave-Trade.

On the call of States, Mr. Banks introduced "a bill (House, No. 490) to carry into effect article thirteen of the Constitution of the United States, and to prohibit the owning or dealing in slaves by American citizens in foreign countries." *House Journal*, 42 Cong. 2 sess. p. 48.

APPENDIX C.

TYPICAL CASES OF VESSELS ENGAGED IN THE AMERICAN SLAVE-TRADE.

1619–1864.

THIS chronological list of certain typical American slavers is not intended to catalogue all known cases, but is designed merely to illustrate, by a few selected examples, the character of the licit and the illicit traffic to the United States.

1619. ———. Dutch man-of-war, imports twenty Negroes into Virginia, the first slaves brought to the continent. Smith, *Generall Historie of Virginia* (1626 and 1632), p. 126.

1645. **Rainbowe,** under Captain Smith, captures and imports African slaves into Massachusetts. The slaves were forfeited and returned. *Massachusetts Colonial Records*, II. 115, 129, 136, 168, 176; III. 13, 46, 49, 58, 84.

1655. **Witte paert,** first vessel to import slaves into New York. O'Callaghan, *Laws of New Netherland* (ed. 1868), p. 191, note.

1736, Oct. ———. Rhode Island slaver, under Capt. John Griffen. *American Historical Record*, I. 312.

1746. ———. Spanish vessel, with certain free Negroes, captured by Captains John Dennis and Robert Morris, and Negroes sold by them in Rhode Island, Massachusetts, and New York; these Negroes afterward returned to Spanish colonies by the authorities of Rhode Island. *Rhode Island Colonial Records*, V. 170, 176–7; Dawson's *Historical Magazine*, XVIII. 98.

1752. **Sanderson,** of Newport, trading to Africa and West Indies. *American Historical Record*, I. 315–9, 338–42. Cf. above, p. 28, note 5.

1788 (*circa*). ———. "One or two" vessels fitted out in Connecticut. W. C. Fowler, *Historical Status of the Negro in Connecticut*, in *Local Law*, etc., p. 125.

1801. **Sally,** of Norfolk, Virginia, equipped slaver; libelled and acquitted; owners claimed damages. *American State Papers, Commerce and Navigation*, I. No. 128.

1803 (?). ———. Two slavers seized with slaves, and brought to Philadelphia; both condemned, and slaves apprenticed. Robert Sutcliff, *Travels in North America*, p. 219.

1804. ———. Slaver, allowed by Governor Claiborne to land fifty Negroes in Louisiana. *American State Papers, Miscellaneous*, I. No. 177.

1814. **Saucy Jack** carries off slaves from Africa and attacks British cruiser. *House Reports*, 17 Cong. 1 sess. II. No. 92, p. 46; 21 Cong. 1 sess. III. No. 348, p. 147.

1816 (*circa*). **Paz, Rosa, Dolores, Nueva Paz,** and **Dorset,** American slavers in Spanish-African trade. Many of these were formerly privateers. *Ibid.*, 17 Cong. 1 sess. II. No. 92, pp. 45–6; 21 Cong. 1 sess. III. No. 348, pp. 144–7.

1817, Jan. 17. **Eugene,** armed Mexican schooner, captured while attempting to smuggle slaves into the United States. *House Doc.*, 15 Cong. 1 sess. II. No. 12, p. 22.

1817, Nov. 19. **Tentativa,** captured with 128 slaves and brought into Savannah. *Ibid.*, p. 38; *House Reports*, 21 Cong. 1 sess. III. No. 348, p. 81. See *Friends' View of the African Slave Trade* (1824), pp. 44–7.

1818. ———. Three schooners unload slaves in Louisiana. Collector Chew to the Secretary of the Treasury, *House Reports*, 21 Cong. 1 sess. III. No. 348, p 70.

1818, Jan. 23. English brig **Neptune,** detained by U. S. S. John Adams, for smuggling slaves into the United States. *House Doc.*, 16 Cong. 1 sess. III. No. 36 (3).

1818, June. **Constitution,** captured with 84 slaves on the Florida coast, by a United States army officer. See references under 1818, June, below.

1818, June. **Louisa** and **Merino,** captured slavers, smuggling from Cuba to the United States; condemned after five years' litigation. *House*

Doc., 15 Cong. 2 sess. VI. No. 107; 19 Cong. 1 sess. VI.–IX. Nos. 121, 126, 152, 163; *House Reports*, 19 Cong. 1 sess. II. No. 231; *American State Papers, Naval Affairs*, II. No. 308; Decisions of the United States Supreme Court in 9 *Wheaton*, 391.

1819. **Antelope,** or **General Ramirez.** The Colombia (or Arraganta), a Venezuelan privateer, fitted in the United States and manned by Americans, captures slaves from a Spanish slaver, the Antelope, and from other slavers; is wrecked, and transfers crew and slaves to Antelope; the latter, under the name of the General Ramirez, is captured with 280 slaves by a United States ship. The slaves were distributed, some to Spanish claimants, some sent to Africa, and some allowed to remain; many died. *House Reports*, 17 Cong. 1 sess. II. No. 92, pp. 5, 15; 21 Cong. 1 sess. III. No. 348, p. 186; *House Journal*, 20 Cong. 1 sess. pp. 59, 76, 123 to 692, *passim*. Gales and Seaton, *Register of Debates*, IV. pt. 1, pp. 915–6, 955–68, 998, 1005; *Ibid.*, pt. 2, pp. 2501–3; *American State Papers, Naval Affairs*, II. No. 319, pp. 750–60; Decisions of the United States Supreme Court in 10 *Wheaton*, 66, and 12 *Ibid.*, 546.

1820. **Endymion, Plattsburg, Science, Esperanza,** and **Alexander,** captured on the African coast by United States ships, and sent to New York and Boston. *House Reports*, 17 Cong. 1 sess. II. No. 92, pp. 6, 15; 21 Cong. 1 sess. III. No. 348, pp. 122, 144, 187.

1820. **General Artigas** imports twelve slaves into the United States. *Friends' View of the African Slave Trade* (1824), p. 42.

1821 (?). **Dolphin,** captured by United States officers and sent to Charleston, South Carolina. *Ibid.*, pp. 31–2.

1821. **La Jeune Eugène, La Daphnée, La Mathilde,** and **L'Elize,** captured by U. S. S. Alligator; **La Jeune Eugène** sent to Boston; the rest escape, and are recaptured under the French flag; the French protest. *House Reports*, 21 Cong. 1 sess. III. No. 348, p. 187; *Friends' View of the African Slave Trade* (1824), pp. 35–41.

1821. **La Pensée,** captured with 220 slaves by the U. S. S. Hornet; taken to Louisiana. *House Reports*, 17 Cong. 1 sess. II. No. 92, p. 5; 21 Cong. 1 sess. III. No. 348, p. 186.

1821. **Esencia** lands 113 Negroes at Matanzas. *Parliamentary Papers*, 1822, Vol. XXII., *Slave Trade, Further Papers*, III. p. 78.

1826. **Fell's Point** attempts to land Negroes in the United States. The Negroes were seized. *American State Papers, Naval Affairs*, II. No. 319, p. 751.

1827, Dec. 20. **Guerrero,** Spanish slaver, chased by British cruiser and grounded on Key West, with 561 slaves; a part (121) were landed at

Key West, where they were seized by the collector; 250 were seized by the Spanish and taken to Cuba, etc. *House Journal*, 20 Cong. 1 sess. p. 650; *House Reports*, 24 Cong. 1 sess. I. No. 268; 25 Cong. 2 sess. I. No. 4; *American State Papers, Naval Affairs*, III. No. 370, p. 210; *Niles's Register*, XXXIII. 373.

1828, March 11. **General Geddes** brought into St. Augustine for safe keeping 117 slaves, said to have been those taken from the wrecked **Guerrero** and landed at Key West (see above, 1827). *House Doc.*, 20 Cong. 1 sess. VI. No. 262.

1828. **Blue-eyed Mary**, of Baltimore, sold to Spaniards and captured with 405 slaves by a British cruiser. *Niles's Register*, XXXIV. 346.

1830, June 4. **Fenix**, with 82 Africans, captured by U. S. S. Grampus, and brought to Pensacola; American built, with Spanish colors. *House Doc.*, 21 Cong. 2 sess. III. No. 54; *House Reports*, 24 Cong. 1 sess. I. No. 223; *Niles's Register*, XXXVIII. 357.

1831, Jan. 3. **Comet**, carrying slaves from the District of Columbia to New Orleans, was wrecked on Bahama banks and 164 slaves taken to Nassau, in New Providence, where they were freed. Great Britain finally paid indemnity for these slaves. *Senate Doc.*, 24 Cong. 2 sess. II. No. 174; 25 Cong. 3 sess. III. No. 216.

1834, Feb. 4. **Encomium**, bound from Charleston, South Carolina, to New Orleans, with 45 slaves, was wrecked near Fish Key, Abaco, and slaves were carried to Nassau and freed. Great Britain eventually paid indemnity for these slaves. *Ibid.*

1835, March. **Enterprise**, carrying 78 slaves from the District of Columbia to Charleston, was compelled by rough weather to put into the port of Hamilton, West Indies, where the slaves were freed. Great Britain refused to pay for these, because, before they landed, slavery in the West Indies had been abolished. *Ibid.*

1836, Aug.–Sept. **Emanuel**, **Dolores**, **Anaconda**, and **Viper**, built in the United States, clear from Havana for Africa. *House Doc.*, 26 Cong. 2 sess. V. No. 115, pp. 4–6, 221.

1837. ———. Eleven American slavers clear from Havana for Africa. *Ibid.*, p. 221.

1837. **Washington**, allowed to proceed to Africa by the American consul at Havana. *Ibid.*, pp. 488–90, 715 ff.; 27 Cong. 1 sess. No. 34, pp. 18–21.

1838. **Prova** spends three months refitting in the harbor of Charleston, South Carolina; afterwards captured by the British, with 225 slaves. *Ibid.*, pp. 121, 163–6.

1838. ———. Nineteen American slavers clear from Havana for Africa. *House Doc.*, 26 Cong. 2 sess. V. No. 115, p. 221.

1838-9. **Venus**, American built, manned partly by Americans, owned by Spaniards. *Ibid.*, pp. 20–2, 106, 124–5, 132, 144–5, 330–2, 475–9.

1839. **Morris Cooper**, of Philadelphia, lands 485 Negroes in Cuba. *Niles's Register*, LVII. 192.

1839. **Edwin** and **George Crooks**, slavers, boarded by British cruisers. *House Doc.*, 26 Cong. 2 sess. V. No. 115, pp. 12–4, 61–4.

1839. **Eagle**, **Clara**, and **Wyoming**, with American and Spanish flags and papers and an American crew, captured by British cruisers, and brought to New York. The United States government declined to interfere in case of the **Eagle** and the **Clara**, and they were taken to Jamaica. The **Wyoming** was forfeited to the United States. *Ibid.*, pp. 92–104, 109, 112, 118–9, 180–4; *Niles's Register*, LVI. 256; LVII. 128, 208.

1839. **Florida**, protected from British cruisers by American papers *House Doc.*, 26 Cong. 2 sess. V. No. 115, pp. 113–5.

1839. ———. Five American slavers arrive at Havana from Africa, under American flags. *Ibid.*, p. 192.

1839. ———. Twenty-three American slavers clear from Havana. *Ibid.*, pp. 190–1, 221.

1839. **Rebecca**, part Spanish, condemned at Sierra Leone. *House Reports*, 27 Cong. 3 sess. III. No. 283, pp. 649–54, 675–84.

1839. **Douglas** and **Iago**, American slavers, visited by British cruisers, for which the United States demanded indemnity. *Ibid.*, pp. 542–65, 731–55; *Senate Doc.*, 29 Cong. 1 sess. VIII. No. 377, pp. 39–45, 107–12, 116–24, 160–1, 181–2.

1839, April 9. **Susan**, suspected slaver, boarded by the British. *House Doc.*, 26 Cong. 2 sess. V. No. 115, pp. 34–41.

1839, July–Sept. **Dolphin** (or **Constitução**), **Hound**, **Mary Cushing** (or **Sete de Avril**), with American and Spanish flags and papers. *Ibid.*, pp. 28, 51–5, 109–10, 136, 234–8; *House Reports*, 27 Cong. 3 sess. III. No. 283, pp. 709–15.

1839, Aug. **L'Amistad**, slaver, with fifty-three Negroes on board, who mutinied; the vessel was then captured by a United States vessel and brought into Connecticut; the Negroes were declared free. *House Doc.*, 26 Cong. 1 sess. IV. No. 185; 27 Cong. 3 sess. V. No. 191; 28 Cong. 1 sess. IV. No. 83; *House Exec. Doc.*, 32 Cong. 2 sess. III. No. 20; *House Reports*, 26 Cong. 2 sess. No. 51; 28 Cong.

1 sess. II. No. 426; 29 Cong. 1 sess. IV. No. 753; *Senate Doc.*, 26 Cong. 2 sess. IV. No. 179; *Senate Exec. Doc.*, 31 Cong. 2 sess. III. No. 29; 32 Cong. 2 sess. III. No. 19; *Senate Reports*, 31 Cong. 2 sess. No. 301; 32 Cong. 1 sess. I. No. 158; 35 Cong. 1 sess. I. No. 36; Decisions of the United States Supreme Court in 15 *Peters*, 518; *Opinions of the Attorneys-General*, III. 484–92.

1839, Sept. **My Boy**, of New Orleans, seized by a British cruiser, and condemned at Sierra Leone. *Niles's Register*, LVII. 353.

1839, Sept. 23. **Butterfly**, of New Orleans, fitted as a slaver, and captured by a British cruiser on the coast of Africa. *House Doc.*, 26 Cong. 2 sess. No. 115, pp. 191, 244–7; *Niles's Register*, LVII. 223.

1839, Oct. **Catharine**, of Baltimore, captured on the African coast by a British cruiser, and brought by her to New York. *House Doc.*, 26 Cong. 2 sess. V. No. 115, pp. 191, 215, 239–44; *Niles's Register*, LVII. 119, 159.

1839. **Asp, Laura**, and **Mary Ann Cassard**, foreign slavers sailing under the American flag. *House Doc.*, 26 Cong. 2 sess. V. No. 115, pp. 126–7, 209–18; *House Reports*, 27 Cong. 3 sess. III. No. 283, p. 688 ff.

1839. **Two Friends**, of New Orleans, equipped slaver, with Spanish, Portuguese, and American flags. *House Doc.*, 26 Cong. 2 sess. V. No. 115, pp. 120, 160–2, 305.

1839. **Euphrates**, of Baltimore, with American papers, seized by British cruisers as Spanish property. Before this she had been boarded fifteen times. *Ibid.*, pp. 41–4; A. H. Foote, *Africa and the American Flag*, p. 152–6.

1839. **Ontario**, American slaver, "sold" to the Spanish on shipping a cargo of slaves. *House Doc.*, 26 Cong. 2 sess. V. No. 115, pp. 45–50.

1839. **Mary**, of Philadelphia; case of a slaver whose nationality was disputed. *House Reports*, 27 Cong. 3 sess. III. No. 283, pp. 736–8; *Senate Doc.*, 29 Cong. 1 sess. VIII. No. 377, pp. 19, 24–5.

1840, March. **Sarah Ann**, of New Orleans, captured with fraudulent papers. *House Doc.*, 26 Cong. 2 sess. V. No. 115, pp. 184–7.

1840, June. **Caballero, Hudson**, and **Crawford**; the arrival of these American slavers was publicly billed in Cuba. *Ibid.*, pp. 65–6.

1840. **Tigris**, captured by British cruisers and sent to Boston for kidnapping. *House Reports*, 27 Cong. 3 sess. III. No. 283, pp. 724–9; *Senate Doc.*, 29 Cong. 1 sess. VIII. No. 377, p. 94.

1840. **Jones**, seized by the British. *Senate Doc.*, 29 Cong. 1 sess. VIII. No. 377, pp. 131–2, 143–7, 148–60.

1841, Nov. 7. **Creole,** of Richmond, Virginia, transporting slaves to New Orleans; the crew mutiny and take her to Nassau, British West Indies. The slaves were freed and Great Britain refused indemnity. *Senate Doc.*, 27 Cong. 2 sess. II. No. 51 and III. No. 137.

1841. **Sophia,** of New York, ships 750 slaves for Brazil. *House Doc.*, 29 Cong. 1 sess. III. No. 43, pp. 3–8.

1841. **Pilgrim,** of Portsmouth, N. H., **Solon,** of Baltimore, **William Jones** and **Himmaleh,** of New York, clear from Rio Janeiro for Africa. *Ibid.*, pp. 8–12.

1842, May. **Illinois,** of Gloucester, saved from search by the American flag; escaped under the Spanish flag, loaded with slaves. *Senate Doc.*, 28 Cong. 2 sess. IX. No. 150, p. 72 ff.

1842, June. **Shakespeare,** of Baltimore, with 430 slaves, captured by British cruisers. *Ibid.*

1843. **Kentucky,** of New York, trading to Brazil. *Ibid.*, 30 Cong. 1 sess. IV. No. 28, pp. 71–8; *House Exec. Doc.*, 30 Cong. 2 sess. VII. No. 61, p. 72 ff.

1844. **Enterprise,** of Boston, transferred in Brazil for slave-trade. *Senate Exec. Doc.*, 30 Cong. 1 sess. IV. No. 28, pp. 79–90.

1844. **Uncas,** of New Orleans, protected by United States papers; allowed to clear, in spite of her evident character. *Ibid.*, 28 Cong. 2 sess. IX. No. 150, pp. 106–14.

1844. **Sooy,** of Newport, without papers, captured by the British sloop Racer, after landing 600 slaves on the coast of Brazil. *House Doc.*, 28 Cong. 2 sess. IV. No. 148, pp. 4, 36–62.

1844. **Cyrus,** of New Orleans, suspected slaver, captured by the British cruiser Alert. *Ibid.*, pp. 3–41.

1844–5. ———. Nineteen slavers from Beverly, Boston, Baltimore, Philadelphia, New York, Providence, and Portland, make twenty-two trips. *Ibid.*, 30 Cong. 2 sess. VII. No. 61, pp. 219–20.

1844–9. ———. Ninety-three slavers in Brazilian trade. *Senate Exec. Doc.*, 31 Cong. 2 sess. II. No. 6, pp. 37–8.

1845. **Porpoise,** trading to Brazil. *House Exec. Doc.*, 30 Cong. 2 sess. VII. No. 61, pp. 111–56, 212–4.

1845, May 14. **Spitfire,** of New Orleans, captured on the coast of Africa, and the captain indicted in Boston. A. H. Foote, *Africa ana the American Flag*, pp. 240–1; *Niles's Register*, LXVIII. 192, 224, 248–9.

1845–6. **Patuxent, Pons, Robert Wilson, Merchant,** and **Panther,** captured by Commodore Skinner. *House Exec. Doc.*, 31 Cong. 1 sess. IX. No. 73.

1847. **Fame**, of New London, Connecticut, lands 700 slaves in Brazil. *House Exec. Doc.*, 30 Cong. 2 sess. VII. No. 61, pp. 5–6, 15–21.

1847. **Senator**, of Boston, brings 944 slaves to Brazil. *Ibid.*, pp. 5–14.

1849. **Casco**, slaver, with no papers; searched, and captured with 420 slaves, by a British cruiser. *Senate Exec. Doc.*, 31 Cong. 1 sess. XIV. No. 66, p. 13.

1850. **Martha**, of New York, captured when about to embark 1800 slaves. The captain was admitted to bail, and escaped. A. H. Foote, *Africa and the American Flag*, pp. 285–92.

1850. **Lucy Ann**, of Boston, captured with 547 slaves by the British. *Senate Exec. Doc.*, 31 Cong. 1 sess. XIV. No. 66, pp. 1–10 ff.

1850. **Navarre**, American slaver, trading to Brazil, searched and finally seized by a British cruiser. *Ibid.*

1850 (*circa*). **Louisa Beaton, Pilot, Chatsworth, Meteor, R. de Zaldo, Chester**, etc., American slavers, searched by British vessels. *Ibid.*, *passim.*

1851, Sept. 18. **Illinois** brings seven kidnapped West India Negro boys into Norfolk, Virginia. *House Exec. Doc.*, 34 Cong. 1 sess. XII. No. 105, pp. 12–14.

1852-62. ———. Twenty-six ships arrested and bonded for slave-trading in the Southern District of New York. *Senate Exec. Doc.*, 37 Cong. 2 sess. V. No. 53.

1852. **Advance** and **Rachel P. Brown**, of New York; the capture of these was hindered by the United States consul in the Cape Verd Islands. *Ibid.*, 34 Cong. 1 sess. XV. No. 99, pp. 41–5; *House Exec. Doc.*, 34 Cong. 1 sess. XII. No. 105, pp. 15–19.

1853. **Silenus**, of New York, and **General de Kalb**, of Baltimore, carry 900 slaves from Africa. *Senate Exec. Doc.*, 34 Cong. 1 sess. XV. No. 99, pp. 46–52; *House Exec. Doc.*, 34 Cong. 1 sess. XII. No. 105, pp. 20–26.

1853. **Jasper** carries slaves to Cuba. *Senate Exec. Doc.*, 34 Cong. 1 sess. XV. No. 99, pp. 52–7.

1853. **Camargo**, of Portland, Maine, lands 500 slaves in Brazil. *Ibid.*, 33 Cong. 1 sess. VIII. No. 47.

1854. **Glamorgan**, of New York, captured when about to embark nearly 700 slaves. *Ibid.*, 34 Cong. 1 sess. XV. No. 99, pp. 59–60.

1854. **Grey Eagle**, of Philadelphia, captured off Cuba by British cruiser. *Ibid.*, pp. 61–3.

1854. **Peerless**, of New York, lands 350 Negroes in Cuba. *Ibid.*, p. 66.

1854. **Oregon**, of New Orleans, trading to Cuba. *Senate Exec. Doc.*, 34 Cong. 1 sess. XV. No. 99, pp. 69–70.

1856. **Mary E. Smith**, sailed from Boston in spite of efforts to detain her, and was captured with 387 slaves, by the Brazilian brig Olinda, at port of St. Matthews. *Ibid.*, pp. 71–3.

1857. ———. Twenty or more slavers from New York, New Orleans, etc. *Ibid.*, 35 Cong. 1 sess. XII. No. 49, pp. 14–21, 70–1, etc.

1857. **William Clark** and **Jupiter**, of New Orleans, **Eliza Jane**, of New York, **Jos. H. Record**, of Newport, and **Onward**, of Boston, captured by British cruisers. *Ibid.*, pp. 13, 25–6, 69, etc.

1857. **James Buchanan**, slaver, escapes under American colors, with 300 slaves. *Ibid.*, p. 38.

1857. **James Titers**, of New Orleans, with 1200 slaves, captured by British cruiser. *Ibid.*, pp. 31–4, 40–1.

1857. ———. Four New Orleans slavers on the African coast. *Ibid.*, p. 30.

1857. **Cortes**, of New York, captured. *Ibid.*, pp. 27–8.

1857. **Charles**, of Boston, captured by British cruisers, with about 400 slaves. *Ibid.*, pp. 9, 13, 36, 69, etc.

1857. **Adams Gray** and **W. D. Miller**, of New Orleans, fully equipped slavers. *Ibid.*, pp. 3–5, 13.

1857–8. **Charlotte**, of New York, **Charles**, of Maryland, etc., reported American slavers. *Ibid.*, *passim*.

1858, Aug. 21. **Echo**, captured with 306 slaves, and brought to Charleston, South Carolina. *House Exec. Doc.*, 35 Cong. 2 sess. II. pt. 4, No. 2. pt. 4, pp. 5, 14.

1858, Sept. 8. **Brothers**, captured and sent to Charleston, South Carolina. *Ibid.*, p. 14.

1858. **Mobile, Cortez, Tropic Bird**; cases of American slavers searched by British vessels. *Ibid.*, 36 Cong. 2 sess. IV. No. 7, p. 97 ff.

1858. **Wanderer**, lands 500 slaves in Georgia. *Senate Exec. Doc.*, 35 Cong. 2 sess. VII. No. 8; *House Exec. Doc.*, 35 Cong. 2 sess. IX. No. 89.

1859, Dec. 20. **Delicia**, supposed to be Spanish, but without papers; captured by a United States ship. The United States courts declared her beyond their jurisdiction. *House Exec. Doc.*, 36 Cong. 2 sess. IV. No. 7, p. 434.

1860. **Erie**, with 897 Africans, captured by a United States ship. *Senate Exec. Doc.*, 36 Cong. 2 sess. I. No. 1, pp. 41–4.

1860. **William**, with 550 slaves, **Wildfire**, with 507, captured on the coast of Cuba. *Senate Journal,* 36 Cong. 1 sess. pp. 478–80, 492, 543, etc.; *Senate Exec. Doc.*, 36 Cong. 1 sess. XI. No. 44; *House Exec. Doc.*, 36 Cong. 1 sess. XII. No. 83; 36 Cong. 2 sess. V. No. 11; *House Reports*, 36 Cong. 1 sess. IV. No. 602.

1861. **Augusta**, slaver, which, in spite of the efforts of the officials, started on her voyage. *Senate Exec. Doc.*, 37 Cong. 2 sess. V. No. 40; *New York Tribune*, Nov. 26, 1861.

1861. **Storm King**, of Baltimore, lands 650 slaves in Cuba. *Senate Exec. Doc.*, 38 Cong. 1 sess. No. 56, p. 3.

1862. **Ocilla**, of Mystic, Connecticut, lands slaves in Cuba. *Ibid.*, pp. 8–13.

1864. **Huntress**, of New York, under the American flag, lands slaves in Cuba. *Ibid.*, pp. 19–21.

APPENDIX D.

BIBLIOGRAPHY.

COLONIAL LAWS.

[The Library of Harvard College, the Boston Public Library, and the Charlemagne Tower Collection at Philadelphia are especially rich in Colonial Laws.]

Alabama and Mississippi Territory. Acts of the Assembly of Alabama, 1822, etc.; J. J. Ormond, Code of Alabama, Montgomery, 1852; H. Toulmin, Digest of the Laws of Alabama, Cahawba, 1823; A. Hutchinson, Code of Mississippi, Jackson, 1848; Statutes of Mississippi etc., digested, Natchez, 1816 and 1823.

Connecticut. Acts and Laws of Connecticut, New London, 1784 [–1794], and Hartford, 1796; Connecticut Colonial Records; The General Laws and Liberties of Connecticut Colonie, Cambridge, 1673, reprinted at Hartford in 1865; Statute Laws of Connecticut, Hartford, 1821.

Delaware. Laws of Delaware, 1700–1797, 2 vols., New Castle, 1797.

Georgia. George W. J. De Renne, editor, Colonial Acts of Georgia, Wormsloe, 1881; Constitution of Georgia; T. R. R. Cobb, Digest of the Laws, Athens, Ga., 1851; Horatio Marbury and W. H. Crawford, Digest of the Laws, Savannah, 1802; Oliver H. Prince, Digest of the Laws, 2d edition, Athens, Ga., 1837.

Maryland. James Bisset, Abridgment of the Acts of Assembly, Philadelphia, 1759; Acts of Maryland, 1753–1768, Annapolis, 1754 [–1768]; Compleat Collection of the Laws of Maryland, Annapolis, 1727; Thomas Bacon, Laws of Maryland at Large, Annapolis, 1765; Laws of Maryland since 1763, Annapolis, 1787, year 1771; Clement Dorsey, General Public Statutory Law, etc., 1692–1837, 3 vols., Baltimore, 1840.

Massachusetts. Acts and Laws of His Majesty's Province of the Massachusetts-Bay in New-England, Boston, 1726; Acts and Resolves . . . of the Province of the Massachusetts Bay, 1692–1780 [Massachusetts Province Laws]; Colonial Laws of Massachusetts, reprinted from the editions of 1660 and 1672, Boston, 1887, 1890; General Court Records; Massachusetts Archives; Massachusetts Historical Society Collections; Perpetual Laws of Massachusetts, 1780–1789, Boston, 1789; Plymouth Colony Records; Records of the Governor and Company of the Massachusetts Bay.

New Jersey. Samuel Allinson, Acts of Assembly, Burlington, 1776; William Paterson, Digest of the Laws, Newark, 1800; William A. Whitehead, editor, Documents relating to the Colonial History of New Jersey, Newark, 1880–93; Joseph Bloomfield, Laws of New Jersey, Trenton, 1811; New Jersey Archives.

New York. Acts of Assembly, 1691–1718, London, 1719; E. B. O'Callaghan, Documentary History of New York, 4 vols., Albany, 1849–51; E. B. O'Callaghan, editor, Documents relating to the Colonial History of New York, 12 vols., Albany, 1856–77; Laws of New York, 1752–1762, New York, 1762; Laws of New York, 1777–1801, 5 vols., republished at Albany, 1886–7.

North Carolina. F. X. Martin, Iredell's Public Acts of Assembly, Newbern, 1804; Laws, revision of 1819, 2 vols., Raleigh, 1821; North Carolina Colonial Records, edited by William L. Saunders, Raleigh, 1886–90.

Pennsylvania. Acts of Assembly, Philadelphia, 1782; Charter and Laws of the Province of Pennsylvania, Harrisburg, 1879; M. Carey and J. Bioren, Laws of Pennsylvania, 1700–1802, 6 vols., Philadelphia, 1803; A. J. Dallas, Laws of Pennsylvania, 1700–1781, Philadelphia, 1797; *Ibid.*, 1781–1790, Philadelphia, 1793; Collection of all the Laws now in force, 1742; Pennsylvania Archives; Pennsylvania Colonial Records.

Rhode Island. John Russell Bartlett, Index to the Printed Acts and Resolves, of . . . the General Assembly, 1756–1850, Providence, 1856; Elisha R. Potter, Reports and Documents upon Public Schools, etc., Providence, 1855; Rhode Island Colonial Records.

South Carolina. J. F. Grimké, Public Laws, Philadelphia, 1790; Thomas Cooper and D. J. McCord, Statutes at Large, 10 vols., Columbia, 1836–41.

Vermont. Statutes of Vermont, Windsor, 1787; Vermont State Papers, Middlebury, 1823.

Virginia. John Mercer, Abridgement of the Acts of Assembly, Glasgow, 1759; Acts of Assembly, Williamsburg, 1769; Collection of Public Acts . . . passed since 1768, Richmond, 1785; Collections of the Virginia Historical Society; W. W. Hening, Statutes at Large, 13 vols., Richmond, etc., 1819–23; Samuel Shepherd, Statutes at Large, New Series (continuation of Hening), 3 vols. Richmond, 1835–6.

UNITED STATES DOCUMENTS.

1789–1836. American State Papers — Class I., *Foreign Relations*, Vols. III. and IV. (Reprint of Foreign Relations, 1789–1828.) Class VI., *Naval Affairs*. (Well indexed.)

1794, Feb. 11. Report of Committee on the Slave Trade. *Amer. State Papers, Miscellaneous*, I. No. 44.

1806, Feb. 17. Report of the Committee appointed on the seventh instant, to inquire whether any, and if any, what Additional Provisions are necessary to Prevent the Importation of Slaves into the Territories of the United States. *House Reports*, 9 Cong. 1 sess. II.

1817, Feb. 11. Joint Resolution for abolishing the traffick in Slaves, and the Colinization [*sic*] of the Free People of Colour of the United States. *House Doc.*, 14 Cong. 2 sess. II. No. 77.

1817, Dec. 15. Message from the President . . . communicating Information of the Proceeding of certain Persons who took Possession of Amelia Island and of Galvezton, [*sic*] during the Summer of the Present Year, and made Establishments there. *House Doc.*, 15 Cong. 1 sess. II. No. 12. (Contains much evidence of illicit traffic.)

1818, Jan. 10. Report of the Committee to whom was referred so much of the President's Message as relates to the introduction of Slaves from Amelia Island. *House Doc.*, 15 Cong. 1 sess. III. No. 46 (cf. *House Reports*, 21 Cong. 1 sess. III. No. 348).

1818, Jan. 13. Message from the President . . . communicating information of the Troops of the United States having taken possession of Amelia Island, in East Florida. *House Doc.*, 15 Cong. 1 sess. III. No. 47. (Contains correspondence.)

1819, Jan. 12. Letter from the Secretary of the Navy, transmitting copies of the instructions which have been issued to Naval Commanders, upon the subject of the Importation of Slaves, etc. *House Doc.*, 15 Cong. 2 sess. IV. No. 84.

1819, Jan. 19. Extracts from Documents in the Departments of State, of the Treasury, and of the Navy, in relation to the Illicit Introduction of Slaves into the United States. *House Doc.*, 15 Cong. 2 sess. VI. No. 100.

1819, Jan. 21. Letter from the Secretary of the Treasury . . . in relation to Ships engaged in the Slave Trade, which have been Seized and Condemned, and the Disposition which has been made of the Negroes, by the several State Governments, under whose Jurisdiction they have fallen. *House Doc.*, 15 Cong. 2 sess. VI. No. 107.

1820, Jan. 7. Letter from the Secretary of the Navy, transmitting information in relation to the Introduction of Slaves into the United States. *House Doc.*, 16 Cong. 1 sess. III. No. 36.

1820, Jan. 13. Letter from the Secretary of the Treasury, transmitting . . . Information in relation to the Illicit Introduction of Slaves into the United States, etc., *Ibid.*, No. 42.

1820, May 8. Report of the Committee to whom was referred . . . so much of the President's Message as relates to the Slave Trade, etc. *House Reports*, 16 Cong. 1 sess. No. 97.

1821, Jan. 5. Message from the President . . . transmitting . . . Information on the Subject of the African Slave Trade. *House Doc.*, 16 Cong. 2 sess. IV. No. 48.

1821, Feb. 7. Report of the Secretary of the Navy. *House Reports*, 17 Cong. 1 sess. No. 92, pp. 15–21.

1821, Feb. 9. Report of the Committee to which was referred so much of the President's message as relates to the Slave Trade. *House Reports*, 16 Cong. 2 sess. No. 59.

1822, April 12. Report of the Committee on the Suppression of the Slave Trade. Also Report of 1821, Feb. 9, reprinted. (Contains discussion of the Right of Search, and papers on European Conference for the Suppression of the Slave Trade.) *House Reports*, 17 Cong. 1 sess. II. No. 92.

1823, Dec. 1. Report of the Secretary of the Navy. *House Doc.*, 18 Cong. 1 sess. I. No. 2, p. 111, ff.; *Amer. State Papers, Naval Affairs*, I. No. 258. (Contains reports on the establishment at Cape Mesurado.)[1]

1824, March 20. Message from the President . . . in relation to the Suppression of the African Slave Trade. *House Doc.*, 18 Cong.

[1] The Reports of the Secretary of the Navy are found among the documents accompanying the annual messages of the President.

1 sess. VI. No. 119. (Contains correspondence on the proposed treaty of 1824.)

1824, Dec. 1. Report of the Secretary of the Navy. *Amer. State Papers, Naval Affairs*, I. No. 249.

1824, Dec. 7. Documents accompanying the Message of the President . . . to both Houses of Congress, at the commencement of the Second Session of the Eighteenth Congress: Documents from the Department of State. *House Doc.*, 18 Cong. 2 sess. I. No. 1. pp. 1–56. Reprinted in *Senate Doc.*, 18 Cong. 2 sess. I. No. 1. (Matter on the treaty of 1824.)

1825, Feb. 16. Report of the Committee to whom was referred so much of the President's Message, of the 7th of December last, as relates to the Suppression of the Slave Trade. *House Reports*, 18 Cong. 2 sess. I. No. 70. (Report favoring the treaty of 1824.)

1825, Dec. 2. Report of the Secretary of the Navy. *House Doc.*, 19 Cong. 1 sess. I. No. 1. p. 98.

1825, Dec. 27. Slave Trade: Message from the President . . . communicating Correspondence with Great Britain in relation to the Convention for Suppressing the Slave Trade. *House Doc.*, 19 Cong. 1 sess. I. No. 16.

1826, Feb. 6. Appropriation — Slave Trade: Report of the Committee of Ways and Means on the subject of the estimate of appropriations for the service of the year 1826. *House Reports*, 19 Cong. 1 sess. I. No. 65. (Contains report of the Secretary of the Navy and account of expenditures for the African station.)

1826, March, 8. Slave Ships in Alabama: Message from the President . . . in relation to the Cargoes of certain Slave Ships, etc. *House Doc.*, 19 Cong. 1 sess. VI. No. 121; cf. *Ibid.*, VIII. No. 126, and IX. Nos. 152, 163; also *House Reports*, 19 Cong. 1 sess. II. No. 231. (Cases of the Constitution, Louisa, and Merino.)

1826, Dec. 2. Report of the Secretary of the Navy. (Part IV. of Documents accompanying the President's Message.) *House Doc.*, 19 Cong. 2 sess. I. No. 2, pp. 9, 10, 74–103.

1827, etc. Colonization Society: Reports, etc. *House Doc.*, 19 Cong. 2 sess. IV. Nos. 64, 69; 20 Cong. 1 sess. III. Nos. 99, 126, and V. No. 193; 20 Cong. 2 sess. I. No. 2, pp. 114, 127–8; 21 Cong. 2 sess. I. No. 2, p. 211–18; *House Reports*, 19 Cong. 2 sess. II. No. 101; 21 Cong. 1 sess. II. No. 277, and III. No. 348; 22 Cong. 1 sess. II. No. 277.

1827, Jan. 30. Prohibition of the Slave Trade: Statement showing the

Expenditure of the Appropriation for the Prohibition of the Slave Trade, during the year 1826, and an Estimate for 1827. *House Doc.*, 19 Cong. 2 sess. IV. No. 69.

1827, Dec. 1 and Dec. 4. Reports of the Secretary of the Navy. *Amer. State Papers, Naval Affairs*, III. Nos. 339, 340.

1827, Dec. 6. Message from the President . . . transmitting . . . a Report from the Secretary of the Navy, showing the expense annually incurred in carrying into effect the Act of March 2, 1819, for Prohibiting the Slave Trade. *Senate Doc.*, 20 Cong. 1 sess. I. No. 3.

1828, March 12. Recaptured Africans: Letter from the Secretary of the Navy . . . in relation to . . . Recaptured Africans. *House Doc.*, 20 Cong. 1 sess. V. No. 193; cf. *Ibid.*, 20 Cong. 2 sess. I. No. 2, pp. 114, 127–8; also *Amer. State Papers, Naval Affairs*, III. No. 357.

1828, April 30. Africans at Key West: Message from the President . . . relative to the Disposition of the Africans Landed at Key West. *House Doc.*, 20 Cong. 1 sess. VI. No. 262.

1828, Nov. 27. Report of the Secretary of the Navy. *Amer. State Papers, Naval Affairs*, III. No. 370.

1829, Dec. 1. Report of the Secretary of the Navy. *House Doc.*, 21 Cong. 1 sess. I. No. 2, p. 40.

1830, April 7. Slave Trade . . . Report: "The committee to whom were referred the memorial of the American Society for colonizing the free people of color of the United States; also, sundry memorials from the inhabitants of the State of Kentucky, and a memorial from certain free people of color of the State of Ohio, report," etc., 3 pp. Appendix. Collected and arranged by Samuel Burch. 290 pp. *House Reports*, 21 Cong. 1 sess. III. No. 348. (Contains a reprint of legislation and documents from 14 Cong. 2 sess. to 21 Cong. 1 sess. Very valuable.)

1830, Dec. 6. Report of the Secretary of the Navy. *House Doc.*, 21 Cong. 2 sess. I. No. 2, pp. 42–3; *Amer. State Papers, Naval Affairs*, III. No. 429 E.

1830, Dec. 6. Documents communicated to Congress by the President at the opening of the Second Session of the Twenty-first Congress, accompanying the Report of the Secretary of the Navy: Paper E. Statement of expenditures, etc., for the removal of Africans to Liberia. *House Doc.*, 21 Cong. 2 sess. I. No. 2, pp. 211–8.

1831 Jan. 18. Spanish Slave Ship Fenix: Message from the President

. . . transmitting Documents in relation to certain captives on board the Spanish slave vessel, called the Fenix. *House Doc.*, 21 Cong. 2 sess. III. No. 54; *Amer. State Papers, Naval Affairs*, III. No. 435.

1831–1835. Reports of the Secretary of the Navy. *House Doc.*, 22 Cong. 1 sess. I. No. 2, pp. 45, 272–4; 22 Cong. 2 sess. I. No. 2, pp. 48, 229; 23 Cong. 1 sess. I. No. 1, pp. 238, 269; 23 Cong. 2 sess. I. No. 2, pp. 315, 363; 24 Cong. 1 sess. I. No. 2, pp. 336, 378. Also *Amer. State Papers, Naval Affairs*, IV. No. 457, R. Nos. 1, 2; No. 486, H. I.; No. 519, R.; No. 564, P.; No. 585, P.

1836, Jan. 26. Calvin Mickle, Ex'r of Nagle & De Frias. *House Reports*, 24 Cong. 1 sess. I. No. 209. (Reports on claims connected with the captured slaver Constitution.)

1836, Jan. 27, etc. [Reports from the Committee of Claims on cases of captured Africans.] *House Reports*, 24 Cong. 1 sess. I. Nos. 223, 268, and III. No. 574. No. 268 is reprinted in *House Reports*, 25 Cong. 2 sess. I. No. 4.

1836, Dec. 3. Report of the Secretary of the Navy. *House Doc.*, 24 Cong. 2 sess. I. No. 2, pp. 450, 506.

1837, Feb. 14. Message from the President . . . with copies of Correspondence in relation to the Seizure of Slaves on board the brigs "Encomium" and "Enterprise." *Senate Doc.*, 24 Cong. 2 sess. II. No. 174; cf. *Ibid.*, 25 Cong. 3 sess. III. No. 216.

1837–1839. Reports of the Secretary of the Navy. *House Doc.*, 25 Cong. 2 sess. I. No. 3, pp. 762, 771, 850; 25 Cong. 3 sess. I. No. 2, p. 613; 26 Cong. 1 sess. I. No. 2, pp. 534, 612.

1839. [L'Amistad Case.] *House Doc.*, 26 Cong. 1 sess. IV. No. 185 (correspondence); 27 Cong. 3 sess. V. No. 191 (correspondence); 28 Cong. 1 sess. IV. No. 83; *House Exec. Doc.*, 32 Cong. 2 sess. III. No. 20; *House Reports*, 26 Cong. 2 sess. No. 51 (case of altered Ms.); 28 Cong. 1 sess. II. No. 426 (Report of Committee); 29 Cong. 1 sess. IV. No. 753 (Report of Committee); *Senate Doc.*, 26 Cong. 2 sess. IV. No. 179 (correspondence); *Senate Exec. Doc.*, 31 Cong. 2 sess. III. No. 29 (correspondence); 32 Cong. 2 sess. III. No. 19; *Senate Reports*, 31 Cong. 2 sess. No. 301 (Report of Committee); 32 Cong. 1 sess. I. No. 158 (Report of Committee); 35 Cong. 1 sess. I. No. 36 (Report of Committee).

1840, May 18. Memorial of the Society of Friends, upon the subject of the foreign slave trade. *House Doc.*, 26 Cong. 1 sess. VI. No. 211. (Results of certain investigations.)

1840, Dec. 5. Report of the Secretary of the Navy. *House Doc.*, 26 Cong. 2 sess. I. No. 2, pp. 405, 450.

1841, Jan. 20. Message from the President . . . communicating . . . copies of correspondence, imputing malpractices to the American consul at Havana, in regard to granting papers to vessels engaged in the slave-trade. *Senate Doc.*, 26 Cong. 2 sess. III. No. 125. (Contains much information.)

1841, March 3. Search or Seizure of American Vessels, etc.: Message from the President . . . transmitting a report from the Secretary of State, in relation to seizures or search of American vessels on the coast of Africa, etc. *House Doc.*, 26 Cong. 2 sess. V. No. 115 (elaborate correspondence). See also *Ibid.*, 27 Cong. 1 sess. No. 34; *House Reports*, 27 Cong. 3 sess. III. No. 283, pp. 478–755 (correspondence).

1841, Dec. 4. Report of the Secretary of the Navy. *House Doc.*, 27 Cong. 2 sess. I. No. 2, pp. 349, 351.

1842, Jan. 20. Message from the President . . . communicating . . . copies of correspondence in relation to the mutiny on board the brig Creole, and the liberation of the slaves who were passengers in the said vessel. *Senate Doc.*, 27 Cong. 2 sess. II. No. 51. See also *Ibid.*, III. No. 137; *House Doc.*, 27 Cong. 3 sess. I. No. 2, p. 114.

1842, May 10. Resolutions of the Legislature of the State of Mississippi in reference to the right of search, and the case of the American brig Creole. *House Doc.*, 27 Cong. 2 sess. IV. No. 215. (Suggestive.)

1842, etc. [Quintuple Treaty and Cass's Protest: Messages of the President, etc.] *House Doc.*, 27 Cong. 2 sess. V. No. 249; *Senate Doc.*, 27 Cong. 3 sess. II. No. 52, and IV. No. 223; 29 Cong. 1 sess. VIII. No. 377.

1842, June 10. Indemnities for slaves on board the Comet and Encomium: Report of the Secretary of State. *House Doc.*, 27 Cong. 2 sess. V. No. 242.

1842, Aug. Suppression of the African Slave Trade — Extradition: Case of the Creole, etc. *House Doc.*, 27 Cong. 3 sess. I. No. 2, pp. 105–136. (Correspondence accompanying Message of President.)

1842, Dec. Report of the Secretary of the Navy. *House Doc.*, 27 Cong. 3 sess. I. No. 2, p. 532.

1842, Dec. 30. Message from the President . . . in relation to the strength and expense of the squadron to be employed on the coast of Africa. *Senate Doc.*, 27 Cong. 3 sess. II. No. 20.

1843, Feb. 28. Construction of the Treaty of Washington, etc.: Message from the President . . . transmitting a report from the Secretary of State, in answer to the resolution of the House of the 22d February, 1843. *House Doc.*, 27 Cong. 3 sess. V. No. 192.

1843, Feb. 28. African Colonization. . . . Report: "The Committee on Commerce, to whom was referred the memorial of the friends of African colonization, assembled in convention in the city of Washington in May last, beg leave to submit the following report," etc. (16 pp.). Appendix. (1071 pp.). *House Reports*, 27 Cong. 3 sess. III. No. 283 [Contents of Appendix: pp. 17–408, identical nearly with the Appendix to *House Reports*, 21 Cong. 1 sess. III. No. 348; pp. 408–478. Congressional history of the slave-trade, case of the Fenix, etc. (cf. *House Doc.*, 21 Cong. 2 sess. III. No. 54); pp. 478–729, search and seizure of American vessels (same as *House Doc.*, 26 Cong. 2 sess. V. No. 115, pp. 1–252); pp. 730–755, correspondence on British search of American vessels, etc.; pp. 756–61, Quintuple Treaty; pp. 762–3, President's Message on Treaty of 1842; pp. 764–96, correspondence on African squadron, etc.; pp. 796–1088, newspaper extracts on the slave-trade and on colonization, report of Colonization Society, etc.]

1843, Nov. 25. Report of the Secretary of the Navy. *House Doc.*, 28 Cong. 1 sess. I. No. 2, pp. 484–5.

1844, March 14. Message from the President . . . communicating . . . information in relation to the abuse of the flag of the United States in . . . the African slave trade, etc. *Senate Doc.*, 28 Cong. 1 sess. IV. No 217.

1844, March 15. Report: "The Committee on the Judiciary, to whom was referred the petition of . . . John Hanes, . . . praying an adjustment of his accounts for the maintenance of certain captured African slaves, ask leave to report," etc. *Senate Doc.*, 28 Cong. 1 sess. IV. No. 194.

1844, May 4. African Slave Trade: Report: "The Committee on Foreign Affairs, to whom was referred the petition of the American Colonization Society and others, respectfully report," etc. *House Reports*, 28 Cong. 1 sess. II. No. 469.

1844, May 22. Suppression of the Slave-Trade on the coast of Africa: Message from the President, etc. *House Doc.*, 28 Cong. 1 sess. VI. No. 263.

1844, Nov. 25. Report of the Secretary of the Navy. *House Doc.*, 28 Cong. 2 sess. I. No. 2, p. 514.

1845, Feb. 20. Slave-Trade, etc.: Message from the President . . . transmitting copies of despatches from the American minister at the court of Brazil, relative to the slave-trade, etc. *House Doc.*, 28 Cong. 2 sess. IV. No. 148. (Important evidence, statistics, etc.)

1845, Feb. 26. Message from the President . . . communicating . . . information relative to the operations of the United States squadron, etc. *Senate Doc.*, 28 Cong. 2 sess. IX. No. 150. (Contains reports of Commodore Perry, and statistics of Liberia.)

1845, Dec. 1. Report of the Secretary of the Navy. *House Doc.*, 29 Cong. 1 sess, I. No. 2, p. 645.

1845, Dec. 22. African Slave-Trade: Message from the President . . . transmitting a report from the Secretary of State, together with the correspondence of George W. Slacum, relative to the African slave trade. *House Doc.*, 29 Cong. 1 sess. III. No. 43. (Contains much information.)

1846, June 6. Message from the President . . . communicating . . . copies of the correspondence between the government of the United States and that of Great Britain, on the subject of the right of search; with copies of the protest of the American minister at Paris against the quintuple treaty, etc. *Senate Doc.*, 29 Cong. 1 sess. VIII. No. 377. Cf. *Ibid.*, 27 Cong. 3 sess. II. No. 52, and IV. No. 223; *House Doc.*, 27 Cong. 2 sess. V. No. 249.

1846–1847, Dec. Reports of the Secretary of the Navy. *House Doc.*, 29 Cong. 2 sess. I. No. 4, p. 377; 30 Cong. 1 sess. II. No. 8, p. 946.

1848, March 3. Message from the President . . . communicating a report from the Secretary of State, with the correspondence of Mr. Wise, late United States minister to Brazil, in relation to the slave trade. *Senate Exec. Doc.*, 30 Cong. 1 sess. IV. No. 28. (Full of facts.)

1848, May 12. Report of the Secretary of State, in relation to . . . the seizure of the brig Douglass by a British cruiser. *Senate Exec. Doc.*, 30 Cong. 1 sess. VI. No. 44.

1848, Dec. 4. Report of the Secretary of the Navy. *House Exec. Doc.*, 30 Cong. 2 sess. I. No. 1, pp. 605, 607.

1849, March 2. Correspondence between the Consuls of the United States at Rio de Janeiro, etc., with the Secretary of State, on the subject of the African Slave Trade: Message of the President, etc. *House Exec. Doc.*, 30 Cong. 2 sess. VII. No. 61. (Contains much evidence.)

1849. Dec. 1. Report of the Secretary of the Navy. *House Exec. Doc.*, 31 Cong. 1 sess. III. pt. 1, No. 5, pt. 1, pp. 427–8.

1850, March 18. Report of the Secretary of the Navy, showing the annual number of deaths in the United States squadron on the coast of Africa, and the annual cost of that squadron. *Senate Exec. Doc.*, 31 Cong. 1 sess. X. No. 40.

1850, July 22. African Squadron: Message from the President . . . transmitting Information in reference to the African squadron. *House Exec. Doc.*, 31 Cong. 1 sess. IX. No. 73. (Gives total expenses of the squadron, slavers captured, etc.)

1850, Aug. 2. Message from the President . . . relative to the searching of American vessels by British ships of war. *Senate Exec. Doc.*, 31 Cong. 1 sess. XIV. No. 66.

1850, Dec. 17. Message of the President . . . communicating . . . a report of the Secretary of State, with documents relating to the African slave trade. *Senate Exec. Doc.*, 31 Cong. 2 sess. II. No. 6.

1851–1853. Reports of the Secretary of the Navy. *House Exec. Doc.*, 32 Cong. 1 sess. II. pt. 2, No. 2, pt. 2, pp. 4–5; 32 Cong. 2 sess. I. pt. 2, No. 1, pt. 2, p. 293; 33 Cong. 1 sess. I. pt. 3, No. 1, pt. 3, pp. 298–9.

1854, March 13. Message from the President . . . communicating . . . the correspondence between Mr. Schenck, United States Minister to Brazil, and the Secretary of State, in relation to the African slave trade. *Senate Exec. Doc.*, 33 Cong. 1 sess. VIII. No. 47.

1854, June 13. Report submitted by Mr. Slidell, from the Committee on Foreign Relations, on a resolution relative to the abrogation of the eighth article of the treaty with Great Britain of the 9th of August, 1842, etc. *Senate Reports*, 34 Cong. 1 sess. I. No. 195. (Injunction of secrecy removed June 26, 1856.)

1854–1855, Dec. Reports of the Secretary of the Navy. *House Exec. Doc.*, 33 Cong. 2 sess. I. pt. 2, No. 1, pt. 2, pp. 386–7; 34 Cong. 1 sess. I. pt. 3, No. 1, pt. 3, p. 5.

1856, May 19. Slave and Coolie Trade: Message from the President . . . communicating information in regard to the Slave and Coolie trade. *House Exec. Doc.*, 34 Cong. 1 sess. XII. No. 105. (Partly reprinted in *Senate Exec. Doc.*, 34 Cong. 1 sess. XV. No. 99.)

1856, Aug. 5. Report of the Secretary of State, in compliance with a resolution of the Senate of April 24, calling for information relative to the coolie trade. *Senate Exec. Doc.*, 34 Cong. 1 sess. XV. No. 99. (Partly reprinted in *House Exec. Doc.*, 34 Cong. 1 sess. XII. No. 105.)

1856, Dec. 1. Report of the Secretary of the Navy. *House Exec. Doc.*, 34 Cong. 3 sess. I. pt. 2, No. 1, pt. 2, p. 407.

1857, Feb. 11. Slave Trade: Letter from the Secretary of State, asking an appropriation for the suppression of the slave trade, etc. *House Exec. Doc.*, 34 Cong. 3 sess. IX. No. 70.

1857, Dec. 3. Report of the Secretary of the Navy. *House Exec. Doc.*, 35 Cong. 1 sess. II. pt. 3, No. 2, pt. 3, p. 576.

1858, April 23. Message of the President . . . communicating . . . reports of the Secretary of State and the Secretary of the Navy, with accompanying papers, in relation to the African slave trade. *Senate Exec. Doc.*, 35 Cong. 1 sess. XII. No. 49. (Valuable.)

1858, Dec. 6. Report of the Secretary of the Navy. *House Exec. Doc.*, 35 Cong. 2 sess. II. pt. 4, No. 2, pt. 4, pp. 5, 13–4.

1859, Jan. 12. Message of the President . . . relative to the landing of the barque Wanderer on the coast of Georgia, etc. *Senate Exec. Doc.*, 35 Cong. 2 sess. VII. No. 8. See also *House Exec. Doc.*, 35 Cong. 2 sess. IX. No. 89.

1859, March 1. Instructions to African squadron: Message from the President, etc. *House Exec. Doc.*, 35 Cong. 2 sess. IX. No. 104.

1859, Dec. 2. Report of the Secretary of the Navy. *Senate Exec. Doc.*, 36 Cong. 1 sess. III. No. 2, pt. 3, pp. 1138–9, 1149–50.

1860, Jan. 25. Memorial of the American Missionary Association, praying the rigorous enforcement of the laws for the suppression of the African slave-trade, etc. *Senate Misc. Doc.*, 36 Cong. 1 sess. No. 8.

1860, April 24. Message from the President . . . in answer to a resolution of the House calling for the number of persons . . . belonging to the African squadron, who have died, etc. *House Exec. Doc.*, 36 Cong. 1 sess. XII. No. 73.

1860, May 19. Message of the President . . . relative to the capture of the slaver Wildfire, etc. *Senate Exec. Doc.*, 36 Cong. 1 sess. XI. No. 44.

1860, May 22. Capture of the slaver "William": Message from the President . . . transmitting correspondence relative to the capture of the slaver "William," etc. *House Exec. Doc.*, 36 Cong. 1 sess. XII. No. 83.

1860, May 31. The Slave Trade . . . Report: "The Committee on the

Judiciary, to whom was referred Senate Bill No. 464, . . . together with the messages of the President . . . relative to the capture of the slavers 'Wildfire' and 'William,' . . . respectfully report," etc. *House Reports*, 36 Cong. 1 sess. IV. No. 602.

1860, June 16. Recaptured Africans: Letter from the Secretary of the Interior, on the subject of the return to Africa of recaptured Africans, etc. *House Misc. Doc.*, 36 Cong. 1 sess. VII. No. 96. Cf. *Ibid.*, No. 97, p. 2.

1860, Dec. 1. Report of the Secretary of the Navy. *Senate Exec. Doc.*, 36 Cong. 2 sess. III. pt. 1, No. 1, pt. 3, pp. 8–9.

1860, Dec. 6. African Slave Trade: Message from the President . . . transmitting . . . a report from the Secretary of State in reference to the African slave trade. *House Exec. Doc.*, 36 Cong. 2 sess. IV. No. 7. (Voluminous document, containing chiefly correspondence, orders, etc., 1855–1860.)

1860, Dec. 17. Deficiencies of Appropriation, etc.: Letter from the Secretary of the Interior, communicating estimates for deficiencies in the appropriation for the suppression of the slave trade, etc. *House Exec. Doc.*, 36 Cong. 2 sess. V. No. 11. (Contains names of captured slavers.)

1861, July 4. Report of the Secretary of the Navy. *Senate Exec. Doc.*, 37 Cong. 1 sess. No. 1, pp. 92, 97.

1861, Dec. 2. Report of the Secretary of the Navy. *Senate Exec. Doc.*, 37 Cong. 2 sess. Vol. III. pt. 1, No. 1, pt. 3, pp. 11, 21.

1861, Dec. 18. In Relation to Captured Africans: Letter from the Secretary of the Interior . . . as to contracts for returning and subsistence of captured Africans. *House Exec. Doc.*, 37 Cong. 2 sess. I. No. 12.

1862, April 1. Letter of the Secretary of the Interior . . . in relation to the slave vessel the "Bark Augusta." *Senate Exec. Doc.*, 37 Cong. 2 sess. V. No. 40.

1862, May 30. Letter of the Secretary of the Interior . . . in relation to persons who have been arrested in the southern district of New York, from the 1st day of May, 1852, to the 1st day of May, 1862, charged with being engaged in the slave trade, etc. *Senate Exec. Doc.*, 37 Cong. 2 sess. V. No. 53.

1862, June 10. Message of the President . . . transmitting a copy of the treaty between the United States and her Britannic Majesty for the suppression of the African slave trade. *Senate Exec. Doc.*, 37 Cong. 2 sess. V. No. 57. (Also contains correspondence.)

1862, Dec. 1. Report of the Secretary of the Navy. *House Exec. Doc.*, 37 Cong. 3 sess. III. No. 1, pt. 3, p. 23.

1863, Jan. 7. Liberated Africans: Letter from the Acting Secretary of the Interior . . . transmitting reports from Agent Seys in relation to care of liberated Africans. *House Exec. Doc.*, 37 Cong. 3 sess. V. No. 28.

1864, July 2. Message of the President . . . communicating . . . information in regard to the African slave trade. *Senate Exec. Doc.*, 38 Cong. 1 sess. No. 56.

1866–69. Reports of the Secretary of the Navy. *House Exec. Doc.*, 39 Cong. 2 sess. IV. No. 1, pt. 6, pp. 12, 18–9; 40 Cong. 2 sess. IV. No. 1, p. 11; 40 Cong. 3 sess. IV. No. 1, p. ix; 41 Cong. 2 sess. I. No. 1, pp. 4, 5, 9, 10.

1870, March 2. [Resolution on the slave-trade submitted to the Senate by Mr. Wilson]. *Senate Misc. Doc.*, 41 Cong. 2 sess. No. 66.

GENERAL BIBLIOGRAPHY.

John Quincy Adams. Argument before the Supreme Court of the United States, in the case of the United States, Appellants, *vs.* Cinque, and Others, Africans, captured in the schooner Amistad, by Lieut. Gedney, delivered on the 24th of Feb. and 1st of March, 1841. With a Review of the case of the Antelope. New York, 1841.

An African Merchant (anon.). A Treatise upon the Trade from Great-Britain to Africa; Humbly recommended to the Attention of Government. London, 1772.

The African Slave Trade: Its Nature, Consequences, and Extent. From the Leeds Mercury. [Birmingham, 183–.]

The African Slave Trade: The Secret Purpose of the Insurgents to Revive it. No Treaty Stipulations against the Slave Trade to be entered into with the European Powers, etc. Philadelphia, 1863.

George William Alexander. Letters on the Slave-Trade, Slavery, and Emancipation, etc. London, 1842. (Contains Bibliography.)

American and Foreign Anti-Slavery Society; Reports.

American Anti-Slavery Society. Memorial for the Abolition of Slavery and the Slave Trade. London, 1841.

—— ——. Reports and Proceedings.

American Colonization Society. Annual Reports, 1818–1860. (Cf. above, United States Documents.)

J. A. Andrew and A. G. Browne, proctors. Circuit Court of the United

States, Massachusetts District, ss. In Admiralty. The United States, by Information, *vs.* the Schooner Wanderer and Cargo, G. Lamar, Claimant. Boston, 1860.

Edward Armstrong, editor. The Record of the Court at Upland, in Pennsylvania. 1676–1681. Philadelphia, 1860. (In *Memoirs* of the Pennsylvania Historical Society, VII. 11.)

Samuel Greene Arnold. History of the State of Rhode Island and Providence Plantations. 2 vols. New York, 1859–60. (See Index to Vol. II., "Slave Trade.")

Assiento, or, Contract for allowing to the Subjects of Great Britain the Liberty of Importing Negroes into the Spanish America. Sign'd by the Catholick King at Madrid, the Twenty sixth Day of March, 1713. By Her Majesties special Command. London, 1713.

R. S. Baldwin. Argument before the Supreme Court of the United States, in the case of the United States, Appellants, *vs.* Cinque, and Others, Africans of the Amistad. New York, 1841.

James Bandinel. Some Account of the Trade in Slaves from Africa as connected with Europe and America; From the Introduction of the Trade into Modern Europe, down to the present Time; especially with reference to the efforts made by the British Government for its extinction. London, 1842.

Anthony Benezet. Inquiry into the Rise and Progress of the Slave Trade, 1442–1771. (In his Historical Account of Guinea, etc., Philadelphia, 1771.)

—— ——. Notes on the Slave Trade, etc. [1780?].

Thomas Hart Benton. Abridgment of the Debates of Congress, from 1789 to 1856. 16 vols. Washington, 1857–61.

Edward Bettle. Notices of Negro Slavery, as connected with Pennsylvania. (Read before the Historical Society of Pennsylvania, Aug. 7, 1826. Printed in *Memoirs* of the Historical Society of Pennsylvania, Vol. I. Philadelphia, 1864.)

W. O. Blake. History of Slavery and the Slave Trade, Ancient and Modern. Columbus, 1859.

Jeffrey R. Brackett. The Status of the Slave, 1775–1789. (Essay V. in Jameson's *Essays in the Constitutional History of the United States, 1775–89*. Boston, 1889.)

Thomas Branagan. Serious Remonstrances, addressed to the Citizens of the Northern States and their Representatives, on the recent Revival of the Slave Trade in this Republic. Philadelphia, 1805.

British and Foreign Anti-Slavery Society. Annual and Special Reports.

—— ——. Proceedings of the general Anti-Slavery Convention, called by the committee of the British and Foreign Anti-Slavery Society, and held in London, . . . June, 1840. London, 1841.

[A British Merchant.] The African Trade, the Great Pillar and Support of the British Plantation Trade in America: shewing, etc. London, 1745.

[British Parliament, House of Lords.] Report of the Lords of the Committee of the Council appointed for the Confederation of all Matters relating to Trade and Foreign Plantations, etc. 2 vols. [London,] 1789.

William Brodie. Modern Slavery and the Slave Trade: a Lecture, etc. London, 1860.

Thomas Fowell Buxton. The African Slave Trade and its Remedy. London, 1840.

John Elliot Cairnes. The Slave Power: its Character, Career, and Probable Designs. London, 1862.

Henry C. Carey. The Slave Trade, Domestic and Foreign: why it Exists and how it may be Extinguished. Philadelphia, 1853.

[Lewis Cass]. An Examination of the Question, now in Discussion, . . . concerning the Right of Search. By an American. [Philadelphia, 1842.]

William Ellery Channing, The Duty of the Free States, or Remarks suggested by the case of the Creole. Boston, 1842.

David Christy. Ethiopia, her Gloom and Glory, as illustrated in the History of the Slave Trade, etc. (1442–1857.) Cincinnati, 1857.

Rufus W. Clark. The African Slave Trade. Boston, [1860.]

Thomas Clarkson. An Essay on the Comparative Efficiency of Regulation or Abolition, as applied to the Slave Trade. Shewing that the latter only can remove the evils to be found in that commerce. London, 1789.

—— ——. An Essay on the Impolicy of the African Slave Trade. In two parts. Second edition. London, 1788.

—— ——. An Essay on the Slavery and Commerce of the Human Species, particularly the African. London and Dublin, 1786.

—— ——. The History of the Rise, Progress, and Accomplishment of the Abolition of the African Slave-Trade, by the British Parliament. 2 vols. Philadelphia, 1808.

Michael W. Cluskey. The Political Text-Book, or Encyclopedia . . . for the Reference of Politicians and Statesmen. Fourteenth edition. Philadelphia, 1860.

T. R. R. Cobb. An Historical Sketch of Slavery, from the Earliest Periods. Philadelphia and Savannah. 1858.

T. R. R. Cobb. Inquiry into the Law of Negro Slavery in the United States of America. Vol. I. Philadelphia and Savannah, 1858.

Company of Royal Adventurers. The Several Declarations of the Company of Royal Adventurers of England trading into Africa, inviting all His Majesties Native Subjects in general to Subscribe, and become Sharers in their Joynt-stock, etc. [London,] 1667.

Confederate States of America. By Authority of Congress: The Statutes at Large of the Provisional Government of the Confederate States of America, from the Institution of the Government, Feb. 8, 1861, to its Termination, Feb. 18, 1862, Inclusive, etc. (Contains provisional and permanent constitutions.) Edited by James M. Matthews. Richmond, 1864.

Constitution of a Society for Abolishing the Slave-Trade. With Several Acts of the Legislatures of the States of Massachusetts, Connecticut and Rhode-Island, for that Purpose. Printed by John Carter. Providence, 1789.

Continental Congress. Journals and Secret Journals.

Moncure D. Conway. Omitted Chapters of History disclosed in the Life and Papers of Edmund Randolph, etc. New York and London, 1888.

Thomas Cooper. Letters on the Slave Trade. Manchester, Eng., 1787.

Correspondence with British Ministers and Agents in Foreign Countries, and with Foreign Ministers in England, relative to the Slave Trade, 1859–60. London, 1860.

The Creole Case, and Mr. Webster's Despatch; with the comments of the New York "American." New York, 1842.

B. R. Curtis. Reports of Decisions in the Supreme Court of the United States. With Notes, and a Digest. Fifth edition. 22 vols. Boston, 1870.

James Dana. The African Slave Trade. A Discourse delivered . . . September, 9, 1790, before the Connecticut Society for the Promotion of Freedom. New Haven, 1791.

Henry B. Dawson, editor. The Fœderalist: A Collection of Essays, written in favor of the New Constitution, as agreed upon by the Fœderal Convention, September 17, 1787. Reprinted from the Original Text. With an Historical Introduction and Notes. Vol. I. New York, 1863.

Paul Dean. A Discourse delivered before the African Society . . . in Boston, Mass., on the Abolition of the Slave Trade . . . July 14, 1819. Boston, 1819.

Charles Deane. The Connection of Massachusetts with Slavery and the Slave-Trade, etc. Worcester, 1886. (Also in *Proceedings* of the American Antiquarian Society, October, 1886.)

Charles Deane. Letters and Documents relating to Slavery in Massachusetts. (In *Collections* of the Massachusetts Historical Society, 5th Series, III. 373.)

Debate on a Motion for the Abolition of the Slave-Trade, in the House of Commons, on Monday and Tuesday, April 18 and 19, 1791. Reported in detail. London, 1791.

J. D. B. De Bow. The Commercial Review of the South and West. (Also De Bow's Review of the Southern and Western States.) 38 vols. New Orleans, 1846–69.

Franklin B. Dexter. Estimates of Population in the American Colonies. Worcester, 1887.

Captain Richard Drake. Revelations of a Slave Smuggler: being the Autobiography of Capt. Richard Drake, an African Trader for fifty years — from 1807 to 1857, etc. New York, [1860.]

Daniel Drayton. Personal Memoir, etc. Including a Narrative of the Voyage and Capture of the Schooner Pearl. Published by the American and Foreign Anti-Slavery Society, Boston and New York, 1855.

John Drayton. Memoirs of the American Revolution. 2 vols. Charleston, 1821.

Paul Dudley. An Essay on the Merchandize of Slaves and Souls of Men. Boston, 1731.

Edward E. Dunbar. The Mexican Papers, containing the History of the Rise and Decline of Commercial Slavery in America, with reference to the Future of Mexico. First Series, No. 5. New York, 1861.

Jonathan Edwards. The Injustice and Impolicy of the Slave Trade, and of the Slavery of the Africans, etc. [New Haven,] 1791.

Jonathan Elliot. The Debates . . . on the adoption of the Federal Constitution, etc. 4 vols. Washington, 1827–30.

Emerson Etheridge. Speech . . . on the Revival of the African Slave Trade, etc. Washington, 1857.

Alexander Falconbridge. An Account of the Slave Trade on the Coast of Africa. London, 1788.

Andrew H. Foote. Africa and the American Flag. New York, 1854.

—— ——. The African Squadron: Ashburton Treaty: Consular Sea Letters. Philadelphia, 1855.

Peter Force. American Archives, etc. In Six Series. Prepared and Published under Authority of an act of Congress. Fourth and Fifth Series. 9 vols. Washington, 1837–53.

Paul Leicester Ford. The Association of the First Congress. (In Political Science Quarterly, VI. 613.)

—— ——. Pamphlets on the Constitution of the United States, published during its Discussion by the People, 1787–8. (With Bibliography, etc.) Brooklyn, 1888.

William Chauncey Fowler. Local Law in Massachusetts and Connecticut, Historically considered; and The Historical Status of the Negro, in Connecticut, etc. Albany, 1872, and New Haven, 1875.

[Benjamin Franklin.] An Essay on the African Slave Trade. Philadelphia, 1790.

[Friends.] Address to the Citizens of the United States of America on the subject of Slavery, etc. (At New York Yearly Meeting.) New York, 1837.

—— ——. An Appeal on the Iniquity of Slavery and the Slave Trade. (At London Yearly Meeting.) London and Cincinnati, 1844.

—— ——. The Appeal of the Religious Society of Friends in Pennsylvania, New Jersey, Delaware, etc., [Yearly Meeting] to their Fellow-Citizens of the United States on behalf of the Coloured Races. Philadelphia, 1858.

—— ——. A Brief Statement of the Rise and Progress of the Testimony of the Religious Society of Friends against Slavery and the Slave Trade. 1671–1787. (At Yearly Meeting in Philadelphia.) Philadelphia, 1843.

—— ——. The Case of our Fellow-Creatures, the Oppressed Africans, respectfully recommended to the Serious Consideration of the Legislature of Great-Britain, by the People called Quakers. (At London Meeting.) London, 1783 and 1784. (This volume contains many tracts on the African slave-trade, especially in the West Indies; also descriptions of trade, proposed legislation, etc.)

—— ——. An Exposition of the African Slave Trade, from the year 1840, to 1850, inclusive. Prepared from official documents. Philadelphia, 1857.

—— ——. Extracts and Observations on the Foreign Slave Trade. Philadelphia, 1839.

—— ——. Facts and Observations relative to the Participation of American Citizens in the African Slave Trade. Philadelphia, 1841.

—— ——. Faits relatifs à la Traite des Noirs, et Détails sur Sierra Leone; par la Société des Ames. Paris, 1824.

—— ——. Germantown Friends' Protest against Slavery, 1688. Facsimile Copy. Philadelphia, 1880.

[Friends.] Observations on the Inslaving, importing and purchasing of Negroes; with some Advice thereon, extracted from the Epistle of the Yearly-Meeting of the People called Quakers, held at London in the Year 1748. Second edition. Germantown, 1760.

—— ——. Proceedings in relation to the Presentation of the Address of the [Great Britain and Ireland] Yearly Meeting on the Slave-Trade and Slavery, to Sovereigns and those in Authority in the nations of Europe, and in other parts of the world, where the Christian religion is professed. Cincinnati, 1855.

—— ——. Slavery and the Domestic Slave Trade in the United States. By the committee appointed by the late Yearly Meeting of Friends held in Philadelphia, in 1839. Philadelphia, 1841.

—— ——. A View of the Present State of the African Slave Trade. Philadelphia, 1824.

Carl Gareis. Das heutige Völkerrecht und der Menschenhandel. Eine völkerrechtliche Abhandlung, zugleich Ausgabe des deutschen Textes der Verträge von 20. Dezember 1841 und 29. März 1879. Berlin, 1879.

—— ——. Der Sklavenhandel, das Völkerrecht, und das deutsche Recht. (In Deutsche Zeit- und Streit-Fragen, No. 13.) Berlin, 1885.

Agénor Étienne de Gasparin. Esclavage et Traite. Paris, 1838.

Joshua R. Giddings. Speech . . . on his motion to reconsider the vote taken upon the final passage of the "Bill for the relief of the owners of slaves lost from on Board the Comet and Encomium." [Washington, 1843.]

Benjamin Godwin. The Substance of a Course of Lectures on British Colonial Slavery, delivered at Bradford, York, and Scarborough. London, 1830.

—— ——. Lectures on Slavery. From the London edition, with additions. Edited by W. S. Andrews. Boston, 1836.

William Goodell. The American Slave Code in Theory and Practice: its Distinctive Features shown by its Statutes, Judicial Decisions, and Illustrative Facts. New York, 1853.

—— ——. Slavery and Anti-Slavery; A History of the great Struggle in both Hemispheres; with a view of the Slavery Question in the United States. New York, 1852.

Daniel R. Goodloe. The Birth of the Republic. Chicago, [1889.]

[Great Britain.] British and Foreign State Papers.

—— ——. Sessional Papers. (For notices of slave-trade in British Sessional Papers, see Bates Hall Catalogue, Boston Public Library, pp. 347 *et seq.*)

William Jay. Miscellaneous Writings on Slavery. Boston, 1853.

—— ——. A View of the Action of the Federal Government, in Behalf of Slavery. New York, 1839.

T. and J. W. Johnson. Inquiry into the Law of Negro Slavery in the United States.

Alexandre Moreau de Jonnès. Recherches Statistiques sur l'Esclavage Colonial et sur les Moyens de le supprimer. Paris, 1842.

M. A. Juge. The American Planter: or The Bound Labor Interest in the United States. New York, 1854.

Friedrich Kapp. Die Sklavenfrage in den Vereinigten Staaten. Göttingen and New York, 1854.

—— ——. Geschichte der Sklaverei in den Vereinigten Staaten von Amerika. Hamburg, 1861.

Frederic Kidder. The Slave Trade in Massachusetts. (In *New-England Historical and Genealogical Register*, XXXI. 75.)

George Lawrence. An Oration on the Abolition of the Slave Trade . . . Jan. 1, 1813. New York, 1813.

William B. Lawrence. Visitation and Search; or, An Historical Sketch of the British Claim to exercise a Maritime Police over the Vessels of all Nations, in Peace as well as in War. Boston, 1858.

Letter from . . . in London, to his Friend in America, on the . . . Slave Trade, etc. New York, 1784.

Thomas Lloyd. Debates of the Convention of the State of Pennsylvania on the Constitution, proposed for the Government of the United States. In two volumes. Vol. I. Philadelphia, 1788.

London Anti-Slavery Society. The Foreign Slave Trade, A Brief Account of its State, of the Treaties which have been entered into, and of the Laws enacted for its Suppression, from the date of the English Abolition Act to the present time. London, 1837.

—— ——. The Foreign Slave Trade, etc., No. 2. London, 1838.

London Society for the Extinction of the Slave Trade, and for the Civilization of Africa. Proceedings at the first Public Meeting, held at Exeter Hall, on Monday, 1st June, 1840. London, 1840.

Theodore Lyman, Jr. The Diplomacy of the United States, etc. Second edition. 2 vols. Boston, 1828.

Hugh M'Call. The History of Georgia, containing Brief Sketches of the most Remarkable Events, up to the Present Day. 2 vols. Savannah, 1811–16.

Marion J. McDougall. Fugitive Slaves. Boston, 1891.

John Fraser Macqueen. Chief Points in the Laws of War and Neutrality, Search and Blockade, etc. London and Edinburgh, 1862.

[Great Britain: Parliament.] Chronological Table and Index o
Statutes, Eleventh Edition, to the end of the Session 52 and 53 Vic
(1889.) By Authority. London, 1890.

[Great Britain: Record Commission.] The Statutes of the R
Printed by command of His Majesty King George the Third
From Original Records and Authentic Manuscripts. 9 vols. Lor
1810–22.

George Gregory. Essays, Historical and Moral. Second ed
London, 1788. (Essays 7 and 8: Of Slavery and the Slave Trad
Short Review, etc.)

Pope Gregory XVI. To Catholic Citizens! The Pope's Bull [fo
Abolition of the Slave Trade], and the words of Daniel O'Conne
American Slavery.] New York, [1856.]

H. Hall. Slavery in New Hampshire. (In *New England Re*
XXIX. 247.)

Isaac W. Hammond. Slavery in New Hampshire in the Olden
(In *Granite Monthly*, IV. 108.)

James H. Hammond. Letters on Southern Slavery: address
Thomas Clarkson. [Charleston, (?)].

Robert G. Harper.. Argument against the Policy of Re-openin
African Slave Trade. Atlanta, Ga., 1858.

Samuel Hazard, editor. The Register of Pennsylvania. 16
Philadelphia, 1828–36.

Hinton R. Helper. The Impending Crisis of the South: H
Meet it. Enlarged edition. New York, 1860.

Lewis and Sir Edward Hertslet, compilers. A Complete Coll
of the Treaties and Conventions, and Reciprocal Regulations, at p
subsisting between Great Britain and Foreign Powers, and of the
Decrees, and Orders in Council, concerning the same; so far as
relate to Commerce and Navigation, . . . the Slave Trade, etc. 17
(Vol. XVI., Index.) London, 1840–90.

William B. Hodgson. The Foulahs of Central Africa, and the A
Slave Trade. [New York, (?)] 1843.

John Codman Hurd. The Law of Freedom and Bondage i
United States. 2 vols. Boston and New York, 1858, 1862.

—— ——. The International Law of the Slave Trade, an
Maritime Right of Search. (In the American Jurist, XXVI. 33

—— ——. The Jamaica Movement, for promoting the Enforc
of the Slave-Trade Treaties, and the Suppression of the Slave-Trade
statements of Fact, Convention, and Law: prepared at the requ
the Kingston Committee. London, 1850.

R. R. Madden. A Letter to W. E. Channing, D. D., on the subject of the Abuse of the Flag of the United States in the Island of Cuba, and the Advantage taken of its Protection in promoting the Slave Trade. Boston, 1839.

James Madison. Letters and Other Writings of James Madison, Fourth President of the United States. In four volumes. Published by order of Congress. Philadelphia, 1865.

—— ——. The Papers of James Madison, purchased by order of Congress; being his Correspondence and Reports of Debates during the Congress of the Confederation and his Reports of Debates in the Federal Convention. 3 vols. Washington, 1840.

Marana (pseudonym). The Future of America. Considered . . . in View of . . . Re-opening the Slave Trade. Boston, 1858.

E. Marining. Six Months on a Slaver. New York, 1879.

George C. Mason. The African Slave Trade in Colonial Times. (In American Historical Record, I. 311, 338.)

Frederic G. Mather. Slavery in the Colony and State of New York. (In *Magazine of American History*, XI. 408.)

Samuel May, Jr. Catalogue of Anti-Slavery Publications in America, 1750–1863. (Contains bibliography of periodical literature.)

Memorials presented to the Congress of the United States of America, by the Different Societies instituted for promoting the Abolition of Slavery, etc., etc., in the States of Rhode-Island, Connecticut, New-York, Pennsylvania, Maryland, and Virginia. Philadelphia, 1792.

Charles F. Mercer. Mémoires relatifs à l'Abolition de la Traite Africaine, etc. Paris, 1855.

C. W. Miller. Address on Re-opening the Slave Trade . . . August 29, 1857. Columbia, S. C., 1857.

George H. Moore. Notes on the History of Slavery in Massachusetts. New York, 1866.

—— ——. Slavery in Massachusetts. (In *Historical Magazine*, XV. 329.)

Jedidiah Morse. A Discourse . . . July 14, 1808, in Grateful Celebration of the Abolition of the African Slave-Trade by the Governments of the United States, Great Britain and Denmark. Boston, 1808.

John Pennington, Lord Muncaster. Historical Sketches of the Slave Trade and its effect on Africa, addressed to the People of Great Britain. London, 1792.

Edward Needles. An Historical Memoir of the Pennsylvania Society, for Promoting the Abolition of Slavery. Philadelphia, 1848.

New England Anti-Slavery Convention. Proceedings at Boston, May 27, 1834. Boston, 1834.

Hezekiah Niles (*et al.*), editors. The Weekly Register, etc. 71 vols. Baltimore, 1811–1847. (For Slave-Trade, see I. 224; III. 189; V. 30, 46; VI. 152; VII. 54, 96, 286, 350; VIII. 136, 190, 262, 302, Supplement, p. 155; IX. 60, 78, 133, 172, 335; X. 296, 400, 412, 427; XI. 15, 108, 156, 222, 336, 399; XII. 58, 60, 103, 122, 159, 219, 237, 299, 347, 397, 411.)

Robert Norris. A Short Account of the African Slave-Trade. A new edition corrected. London, 1789.

E. B. O'Callaghan, translator. Voyages of the Slavers St. John and Arms of Amsterdam, 1659, 1663; with additional papers illustrative of the Slave Trade under the Dutch. Albany, 1867. (New York Colonial Tracts, No. 3.)

Frederick Law Olmsted. A Journey in the Back Country. New York, 1860.

—— ——. A Journey in the Seaboard Slave States, etc. New York, 1856.

—— ——. A Journey through Texas, etc. New York, 1857.

—— ——. The Cotton Kingdom, etc. 2 vols. New York, 1861.

Sir W. G. Ouseley. Notes on the Slave Trade; with Remarks on the Measures adopted for its Suppression. London, 1850.

Pennsylvania Historical Society. The Charlemagne Tower Collection of American Colonial Laws. (Bibliography.) Philadelphia, 1890.

Edward A. Pollard. Black Diamonds gathered in the Darkey Homes of the South. New York, 1859.

William F. Poole. Anti-Slavery Opinions before the Year 1800. To which is appended a fac-simile reprint of Dr. George Buchanan's Oration on the Moral and Political Evil of Slavery, etc. Cincinnati, 1873.

Robert Proud. History of Pennsylvania. 2 vols. Philadelphia. 1797–8.

[James Ramsay.] An Inquiry into the Effects of putting a Stop to the African Slave Trade, and of granting Liberty to the Slaves in the British Sugar Colonies. London, 1784.

—— ——. Objections to the Abolition of the Slave Trade, with Answers, etc. Second edition. London, 1788.

[John Ranby.] Observations on the Evidence given before the Committees of the Privy Council and House of Commons in Support of the Bill for Abolishing the Slave Trade. London, 1791.

Remarks on the Colonization of the Western Coast of Africa, by the Free Negroes of the United States, etc. New York, 1850.

Right of Search. Reply to an "American's Examination" of the "Right of Search, etc." By an Englishman. London, 1842.

William Noel Sainsbury, editor. Calendar of State Papers, Colonial Series, America and the West Indies, 1574–1676. 4 vols. London, 1860–93.

George Sauer. La Traite et l'Esclavage des Noirs. London, 1863.

George S. Sawyer. Southern Institutes; or, An Inquiry into the Origin and Early Prevalence of Slavery and the Slave-Trade. Philadelphia, 1858.

Selections from the Revised Statutes: Containing all the Laws relating to Slaves, etc. New York, 1830.

Johann J. Sell. Versuch einer Geschichte des Negersclavenhandels. Halle, 1791.

[Granville Sharp.] Extract of a Letter to a Gentleman in Maryland; Wherein is demonstrated the extreme wickedness of tolerating the Slave Trade. Fourth edition. London, 1806.

A Short Account of that part of Africa Inhabited by the Negroes, . . . and the Manner by which the Slave Trade is carried on. Third edition. London, 1768.

A Short Sketch of the Evidence for the Abolition of the Slave-Trade. Philadelphia, 1792.

Joseph Sidney. An Oration commemorative of the Abolition of the Slave Trade in the United States. . . . Jan, 2. 1809. New York, 1809.

[A Slave Holder.] Remarks upon Slavery and the Slave-Trade, addressed to the Hon. Henry Clay. 1839.

The Slave Trade in New York. (In the *Continental Monthly*, January, 1862, p. 86.)

Joseph Smith. A Descriptive Catalogue of Friends' Books. (Bibliography.) 2 vols. London, 1867.

Capt. William Snelgrave. A New Account of some Parts of Guinea, and the Slave-Trade. London, 1734.

South Carolina. General Assembly (House), 1857. Report of the Special Committee of the House of Representatives . . . on so much of the Message of His Excellency Gov. Jas. H. Adams, as relates to Slavery and the Slave Trade. Columbia, S. C., 1857.

L. W. Spratt. A Protest from South Carolina against a Decision of the Southern Congress: Slave Trade in the Southern Congress. (In Littell's *Living Age*, Third Series, LXVIII. 801.)

—— ——. Speech upon the Foreign Slave Trade, before the Legislature of South Carolina. Columbia, S. C., 1858.

L. W. Spratt. The Foreign Slave Trade the Source of Political Power, etc. Charleston, 1858.

William Stith. The History of the First Discovery and Settlement of Virginia. Virginia and London, 1753.

George M. Stroud. A Sketch of the Laws relating to Slavery in the Several States of the United States of America. Philadelphia, 1827.

James Swan. A Dissuasion to Great-Britain and the Colonies: from the Slave-Trade to Africa. Shewing the Injustice thereof, etc. Revised and Abridged. Boston, 1773.

F. T. Texugo. A Letter on the Slave Trade still carried on along the Eastern Coast of Africa, etc. London, 1839.

R. Thorpe. A View of the Present Increase of the Slave Trade, the Cause of that Increase, and a mode for effecting its total Annihilation. London, 1818.

Jesse Torrey. A Portraiture of Domestic Slavery . . . and a Project of Colonial Asylum for Free Persons of Colour. Philadelphia, 1817.

Drs. Tucker and Belknap. Queries respecting the Slavery and Emancipation of Negroes in Massachusetts, proposed by the Hon. Judge Tucker of Virginia, and answered by the Rev. Dr. Belknap. (In Collections of the Massachusetts Historical Society, First Series, IV. 191.)

David Turnbull. Travels in the West. Cuba; with Notices of Porto Rico, and the Slave Trade. London, 1840.

United States Congress. Annals of Congress, 1789–1824; Congressional Debates, 1824–37; Congressional Globe, 1833–73; Congressional Record, 1873–; Documents (House and Senate); Executive Documents (House and Senate); Journals (House and Senate); Miscellaneous Documents (House and Senate); Reports (House and Senate); Statutes at Large.

United States Supreme Court. Reports of Decisions.

Charles W. Upham. Speech in the House of Representatives, Massachusetts, on the Compromises of the Constitution, with an Appendix containing the Ordinance of 1787. Salem, 1849.

Virginia State Convention. Proceedings and Debates, 1829–30. Richmond, 1830.

G. Wadleigh. Slavery in New Hampshire. (In *Granite Monthly*, VI. 377.)

Emory Washburn. Extinction of Slavery in Massachusetts. (In Proceedings of the Massachusetts Historical Society, May, 1857. Boston, 1859.)

William B. Weeden. Economic and Social History of New England, 1620–1789. 2 vols. Boston, 1890.

Henry Wheaton. Enquiry into the Validity of the British Claim to a Right of Visitation and Search of American Vessels suspected to be engaged in the African Slave-Trade. Philadelphia, 1842.

William H. Whitmore. The Colonial Laws of Massachusetts. Reprinted from the Edition of 1660, with the Supplements to 1772. Containing also the Body of Liberties of 1641. Boston, 1889.

George W. Williams. History of the Negro Race in America from 1619 to 1880. 2 vols. New York, 1883.

Henry Wilson. History of the Antislavery Measures of the Thirty-seventh and Thirty-eighth United-States Congresses, 1861–64. Boston, 1864.

——. History of the Rise and Fall of the Slave Power in America. 3 vols. Boston, 1872–7.

INDEX.

A CATALOG OF SELECTED
DOVER BOOKS
IN ALL FIELDS OF INTEREST

A CATALOG OF SELECTED DOVER BOOKS IN ALL FIELDS OF INTEREST

FRANK LLOYD WRIGHT'S HOLLYHOCK HOUSE, Donald Hoffmann. Lavishly illustrated, carefully documented study of one of Wright's most controversial residential designs. Over 120 photographs, floor plans, elevations, etc. Detailed perceptive text by noted Wright scholar. Index. 128pp. 9¼ x 10¾. 27133-1 Pa. $11.95

THE MALE AND FEMALE FIGURE IN MOTION: 60 Classic Photographic Sequences, Eadweard Muybridge. 60 true-action photographs of men and women walking, running, climbing, bending, turning, etc., reproduced from rare 19th-century masterpiece. vi + 121pp. 9 x 12. 24745-7 Pa. $10.95

1001 QUESTIONS ANSWERED ABOUT THE SEASHORE, N. J. Berrill and Jacquelyn Berrill. Queries answered about dolphins, sea snails, sponges, starfish, fishes, shore birds, many others. Covers appearance, breeding, growth, feeding, much more. 305pp. 5¼ x 8¼. 23366-9 Pa. $8.95

GUIDE TO OWL WATCHING IN NORTH AMERICA, Donald S. Heintzelman. Superb guide offers complete data and descriptions of 19 species: barn owl, screech owl, snowy owl, many more. Expert coverage of owl-watching equipment, conservation, migrations and invasions, etc. Guide to observing sites. 84 illustrations. xiii + 193pp. 5⅜ x 8½. 27344-X Pa. $8.95

MEDICINAL AND OTHER USES OF NORTH AMERICAN PLANTS: A Historical Survey with Special Reference to the Eastern Indian Tribes, Charlotte Erichsen-Brown. Chronological historical citations document 500 years of usage of plants, trees, shrubs native to eastern Canada, northeastern U.S. Also complete identifying information. 343 illustrations. 544pp. 6½ x 9¼. 25951-X Pa. $12.95

STORYBOOK MAZES, Dave Phillips. 23 stories and mazes on two-page spreads: Wizard of Oz, Treasure Island, Robin Hood, etc. Solutions. 64pp. 8¼ x 11. 23628-5 Pa. $2.95

NEGRO FOLK MUSIC, U.S.A., Harold Courlander. Noted folklorist's scholarly yet readable analysis of rich and varied musical tradition. Includes authentic versions of over 40 folk songs. Valuable bibliography and discography. xi + 324pp. 5⅜ x 8½. 27350-4 Pa. $9.95

MOVIE-STAR PORTRAITS OF THE FORTIES, John Kobal (ed.). 163 glamor, studio photos of 106 stars of the 1940s: Rita Hayworth, Ava Gardner, Marlon Brando, Clark Gable, many more. 176pp. 8⅜ x 11¼. 23546-7 Pa. $12.95

BENCHLEY LOST AND FOUND, Robert Benchley. Finest humor from early 30s, about pet peeves, child psychologists, post office and others. Mostly unavailable elsewhere. 73 illustrations by Peter Arno and others. 183pp. 5⅜ x 8½. 22410-4 Pa. $6.95

YEKL and THE IMPORTED BRIDEGROOM AND OTHER STORIES OF YIDDISH NEW YORK, Abraham Cahan. Film Hester Street based on Yekl (1896). Novel, other stories among first about Jewish immigrants on N.Y.'s East Side. 240pp. 5⅜ x 8½. 22427-9 Pa. $6.95

SELECTED POEMS, Walt Whitman. Generous sampling from *Leaves of Grass*. Twenty-four poems include "I Hear America Singing," "Song of the Open Road," "I Sing the Body Electric," "When Lilacs Last in the Dooryard Bloom'd," "O Captain! My Captain!"–all reprinted from an authoritative edition. Lists of titles and first lines. 128pp. 5³⁄₁₆ x 8¼. 26878-0 Pa. $1.00

MY BONDAGE AND MY FREEDOM, Frederick Douglass. Born a slave, Douglass became outspoken force in antislavery movement. The best of Douglass' autobiographies. Graphic description of slave life. 464pp. 5⅜ x 8½. 22457-0 Pa. $8.95

FOLLOWING THE EQUATOR: A Journey Around the World, Mark Twain. Fascinating humorous account of 1897 voyage to Hawaii, Australia, India, New Zealand, etc. Ironic, bemused reports on peoples, customs, climate, flora and fauna, politics, much more. 197 illustrations. 720pp. 5⅜ x 8½. 26113-1 Pa. $15.95

THE PEOPLE CALLED SHAKERS, Edward D. Andrews. Definitive study of Shakers: origins, beliefs, practices, dances, social organization, furniture and crafts, etc. 33 illustrations. 351pp. 5⅜ x 8½. 21081-2 Pa. $8.95

THE MYTHS OF GREECE AND ROME, H. A. Guerber. A classic of mythology, generously illustrated, long prized for its simple, graphic, accurate retelling of the principal myths of Greece and Rome, and for its commentary on their origins and significance. With 64 illustrations by Michelangelo, Raphael, Titian, Rubens, Canova, Bernini and others. 480pp. 5⅜ x 8½. 27584-1 Pa. $9.95

PSYCHOLOGY OF MUSIC, Carl E. Seashore. Classic work discusses music as a medium from psychological viewpoint. Clear treatment of physical acoustics, auditory apparatus, sound perception, development of musical skills, nature of musical feeling, host of other topics. 88 figures. 408pp. 5⅜ x 8½. 21851-1 Pa. $11.95

THE PHILOSOPHY OF HISTORY, Georg W. Hegel. Great classic of Western thought develops concept that history is not chance but rational process, the evolution of freedom. 457pp. 5⅜ x 8½. 20112-0 Pa. $9.95

THE BOOK OF TEA, Kakuzo Okakura. Minor classic of the Orient: entertaining, charming explanation, interpretation of traditional Japanese culture in terms of tea ceremony. 94pp. 5⅜ x 8½. 20070-1 Pa. $3.95

LIFE IN ANCIENT EGYPT, Adolf Erman. Fullest, most thorough, detailed older account with much not in more recent books, domestic life, religion, magic, medicine, commerce, much more. Many illustrations reproduce tomb paintings, carvings, hieroglyphs, etc. 597pp. 5⅜ x 8½. 22632-8 Pa. $12.95

SUNDIALS, Their Theory and Construction, Albert Waugh. Far and away the best, most thorough coverage of ideas, mathematics concerned, types, construction, adjusting anywhere. Simple, nontechnical treatment allows even children to build several of these dials. Over 100 illustrations. 230pp. 5⅜ x 8½. 22947-5 Pa. $8.95

DYNAMICS OF FLUIDS IN POROUS MEDIA, Jacob Bear. For advanced students of ground water hydrology, soil mechanics and physics, drainage and irrigation engineering, and more. 335 illustrations. Exercises, with answers. 784pp. 6⅛ x 9¼. 65675-6 Pa. $19.95

SONGS OF EXPERIENCE: Facsimile Reproduction with 26 Plates in Full Color, William Blake. 26 full-color plates from a rare 1826 edition. Includes "TheTyger," "London," "Holy Thursday," and other poems. Printed text of poems. 48pp. 5¼ x 7. 24636-1 Pa. $4.95

OLD-TIME VIGNETTES IN FULL COLOR, Carol Belanger Grafton (ed.). Over 390 charming, often sentimental illustrations, selected from archives of Victorian graphics–pretty women posing, children playing, food, flowers, kittens and puppies, smiling cherubs, birds and butterflies, much more. All copyright-free. 48pp. 9¼ x 12¼. 27269-9 Pa. $7.95

PERSPECTIVE FOR ARTISTS, Rex Vicat Cole. Depth, perspective of sky and sea, shadows, much more, not usually covered. 391 diagrams, 81 reproductions of drawings and paintings. 279pp. 5⅜ x 8½. 22487-2 Pa. $7.95

DRAWING THE LIVING FIGURE, Joseph Sheppard. Innovative approach to artistic anatomy focuses on specifics of surface anatomy, rather than muscles and bones. Over 170 drawings of live models in front, back and side views, and in widely varying poses. Accompanying diagrams. 177 illustrations. Introduction. Index. 144pp. 8⅝ x11¼. 26723-7 Pa. $8.95

GOTHIC AND OLD ENGLISH ALPHABETS: 100 Complete Fonts, Dan X. Solo. Add power, elegance to posters, signs, other graphics with 100 stunning copyright-free alphabets: Blackstone, Dolbey, Germania, 97 more–including many lower-case, numerals, punctuation marks. 104pp. 8⅛ x 11. 24695-7 Pa. $8.95

HOW TO DO BEADWORK, Mary White. Fundamental book on craft from simple projects to five-bead chains and woven works. 106 illustrations. 142pp. 5⅜ x 8. 20697-1 Pa. $4.95

THE BOOK OF WOOD CARVING, Charles Marshall Sayers. Finest book for beginners discusses fundamentals and offers 34 designs. "Absolutely first rate . . . well thought out and well executed."–E. J. Tangerman. 118pp. 7¾ x 10⅝. 23654-4 Pa. $6.95

ILLUSTRATED CATALOG OF CIVIL WAR MILITARY GOODS: Union Army Weapons, Insignia, Uniform Accessories, and Other Equipment, Schuyler, Hartley, and Graham. Rare, profusely illustrated 1846 catalog includes Union Army uniform and dress regulations, arms and ammunition, coats, insignia, flags, swords, rifles, etc. 226 illustrations. 160pp. 9 x 12. 24939-5 Pa. $10.95

WOMEN'S FASHIONS OF THE EARLY 1900s: An Unabridged Republication of "New York Fashions, 1909," National Cloak & Suit Co. Rare catalog of mail-order fashions documents women's and children's clothing styles shortly after the turn of the century. Captions offer full descriptions, prices. Invaluable resource for fashion, costume historians. Approximately 725 illustrations. 128pp. 8⅜ x 11¼. 27276-1 Pa. $11.95

THE 1912 AND 1915 GUSTAV STICKLEY FURNITURE CATALOGS, Gustav Stickley. With over 200 detailed illustrations and descriptions, these two catalogs are essential reading and reference materials and identification guides for Stickley furniture. Captions cite materials, dimensions and prices. 112pp. 6½ x 9¼. 26676-1 Pa. $9.95

EARLY AMERICAN LOCOMOTIVES, John H. White, Jr. Finest locomotive engravings from early 19th century: historical (1804–74), main-line (after 1870), special, foreign, etc. 147 plates. 142pp. 11⅜ x 8¼. 22772-3 Pa. $10.95

THE TALL SHIPS OF TODAY IN PHOTOGRAPHS, Frank O. Braynard. Lavishly illustrated tribute to nearly 100 majestic contemporary sailing vessels: Amerigo Vespucci, Clearwater, Constitution, Eagle, Mayflower, Sea Cloud, Victory, many more. Authoritative captions provide statistics, background on each ship. 190 black-and-white photographs and illustrations. Introduction. 128pp. 8⅞ x 11¾. 27163-3 Pa. $14.95

EARLY NINETEENTH-CENTURY CRAFTS AND TRADES, Peter Stockham (ed.). Extremely rare 1807 volume describes to youngsters the crafts and trades of the day: brickmaker, weaver, dressmaker, bookbinder, ropemaker, saddler, many more. Quaint prose, charming illustrations for each craft. 20 black-and-white line illustrations. 192pp. 4⅝ x 6. 27293-1 Pa. $4.95

VICTORIAN FASHIONS AND COSTUMES FROM HARPER'S BAZAR, 1867–1898, Stella Blum (ed.). Day costumes, evening wear, sports clothes, shoes, hats, other accessories in over 1,000 detailed engravings. 320pp. 9⅜ x 12¼. 22990-4 Pa. $15.95

GUSTAV STICKLEY, THE CRAFTSMAN, Mary Ann Smith. Superb study surveys broad scope of Stickley's achievement, especially in architecture. Design philosophy, rise and fall of the Craftsman empire, descriptions and floor plans for many Craftsman houses, more. 86 black-and-white halftones. 31 line illustrations. Introduction 208pp. 6½ x 9¼. 27210-9 Pa. $9.95

THE LONG ISLAND RAIL ROAD IN EARLY PHOTOGRAPHS, Ron Ziel. Over 220 rare photos, informative text document origin (1844) and development of rail service on Long Island. Vintage views of early trains, locomotives, stations, passengers, crews, much more. Captions. 8⅞ x 11¾. 26301-0 Pa. $13.95

THE BOOK OF OLD SHIPS: From Egyptian Galleys to Clipper Ships, Henry B. Culver. Superb, authoritative history of sailing vessels, with 80 magnificent line illustrations. Galley, bark, caravel, longship, whaler, many more. Detailed, informative text on each vessel by noted naval historian. Introduction. 256pp. 5⅜ x 8½. 27332-6 Pa. $7.95

TEN BOOKS ON ARCHITECTURE, Vitruvius. The most important book ever written on architecture. Early Roman aesthetics, technology, classical orders, site selection, all other aspects. Morgan translation. 331pp. 5⅜ x 8½. 20645-9 Pa. $8.95

THE HUMAN FIGURE IN MOTION, Eadweard Muybridge. More than 4,500 stopped-action photos, in action series, showing undraped men, women, children jumping, lying down, throwing, sitting, wrestling, carrying, etc. 390pp. 7⅞ x 10⅝. 20204-6 Clothbd. $27.95

TREES OF THE EASTERN AND CENTRAL UNITED STATES AND CANADA, William M. Harlow. Best one-volume guide to 140 trees. Full descriptions, woodlore, range, etc. Over 600 illustrations. Handy size. 288pp. 4½ x 6⅜. 20395-6 Pa. $6.95

SONGS OF WESTERN BIRDS, Dr. Donald J. Borror. Complete song and call repertoire of 60 western species, including flycatchers, juncoes, cactus wrens, many more–includes fully illustrated booklet. Cassette and manual 99913-0 $8.95

GROWING AND USING HERBS AND SPICES, Milo Miloradovich. Versatile handbook provides all the information needed for cultivation and use of all the herbs and spices available in North America. 4 illustrations. Index. Glossary. 236pp. 5⅜ x 8½. 25058-X Pa. $7.95

BIG BOOK OF MAZES AND LABYRINTHS, Walter Shepherd. 50 mazes and labyrinths in all–classical, solid, ripple, and more–in one great volume. Perfect inexpensive puzzler for clever youngsters. Full solutions. 112pp. 8⅛ x 11. 22951-3 Pa. $4.95

PIANO TUNING, J. Cree Fischer. Clearest, best book for beginner, amateur. Simple repairs, raising dropped notes, tuning by easy method of flattened fifths. No previous skills needed. 4 illustrations. 201pp. 5⅜ x 8½. 23267-0 Pa. $6.95

A SOURCE BOOK IN THEATRICAL HISTORY, A. M. Nagler. Contemporary observers on acting, directing, make-up, costuming, stage props, machinery, scene design, from Ancient Greece to Chekhov. 611pp. 5⅜ x 8½. 20515-0 Pa. $12.95

THE COMPLETE NONSENSE OF EDWARD LEAR, Edward Lear. All nonsense limericks, zany alphabets, Owl and Pussycat, songs, nonsense botany, etc., illustrated by Lear. Total of 320pp. 5⅜ x 8½. (USO) 20167-8 Pa. $7.95

VICTORIAN PARLOUR POETRY: An Annotated Anthology, Michael R. Turner. 117 gems by Longfellow, Tennyson, Browning, many lesser-known poets. "The Village Blacksmith," "Curfew Must Not Ring Tonight," "Only a Baby Small," dozens more, often difficult to find elsewhere. Index of poets, titles, first lines. xxiii + 325pp. 5⅝ x 8¼. 27044-0 Pa. $8.95

DUBLINERS, James Joyce. Fifteen stories offer vivid, tightly focused observations of the lives of Dublin's poorer classes. At least one, "The Dead," is considered a masterpiece. Reprinted complete and unabridged from standard edition. 160pp. 5³⁄₁₆ x 8¼. 26870-5 Pa. $1.00

THE HAUNTED MONASTERY and THE CHINESE MAZE MURDERS, Robert van Gulik. Two full novels by van Gulik, set in 7th-century China, continue adventures of Judge Dee and his companions. An evil Taoist monastery, seemingly supernatural events; overgrown topiary maze hides strange crimes. 27 illustrations. 328pp. 5⅜ x 8½. 23502-5 Pa. $8.95

THE BOOK OF THE SACRED MAGIC OF ABRAMELIN THE MAGE, translated by S. MacGregor Mathers. Medieval manuscript of ceremonial magic. Basic document in Aleister Crowley, Golden Dawn groups. 268pp. 5⅜ x 8½. 23211-5 Pa. $9.95

NEW RUSSIAN-ENGLISH AND ENGLISH-RUSSIAN DICTIONARY, M. A. O'Brien. This is a remarkably handy Russian dictionary, containing a surprising amount of information, including over 70,000 entries. 366pp. 4½ x 6⅛. 20208-9 Pa. $9.95

HISTORIC HOMES OF THE AMERICAN PRESIDENTS, Second, Revised Edition, Irvin Haas. A traveler's guide to American Presidential homes, most open to the public, depicting and describing homes occupied by every American President from George Washington to George Bush. With visiting hours, admission charges, travel routes. 175 photographs. Index. 160pp. 8¼ x 11. 26751-2 Pa. $11.95

NEW YORK IN THE FORTIES, Andreas Feininger. 162 brilliant photographs by the well-known photographer, formerly with *Life* magazine. Commuters, shoppers, Times Square at night, much else from city at its peak. Captions by John von Hartz. 181pp. 9¼ x 10¾. 23585-8 Pa. $12.95

INDIAN SIGN LANGUAGE, William Tomkins. Over 525 signs developed by Sioux and other tribes. Written instructions and diagrams. Also 290 pictographs. 111pp. 6⅛ x 9¼. 22029-X Pa. $3.95

PHOTOGRAPHIC SKETCHBOOK OF THE CIVIL WAR, Alexander Gardner. 100 photos taken on field during the Civil War. Famous shots of Manassas Harper's Ferry, Lincoln, Richmond, slave pens, etc. 244pp. 10⅜ x 8¼. 22731-6 Pa. $9.95

FIVE ACRES AND INDEPENDENCE, Maurice G. Kains. Great back-to-the-land classic explains basics of self-sufficient farming. The one book to get. 95 illustrations. 397pp. 5⅜ x 8½. 20974-1 Pa. $7.95

SONGS OF EASTERN BIRDS, Dr. Donald J. Borror. Songs and calls of 60 species most common to eastern U.S.: warblers, woodpeckers, flycatchers, thrushes, larks, many more in high-quality recording. Cassette and manual 99912-2 $9.95

A MODERN HERBAL, Margaret Grieve. Much the fullest, most exact, most useful compilation of herbal material. Gigantic alphabetical encyclopedia, from aconite to zedoary, gives botanical information, medical properties, folklore, economic uses, much else. Indispensable to serious reader. 161 illustrations. 888pp. 6½ x 9¼. 2-vol. set. (USO) Vol. I: 22798-7 Pa. $9.95
Vol. II: 22799-5 Pa. $9.95

HIDDEN TREASURE MAZE BOOK, Dave Phillips. Solve 34 challenging mazes accompanied by heroic tales of adventure. Evil dragons, people-eating plants, blood-thirsty giants, many more dangerous adversaries lurk at every twist and turn. 34 mazes, stories, solutions. 48pp. 8¼ x 11. 24566-7 Pa. $2.95

LETTERS OF W. A. MOZART, Wolfgang A. Mozart. Remarkable letters show bawdy wit, humor, imagination, musical insights, contemporary musical world; includes some letters from Leopold Mozart. 276pp. 5⅜ x 8½. 22859-2 Pa. $7.95

BASIC PRINCIPLES OF CLASSICAL BALLET, Agrippina Vaganova. Great Russian theoretician, teacher explains methods for teaching classical ballet. 118 illustrations. 175pp. 5⅜ x 8½. 22036-2 Pa. $5.95

THE JUMPING FROG, Mark Twain. Revenge edition. The original story of The Celebrated Jumping Frog of Calaveras County, a hapless French translation, and Twain's hilarious "retranslation" from the French. 12 illustrations. 66pp. 5⅜ x 8½. 22686-7 Pa. $3.95

BEST REMEMBERED POEMS, Martin Gardner (ed.). The 126 poems in this superb collection of 19th- and 20th-century British and American verse range from Shelley's "To a Skylark" to the impassioned "Renascence" of Edna St. Vincent Millay and to Edward Lear's whimsical "The Owl and the Pussycat." 224pp. 5⅜ x 8½. 27165-X Pa. $5.95

COMPLETE SONNETS, William Shakespeare. Over 150 exquisite poems deal with love, friendship, the tyranny of time, beauty's evanescence, death and other themes in language of remarkable power, precision and beauty. Glossary of archaic terms. 80pp. 5³⁄₁₆ x 8¼. 26686-9 Pa. $1.00

BODIES IN A BOOKSHOP, R. T. Campbell. Challenging mystery of blackmail and murder with ingenious plot and superbly drawn characters. In the best tradition of British suspense fiction. 192pp. 5⅜ x 8½. 24720-1 Pa. $6.95

AUTOBIOGRAPHY: The Story of My Experiments with Truth, Mohandas K. Gandhi. Boyhood, legal studies, purification, the growth of the Satyagraha (nonviolent protest) movement. Critical, inspiring work of the man responsible for the freedom of India. 480pp. 5⅜ x 8½. (USO) 24593-4 Pa. $8.95

CELTIC MYTHS AND LEGENDS, T. W. Rolleston. Masterful retelling of Irish and Welsh stories and tales. Cuchulain, King Arthur, Deirdre, the Grail, many more. First paperback edition. 58 full-page illustrations. 512pp. 5⅜ x 8½. 26507-2 Pa. $9.95

THE PRINCIPLES OF PSYCHOLOGY, William James. Famous long course complete, unabridged. Stream of thought, time perception, memory, experimental methods; great work decades ahead of its time. 94 figures. 1,391pp. 5⅜ x 8½. 2-vol. set.
Vol. I: 20381-6 Pa. $13.95
Vol. II: 20382-4 Pa. $14.95

THE WORLD AS WILL AND REPRESENTATION, Arthur Schopenhauer. Definitive English translation of Schopenhauer's life work, correcting more than 1,000 errors, omissions in earlier translations. Translated by E. F. J. Payne. Total of 1,269pp. 5⅜ x 8½. 2-vol. set. Vol. 1: 21761-2 Pa. $12.95
Vol. 2: 21762-0 Pa. $12.95

MAGIC AND MYSTERY IN TIBET, Madame Alexandra David-Neel. Experiences among lamas, magicians, sages, sorcerers, Bonpa wizards. A true psychic discovery. 32 illustrations. 321pp. 5⅜ x 8½. (USO) 22682-4 Pa. $9.95

THE EGYPTIAN BOOK OF THE DEAD, E. A. Wallis Budge. Complete reproduction of Ani's papyrus, finest ever found. Full hieroglyphic text, interlinear transliteration, word-for-word translation, smooth translation. 533pp. 6½ x 9¼.
21866-X Pa. $11.95

MATHEMATICS FOR THE NONMATHEMATICIAN, Morris Kline. Detailed, college-level treatment of mathematics in cultural and historical context, with numerous exercises. Recommended Reading Lists. Tables. Numerous figures. 641pp. 5⅜ x 8½.
24823-2 Pa. $11.95

THEORY OF WING SECTIONS: Including a Summary of Airfoil Data, Ira H. Abbott and A. E. von Doenhoff. Concise compilation of subsonic aerodynamic characteristics of NACA wing sections, plus description of theory. 350pp. of tables. 693pp. 5⅜ x 8½. 60586-8 Pa. $14.95

THE RIME OF THE ANCIENT MARINER, Gustave Doré, S. T. Coleridge. Doré's finest work; 34 plates capture moods, subtleties of poem. Flawless full-size reproductions printed on facing pages with authoritative text of poem. "Beautiful. Simply beautiful."–*Publisher's Weekly*. 77pp. 9¼ x 12. 22305-1 Pa. $7.95

NORTH AMERICAN INDIAN DESIGNS FOR ARTISTS AND CRAFTSPEOPLE, Eva Wilson. Over 360 authentic copyright-free designs adapted from Navajo blankets, Hopi pottery, Sioux buffalo hides, more. Geometrics, symbolic figures, plant and animal motifs, etc. 128pp. 8⅜ x 11. (EUK) 25341-4 Pa. $8.95

SCULPTURE: Principles and Practice, Louis Slobodkin. Step-by-step approach to clay, plaster, metals, stone; classical and modern. 253 drawings, photos. 255pp. 8⅛ x 11.
22960-2 Pa. $11.95